The Pragmatic Dragon

Contemporary Chinese Studies

This series provides new scholarship and perspectives on modern and contemporary China, including China's contested borderlands and minority peoples; ongoing social, cultural, and political changes; and the varied histories that animate China today.

A list of titles in this series appears at the end of this book.

The Pragmatic Dragon

China's Grand Strategy and Boundary Settlements

Eric Hyer

UBCPress · Vancouver · Toronto

22 21 20 19 18 17 16 15   5 4 3 2 1

Printed in Canada on FSC-certified ancient-forest-free paper (100% post-consumer recycled) that is processed chlorine- and acid-free.

Library and Archives Canada Cataloguing in Publication

Hyer, Eric, author
    The pragmatic dragon : China's grand strategy and boundary settlements / Eric Hyer.

(Contemporary Chinese studies)
Includes bibliographical references and index.
Issued in print and electronic formats.
ISBN 978-0-7748-2635-8 (bound). – ISBN 978-0-7748-2636-5 (pbk.)
ISBN 978-0-7748-2637-2 (pdf). – ISBN 978-0-7748-2638-9 (epub)

    1. China – Boundaries – History – 20th century I. Title II. Series: Contemporary Chinese studies

DS737.H93 2015   951   C2014-905841-1
                                                         C2014-905842-X

Canadä

UBC Press gratefully acknowledges the financial support for our publishing program of the Government of Canada (through the Canada Book Fund) and the British Columbia Arts Council. Funding was also provided by the David M. Kennedy Center for International Studies and the College of Family, Home, and Social Sciences, Brigham Young University. Financial support from the Chiang Ching-kuo Foundation is also greatly appreciated.

Printed and bound in Canada by Friesens
Set in Museo and Warnock by Artegraphica Design Co. Ltd.
Copy editor and proofreader: Frank Chow
Indexer: Marnie Lamb
Cartographer: Eric Leinberger

UBC Press
The University of British Columbia
2029 West Mall
Vancouver, BC V6T 1Z2
www.ubcpress.ca

To the memory of my mother
Harriet Catherine Johns Hyer (1926-90)

and for my father
Paul Van Hyer

Contents

List of Maps

Acknowledgments

I was mentored by a group of excellent sinologists who adhered to what I call the *exotica sinica* school of China studies, but belong to the next generation of scholars committed to the rigorous application of social science theory and methods to the study of Chinese politics and foreign relations. In this book, I have attempted to strike a balance between the rich tradition of sinology and the rigorous analysis of China's foreign policy within a theoretical framework, by placing Chinese policy toward territorial issues and boundary disputes within the context of China's strategic imperatives.

This book is the culmination of research and writing over a good portion of my academic career. For many years I researched China's boundary disputes and settlements, but the major disputes with the Soviet Union and India seemed to have reached a stasis rooted in ideological and historical differences. The dramatic end of the Cold War with the collapse of the Soviet Union in December 1991 brought about a sea change in China's strategic environment. Relations with Russia began to improve, while at the same time tensions with the United States increased. At the time, I set aside this research project to wait for the dust to settle and Beijing to make its next move. Negotiations with the new Russian Federation eventually resolved their remaining boundary disputes, and Beijing also negotiated boundaries with its new Eurasian neighbours. This dramatic shift in the structure of the international system stimulated renewed efforts to resolve the Sino-Indian boundary as well. Although the Sino-Indian dispute remains unresolved, a stable status quo exists along the Line of Actual Control and negotiations continue. This will remain the case until a larger strategic imperative sets the context for a final resolution. China's growing military power and assertiveness has recently focused attention on the South China Sea disputes. In light of these developments, I renewed work on the manuscript to include analysis of China's post–Cold War settlements, the pending settlement of the Sino-Indian dispute, and the ongoing South China Sea disputes.

During the years this manuscript sat on the shelf, other scholars took up research on China's boundary disputes and settlement. This book is my response to alternative arguments other scholars have advanced seeking to explain China's approach to boundary disputes and settlement from different perspectives, and includes my analysis of China's post–Cold War boundary settlements and the ongoing disputes.

Over the years of working on this book, I have been supported and assisted by family members, colleagues, students, friends, and other scholars too numerous to list. Columbia University's East Asian Institute provided an intellectually stimulating environment and generous funding during my graduate student days. Brigham Young University's College of Family, Home and Social Sciences, the David M. Kennedy Center for International Studies, and the Political Science Department have offered collegial support and generous research funding. As a Fulbright Scholar at China's Foreign Affairs College, I formed enduring friendships that have resulted in scholarly collaboration. A generous grant from the Chiang Ching-kuo Foundation for International Scholarly Exchange supported the publication of this book.

I'm grateful to the reviewers (anonymous and known to me) who read and commented on multiple drafts of the manuscript. I've incorporated many of your suggestions. The work of many other scholars has informed and enriched my analysis, and the numerous citations in this book are a testament to their contributions. The staff at UBC Press has been most helpful in guiding this project to publication. Senior editor Emily Andrew coached me through the external review process and negotiations with the UBC Press Publications Board. My editor, Megan Brand, orchestrated the production process and was patient with me when my responses to her requests were delayed. Francis Chow's meticulous editing made the text more readable. Eric Leinberger's maps illustrate what would otherwise have been only abstract descriptions of complex terrain along China's borders. As with all scholarly work, however, I alone am responsible for any shortcomings that remain.

PART 1
The Strategic and Historical Context

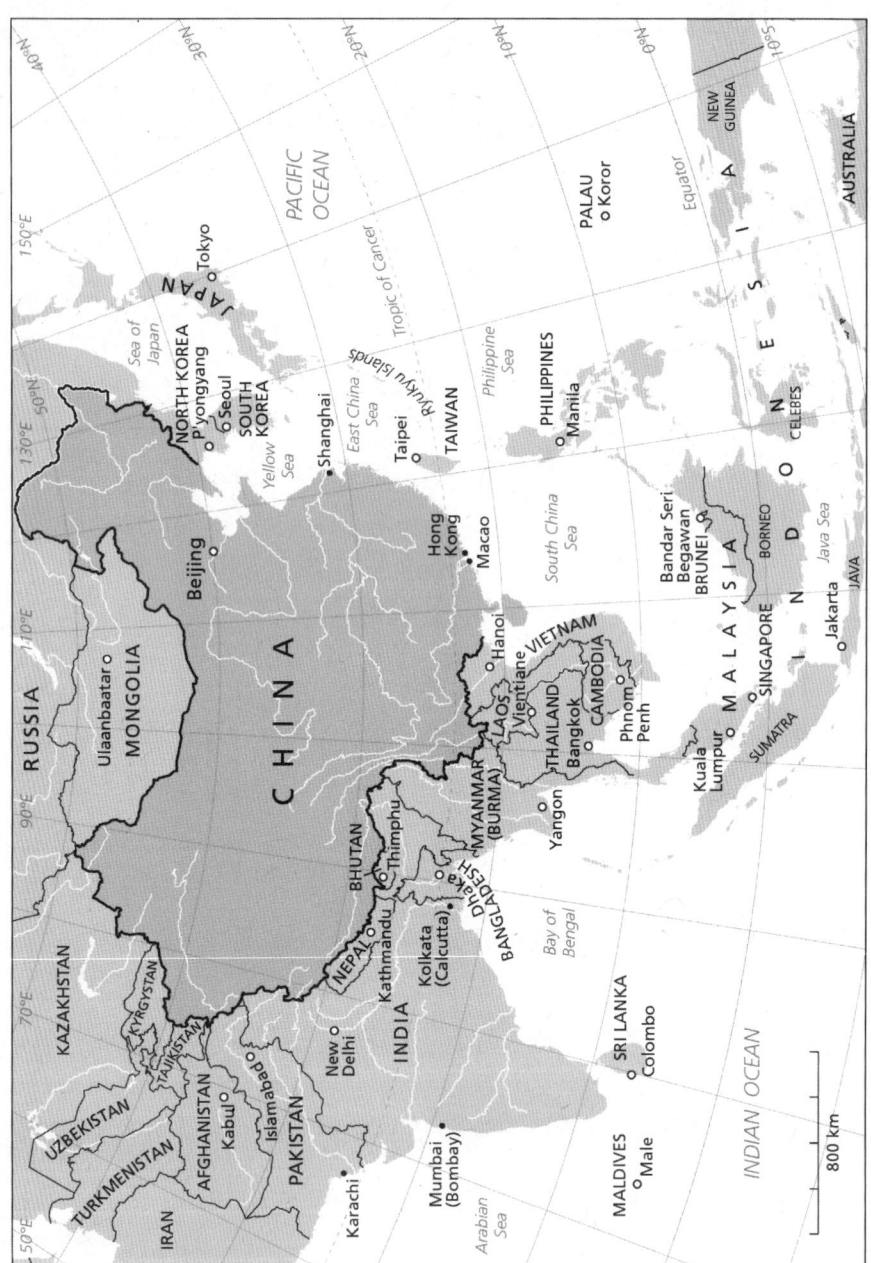

Map 1 China

Introduction
Grand Strategy and Boundary Settlements

Boundary disputes are a "primary cause of rivalry between states" and have long been a fundamental cause of war. Territorial disputes persist in many regions of the world, with the potential to erupt into armed conflict.[1] The likelihood of war is high because territorial differences are "intractable" and "tend to give rise ... to the foreign policy practices of power politics." On the bright side, however, "if claims over contiguous territory are settled amicably ... it is highly unlikely that ... war will break out between the two neighbors regardless of issues that may arise in the future."[2] These observations seem especially relevant to China, a country that has settled land boundaries with twelve of its neighbours but continues to have a major boundary dispute with India and maritime boundary disputes involving numerous islands in the East China Sea and the South China Sea (see Map 1). To date, however, there has been no comprehensive and systematic study of China's boundary disputes and settlements.

There have been numerous studies of various disputes but only recently have more systematic ones been published. Earlier studies of China's boundary disputes and settlements made little use of the theories and methodology of international relations to enhance our understanding of China's behaviour, whereas more recent studies have adopted theoretical frameworks for analysis.[3] This study adds to this new literature by explaining the significance of the boundary settlements within the larger context of the shifting balance of power and China's strategic imperatives. It thus highlights Beijing's changing policy toward boundary disputes and settlements in response to international systemic constraints.

The central question of this book is how the strategic environment of the People's Republic of China (PRC) influences its policy on boundary disputes. There are several related questions: When seeking to settle disputes, how is China motivated or constrained by strategic considerations? Under what circumstances do territorial issues become part of Beijing's foreign policy "agenda"? What factors determine Beijing's willingness to compromise? For example, one distinguishing characteristic of the PRC's boundary settlements is that only some compensating strategic gain appears to motivate China to seek a settlement.[4]

When confronted by an external threat, states adopt policies designed to reduce the threat. Resolving a territorial dispute may help a state avoid war, and in many cases may even pave the way for an alliance or a non-aggression treaty.[5] To enhance its security, China sought to reduce tensions in bilateral relations and facilitate alliances with neighbouring states by concluding boundary settlements in the early 1960s, the 1970s, and after 1990.[6] Although states may have many reasons for particular policies on specific issues, I argue, based on the evidence, that Beijing's primary motivation was the shifting balance of power, and that its objective was to enhance China's security vis-à-vis its primary adversaries.

This book analyzes China's approach to its boundary disputes in the context of international systemic forces. One of the major obstacles to achieving settlements has been Beijing's far-reaching historical claims, which, understandably, have alarmed China's neighbours despite Beijing's professed willingness to conclude boundary treaties based on realistic historical, geographic, and security considerations. In the end, China has proved to be very pragmatic and willing to compromise in order to establish legitimate boundaries through peaceful negotiations, even ceding territory believed by both parties to belong to China historically. Knowledge of China's approach toward boundary and territorial settlements will increase our understanding of China's foreign policy, an important result for scholars of international relations and China studies given that country's growing importance in world politics and the concerns that it has given rise to.

Other studies analyze China's boundary disputes and settlements from different theoretical paradigms by adopting constructivist and domestic politics perspectives. Allen Carlson examines the Chinese concept of sovereignty in order to determine whether China's internalization of evolving international norms has effected a change in its attitude toward settling its borders. He argues that, despite China's "historically conditioned sovereignty-centric values, rational cost-benefit calculations, and external pressures ... brought to bear on China by reform and opening" have resulted in a shifting stance on sovereignty. As Beijing has become more confident and has come to place greater value on international acceptance, it has become more willing to compromise and has sought territorial settlements, resulting in an unprecedented relaxation of tensions along China's borders. Nevertheless, although it has not pushed revanchist claims, Beijing has insisted on "maintaining and reinscribing conventional boundaries," which, Carlson concludes, "reflects the strict limits on its willingness to cooperate and compromise with its continental and maritime neighbors."[7]

Chien-peng Chung analyzes Beijing's behaviour by tracing the influence of "bargaining space in the presence or absence of certain domestic, institutional and leadership factors." This approach assumes that domestic politics is the major determinant of Beijing's policy toward boundary disputes. Chung admits, however, that such an approach "cannot explain when or why a disagreement, dispute or conflict arose ... or for that matter its duration, let alone predict future occurrence of such disputes or conflicts," and therefore cannot explain or predict the circumstances under which China seeks settlements of such disputes.[8] Chung's analysis based on "culture" and the so-called moral basis of China's foreign policy ignores the systemic determinants of Chinese foreign policy, relying instead on ideological and Sinocentric variables to explain Beijing's behaviour. Thus, while the analysis of each individual dispute may ring true in the context of an overarching cultural explanation, it offers no generalizable explanation of China's behaviour.

M. Taylor Fravel's analysis sees Beijing's concerns over regime insecurity as motivating China to seek compromise settlements, arguing that Beijing is "willing to cooperate with other states in exchange for assistance in countering [its] domestic sources of insecurity" and has made "territorial concessions [in exchange] for assistance from neighboring states" to quell domestic unrest. He concludes that once domestic unrest has threatened the regime's control over border regions, Beijing has compromised in order to facilitate a settlement and cooperation with neighbouring states to dampen ethnic unrest.[9] However, the fact that there has not been local ethnic unrest in all cases raises questions about such a conclusion.

This book offers an alternative to these explanations by drawing on contemporary realist balance-of-power theories. According to Quincy Wright, "changes in the political map have always been disturbing to the balance of power. Such changes and demands for them have been the main problem with which power politics has dealt."[10] The survival of states and the maintenance of their boundaries require constant vigilance and self-strengthening.

When a nation's power is inadequate vis-à-vis that of an opponent, adroit use of alliances and other means becomes necessary, and Beijing has adopted such strategies.[11]

Systemic Constraints and China's Boundary Settlements

China's policy toward boundary disputes cannot be understood by studying a particular boundary dispute in an idiosyncratic way. A systemic approach requires consideration of the impact of the structure of the international system on China's behaviour. Such a deductive explanation assumes that a state's "decisions are shaped by the very presence of other states as well as by interactions with them."[12] One sinologist has concluded that "the whole development of modern China ... has been circumscribed by its external environment, and ... this wider setting has continued to preoccupy the Chinese leadership" since 1949.[13] The international structure conditions China's calculations and approach. "Singular Sinocentrism has no place in analysis" and the "important impact of the international system ... justifies linking theory with sinology in the analytic scheme."[14] I therefore adopt a structural realist explanation of China's approach to boundary disputes and settlements, while remaining sensitive to the impact of China's historical legacy on its foreign policy.

The structure of the international system and the balance of power determine China's behaviour, and ideology does not seem to affect Chinese perceptions in any concrete way. Despite some idiosyncrasies, Beijing's foreign policy follows certain predictable patterns because of general strategic constraints and limits imposed by the "regularities" of the international system. Beijing is sensitive to the constantly shifting balance of power and responds to these changes by seeking to improve relations with its neighbours despite ideological differences.[15] Careful study of China's foreign policy shows that Mao Zedong's "policies reflected ... strategic balance of power maneuvers."[16]

Because of Chinese hypersensitivity to territorial issues, leaders may have rationalized territorial settlements by invoking Mao's "united front" doctrine, which justified cooperation with less threatening and even ideologically shunned states, but this appeal to Maoist doctrines obscured the strategic calculations behind the historically painful compromises that made settlement possible. In some cases, the government did not publicize settlements for fear of undermining the Communist Party's role as an uncompromising defender of Chinese sovereignty against imperialist encroachment.

Externally, China presented these settlements as examples of its reasonableness or magnanimity.

In this book, I present a systematic explanation focusing on the influence of Beijing's strategic concerns on boundary settlements. In the early 1960s, with China confronted by a hostile United States, Soviet Union, and India, Mao sought improved relations with many smaller neighbouring states as a means of breaking China's isolation and tilting the balance of power in China's direction. The potential cost of continued confrontation "implies that leaders will think ... in terms of what the security implications will be of worsening relations" with neighbouring states, and this "provides incentives to ... reduce the levels of diplomatic and military conflict in a dispute in order to secure the continued support" of these potential allies.[17] This deeper strategic rationale for the settlements or attempted settlements is clear from a careful study of the boundary settlements concluded in the early 1960s. The same strategic analysis is used to explain China's behaviour in the late 1970s, as the Soviet threat to China escalated, and during a third period of boundary settlement following the Cold War, which changed the international dynamic and Beijing's strategic calculations, especially along China's western boundary and in Southeast Asia.

As the position of various states in the regional balance of power shifted, China adjusted its foreign policy tactics and alliances accordingly, and these adaptations were reflected in its changing attitude toward the settlement of specific boundary questions. In a sense, then, this study encompasses not only China's boundary disputes and settlements but also its evolving interactions with neighbouring states, with the boundary disputes and settlements providing a lens through which to analyze China's strategic behaviour, how it is influenced by relations with other states, and how China has used boundary settlements to further larger strategic goals.

Despite the fact that irredentist views were common among China's communist elite, there is clear evidence of a correlation between the dynamics of the international system and China's adoption of a conciliatory boundary policy. This book demonstrates that Beijing has been much more pragmatic in approaching territorial and boundary disputes than many had assumed. In fact, China obtained less than 30 percent of the territory it claimed in the already concluded settlements, and is seeking only 25 percent of the disputed territory in its outstanding disputes with India and Bhutan.[18] These claims and settlements exclude the vast territories that Chinese believe were historically part of imperial China before being carved off by imperialist powers, and Beijing has not insisted on the far-reaching historical claims it initially asserted. It is clear that a "chauvinistic nationalist" posture did not get in the way of a pragmatic approach in the already concluded settlements, and there is no sign that such pragmatism will be missing in the future.

Methodology

Although each case is unique, they are comparable when placed within a larger strategic framework. Using a detailed historical comparative mode of analysis for each case, I identify the "causal nexus" between the structural constraints of the international system and Beijing's policy toward specific disputes and settlements. The scope of analysis is restricted to the key variables of comparable cases, making it possible to "bound the domain of our concern, to organize it, to simplify the materials we deal with, to concentrate on central tendencies, and to single out the strongest propelling forces."[19] The structural realist assumptions and comparable-cases approach enable us to focus on Beijing's larger strategic concerns and how these influenced policy toward boundary disputes and settlements. In turn, the comparative analysis of individual cases makes generalizations possible, and we can engage the larger debates in the field of international relations.

I am aware that domestic politics and individual levels of analysis are important to a complete analysis, but this is beyond the scope of this book. Foreign policy was closely controlled by Mao and a small circle of foreign policy elite, so domestic politics in the sense of "bureaucratic politics" and "public opinion" did not constrain decision-making in any significant way. A. Doak Barnett observes that "Mao was totally dominant and made all of the 'big decisions.'"[20] Although China's foreign policy bureaucracy became more complex in the post-Mao era, Chinese foreign policy scholar Zhang Qingmin argues that "Deng [Xiaoping] also enjoyed similar authority in foreign policy" and he "retained the final say on any details of ... policy."[21] The consensus among scholars and practitioners of Chinese foreign policy is that in the post-Deng era, Beijing's policy remains "based on practical rather than ideological considerations," and that decision making characterized by "oligarchical consensus" is "highly centralized in the hands of a few or even one top leader, with very little delegation of decision power." As in the Mao and Deng eras, decisions on major issues, such as boundary disputes, are "decided at the very top by party leaders or the elders who command real power behind the scenes." The foreign policy bureaucracy can deploy research and analysis to exercise "recommending power" on issues such as boundary disputes, but a high level of control makes "subversion of a decision" difficult.[22] As Zhang points out, "so long as the Chinese hierarchical decision-making structure remains along with its authoritarian political system, the role of the core leader will continue to be the center to understand Chinese foreign policy."[23]

A new layer of domestic politics that complicates post-Deng foreign policy is the growing role of social media and publically expressed opinion. Even some People's Liberation Army (PLA) generals speak more freely to the press, especially the press that caters to popular opinion, and this can inflame nationalistic sentiments among the public, supported by conservative and nationalistic scholars. The impact of this relatively new phenomenon on the foreign policy process is hotly debated among Chinese and Western scholars of Chinese foreign policy. Statements attributed to outspoken PLA officers and published in "commercial" outlets, such as the *Global Times*, that cater to public opinion, have become common in the post-Deng era, but such extreme statements do not appear in the "official press," such as the Party's flagship paper, the *People's Daily*. Many scholars conclude that this is a key indicator that although public expressions of foreign policy views are now more common, the official Party-controlled media carefully represents the central leadership's measured views on foreign policy.[24] In addition, recent research has concluded that over the past fifteen years, the PLA's influence on foreign policy has waned as the PLA has become a more professional organization with clear defence duties – the result of a "deliberate decision to remove the military from elite politics and the most powerful decision-making councils." This could be one reason why the Party now tolerates more public expressions of opinion by PLA officers than was the case a decade ago. However, on "fundamental" national security issues the influence of the PLA has diminished because "the PLA today wields far less political power than it did during the Mao Zedong and Deng Xiaoping eras. Moreover, ultimate decision-making authority regarding fundamental foreign relations ... resides in the CCP Politburo Standing Committee."[25]

Popular expressions on foreign policy issues are also more common and tolerated than in the past. Boundary issues, such as the unsettled territorial dispute with Japan over the Senkaku/Diaoyu Islands and the South China Sea disputes, are especially likely to inflame public sentiment. Recent scholarship has concluded that public opinion does influence China's foreign policy, but there is no "general framework for understanding the interactive effects between popular sentiments and foreign policy in China," and very little research that "critically assesses the Chinese state's capacity to shape public opinion on foreign policy issues."[26] One new careful study concludes that, whereas China's foreign policy leaders respond to short-lived public outcry over highly emotional issues, they will not allow "popular activism" to "threaten core foreign policy interests" and have quickly adopted policies of "moderation and engagement once public mobilization levels died down."[27] Public activism does affect negotiations, however, and can slow progress toward a resolution. According to one Chinese scholar, the attentive public reduces the "space and flexibility to implement policy ... from a long-term, reasonable, strategic perspective ... even though Chinese leaders needed to take a stance on the basis of China's national interests [they] could not ignore the strong feelings of this part of the population."[28]

However, while keeping in the background this "second-level" influence on Chinese foreign policy toward boundary disputes and settlements, adopting a rational actor model makes it possible to focus on the *general pattern* of China's behaviour and the role of Beijing's strategic calculations when resolving boundary disputes. Structural realist explanations of Chinese foreign policy have proven to be robust. Allen S. Whiting, doyen of Chinese foreign policy studies, observes that "motivational analysis is necessarily tentative, especially when the event is long past, the evidence is partial, and the actors are unavailable"; moreover, "reading the mind of Mao Zedong is contentious under the best of circumstances." However, studying China's foreign policy is possible using "inferential analysis of published material [that] can provide valuable clues to strategy and tactics." And "parsimony in theory, if enriched with area study and cultural knowledge, can illuminate ... systemic and national actor levels of realpolitik analysis."[29]

China's Grand Strategy and Boundary Disputes

The analytical thread that ties together Beijing's consistent behaviour in different boundary disputes is the larger strategic context of such behaviour. Understanding China's grand strategy facilitates the analysis of how China's changing strategic environment influences Beijing's boundary settlements. An axiom of international politics is that a fundamental objective of states is to maintain their borders. When the communists took power in 1949, they extended central control to China's border regions for the first time in over a century. In Beijing's eyes, China's boundaries were either historically established "traditional customary" boundaries or boundaries imposed on China by unequal treaties.[30] Beijing disputed most every boundary, rejecting the current location of the boundary line with its neighbours or arguing that no treaty or historical documents had established a boundary.[31]

To understand the approach of the People's Republic of China to boundary disputes, one must first place these disputes in the context of China's fundamental strategic concerns, such as the balance of power. Many scholars conclude that Beijing is preoccupied with the "constant change in international relations and [shows] acute sensitivity to situational change" as well as "balance-of-power politics" and "geopolitical struggle." It follows that Chinese leaders have an "appreciation of ... the use of pragmatic balance-of-power politics."[32] Their perceptions of threats do not "correspond with any permanent moral quality" of a state but are determined by shifts in the balance of power that affect their view of the character and behaviour of other states.[33]

According to John Mearsheimer, "if a great power confronts two or more aggressors at the same time, but has neither the resources to check all of them nor an ally to which it can pass the buck, the besieged state probably should prioritize between its threats ... so as to free up resources to deal with the primary threat."[34] Despite Mearsheimer's avowal of "offensive realist" arguments, this statement is more an expression of "defensive realism," which is exhibited by China's foreign policy behaviour.[35] Mao's "united front" doctrine, adopted during the communists' protracted struggle for power, explicitly defined primary and secondary threats and called for the subordination of minor threats in order to form a united front against perceived primary threats to China's national security – a strategy of external balancing. This doctrine continues to influence China's foreign policy calculations; whenever strategic imperatives have dictated, Beijing has subordinated a secondary goal (such as revolution in Burma in the early 1960s) to a primary national security goal, such as a more favourable balance of power vis-à-vis other threatening states (for example, Sino-Japanese rapprochement in the 1970s to balance the threat from the Soviet Union), and Beijing has generally signalled its intentions rather clearly to its adversaries and potential allies.[36]

A fundamental shift in the East Asian regional balance of power took place during the early 1960s, which saw the Sino-Soviet split, improved Soviet-Indian relations, and the escalating involvement of the United States in Southeast Asia. There is a correlation between this shift in the strategic environment and Beijing's efforts to settle boundary disputes during this period. At the time of a second major shift in the 1970s, the dispute with

Vietnam escalated into violence; at the same time, Beijing sidestepped territorial disputes with Japan and the Philippines, which it considered potential allies against the Soviet Union. With the end of the Cold War, a third major shift in the strategic environment in the early 1990s prompted the settlement of the Sino-Russian boundary, settlements with Central Eurasian states, as well as agreements with Vietnam on the land boundary and the Gulf of Tonkin.

Although China was unable to resolve its disputes with India and the Soviet Union, during the 1960s it negotiated a compromise settlement with most of the other neighbouring states, which permitted bilateral relations to develop unhindered. This pattern can be explained by the hypothesis that Beijing's perception of strategic imperatives and corresponding foreign policy determine its policy in a specific dispute; thus, Beijing prioritized threats and adjusted its policy accordingly to deal with the primary threat from the Soviet Union, India, and, to a lesser extent, the United States. The boundary settlements with Burma, Nepal, Mongolia, Pakistan, and Afghanistan illustrate this pattern. China certainly had the military capability to seize the disputed territories, but did not resort to the use of force because control of the disputed territories was not, on balance, strategically important, whereas settlement of the disputes served larger important strategic objectives.

Beijing showed great flexibility in its approach to boundary disputes in order to reach a compromise settlement and bolster amicable relations with a particular state, thereby maintaining a favourable balance of power and achieving its strategic objectives. It expected at most only tacit recognition of China's victimization by imperialism, and was more interested in stable and legitimate boundaries than in asserting historical claims. Borders that were a legacy of China's humiliation at the hands of imperialist powers left China frustrated and its neighbours apprehensive over the possibility that Beijing would behave expansively in order to satisfy irredentist aspirations. However, Beijing was willing to cede territory in order to achieve larger strategic goals, as long as this did not diminish China's boundary security or hamper its ability to defend the heartland.[37]

At the 1955 non-aligned conference in Bandung, Indonesia, Zhou Enlai stated that China was prepared to move forward and peacefully negotiate new boundary treaties.[38] Progress toward settlement of boundary disputes did not gain much momentum until the 1960s, however. Despite the radical tone of Chinese domestic politics at the time, China's domestic economic crisis and the perception of a heightened foreign threat (*neiluan waihuan*) necessitated adjustments in foreign policy. In the face of deteriorating relations with India, a growing threat from the Soviet Union after 1960, and increasing US involvement in Southeast Asia, Beijing moved quickly to negotiate boundary settlements (unsuccessfully in the case of India) in order to strengthen relations with its neighbours and offset the threat posed by the two superpowers. China was facing a possible Soviet-Indian alliance with an anti-China raison d'être; moreover, beginning in the late 1950s, its radical policies had led to strained relations with most of its other neighbours. Seen in the context of Beijing's larger strategic concerns at the time, boundary settlements were a way for Beijing to balance power and enhance its national security.

Despite China's radical domestic policies, international realities necessitated better relations with its neighbours. To offset the growing confrontation with the Soviet Union, India, and the United States, Beijing moved to settle boundaries with all of its neighbours, concluding treaties with Burma, Nepal, Pakistan, Afghanistan, and Mongolia during the 1960s, and attempting to reach some agreement with India too. As early as 1959, when the Sino-Indian boundary dispute began causing friction between the two countries, Beijing clearly expressed its alarm over the increasingly hostile international environment in a diplomatic note to India: "China will not be so foolish as to antagonize the United States in the east and again antagonize India in the west ... We cannot have two centers of attention, nor can we take friend for foe."[39] To prevent further deterioration in Sino-Indian relations, Zhou Enlai initiated negotiations to settle the boundary dispute.[40] In February 1963, at a state banquet honouring Cambodian Prince Norodom Sihanouk, Liu Shaoqi, the president of the PRC and ranking Politburo Standing Committee member, stated that "it has always been the sincere desire of the Chinese Government to live in peace and friendship with the countries of the world, settle complicated questions left over by history through negotiations with its Asian neighbors and strive for a peaceful international environment favorable to socialist construction."[41] PLA documents also attest to the fact that China adopted a conciliatory policy toward India.[42] The series of boundary settlements between 1960 and 1964 suggest a causal relationship between such settlements and larger strategic concerns. China, however, failed to settle its boundaries with India, the Soviet Union, and Vietnam, resulting in war in these cases.

At the peak of the Cultural Revolution in 1969, the Sino-Soviet confrontation over Zhenbao Island in March made it clear that China and the Soviet

Union were on the brink of a larger war, although a summit in mid-September initiated Sino-Soviet negotiations on boundary issues. This confrontation also resulted in renewed flexibility on China's part in territorial settlements with neighbouring states in order to counterbalance the growing Soviet threat. Most notable were China's willingness to shelve the Senkaku/Diaoyu Islands dispute with Japan to facilitate normalization of relations in 1972 and the Treaty of Peace and Friendship in 1978, and China's readiness to sidestep its dispute with the Philippines in the South China Sea in order to facilitate improved relations. It became clear that Beijing would not allow festering territorial differences to derail a higher foreign policy objective: allying with less threatening neighbours in order to strengthen China's developing anti-Soviet alliances.

By the early 1980s, China adopted an "independent foreign policy" and distanced itself from the United States due to continuing differences over the Taiwan issue. "New thinking" in Soviet foreign policy led to a rapid improvement in US-Soviet relations in the late 1980s. China could not afford to have a boundary dispute get in the way of better Sino-Soviet relations, not if it did not want to again become the odd man out in the three-way relationship. The Soviet Union responded to China's initiatives and relations between the two countries improved significantly. Boundary negotiations gained momentum in 1989 when Mikhail Gorbachev travelled to Beijing to normalize relations after three decades of hostility.

The dramatic end of the Cold War with the collapse of the Soviet Union in December 1991 brought about a sea change in China's strategic environment. Although China and Russia concluded a boundary agreement in 1991, it was not as critical as it would have been in the early 1960s or in the 1970s. The end of the Cold War prompted Beijing to renew boundary negotiations with Hanoi even as Hanoi's relations with Washington began to improve. China also moved quickly to develop relations with its Eurasian neighbours following the disintegration of the Soviet Union. Boundary settlements with these newly independent states were an important way for China to remain a key player in a region where US and European pressure was increasing on its western frontier. Relations with India have improved in recent years, although progress on a boundary settlement has been limited to a tacit agreement on the Tibet-Sikkim boundary reached in 2003. These developments demonstrate Beijing's efforts to maintain a favourable balance of power in the post–Cold War world.

The complicated disputes in the South China Sea remain unsettled, but bilateral and multilateral talks have achieved some degree of accommodation. In November 2002, China signed the Declaration on the Conduct of Parties in the South China Sea, pledging to "promote a peaceful and harmonious environment in the South China Sea between ASEAN [Association of Southeast Asian Nations] and China for the enhancement of peace, stability, economic growth and prosperity in the region" in order to "enhance favorable conditions for a peaceful and durable solution of differences and disputes among countries concerned."[43] Nonetheless, the complex multilateral dispute over territory potentially rich in natural resources has all parties continuing to dance a complex minuet of military and diplomatic moves.

Although possible, future military confrontations over boundary disputes with India, Bhutan, and Japan as well as in the South China Sea are unlikely despite the recent spike in tensions because negotiations have been ongoing for several decades and the parties have concluded interim agreements calling for the peaceful settlement of these disputes.[44]

Overview of the Case Studies

Boundary settlements reached in the early 1960s and the manner in which the dispute with Japan over the Senkaku/Diaoyu Islands was handled in the 1970s show remarkable similarities in terms of Beijing's strategic objectives and response to shifts in the balance of power. Settlement of the Sino-Russian border and renewed Sino-Vietnamese boundary negotiations in the early 1990s also came at a time of significant change in the international system. This presents an interesting parallel: although separated by more than a decade in each instance, the cases are comparable in that boundary settlements coincided with important shifts in Beijing's strategic assessment and its corresponding efforts to resolve boundary disputes. These systemic changes, I argue, were a decisive factor influencing Beijing's policy toward its territorial disputes and boundary settlements.

Although the political dynamics of the outstanding territorial and boundary disputes – with India, Bhutan, and Japan as well as in the South China Sea – have been significantly transformed with the end of the Cold War, historical legacies and growing nationalistic sentiments still make the resolution of these disputes very problematic; in some instances, they are flashpoints of potential military confrontation. Beginning in the latter 1990s, however, in an effort to counterbalance the United States' dominant position in Asia,

China has actively sought to improve relations with its regional neighbours. Under a "New Security Concept," Beijing has fostered a "strategic partnership" with Russia, and through the Shanghai Cooperation Organization it has established a security partnership with its Eurasian neighbours. Efforts to improve relations have made significant progress, symbolized by the ASEAN Treaty of Amity and Cooperation in Southeast Asia that China signed in 2003, renouncing the use of force and committing to settle disputes peacefully.

The shifting balance of power and strategic concerns were decisive factors in China's conclusion of boundary settlements in the 1960s and sidestepping of disputes in the 1970s. The settlements concluded in the 1990s exhibit a similar pattern to earlier settlements despite the significant change in the international system with the end of the Cold War. Even the Sino-Indian dispute, which resulted in a border war in 1962 and is still unresolved, is comparable to the others because of the strikingly similar pattern in China's behaviour and approach. The improvement in US-Indian relations in recent years has given China greater incentive to improve relations with India, but a boundary settlement is necessary before this can happen. The 2003 tacit agreement on the Tibet-Sikkim boundary is a clear example of China's willingness to make concessions in order to build momentum toward a comprehensive resolution. These examples support the conclusion that China's behaviour is not idiosyncratic but rather follows a predictable pattern dictated by fundamental strategic imperatives that have impelled Beijing to engage in balancing behaviour.

Because of the relationship between China's behaviour in each of the various boundary disputes and settlements and these fundamental strategic imperatives, the cases discussed here are grouped according to the larger strategic context, the logic of Beijing's grand strategy, and China's primary security concerns at the time: deteriorating relations with India in the early 1960s, trepidation over US involvement in Southeast Asia and ongoing concerns about the Soviet threat in the 1960s and 1970s, and the post–Cold War strategic environment after 1990.

In Part 2, I consider boundary disputes settled with South Asian countries in the early 1960s (Chapters 2 to 6) in the context of Sino-Indian relations and the larger context of escalating tensions with the Soviet Union – a key factor throughout the 1960s – and China's overall concern with the growing presence of the United States in South and Southeast Asia. In other words, Sino-Indian negotiations in the late 1950s and early 1960s were not merely a function of the bilateral relationship, and China's handling of boundary disputes with other South Asian countries was not solely a function of the Sino-Indian boundary dispute, as other scholars have argued; rather, China's larger security concerns and strategic imperatives were paramount.

During the Cold War, the Soviet Union considered India geopolitically important as a non-aligned South Asian power. In the mid-1950s, Moscow began nurturing closer ties with India, providing India with significant economic assistance and political support. Soviet and Indian interests were complementary: Moscow supplied India with much-needed military and technical assistance, while India formed a bulwark against Chinese and American expansion into South Asia. Sino-Indian relations were exacerbated as the Soviets cultivated India as a counterweight to the United States and China by enlisting Indian military strength as a deterrent force and encouraging India to exclude US and Chinese influence from the region.[45]

The deterioration of Sino-Soviet relations during the late 1950s was accompanied by Chinese alarm at the growing warmth of Soviet-Indian relations. "One of Beijing's overriding strategic objectives" was "to prevent the greater threat emanating from the ... north from linking up with a threat to the PRC's southern borders." China sought to prevent further decline in its relations with India by attempting to settle the boundary dispute that had been a significant cause of conflict between the two countries. By the late 1950s, however, Sino-Indian relations had fallen to such a point that the dispute proved intractable.[46] China then sought to bolster relations with other South Asian states, using boundary settlements as a primary means of accomplishing this.

Many scholars have hypothesized that China's approach to these boundary disputes was a function of the Sino-Indian dispute, arguing that China "had incentives to avoid confrontation with some states and thereby convince those states to support [its] claims in a dispute with another adversary," in this case India. China, the thinking goes, "pursued accommodative policies in disputes with some states in order to foster an image of reasonableness and peaceful intentions, so as to build greater international support for [its] territorial claims" against India and, in other cases, the Soviet Union.[47] A more satisfactory explanation of China's behaviour can be found, however, by placing China's relations with its South Asian neighbours in the broader context of the challenges confronting Beijing as a result of growing US influence and deteriorating Sino-Soviet relations.

As Beijing worried about worsening relations with India, China suffered one of its greatest domestic economic disasters as a result of the Great Leap Forward. At the same time, it faced a growing Soviet threat along its northern border; increasing US involvement in Vietnam along its southern border as well as the US-supported Tibetan resistance based in Nepal; and the Nationalist Chinese government's desire to "retake the mainland" from its base on Taiwan as well as the Guomindang army's continued operations in Burma. This combination of internal political and economic challenges and growing external threats to China's security set the stage for a quick succession of boundary settlements in the early 1960s. The glaring exception is China's failure to achieve a compromise settlement with India, which precipitated the brief 1962 border war. Since the analysis of these disputes and settlements is placed within the broader framework of Sino-Indian relations, I will begin with a discussion of the Sino-Indian boundary dispute and the failure to achieve a settlement, then consider the cases settled in the early 1960s with China's other South Asian neighbours.

The next group of boundary disputes and settlements (Part 3, Chapters 7 to 10) fall along the Sino-Soviet/Russian dimension and are therefore analyzed in the larger context of this bilateral relationship. Although the Sino-Soviet boundary dispute became public only after China had negotiated settlements with several other states and the dispute with India had flared into a border war, relations with Moscow had already deteriorated over the previous several years. The crescendo in Sino-Soviet tensions necessitated a new tack in China's foreign policy and altered Beijing's approach toward boundary disputes and settlements with Mongolia, Japan, and Vietnam during the 1960s and 1970s.

As Sino-Soviet relations deteriorated in the late 1950s and the balance of power in East Asia began to shift, China attempted to counter the growing Soviet threat by developing better relations with other states in the region and with the United States.[48] A 1962 boundary settlement with the Mongolian People's Republic, like settlements with Burma and other neighbouring states, was part of Beijing's strategy to surround itself with friendly, or at least neutral, states. A decade after the Sino-Soviet boundary dispute became public, the dispute with Japan over the Senkaku/Diaoyu Islands erupted. China's national security concerns and strategies as well as its behaviour in this dispute paralleled those in the early 1960s. The Sino-Vietnamese dispute initially flared up in the 1970s and culminated in a border war in 1979. A final settlement on the land boundary was negotiated in December 1999 and the two countries agreed to a boundary in the Gulf of Tonkin a year later, after the collapse of the Soviet Union and the end of the Cold War; nevertheless, this case also shows how Beijing's concern over growing Soviet influence in the region drove China's initial efforts to settle the boundary dispute.

Since the analysis of these disputes and negotiations is placed within the broader framework of Sino-Soviet/Russian relations, I will begin with a discussion of the Sino-Soviet boundary dispute and the settlement that was negotiated with Russia during the 1990s and finalized in 2005. The Sino-Korean boundary settlement is quite mysterious for lack of significant documentation, but is discussed briefly with the Sino-Russian boundary settlement. I then turn to the settlement negotiated with Mongolia in the early 1960s. This is followed by analysis of the unsettled disputes with Japan because the timing of the initial negotiations relates China's behaviour to larger strategic concerns with the Soviet Union. The final chapter in Part 3 considers the settlement with Vietnam in the latter 1990s. The situation along the boundary with Laos is also inscrutable for lack of significant documentation, but is discussed briefly with the Sino-Vietnamese boundary settlement.

In Part 4, I analyze the contemporary settlements with China's Eurasian neighbours (Chapter 11) and the South China Sea disputes (Chapter 12). Following the collapse of the Soviet Union, Beijing moved deftly to establish close security and economic relations with the newly independent Eurasian states. Uppermost in China's mind was the post–Cold War strategic environment in the region and security along its Eurasian frontier. A primary concern was the security vacuum left by the collapse of the Soviet Union and the subsequent increase in US influence in the region. An editorial critical of NATO expansion into Eurasia highlights China's threat perception: "NATO is actively expanding itself ... [and] constitutes a new threat." Explicitly identifying the United States, the editorial concluded that "instead of restraining its power politics and hegemonism, the superpower is intensifying its efforts to continue to pursue them."[49] The fluid security environment in the region threatened China's western frontier, and it became Beijing's goal to establish a security perimeter in Eurasia by improving relations and establishing closer security cooperation with these newly independent neighbours.[50] Key to enhancing relations with Kazakhstan, Kyrgyzstan, and Tajikistan were boundary settlements to reassure them that China was not planning to lay claim to territories that it believed Russia had taken by force or "unequal treaties" over the past century. Eliminating the Eurasian countries' concerns over Chinese irredentism was the first step in strengthening China's role as a major player in regional security, and in building the economic relations necessary for China's development and meeting its growing energy needs.

The South China Sea disputes involve hundreds of uninhabitable small islets, coral atolls, reefs, shoals, and submerged rocks scattered across the South China Sea; China's total maritime claims cover approximately 3.5 million square kilometres. When analyzing these disputes, it is important to distinguish two separate issues: the Sino-Vietnamese dispute over the Paracel Islands, about 150 miles southwest of Hainan Island, and the multilateral dispute over the Spratly Islands. The issue of sovereignty over the Spratlys is unique and more complex because it involves claims by the People's Republic of China, Vietnam, the Philippines, Malaysia, and Brunei, complicated by the claim by Taiwan, the Republic of China. Placing these disputes in a larger strategic context illustrates how China's behaviour has paralleled its behaviour in earlier cases. Finally, the concluding chapter highlights the correlation of China's behaviour in all of these disputes and settlements with its broader strategic concerns that forms the main analytical thread running through this book.

Before we turn to the case studies, Chapter 1 will establish a historical vantage point. State boundaries have fundamental historical significance because they affirm a state's power. Boundary lines are "not a product of nature but a product of histories and struggle between competing authorities over power to organize, occupy, and administer political space," and imperial China "exercised [its] power through [its] ability to impose order and meaning upon space."[51] According to Henry Kissinger:

> Any international settlement represents a stage in a process by which a nation reconciles its vision of itself with the vision of it by other powers ... But an exact balance is impossible ... because while powers may appear to outsiders as factors in a security arrangement, they appear domestically as expressions of a historical existence. No power will submit to a settlement, however well-balanced and however "secure," which seems totally to deny its vision of itself.[52]

This observation seems especially relevant to China since its past wields an imposing power over the present. An understanding of contemporary boundary disputes and settlements is impossible without some understanding of the historical legacy inherited by the People's Republic of China.

1 The Historical Legacy

The understandable alarm on the part of China's neighbours over Beijing's historical claims to territory far beyond the borders it actually controlled has been one of the major obstacles to the achievement of boundary settlements, despite Beijing's apparent willingness to conclude treaties based on realistic historical, geographic, and security considerations. The People's Republic of China inherited a dual legacy of pre-nineteenth-century regional hegemony followed by colonial domination by the West. The former had lasted for millennia, whereas the latter, characterized by the "one hundred years of humiliation" beginning with the 1842 Treaty of Nanjing following the First Opium War, lasted until 1943, when the major Western powers renounced the unequal treaties. Throughout its history, China's geographical dimensions expanded and contracted as the power of the ruling dynasty waxed or waned and peripheral regions slipped from control, or China ceded territory to imperialist powers. The residual effects of this dual legacy continue to the present. Like other post-colonial nations, the People's Republic of China is hypersensitive to issues concerning sovereignty and territorial integrity, and harbours irredentist sentiments. These underlying historical and nationalistic obsessions have complicated the negotiation of boundary settlements. Despite the ideological commitment and irredentist views common among Chinese leaders, however, Beijing, acutely aware of strategic imperatives, has shown pragmatism and compromised on boundary issues in order to achieve more fundamental security objectives. What is the PRC's vision of the geographical bounds of "China" and how has this changed over time? What is Beijing's policy regarding the recovery of "lost" territory? This chapter analyzes the historical legacy inherited by the PRC, focusing on the influence of both the ideological aspects of this legacy and the impact of international politics on Beijing's contemporary territorial and boundary policy.

The Introduction concluded with the assertion that history is one determining factor in any country's foreign policy. In China's case, understanding this historical legacy is perhaps even more important because this legacy is "one of the most impressive instances" of the power of the past over the present.[1] According to historian John K. Fairbank, to disregard China's history and "especially the tradition in foreign policy, is truly to be flying blind."[2] What is commonly referred to as the traditional "Chinese world order" has, despite centuries of interaction with the outside world, "persisted as a symbol of the world as the Chinese elite imagined it should be," even after any semblance of this Sinocentric "world order" has ceased to exist.[3] Thus, when studying China's boundary disputes and settlements, we must distinguish historical "myth" from political "reality" while recognizing that both influence China's behaviour.[4]

The political elites of China retain the "distilled essence" of China's Sinocentric world order; a notion of the geographical realm and the historical setting based primarily on the Qing Empire forms their mindset.[5] Although this cultural and psychological mindset may provide the substance of a unique Chinese world view that is an important variable in foreign policy, it is only one factor influencing Beijing's foreign policy and is constrained by the dynamics and structure of the international system – the political reality that "conditions their calculations, their behavior, and their interactions."[6] These systemic factors and the boundaries inherited from the Qing Empire that China feels obligated to defend, along with an acute consciousness of past colonial infringement on its sovereignty, have a significant impact on China's foreign policy and together determine its policy on specific boundary disputes and settlements.[7] The Chinese, however, have demonstrated a remarkable "capacity to compromise" when necessary, in order to strike a balance between, on the one hand, controlling peripheral areas believed to have belonged to China historically and culturally and, on the other hand, consolidating borders to facilitate alliances and ensure the security of the heartland.[8]

Tu Wei-ming, the renowned Chinese historian, argues that Chinese "know reflexively what China proper refers to," and the "impression that geopolitical China evolved through a long process centering around a definable core remains deeply rooted."[9] Even before taking power in 1949, Mao Zedong identified foreign-controlled territory that he believed was historically China's. On the heels of the "one hundred years of humiliation," the

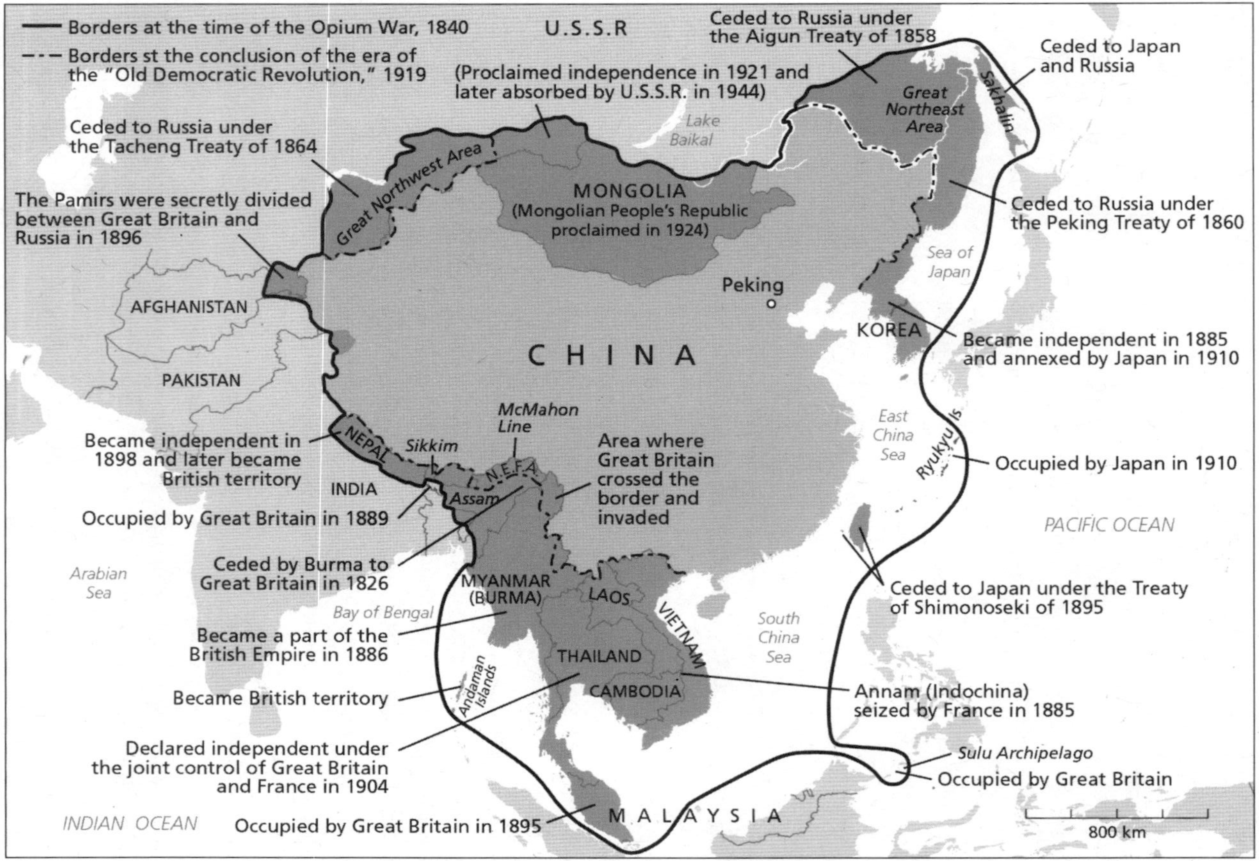
Borders at the time of the Opium War, 1840
Borders st the conclusion of the era of the "Old Democratic Revolution," 1919
U.S.S.R
Ceded to Russia under the Aigun Treaty of 1858
Ceded to Japan and Russia
Sakhalin
Great Northeast Area
(Proclaimed independence in 1921 and later absorbed by U.S.S.R. in 1944)
Lake Baikal
Ceded to Russia under the Tacheng Treaty of 1864
Great Northwest Area
MONGOLIA
(Mongolian People's Republic proclaimed in 1924)
Ceded to Russia under the Peking Treaty of 1860
The Pamirs were secretly divided between Great Britain and Russia in 1896
Sea of Japan
Peking
AFGHANISTAN
KOREA
Became independent in 1885 and annexed by Japan in 1910
C H I N A
PAKISTAN
McMahon Line
East China Sea
Became independent in 1898 and later became British territory
NEPAL
Sikkim
N.E.F.A.
Area where Great Britain crossed the border and invaded
Ryukyu Is
Occupied by Japan in 1910
INDIA
Assam
Occupied by Great Britain in 1889
PACIFIC OCEAN
Ceded by Burma to Great Britain in 1826
Arabian Sea
MYANMAR (BURMA)
LAOS
VIETNAM
Ceded to Japan under the Treaty of Shimonoseki of 1895
Bay of Bengal
South China Sea
Became a part of the British Empire in 1886
THAILAND
Andaman Islands
CAMBODIA
Annam (Indochina) seized by France in 1885
Became British territory
Declared independent under the joint control of Great Britain and France in 1904
Sulu Archipelago
Occupied by Great Britain
INDIAN OCEAN
Occupied by Great Britain in 1895
M A L A Y S I A
800 km

Map 2 "Lost" Territory. *Source:* Adapted from the original published in Liu Peihua, *Zhongguo jindaishi* (Beijing: Yichang shuju, 1954).

communists came to power harbouring a hypersensitivity about "lost territory." Li Jijun, a former lieutenant general and vice president of the People's Liberation Army Academy of Military Sciences, explains that "this was a period of humiliation that the Chinese people can never forget. This is why the people of China show such strong emotions in matters concerning our ... integrity of territory, and sovereignty. This is also why the Chinese are so determined to safeguard them under any circumstances and at all costs."[10] This strong sense of territoriality, buttressed by an image of the past glory of a "united" empire and often bellicose and extensive territorial claims, alarmed the PRC's neighbours (see Map 2). Beijing, however, has shown sensitivity to the realities of international politics. When engaging with neighbouring countries, officials have intuitively assumed the legitimacy of Beijing's territorial claims but, cognizant of strategic imperatives, have adopted pragmatic policies to resolve boundary disputes.

China's Territorial Legacy

China's nationalistic historiography adopts an "essentialist view" of the contemporary Chinese state, which Chinese believe evolved historically, without any "fundamental alteration"; they also assume that the Qing Empire's boundaries should constitute the modern state.[11] This nationalist myth is embraced by the PRC, but historically China did conclude boundary treaties defining the territorial extent of China. As early as the Tang Dynasty (618-907), treaties delineated China's boundaries. These treaties constituted "clearly demarcated borderlines" and stipulated how boundary disputes were to be handled, demonstrating that China did "think in terms of ownership of territory" and was "concerned about precise border designations and apprehensive about military maneuvers and the construction of new military facilities along these borders."[12]

By the late eighteenth century, China had developed an inclusive "territorial ideology" that was crucial in the formation of the modern Chinese national identity, even if its validation was based on self-serving historical evidence.[13] Ho Ping-ti concludes that the Manchu were of the "greatest importance to the formation of modern China as a geographic entity," asserting that "the Ch'ing [Qing] is without doubt the most successful dynasty of conquest in Chinese history."[14] During the Simla Conference held in 1914 to negotiate a boundary between China and British India, the Republic of China resisted any compromise, arguing that "the Republic has no right to alienate any part of the territory which she has inherited from the Manchu dynasty, and she must maintain the extent of her territory the same as before."[15]

Published in 1925, *Zhongguo sangdi shi (History of China's Lost Territory)* is an example of grandiose Chinese claims regarding "lost" territory.[16] Although the author cites the great expanse of the Mongol Empire, he argues that China should claim only territory included in the Manchu Empire, for two reasons:

> First, the territory inherited by the Republic [of China] comes directly from what was controlled by the Qing during its final days ... and secondly, all areas inhabited by the Han, Manchu, Mongols, Muslims and Tibetans are in fact unified, which was completed during the Qing.[17]

The PRC expressed similar views on China's historical frontiers in a lengthy *Renmin ribao (People's Daily)* article:

> During the reign of the Kangxi, Yongzheng and Qianlong Emperors ... the government of the Qing Dynasty ... consolidated its rule over the North Desert [Mongolia], Xizang [Tibet] and Xinjiang. All of these constituted indelible historical contributions to safeguarding the vast territory of China.

The same article emphasized that the territorial integrity of China was key to national security:

> Only national unification can effectively resist the invasions of foreign countries and safeguard the independence of the motherland ... During the reigns of the Ming and Qing Dynasties, colonists from the West and expansionists of Tsarist Russia all stretched their claws of aggression into China. If China at that time had not been a powerful unified country, it could hardly have resisted their nibbling.[18]

Furthermore:

> Patriotism is a kind of profound feeling towards the motherland shaped and cultivated over hundreds of years. The people in our country have patriotic traditions, and this is closely related to the fact that China has been a constantly developed and consolidated unified country since ancient times.[19]

In the words of one sinologist, therefore, the PRC is "clinging to the ways of empire" because it believes in the notion of "China as old, unchanging, united, and consistent," not unlike classical Chinese cartography, which "tended to depict the world not so much in terms of how it 'actually' was, but rather in terms of how they wanted it to be."[20] The power of this historical identity is clear from the fact that the PRC embraces a normative vision of a China with boundaries that correspond to the borders of the Qing Empire. The persistence of this territorial ideology in the minds of Chinese and the trepidation this engenders among China's neighbours was articulated by the former prime minister of Singapore, Lee Kuan Yew: "As China's development nears the point when it will have enough weight to elbow its way into the region ... all countries in Asia, medium and small, have this concern: will China seek to re-establish its traditional pattern on international relations of vassal states in a tributary relationship with the Middle Kingdom?"[21]

Evolution of the Communists' Territorial Policy

The PRC embraced the view that the boundaries of China were the "outgrowth of the historical development of the past several thousand years."[22] This territorial vision of China is in fact the fusion of the historical legacy of a traditional Sinocentric worldview and modern nationalism inherited by the communists.[23] Before it came to power in 1949, the Chinese Communist Party (CCP) supported the right of self-determination and, at least publicly, accepted the possibility that certain regions would seek independent statehood. However, Mao Zedong harboured a deep obsession with the inclusion of the vast territories of the Qing Empire within the boundaries of modern China, and although he initially supported national self-determination and a Chinese federation, the historical unity of China became paramount after 1949.

The Manifesto of the Second National Congress, held in July 1922, spelled out the CCP's vision of the eventual territorial boundaries of China: "The unification of China proper (including Manchuria) into a genuine democratic republic ... The establishment of a Chinese Federated Republic by the unification of China proper, Mongolia, Tibet, and Sinkiang into a free federation."[24] In 1928, the Sixth National Congress called for the unity of China but supported the right of national self-determination.[25] At the First All-China Congress of Soviets, held in November 1931, a resolution on the "Question of National Minorities" declared:

In the Fundamental Law (constitution) of the Chinese Soviet Republic it shall be clearly stated that all national minorities within the confines of China shall have the right to national self-determination, including secession from China and the formation of independent states, and that the Chinese Soviet Republic fully and unconditionally recognizes the independence of the Outer Mongolian People's Republic.[26]

Despite his initial support for the right of independence and national self-determination, Mao revealed his views on the future territorial dimensions of China in an interview with Edgar Snow in July 1936:

It is the immediate task of China to regain all our lost territories, not merely to defend our sovereignty below the great wall [sic]. This means that Manchuria must be regained ... As for Inner Mongolia, we will struggle to drive Japan from there and help Inner Mongolia to establish an autonomous state.

But Mao believed that:

When the people's revolution has been victorious in China, the Outer Mongolian republic will automatically become a part of the Chinese federation, at its own will. The Mohammedan and Tibetan peoples, likewise, will form autonomous republics attached to the Chinese federation.[27]

In a 1944 interview with Gunther Stein, Mao excluded Manchuria and Taiwan from areas that should be granted autonomy:

Outer Mongolia is part of China. But it is a nation ... China must first recognize Outer Mongolia as a national entity. Then organize a sort of United States of China to meet their aspirations. We believe they will come to join.

The same is true concerning Tibet ... The Mohammedans should also be given a chance to form their state. Manchurians are no longer a separate nationality. Nor are Formosans.[28]

Mao clearly believed that territory included in the Qing Empire belonged to China.

The CCP's more nationalistic and inclusive view of China is evident in the textbook *The Chinese Revolution and the Chinese Communist Party*. Originally published in 1939, the book describes China's territorial boundaries:

The present boundaries of China are: Bordering on the Union of Soviet Socialist Republics in the northeast, northwest and a portion of the west. In a portion of the west and the southwest bordering on India, Bhutan and Nepal. In the south bordering on Siam, Burma, Annam and close to Taiwan. In the east close to Japan and bordering Korea.

This paragraph was revised in the 1952 edition:

The present boundaries of China are: Bordering on the Union of Soviet Socialist Republics in the northeast, northwest and a portion of the west. Bordering on the Mongolian People's Republic in the north. In a portion of the west and the southwest bordering on Afghanistan, India, Bhutan and Nepal. In the south bordering on Burma and Vietnam. In the east bordering on Korea and close to Japan and the Philippines.

The earlier edition classified several neighbouring states as "vassal states" *(fan)*:

After defeating China in war, the imperialist states then stole several of China's vassal states and a portion of her territory. Japan occupied Korea, Taiwan, the Ryukyus, Penghu islands and Port Arthur; England occupied Burma, Bhutan, Nepal and Hong Kong; France occupied Annam; and a tiny state like Portugal even occupied Macao.

The revised edition changed this to:

After defeating China in war, the imperialist states not only occupied several surrounding states that originally received the protection of China, but also stole or "leased" a portion of China. For example, Japan occupied Taiwan and the Penghu islands and "leased" Port Arthur; England occupied Hong Kong; and France "leased" Guangzhouwan.[29]

In 1949, the establishment of a centralized state of multiple nationalities was the culmination of the dual forces of the myth of a historically united centralized state and modern nationalism. The constitution of the People's Republic of China characterized the new nation as a "big fraternal and co-operative family composed of all nationalities," and prohibited "splitting of the unity of the various nationalities."[30] Secession was no longer considered a legitimate right and autonomous regions were considered "inalienable parts of the People's Republic of China."[31] The following rationalization was given:

> Led and instructed by the Chinese Communist Party, the people of each nationality had already greatly heightened their ... patriotic consciousness, greatly changed and transcended their original situation of mutual antagonism, and gradually formed bonds of equality, unity, mutual help, and cooperation as a basis for realizing common political aims and interests. Therefore, the establishment of a united, multinational state was the desire of the great bulk of the people of all nationalities in our country.[32]

Ho Ping-ti concludes that because of the historical legacy of foreign encroachment, "every party had learned from *Realpolitik* that the true status of any of China's peripheral areas depended on China's ability to exert effective control. It is this rude historical lesson that prompted the People's Republic of China to seize the earliest possible opportunities to rush its army into Sinkiang and Tibet."[33]

Development of the PRC's Boundary Policy

The PRC's expansive territorial vision of China alarmed its neighbours. In the early 1950s, the PRC continued to publish books describing "lost" territories far beyond the borders of the Qing Empire. A 1954 textbook on modern Chinese history recounted the British and French invasions of Southeast Asia that ended those countries' tributary relations with the Qing court, and concluded: "From this, China completely lost its southwestern line of defense."[34] The territories "lost" by China are "the vassal states of Ryukyu, Vietnam, Burma and Thailand, which originally belonged with the territory of China, but were all lost as colonies to the aggressors."[35] A *Renmin ribao* article illustrated China's sensitivity toward boundary issues: "Everybody knows that India used the first opportunity, when at the early establishment of the People's Republic of China, [we] had no time to pay attention to the ... border question, to do things which not even British imperialism dared to do ... to cut off part of the territory of China."[36]

As in the past, however, the PRC's territorial policy was necessarily tempered by the "rude historical lessons" of realpolitik and the dynamics of the international system. While in Moscow negotiating the Sino-Soviet treaty in 1950, Mao was obliged to recognize the independence of the Mongolian

People's Republic – a "bitter pill to swallow for a man who had been obsessed since his earliest boyhood with the disintegration of the Chinese empire, and who had always defined the empire in the broadest possible terms."[37] Accepting Mongolia's independence is difficult for any Chinese government because of the dissonance caused in the normative image of what should constitute China's territoriality. A contemporary Chinese scholar underlines this point:

> Such unbridled annexation of territory is rare in history. Moreover, people ... in today's China still remember how China's map was turned from a "mulberry leaf," as the school textbooks described it before 1945, into a "rooster," as current Chinese geographers characterize it, due to the nibbling away of Outer Mongolia by the Soviet worm.[38]

Yet this is a clear example of how the PRC's territorial claims are tempered by larger strategic imperatives.

Beijing's position regarding other "lost" territories became clear through a process of "denial" and "affirmation." After 1949, Beijing readily recognized several states considered former "vassals" of imperial China. This denial of suzerainty "established an important discontinuity with its imperial past."[39] The PRC also affirmed its claim to other areas:

> Some people inquire: "Since we recognized Mongolia's independence, in the future shouldn't we recognize the independence of Inner Mongolia, Tibet, etc.?" We respond by saying ... Mongolia gained independence under these historical conditions ... Therefore, our position is to continue to recognize and guarantee their independence, and [we] do not need them to be reunified with China as one country ... What of Inner Mongolia, Tibet and other nationalities presently within China? We were liberated at about the same time. The present problem is to join forces to build a strong new China together, not to be divided and independent ... Only in this way will the best interests of all nationalities presently within China be served. We must not forget that specific historical conditions derive from the basic interests of the people. This should be the basis upon which we view issues.[40]

Thus, Beijing's vision of China's boundaries came into sharper focus, and in the ensuing decade China demonstrated its willingness to use military force to assert its claims but also to negotiate boundary treaties with its neighbours based on "historical customary" boundaries.

Any consideration of Beijing's boundary policy must include a discussion of "unequal treaties" because of the pivotal role they play in nearly all of China's boundary disputes and settlements. The PRC's definition of an unequal treaty is neither clear nor consistent; Beijing has never spelled out the principles of an unequal treaty, merely listing treaties it considers unequal, and even this list has changed according to political expediency.[41] According to one Chinese scholar, however:

> The Unequal Treaties have become a symbol invested with a host of meanings extended well beyond the implications of the first treaty encounter between China and Britain in 1842 ... The question of the Unequal Treaties is consequently a matter not only of historical, academic, and diplomatic debate, but also of current political and cultural interest.[42]

General Li Jijun expressed China's sensitivity over this historical legacy:

> Before 1949, when the People's Republic of China was established, more than 1000 treaties and agreements, most of which were unequal in their terms, were forced on China by the Western powers. As many as 1.8 million square kilometers were also taken away from Chinese territory. This was a period of humiliation that the Chinese people can never forget.[43]

During the pre-modern period, China did negotiate boundary treaties determined by the balance of power and based on "equality or diplomatic parity."[44] In modern times, China initiated the practice of establishing boundaries by treaty when it signed the Treaty of Nerchinsk with Russia in 1689, establishing the boundary between the Manchu Empire and the Russian Empire. This treaty and several Sino-Russian boundary treaties that followed were, in the view of some Chinese writers, all equal treaties, but other Chinese scholars consider them unequal based on modern international law.[45] China established treaty relations with other Western nations in the mid-nineteenth century. The 1842 Treaty of Nanjing concluded with Great Britain at the end of the First Opium War was the first quintessential unequal treaty forced on China.

The PRC's position on the question of the legitimacy of the boundary treaties signed by previous governments was initially left in limbo. On the eve of the establishment of the PRC, the CCP declared that it would reconsider previous treaties concluded with foreign powers, especially those concluded by the Nationalist government, but did not clearly specify which treaties it would reconsider. Addressing the Bandung Conference in 1955, Zhou Enlai stated: "With some ... countries we have not yet finally fixed our border line and we are ready to do so ... But before doing so, we are willing to maintain the present situation by acknowledging that those parts of our border are parts which are undetermined."[46] This rejection of older boundary treaties fuelled speculation about Chinese irredentism and set the stage for future boundary disputes with virtually every neighbouring state by making it clear that China did not accept the earlier boundary treaties as legitimate treaties.

Other actions compounded the apprehension felt by China's neighbours. A week following the Bandung Conference, during which Sino-Indian cooperation appeared unshakable, Indian trade union representatives cut short their attendance at May Day celebrations in Beijing to protest map displays that included Aksai Chin within China. China's *World Knowledge Handbook* published in 1957 enumerated countries neighbouring China, but did not list Bhutan and Sikkim. A *Renmin ribao* article even clouded the PRC's view of Korea when it listed the 1895 Treaty of Shimonoseki, in which China recognized the independence of Korea, as an unequal treaty.[47] In an 8 March 1963 *Renmin ribao* editorial, the 1957 statement was revived and the editorial included the boundary treaties signed with Czarist Russia as unequal treaties.[48] Mao's famous 1964 statement about presenting a "bill" to the Soviet Union for vast regions of Siberia once included in the Manchu Empire alarmed Moscow.[49]

Beijing never enunciated a clear position on the recovery of "lost" territory. Although the above statements and intimations caused apprehension among its neighbours, Beijing clearly did not claim sovereignty over all regions that China's *ancien régime* may have considered suzerain territories. And in practice Beijing has never insisted on the return of this territory, only the recognition that in many cases it was taken from China by "unequal treaty" or imperialist force. Nevertheless, this obsession with "lost" territory underscores the deep sensitivity of Chinese over China's territorial legacy and historical "injustices," complicated further by nationalism as a potent force in contemporary China.

In the late 1950s, as Beijing moved to solve boundary problems "left over by history," China first placed the disputes in a larger context taking "politics, strategies, diplomacy and the nation's security into account."[50] It then adopted four principles to guide boundary negotiations: (1) recognizing that boundary

disputes were the result of imperialism and unequal treaties; (2) not asserting claims to traditional tributary areas or older historical claims; (3) negotiating new boundaries based on earlier boundary treaties (despite the fact
that imperialist powers forced these unequal treaties on a weak China); and
(4) maintaining China's "national stand" in negotiations, but at the same
time avoiding "big nation chauvinism."[51] Beijing advocated adopting modern techniques to delimit the boundaries precisely in order to maintain
"distinct and stable" boundary lines, believing that this would "promote
understanding and deepen friendship" with its neighbours because they
would "recognize China's consistent policy of respect for sovereignty and
territorial integrity, mutual equality, mutual understanding and mutual
compromise, and solving boundary disputes peacefully through friendly
consultations."[52] Therefore, "even though parts of Chinese territory are still
occupied by its neighbors, China has shown great restraint and patience
as it calls for peaceful solutions to the territorial disputes left by history."[53]

Conclusion

The leaders of the People's Republic of China are slaves to their image of
the past grandeur of the Chinese empire. The CCP's territorial policy initially
supported self-determination and secession, but was abandoned as the communists faced possible loss of territory. The forces of hypernationalism and
China's imperial legacy influenced the communists' policy toward boundary
disputes and settlements, but this was tempered by international systemic
constraints and the strategic imperatives they faced once in power.

The boundaries the PRC inherited were reminders of the "century of
humiliation" China had suffered. After 1949, when the PRC asserted traditional historical claims conflict with neighbouring states became inevitable.
How the PRC would approach the settlement of these disputes was not clear
at the time, and rejection of the boundary treaties signed by previous governments fuelled apprehensions that the PRC was revanchist and would
attempt to recover "lost" territories. Although Beijing never insisted that it
should regain these "lost" territories, historical pride in the former imperial
greatness of China, and mention of this in textbooks or other publications,
caused understandable apprehension among China's neighbours, a feeling
that persists among some today.

The boundary disputes between China and its neighbours are one legacy
of the age of imperialism: imposed boundaries that may ignore "historical
customary" divisions or boundaries that were never clearly delimited and

often never demarcated. When the PRC emerged as a strong, united nation in 1949, its leaders faced the task of negotiating its boundaries, often with states that had also recently emerged from a colonial past. Under such circumstances, acute sensitivity to issues of sovereignty and territorial integrity made boundary settlements even more difficult.

An understanding of the influence of China's historical legacy on the PRC's contemporary boundary policy is fundamental. An obsession with the historical dimensions of China made the resolution of historical boundary disputes difficult, but international factors compelled Beijing to make territorial compromises in order to meet strategic imperatives. Despite unique national characteristics due to this historical legacy, the PRC, like all other states in the international system, responds to fundamental systemic structural constraints that dictate its policy toward boundary disputes and settlements. The case studies in the following chapters are analyzed in the larger context of international systemic forces and Beijing's strategic considerations.

PART 2
The Sino-Indian Dimension

2 Sino-Indian Relations and Boundary Disputes

The Sino-Indian boundary dispute has received more attention than any of China's other boundary disputes, with the possible exception of the dispute with Russia. Certainly more official government documents are available on the Sino-Indian dispute than on any other. The 1962 border war with India was only the second sizable military engagement involving troops of the People's Republic of China, and the first ostensibly undertaken to defend China's "sovereignty and territorial integrity." This chapter analyzes the development of the Sino-Indian boundary dispute, focusing primarily on the larger strategic context of the dispute's genesis and evolution but also considering domestic political factors.

Historical Background

Throughout history, India and China have shared an ill-defined frontier. China extended its control into South and Central Asia during periods of dynastic expansion, only to withdraw as central power declined. Before the British colonization of India, various Chinese dynasties united parts of the subcontinent but never exercised control to the same extent as the British Raj, which extended its control over the Himalayan states and secured special privileges in Tibet. With few exceptions, attempts to delimit the boundary between China and British India were unsuccessful.

Kashmiri and Tibetan officials delimited the frontier between Ladakh and Tibet as early as 1684, and again in 1842. The fact that these agreements contain no detailed descriptions of the boundary and mention only general landmarks suggests the clear recognition of a traditional customary boundary. Whereas India claims that these are legitimate treaties, China contends that no authentic texts of these treaties exist and that they are therefore not valid. Chinese sources cite volume 12 of *Aitchison's Treaties*, compiled by British authorities, which concludes: "The northern and eastern borders of the State of Jammu and Kashmir have not been delimited."[1] In any case, these early agreements are so vague that they are not helpful in delimiting the boundary and have only muddied the historical waters, adding to the intractable nature of the present boundary dispute.

Chinese authority in Tibet grew following the 1911 revolution establishing the Republic of China. Concerned about securing the northeastern boundary of the Raj, British authorities began to push beyond Britain's so-called outer line of control into the tribal areas along the foothills of the Himalayas where neither British authorities nor Tibetan officials exercised effective control. This was truly a frontier area that formed a buffer between the Chinese empire and British-controlled India, and there were no clear boundaries. The historically complex religious authority exercised by Tibet over some localities in the area further complicates contemporary Chinese and Indian claims.

The 1913-14 Simla Conference was Great Britain's final attempt to delimit the eastern sector of the boundary between India and China. British, Tibetan, and Chinese representatives considered establishing the boundary along the Himalayan watershed, known as the McMahon Line after Sir Henry McMahon, the British representative at the conference. This attempt failed, however, because China's representative refused to sign the convention and the Chinese government did not recognize the authority of the Tibetan negotiator. After several subsequent attempts by Britain to gain China's approval of the Simla Convention were firmly rebuffed, Britain unilaterally published the agreement in 1934. Tibetan leaders were also unhappy with the convention, and after the British departure from India, they requested that the Indian government return areas that the British had occupied, such as Ladakh, Bhutan, Sikkim, and even Darjeeling. The Indian response was equivocal.[2] Even after fleeing to India in 1959, the Dalai Lama chided the Indians for claiming that the McMahon Line was the legitimate boundary between China and India: "If you deny sovereign status to Tibet, you deny the validity of the Simla Convention, and therefore you deny the validity of the McMahon Line."[3]

China-India Rivalry

The British exit from India in 1947 and the communists' rise to power in China two years later set the stage for confrontation between two newly independent and hypernationalistic nations. In the words of one Indian scholar, this was the legacy left to these two young nation-states "because neither of the two past governments really got to grips with the question.

The question of a definitive map was left suspended, only to become a bone of contention between the two succeeding national governments."⁴ The result was tragic conflict as both states sought to establish national boundaries based on historical occupation or control couched in competing national myths. Despite attempts to establish amicable relations, India and China appeared destined to become opposing regional powers. This broader political context is critical to understanding the contemporary boundary dispute.

Although India and China established diplomatic relations, Beijing's attitude toward India remained somewhat tentative and skeptical for several years. Outwardly, relations were good, but Chinese leaders viewed Prime Minister Jawaharlal Nehru as a national bourgeois "running dog" of imperialism. Beijing supported the Indian communists, predicting that a socialist revolution would eventually succeed in India. Nehru believed that, culturally and politically, the "basic challenge in South Asia is between India and China."⁵ K.M. Panikkar, the last Indian ambassador to the Nationalist government, returned to Beijing as his country's ambassador to the People's Republic of China. Aware of the tendency toward "rivalry" and "misunderstanding" between China and India, he believed that "cordial and intimate relations" between the two states would be all but impossible.⁶ Krishna Menon, a leading figure in India's foreign policy establishment, was also pessimistic about Sino-Indian relations. Writing in 1947, several years before the communists came to power and seized control of Tibet, he concluded: "Kautiliya, known as the Indian Machiavelli, defined an enemy 2,200 years ago as 'that state which is situated on the border of one's own state.' In other words, what constitutes a state an enemy actual or potential, is not its conduct but its proximity. A brutal definition ... borne out by history ... [T]he realism of Kautiliya is a useful corrective to our idealism in international politics."⁷

Cultural rivalry and geographical propinquity impelled the two countries toward misunderstanding and conflict. An immediate cause of friction between New Delhi and Beijing in the early 1950s was China's assertion of control over Tibet. India had assumed Britain's treaty privileges in Tibet after 1947, and Nehru himself advocated the independence of Tibet during the Chinese civil war; New Delhi also cooperated with Britain and the United States to support a fledgling Tibetan independence movement.⁸ Following China's assertion of control over Tibet in 1950, Nehru's sympathies lay with the Tibetans, and this continued to influence his view of the issue throughout the 1950s.⁹ During the "liberation" of Tibet, Beijing accused India of being "affected by foreign influences hostile to China," while New Delhi felt that

China had acted with "extreme discourtesy." The Tibet issue necessitated early Sino-Indian negotiations. Despite sympathizing with Tibet, India realized it would have to recognize China's domination of Tibet and relinquish the special privileges it had inherited from Britain. In 1954, India and China reached an agreement on Tibet that legitimized Indian trade and cultural interests but recognized Chinese control.[10]

Even before the 1954 negotiations, New Delhi was alarmed by China's claim that "China's western borders were consolidated." In November 1950, speaking before the Indian Parliament, Nehru declared:

> The frontier from Bhutan eastward has been clearly defined by the McMahon Line ... The frontier from Ladakh to Nepal is defined chiefly by long usage and custom ... [T]hat is our boundary – map or no map. That fact remains and we stand by that boundary, and we will not allow anybody to come across that boundary.[11]

Nehru's vision of India as an ancient nation and an internalized historical vision of Indian geography informed his view of the boundary. Moreover, he believed that the British had been, for geopolitical expediency, willing to surrender territory that was historically Indian. This national mythology of sacred territory resulted in an inflexibility that prevented India from making any territorial concessions.[12] China controlled Aksai Chin, located north of the Karakoram mountain range, which is an extension of the ancient northeastern Kashmir kingdom of Ladakh. In 1953, New Delhi rejected the 1899 British decision to draw the northern boundary of Ladakh along the Karakoram, which left Aksai Chin outside of British India. Using older maps, Indian officials redrew their country's boundary along the northern edge of Aksai Chin and rejected the notion that the border of Aksai Chin and the middle sector near the border with Nepal was "undefined." In the eastern sector, India changed the broken line depicting the McMahon Line as "defined but undemarcated" to a solid line, thus portraying the entire Sino-Indian boundary as much more formalized than was actually the case.[13] On several occasions even in the late 1940s, the Republic of China government had protested British and then Indian encroachment into areas claimed by China south of the McMahon Line (see Map 3).[14]

At this early date, both China and India clearly realized that a boundary dispute existed. Senior officials in India's Ministry of External Affairs wanted Sino-Indian negotiations over Tibet to include the entire boundary issue.

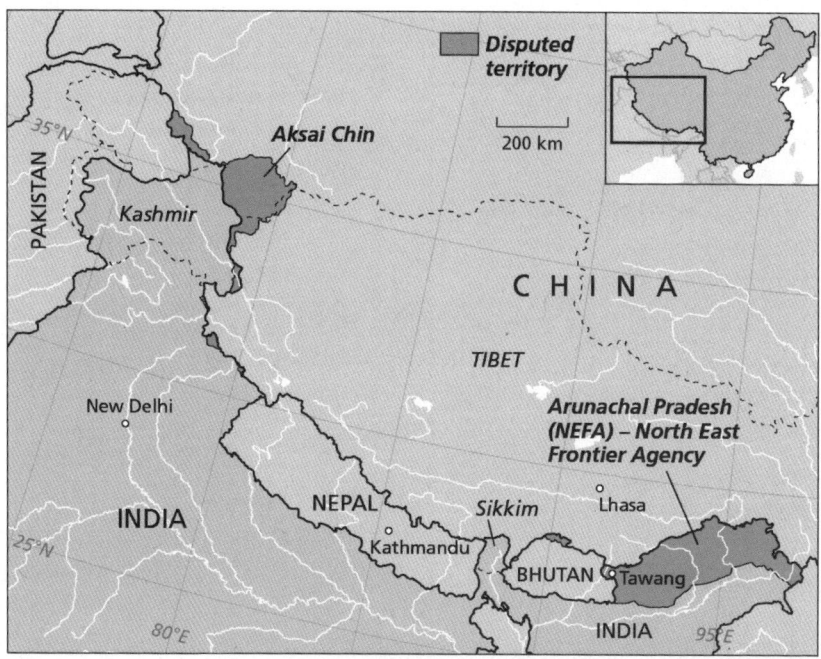

Map 3 India

Nehru supported this policy initially but Beijing resisted. Although China did not want to open the boundary question at the time, Zhou Enlai, recognizing the existence of a dispute, stated that "big countries like India and China with long frontiers were bound to have many questions at issue." Zhou believed, however, that conditions were not yet "ripe for settlement" because the Chinese side had had no time to "study the question." China's unwillingness to discuss the issue at the time or to make any adjustments without a joint survey kept the question open for future negotiations.[15] Nehru wanted an explicit commitment from Beijing on the boundary, but Ambassador Panikkar persuaded him not to press for negotiations but to simply assert that the border was completely settled by historical treaties, forcing the Chinese to raise the issue of the border's legitimacy. Other Indian officials disagreed. Former foreign secretary and national security adviser J.N. Dixit argued:

> The first occasion when we could have negotiated a realistic deal with China was when Nehru acquiesced with the Chinese resuming their suzerainty and jurisdiction over Tibet ... We could have and should have demanded the *quid*

pro quo of their not questioning the delineated boundary ... We did not utilize the opportunity of our agreeing to China resuming authority in Tibet to safeguard our territorial interests ... [W]e did not take a firmer stance against the Chinese early enough when signals were discerned about their territorial ambitions ... Our approach, which was marked by caution and politeness, contributed to the Chinese consolidating their position on the ground and their political conviction that they could deal with any Indian challenge.[16]

The more pressing issue at the time, however, was India's interests in Tibet, and pushing the boundary question would only have made the Tibet issue more difficult to settle.[17] Not addressing the sensitive boundary issue at this time had negative consequences; what India perceived as tacit acceptance by China of India's position on the boundary only made India's later sense of betrayal more intense.[18]

Zhou sought to "identify common ground and set aside differences" to avoid becoming "entangled in disputes."[19] This was the objective of the Five Principles of Peaceful Coexistence, or *Panchsheel* (mutual respect for territorial integrity and sovereignty, mutual non-aggression, non-interference in others' internal affairs, equality and mutual benefit, and peaceful coexistence). Outlined in the Sino-Indian agreement on Tibet, the Five Principles were formally announced two months later, in June 1954. This agreement signalled an improvement in Sino-Indian relations that, however, lasted only through the mid-1950s. Although underlying tensions continued, during this period of *"Hindi-China Bhai-Bhai,"* Sino-Indian relations were outwardly very cordial.

By early 1959, the amicable relations between the two countries reached an important watershed. Two factors played an important role: the Tibetan rebellion and growing Soviet-Indian cooperation in the face of increasing Sino-Soviet tension. China's forceful suppression of rebellion in Tibet was a specific cause of friction. India sympathized with the Tibetan uprising and gave the Dalai Lama sanctuary. In response, Beijing began a vitriolic anti-India campaign, criticizing New Delhi for interfering in China's internal affairs and violating the principles agreed on in 1954. Nehru believed that the Chinese had become "rigid and increasingly arrogant and were inclined to throw their weight about," and that China "was passing through one of the phases of expansionism which occurred regularly in Chinese history whenever the country was strong and united."[20] The boundary dispute, sidestepped for several years while relations were cordial, now became the focus of contention, rooted in larger strategic concerns such as the Sino-Indian regional rivalry, the Sino-Soviet dispute, and the symptoms of other strains in Sino-Indian relations, such as differences over Tibet.

The impact of China's takeover of Tibet on Indian public opinion affected the dynamics of future boundary negotiations. Negotiations over minor boundary issues that had begun quietly as early as the mid-1950s revealed China's sensitivity to boundary differences as well as Beijing's uncertain understanding regarding the boundary line, but when the boundary dispute became public, Indians felt betrayed. Nehru's inflexible stand on India's boundaries led Indians to believe that the "sanctified" Sino-Indian border was firmly established – "searing the lineaments of India's territorial boundaries deep into the national consciousness" and resulting in the "popular sacralization of territory."[21] Politically, Nehru could not seek a compromise settlement even if he might have realized that it was necessary notwithstanding his personal disinclination to make concessions.

Keep in mind that these developments – the worsening Sino-Soviet dispute and growing Soviet-Indian cooperation, as well as the increase in US covert activities in Tibet – occurred simultaneously. The Soviets attempted to maintain a neutral position as Sino-Indian tensions escalated over the boundary issue in 1959 and were reluctant to support China. After the military confrontation across the Sino-Indian border in 1959, Moscow issued a very even-handed statement calling for a peaceful settlement:

> Soviet leaders express the conviction that governments of the Chinese People's Republic and the Republic of India will not let this incident further the aims of those who want the international situation ... to degenerate and who aspire not to permit the emergent lessening of tensions in relations between states ... [Soviet leaders] express the conviction that both governments will settle the misunderstanding that has arisen, taking into account their mutual interests in the spirit of traditional friendship between the peoples of China and India.[22]

China reacted strongly, accusing the Soviets of not upholding socialist solidarity, of being "partial toward India, condemning China, and revealing Sino-Soviet differences to the world."[23] Foreign Minister Chen Yi told Soviet premier Nikita Khrushchev that China's policy toward India was one of "unity cum struggle rather than appeasement" and that Soviet so-called neutrality made China indignant.[24] In fact, however, even after numerous

Indian protests, Soviet maps continued to depict the Sino-Indian boundary more in harmony with China's position. It was not until 1972, after signs of a possible Sino-Indian rapprochement, that the Soviets took measures to appease India over the boundary controversy.[25]

In this deteriorating strategic environment, Mao Zedong initiated efforts to ease Sino-Indian tensions by settling the boundary dispute, and made it clear that he did not want the boundary dispute to exacerbate growing Sino-Indian friction.[26] In May 1959, China's ambassador to India, Pan Zili, revealed that Beijing was cognizant of the larger strategic context when formulating its India policy: "China will not be so foolish as to make another enemy of India to the west after having the United States an enemy to the east. We cannot have two centers of attention, nor can we take friend for foe."[27] To improve relations with India, Beijing initiated boundary negotiations and Mao authorized Zhou to propose territorial compromises in order to reach an early settlement. Although no Chinese government had ever recognized the McMahon Line as a legitimate boundary and Mao believed that it was an artifact of British imperialism, he was willing to accept it as a basis for compromise.[28]

From the outset of the dispute, China showed continued willingness to negotiate a settlement and, pending an agreement, to take measures to reduce tensions. In his April 1959 "Report on the Work of the Government," Zhou expressed Beijing's fear that boundary disputes could be manipulated by outside powers and confirmed China's desire for a peaceful settlement of the disputes through negotiations:

> The undetermined boundary lines between our country and certain neighboring ... countries ... have been used by mischief-makers as propaganda material ... We consider it to be in the interests of both parties to ... not let the imperialists succeed in their scheme of sowing discord between us.[29]

Boundary Dispute

In the 1954 Sino-Indian agreement on Tibet, several important mountain passes between Tibet and India west of Nepal (middle sector) were mentioned but were not defined as either Chinese or Indian territory, and Beijing declined to negotiate the issue.[30] This led to the first protests over border violations. In July 1954, China protested the presence of Indian troops in areas it considered part of Tibet, but India rejected this protest, which, along with the Zhou-Nehru communications, were kept secret until 1959.[31] By

October 1954, tensions along the border were such that when Zhou and Nehru met in Beijing, Nehru raised the boundary issue and protested that maps of the People's Republic of China included Indian territory. Zhou responded that they were "reproductions of old pre-liberation maps" and that China "had had no time to revise them."[32] Nehru did not press the issue or challenge Zhou because he perceived that China was truly unclear about the boundary alignment.[33]

These latent tensions rose closer to the surface when China constructed the Xinjiang-Tibet Highway traversing the Aksai Chin region claimed by India. Built in 1956-57, this was a strategically important road for China connecting Tibet with Xinjiang, especially considering the growing Tibetan resistance movement. India was aware of Chinese activity in Aksai Chin, but deliberately chose to downplay it and preserve Sino-Indian amity. However, once completion of the highway became public with the publication of a map in *China Pictorial* in July 1958, India could no longer ignore the issue. New Delhi raised the issue with Beijing and sent patrols to the area.[34]

In August 1958, India protested that the Chinese map included portions of Indian territory. In November, China responded that the map was based on older maps, but emphasized its willingness to discuss a "new way of drawing the boundary" following "consultations and survey." Tension grew when Nehru responded to the Chinese note by personally writing Zhou and asserting that India's boundaries were not even in question. He claimed there was "no question of these large parts of India being anything but India," and rejected China's position that a survey would "affect the well-known and fixed boundaries." Referring to the 1954 Tibet agreement, Nehru stated: "No border questions were raised at that time and we were under the impression that there were no border disputes between our respective countries. In fact, we thought that the Sino-Indian Agreement ... had settled all outstanding problems between our two countries." Nehru's position appeared to foreclose any possibility of a compromise settlement. Zhou responded that China never believed that a border dispute did not exist, but that in 1954 the time was "not yet ripe for its settlement."[35]

Nehru had been aware of the Chinese maps for some time but withheld the information from Parliament, fearing that it would inflame Indian public opinion against any territorial compromise and complicate any settlement. Once the dispute became public, however, New Delhi took an even more inflexible position just as negotiations were about to begin, arguing that no territorial dispute existed. A careful study of available documents makes clear that India missed several opportunities to seek a settlement of the boundary question and, whether sincere or not, tried to maintain that since Beijing had not rejected India's position earlier, it had tacitly accepted it.

By 1958, it was obvious the entire Sino-Indian boundary was disputed. More than two thousand miles long, the boundary is divided into three sectors, with disputed areas in each sector.[36] The western sector, from the Karakoram Pass to the Parigas salient, includes the strategically important Aksai Chin plateau. It extends for a thousand miles and the total disputed area is approximately fifteen thousand square miles. It is more strategically important to China than to India because of the Xinjiang-Tibet Highway. India argues that the entire sector was delimited by treaties concluded in 1684 between Ladakh and Tibet and in 1842 between Tibet and the authorities of Jammu and Kashmir. Beijing rejects those agreements, arguing that a treaty with a Chinese government had never been concluded, and that, in any case, earlier agreements negotiated by local authorities are vague and imprecise.[37] While New Delhi has asserted what it considers a historical and legal claim to Aksai Chin, for China it is a strategically important region and China views New Delhi's claim as driven more by its desire to undermine China's hold on Tibet than by a principled position based on dubious historical and legal factors.[38]

The middle sector, comprising the area from Parigas to Nepal, is the least controversial. This sector is approximately four hundred miles long, and neither India nor China claims that it was ever delimited by a boundary convention; both countries recognize that a traditional line does exist. The dispute is over the exact location of this historical boundary. India claims that the 1954 agreement on Tibet that listed six passes proves that a recognizable boundary exists. China argues that the 1954 agreement did not concern the boundary question and that the mention of the passes does not demonstrate the existence of any agreement on the location of the boundary.[39]

The eastern sector runs from Bhutan to Burma across the region originally called the North East Frontier Agency (NEFA) that became the Indian state of Arunachal Pradesh in 1987 (but is sometimes referred to as "South Tibet" by the Chinese). This sector involves approximately 32,000 square miles of disputed territory. India maintains that the boundary following the McMahon Line is legitimate, negotiated between British, Tibetan, and Chinese officials at the Simla Conference in 1914. According to New Delhi, the boundary was delimited by treaty either before or during the British Raj.

The only issue, Nehru argued, was for China to observe the "well known and fixed boundaries."[40] China rejects the McMahon Line as a "product of imperialism."[41] No Chinese government has ever recognized this boundary convention, and Beijing maintains that the entire border is undelimited and that only a traditional customary boundary exists. The major town in this disputed area is Tawang, important to China because it is home to one of the most important monasteries in Tibetan Buddhism and is the birthplace of the Sixth Dalai Lama; control of Tawang would enhance China's claims over Tibet. China's strategic interests in Tawang arise from the fact that access to southern Tibet runs through Tawang. Moreover, the area is ethnically and religiously diverse, and Indian control has often been challenged by local groups (see Map 3).[42]

India has persistently voiced concerns about Chinese maps that included large areas of land also claimed by India. In a speech before the Standing Committee of the National People's Congress, Foreign Minister Chen Yi denounced the Indian government's position as a "legacy of British imperialism."[43] By late 1959, rising tensions along the border had already resulted in several military incidents.[44] It was obvious that boundary negotiations were necessary if an armed conflict was to be avoided.

Boundary Negotiations

In concluding the 1954 agreement on Tibet, Nehru inferred China's acceptance of the Indian position on the boundary – the "traditional frontier." At the time, Zhou Enlai did not strongly object to India's assumption, and this only exacerbated later disagreements. Beijing also misjudged New Delhi's inflexible approach to boundary questions. Following the 1954 meeting between Nehru and Zhou in Beijing, no formal discussion of the boundary occurred until late 1956, when the two men met again in New Delhi. This time, Zhou indicated that China would move forward to settle its boundary dispute with Burma based on the "traditional customary line" (i.e., the McMahon Line). He expressed a willingness to do the same with India in the NEFA (the eastern sector), but refused to recognize the legitimacy of the McMahon Line, insisting that it was an inherited legacy of imperialism that must be resolved.[45] In April 1958, talks were held regarding specific areas in the middle sector in an attempt to reduce the possibility of confrontation between border patrols. A month after the publication of the July 1958 *China Pictorial* article, New Delhi asked Beijing to clarify its "official stand" on the boundary, asserting that ten years was ample time for the People's Republic of China to revise its maps that continued to include large areas of Indian territory within China. Beijing responded by reiterating that the maps were based on old maps, and argued that the boundaries were not delimited because the countries concerned had not been consulted. Zhou said that China would "act with prudence and needs time to deal with this matter."[46]

India maintained that "there is *no major boundary dispute* between China and India. There never has been such a dispute so far as we are concerned." At times, Nehru appeared to concede that a boundary question did exist, but, alarmed by China's extensive claims, he was unwilling to lend legitimacy to its larger claims by accepting a compromise agreement even in the middle sector. Nehru therefore denied that a boundary question existed, and argued that agreement on the Five Principles of Peaceful Coexistence affirmed this.[47] That China misjudged India's firm resolve is clear from Zhou's comment in September 1959 that because of their common objection to "imperialist aggression," he assumed both countries would adopt "an attitude of mutual sympathy, mutual understanding and fairness and reasonableness in dealing with the boundary question."[48]

In a note to Nehru dated 7 November 1959, Zhou proposed that military personnel withdraw twenty kilometres in all sectors and that negotiations begin immediately. Nehru wanted withdrawal only in the western sector, where the Chinese actually controlled territory claimed by India, and was reluctant to meet for negotiations.[49] U Nu of Burma offered his services and was willing to go to Beijing to set the stage for negotiations. Nehru turned down the offer, saying that India would not accept China's "absurd" claims and believing that any agreement to negotiate would only "harden the Chinese attitude by suggesting that India was frightened and anxious to find some way out."[50]

Beijing clearly wanted a boundary settlement but insisted on negotiating a new treaty. China showed its willingness to accept earlier treaties and the traditional customary line as the basis for a new treaty during boundary negotiations, but as a matter of principle would not recognize the validity of the earlier treaties, which it considered unequal and the legacy of imperialism. Zhou told Nehru that China was willing to "take a more or less realistic attitude towards the McMahon Line."[51] He made it clear that although China did not accept the McMahon Line, Chinese troops would not cross the line in order to "facilitate negotiations and [a compromise] settlement of the boundary question."[52] By 1959, however, quiet attempts to resolve the dispute had failed and a long and acrimonious exchange of accusations began. There was an exchange of fire between border guards on 25 August, followed by a more intense confrontation on 21 September.[53] These two incidents illustrated the risk of a larger military confrontation.

In his report to the National People's Congress in September 1959, Zhou stated that the Chinese desired a negotiated boundary settlement. He believed that peaceful coexistence was still possible if India was willing to "maintain the longstanding status quo of the border" and negotiate a compromise settlement.[54] At a January 1960 Politburo Standing Committee meeting, China's top leadership agreed that a compromise settlement should be negotiated without delay by settling differences according to the principle of "mutual understanding and mutual accommodation" *(huliang hurang)* and making the necessary territorial concessions.[55] Beijing's miscalculation of India's willingness to negotiate a compromise boundary settlement was rooted in the belief that India too felt victimized by imperialism and recognized the illegitimacy of the current Sino-Indian boundary. Beijing understood neither Nehru's views of historical India nor the domestic political factors that made compromise all but impossible once the dispute became public.

China viewed the Sino-Indian dispute in the context of its larger strategic concerns – the unravelling Sino-Soviet relationship and the escalating US involvement in the region, which exacerbated Beijing's economic, military, and diplomatic challenges. Beijing did not want poor relations with India to further complicate this difficult strategic environment.[56] That the larger strategic context was a major concern was made clear in Zhou's November 1959 letter to Nehru, expressing apprehension over the very real possibility that "it will be made use of by people who are hostile to the friendship of our two countries to attain their ulterior objectives," and arguing that India and China "have no reason to allow the tension on the border ... to continue."[57]

Eventually, after the two skirmishes in late 1959, Nehru agreed to a summit and Zhou travelled to New Delhi in April 1960. He made clear his belief that the boundary dispute was not the primary cause of conflict and that a settlement could ease the more fundamental causes of tension:

> As to the boundary question between our two countries, it is in our opinion, only an issue of limited and temporary nature compared with the fundamental question of preserving friendly co-operation between our two countries. To use a common Chinese expression, it concerns only one finger out of ten.[58]

Zhou emphasized China's desire to settle the boundary question because China needed "peace" and "friends."[59] During the summit, he offered a six-point proposal:

1 A boundary dispute does exist.
2 There is an "actual line of control," and while there are differences of opinion about this, there are few differences over the actual location of the line.
3 The same principle of determining the boundary (watershed, mountain passes, etc.) should apply in all cases.
4 National sentiments regarding the Himalayan and Karakoram mountain ranges should be considered.
5 Before a final boundary settlement, the line of actual control should be observed, but certain adjustments can be negotiated. Neither side should assert territorial claims as preconditions.
6 In order to preserve peace along the boundary and facilitate negotiations, both sides should refrain from patrolling the boundary.[60]

Nehru rejected the six-point proposal even though it included points that he himself had made, but he agreed to continue talks at a lower level.

Nehru's uncompromising position was due in part to his belief that China would be restrained by the Soviet Union and that China would not use force against India. This view was supported by the Indian military, which believed that "India was too big, the Chinese had too many problems, and the Himalayas were still a formidable barrier."[61] In addition, Indian domestic politics made any compromise extremely difficult and reinforced New Delhi's inflexibility before the border war.[62] In May 1960, Deng Xiaoping told the Soviet ambassador to China, S.V. Chervonenko, that China had concluded that Nehru was not constrained by "rightists and other reactionaries"; rather Nehru himself did not want to settle the boundary question in order to gain leverage against the Indian Communist Party.[63] However, China also attributed this failure to make progress toward a settlement to the influence of "American reactionaries" on Nehru, because a Sino-Indian boundary settlement "would be a blow to the aggressive Asia policy of America and the other imperialist states" and "could hinder their aggression."[64]

Zhou's approach to the negotiations followed a pattern set by the recently concluded successful negotiations with Burma. He had come to New Delhi to discuss "principles" and not the details on the ground.[65] It was clear that

China would accept the "traditional customary line" – the McMahon Line – in the eastern sector if India would compromise in the western sector. After all, China's greatest security concerns were in Aksai Chin because of the Xinjiang-Tibet Highway, and India's security concerns were more acute in the NEFA, which controlled the high ground north of Assam and gave China direct access to the narrow Siliguri corridor ("chicken's neck"), a strategic bottleneck in India's defence of the northeastern frontier. China had proved its willingness to compromise by accepting the McMahon Line as the boundary with Burma in January 1960.[66] Although Zhou gave no details of any compromise proposal, he indicated to Nehru that Beijing would accept such a settlement. In his press conference before returning to Beijing, he made it clear that China was willing to give up its claim to the eastern sector if India would reciprocate in the western sector.[67] In Beijing's view this represented a settlement based on geopolitical interests and avoided the thicket of complex historical claims and the geographical vagaries of poorly mapped frontier regions.

There is evidence that China was willing to compromise even further to achieve a boundary settlement. While Zhou was in New Delhi, there were no arrangements for him to meet with Krishna Menon, the Indian defence minister. Among Indian elites, Menon was suspected of advocating a compromise settlement to avoid further tensions with China because he believed Pakistan to be the primary military threat. Despite measures to prevent private discussions between the two men, Menon went directly to Zhou's private suite. Some accounts claim that during their conversation regarding the impasse in negotiations, Zhou even offered to cede the Chumbi Valley salient between Sikkim and Bhutan if India was willing to accept China's position in the Aksai Chin. Other accounts attribute the compromise proposal to Menon, who suggested a long-term lease exchange of the two areas, an idea rejected by other members of the Indian government but considered by Nehru.[68]

The Chumbi Valley was strategically important for India's defence because the only road from Assam to Bhutan passed through the valley, while Aksai Chin was vital to China because of the Xinjiang-Tibet Highway. India's Chief of the Army Staff, Thimayya, considered the Xinjiang-Tibet Highway of no strategic value to India, while Krishna Menon believed that the Chinese territorial claims had merit and should be considered.[69] A precedent was set when Beijing ceded the Namwan Assigned Tract to Burma in exchange for several villages during negotiation of the Sino-Burmese boundary settlement.

According to different accounts, Zhou went to New Delhi "ready and anxious to reach an agreement." Nevertheless, Nehru opined, "I see no reason why we should weaken in it [India's position] at any point."[70] Once the dispute became public, Nehru was watched closely and pressured by the public as well as influential government officials not to make any concessions to China. Beijing exhibited flexibility and was willing to compromise to reach a settlement, but New Delhi was inflexible, agreeing only to continue talks.[71] Even evidence of China's willingness to compromise provided by the recent agreement with Burma was dismissed by Nehru, who argued that there was "no room for negotiations with China" and that China's compromise agreement with Burma was simply an attempt to pressure India to accept China's expansive territorial claims in India.[72]

Lower-level negotiations were held from June to December 1960. Forty-seven meetings were held but no substantive progress was made. A five-hundred-page "red book" was compiled, and in the joint report both sides generally restated their previous positions; there have been no substantive changes in negotiating positions since then.[73] Despite the lack of success, a Chinese diplomat observed that "the seemingly fruitless negotiations kept the negotiation door open – and the opening, from a long-term point of view, was not insignificant."[74]

Nevertheless, China did continue to seek a compromise settlement and continued dialogue.[75] A territorial compromise was discussed on two subsequent occasions. In July 1961, while returning from Mongolia, R.K. Nehru, secretary-general of the Ministry of External Affairs and former ambassador to China, met with Zhou Enlai and Foreign Minister Chen Yi. He favoured a negotiated settlement and may have hinted at Indian willingness to accept the proposal originally discussed by Krishna Menon and Zhou Enlai in 1960, to drop India's claim to Aksai Chin in exchange for China's cession of the Chumbi Valley.[76] A near-breakthrough in the stalemate came in July 1962 during the Geneva Conference on the Question of Laos, when Krishna Menon and Chen Yi discussed the boundary question. China made it clear that the McMahon Line in the eastern sector was acceptable, but that the Aksai Chin region was strategically important to China. Menon agreed to an exchange, but was concerned by the strong domestic public opinion, including even the Indian communists, against any territorial compromise.[77] Possibly to reduce New Delhi's opposition to a territorial compromise, Menon sought a renewed counter-offer of Chinese territory, such as the Chumbi Valley, in exchange for the Indian "concession" in Aksai Chin. China agreed and negotiations were set to continue. However, an outcry in the Indian Parliament against such a compromise and against Krishna Menon's negotiating with the Chinese at all forced Nehru to deny that any negotiations had ever taken place. Three times false hopes had been raised about a compromise settlement; Beijing concluded that Nehru had repudiated the idea of a territorial compromise and that further negotiations were fruitless.[78]

The Border War

In late 1961, India forced the boundary issue militarily by adopting a "forward policy." Nehru, with the support of Indian intelligence despite grave reservations by the military and the foreign ministry, decided to build additional outposts and increase military patrols in disputed areas. The intent was not to establish military superiority in those areas but rather to make a political statement, "a symbol of sovereignty."[79] Publicly, Nehru also left some doubt about the purpose of the forward policy. Just one week before the People's Liberation Army (PLA) launched a blitz against the border patrols on 20 October 1962, he told the press that Indian forces "are to free our territory," but left the timing "entirely for the Army" to decide. In his memoirs, Indian general B.M. Kaul wondered whether "Nehru's statement did not precipitate their [China's] attack."[80] Mao's response to India's forward policy was motivated by two conflicting emotions. He felt that "belligerence towards India was dictated by the desire to take revenge for the century of humiliation at the hands of the European great powers" and believed that India's territorial claims represented boundaries established by European imperialism. On the other hand, Mao was reluctant to go to war, arguing that while China should "never give in to the Indian invasion," it should nevertheless "try to avoid bloodshed, and be prepared for armed coexistence along a jagged line."[81] Mao made this clear when he told the Russians that China "would never go beyond the Himalayas. This is a dispute over insignificant patches of territory."[82]

Several skirmishes had occurred earlier, but on 20 October Chinese troops attacked and overran Indian positions. In the NEFA, China penetrated as far as one hundred miles beyond the McMahon Line. On 24 October, China called for a ceasefire, withdrawal, and the resumption of boundary negotiations. New Delhi immediately rejected Beijing's call for negotiations and accused China of attempting to "force a settlement on their own terms."[83]

On 21 November, China responded by announcing that it would unilaterally withdraw its troops twenty kilometres behind the actual 1959 line of control, that is, north of the McMahon Line in the eastern sector, even if India did not agree to a ceasefire. It also called for renewed negotiations at the highest level, in either Beijing or New Delhi.[84] This proposal clearly showed that Beijing was not bent on occupying more disputed territory but rather sought a boundary settlement and launched the invasion in a desperate attempt to force India back to the negotiating table. Foreign Minister Chen Yi summed up China's policy as an attempt to "achieve unity through struggle and make Nehru agree to negotiate so that a relatively permanent and peaceful boundary-line could be drawn and fixed. Our purpose was to pacify a front, namely the southwest frontier, so that we could concentrate our attention on the eastern front. Our strategic concern is mainly the United States."[85] Despite the Chinese retreat, India remained unwilling to negotiate.

Postwar Developments

The years since the border war have seen only minimal progress toward a settlement. Indian Prime Minister Indira Gandhi made an overture to improve Sino-Indian relations in 1969.[86] The following year, when China was also seeking to improve relations with the United States to offset escalating tensions with the Soviet Union, Mao personally signalled his desire for improved relations with India. Engaging in "Tiananmen diplomacy," while greeting guests atop Tiananmen Square on 1 May 1970, Mao shook hands with the Indian charge d'affaires and told him that "India is a great country ... We should be friendly."[87] However, this initiative was soon overshadowed by the civil war in Pakistan and the conclusion of a Soviet-Indian Treaty of Peace, Friendship, and Cooperation in August 1970. Zhou Enlai made a second gesture to open a dialogue in March 1971, but there was no significant movement until several years later, when diplomatic relations improved.

China and India re-established relations at the ambassador level in 1976. Boundary negotiations were reinitiated in September 1977, and the first high-level talks in March 1978 resulted in an agreement to settle the boundary through biannual negotiations. Early on, a settlement appeared possible when Prime Minister Morarji Desai hinted that India was prepared to recognize the present line of actual control as the border, accepting China's position of "mutual understanding and mutual accommodation" *(huliang hurang)* by recognizing China's claims in Aksai Chin in exchange for Chinese recognition of India's control in the eastern sector, contingent on the overall improvement in Sino-Indian relations.[88] Deng Xiaoping pushed to improve relations in other areas and again presented the "package deal"; however,

Indian Foreign Minister Atal Bihari Vajpayee's February 1979 visit to Beijing ended abruptly when China invaded Vietnam to "teach a lesson." China certainly also viewed the invasion as a reminder to India of the consequences in 1962 of India's unwillingness to settle their boundary dispute through negotiations. Possibly hoping that India would still have this "lesson" in mind, Chinese Premier Hua Guofeng raised the boundary issue with Indira Gandhi when they met in Belgrade in May 1980, and the two leaders issued a joint communiqué stressing the necessity of reducing tensions along the border. The following month, while speaking with Indian journalists, Deng resurrected Zhou Enlai's 1960 offer of a package deal that would swap China's claims in the eastern sector for Indian acceptance of its claims in Aksai Chin – basically accepting the status quo. Deng said that China was not asking for the "return of all the territory illegally incorporated into India by the old colonialists," and that the dispute could be settled by "respect[ing] the present state of the border."[89] To jumpstart relations, Deng took a more neutral position on the India-Pakistan dispute over Kashmir, stating that the dispute was a "bilateral" issue and should be solved peacefully, thus dropping Beijing's previous pro-Pakistan position supporting Kashmir's right to self-determination. In Beijing the previous year, Vajpayee had informed the Chinese that their support for Pakistan on this issue was an additional complicating factor in improving Sino-Indian relations.[90]

India rejected China's proposal, showing no willingness to make "mutual concessions" on the boundary and continuing to insist that Beijing unilaterally retreat from Aksai Chin. India did not view such a compromise settlement as a Chinese "concession" because it did not accept the Chinese premise that the territory was "illegally incorporated into India."[91] The Chinese believed, however, that the proposal of a swap was fair and reasonable; both sides would make accommodations in light of each other's security interests, China would even implicitly recognize the "imperialist McMahon Line" in the eastern sector while India would accept China's strategically important control of Aksai Chin, which India had never controlled in any case. In the eyes of the Chinese, "by rejecting China's reasonable proposal, India demonstrated, once again, its arrogant attitude: what's mine is mine, and what's yours is mine too ... The perceptual gulf between India and China on the issue of rejection of the east-west swap remains huge."[92]

Foreign Minister Huang Hua travelled to New Delhi in June 1981 prepared to discuss other bilateral questions even if India was unwilling to accept China's offer of "mutual understanding and mutual accommodation" and a "package deal" settlement *(huliang hurang, yilanzi jiejue)*. Huang's visit, the first by a minister-level Chinese official since Zhou Enlai's visit in 1960, signalled a gradual improvement in Sino-Indian relations by initiating a series of negotiations that continued from December 1981 to 1988.[93] During the discussions, China continued to call for understanding and accommodation and offered to legitimize the status quo. The talks made no progress, as India was unwilling to discuss the Chinese proposal for a claims swap. India's stubbornness irritated the Chinese, who criticized New Delhi's "ideological" approach to the boundary disputes, claiming that the location of the boundary was clear but that India was simply unwilling to negotiate a compromise settlement.[94] Despite lack of progress on the boundary issue, however, Beijing demonstrated its desire for improved relations in other areas and agreed to allow Indian pilgrimages to Tibet.

As in the past, Indian domestic politics were an obstacle to progress. Indira Gandhi was primarily concerned about the domestic political repercussions of any territorial concessions. After her assassination in 1984, the new government, headed by Rajiv Gandhi, initially supported improved Sino-Indian relations but in the end proved unwilling to make any concessions to China.[95] China in turn hardened its position in 1986, rejecting the McMahon Line and calling for Indian concessions in the eastern sector, a retreat from Beijing's earlier offer of a package deal. The Chinese view was that Zhou offered a swap in 1960 when China was weak and sought to shore up relations with its neighbours; India did not take the opportunity then, and China was no longer bound by its offer of a package deal.[96] The boundary negotiations were further complicated in December 1986 when the Indian National Congress voted to elevate the Northeast Frontier Agency to Arunachal Pradesh state. China strongly protested this move and asked rhetorically whether India thought China would "submissively obey and hand over its territory."[97]

At the same time, the two countries engaged in military manoeuvres along the Line of Actual Control in the Sumdorong Chu Valley, located near the China-Bhutan-India border, which led to a war scare in 1986-87.[98] Beijing warned New Delhi that "history shows that it is unwise to try to solve border disputes by force of arms. The border conflict of 1962 may serve as a lesson."[99] This was the closest China and India came to a repeat of October 1962. Deng Xiaoping, through US Secretary of Defense Caspar Weinberger and Secretary of State George Shultz, conveyed the message that China would "teach India a lesson" if the crisis was not resolved.[100] The crisis was defused when Indian Minister of External Affairs N.D. Tiwari stopped in Beijing after attending a non-aligned conference in Pyongyang. A statement was issued on avoiding conflict and working toward a complete settlement of the boundary.[101]

Even before the Cold War ended, Sino-Soviet relations began to improve following Leonid Brezhnev's overtures to Beijing in 1982 and the renewal of Sino-Soviet boundary talks. This made New Delhi anxious over maintaining balance in the triangular relationship.[102] Visiting New Delhi in November 1988, Mikhail Gorbachev expressed the view that China would no longer be confrontational and encouraged Prime Minister Rajiv Gandhi to improve relations with China.[103] India was compelled to adjust to the changing balance of power, and Gandhi dropped India's earlier insistence on a boundary settlement as a precondition for general improvement in bilateral relations. His visit to Beijing in December 1988 was followed by the historic Sino-Soviet summit in May 1989. The objective of this first visit to China by an Indian prime minister since Nehru's in 1954 was to preserve India's bargaining power in boundary negotiations. Although the summit made no real progress on the boundary question, it led to a significant breakthrough in bilateral relations in the form of an agreement to establish the Joint Working Group mechanism for boundary negotiations.[104] India had reordered its priorities, dropping its position that a precondition to any improvement in relations was recovering "every inch of lost territory," and the joint communiqué indicated a willingness to seek "a fair and reasonable settlement ... while seeking a mutually acceptable solution to this question."[105]

Progress in the boundary negotiations depended on larger international developments, such as Beijing's isolation following the Tiananmen Square massacre in June 1989 and the shift in the balance of power with the collapse of the Soviet Union shortly after. This systemic change gave Beijing greater incentive to resolve the boundary dispute in order to safeguard its more fundamental strategic interests. Premier Li Peng visited India in December 1992. The strategic importance of improving Sino-Indian relations became clear when New Delhi and Beijing rejected an "international oligarchy" and US hegemony. The following September, during Prime Minister P.V. Narasimha Rao's visit to Beijing, the two countries concluded a landmark "Agreement on the Maintenance of Peace along the Line of Actual Control [LAC] in the India-China Border." The agreement stated that "pending an ultimate solution to the boundary question between the two countries, the two sides shall strictly respect and observe the line of actual control between the two sides" and "when necessary, the two sides shall jointly check and determine the segments of the line of actual control where they have different views as to its alignment."[106] Other agreements reached at the same summit included "confidence-building measures," such as regular meetings of field commanders and establishment of a hotline for communications and troop reductions based on "mutual and equal security to ceilings to be mutually agreed." Troop reduction negotiations were initiated in February 1994.[107] In July 1994, Foreign Minister Qian Qichen and Rao "agreed to disagree" and Qian said he did not "expect any overnight solutions," but Rao predicted that China and India would soon achieve a breakthrough to end the "eyeball-to-eyeball confrontation" along the border.[108] During Jiang Zemin's November 1996 visit to India, the two countries signed the "Agreement on Confidence-Building Measures in the Military Field along the Line of Actual Control." These significant confidence-building agreements brought greater stability to the border regions and created an atmosphere of progress toward an eventual boundary agreement. In April 1998, PLA general Fu Quanyou visited India to ease mutual suspicions and expressed the view that boundary negotiations would not be delayed; he was confident that there would be "gradual realization of boundary demarcation."[109]

From the Chinese perspective, however, Beijing's willingness to compromise has not been reciprocated by a recalcitrant India because of its deeply rooted suspicions. According to one of China's leading analysts of Sino-Indian relations, "mutual understanding and trust between the two countries is still far from adequate, especially because in India a considerable group of people *(xiangdang yibufen ren)* have been influenced by the 'China's threat theory' ... and still have suspicions about China. Added to which is the fact that the negative influence of the 1962 war has not been entirely eliminated."[110]

These underlying tensions in Sino-Indian relations were exacerbated in May 1998 when Indian Defence Minister George Fernandes, referring to China as India's "potential threat 1," said that to "underplay the situation across the Himalayas is not in the national interest"; within days, India conducted five nuclear tests. Prime Minister Vajpayee justified the tests by saying that "we have an overt nuclear weapons state on our borders, a state which committed armed aggression against India in 1962," and "an atmosphere of distrust persists mainly due to the unresolved border problems."[111] China suspended negotiations on the boundary that had been given renewed momentum with Rajiv Gandhi's 1988 visit, but steps were quickly taken to put relations on an even keel and Minister of External Affairs Jaswant Singh visited China in June 1999. Singh stated that India did not consider China a threat, and Foreign Minister Tang Jiaxuan responded that "Sino-Indian relations have entered a phase of improvement ... A precondition of the development of Sino-Indian relations is ensuring the two sides do not see each other as a threat."[112] Singh's visit was followed by a succession of high-level exchanges, including a visit to Beijing by President K.R. Narayanan from 28 May to 3 June 2000 and an agreement to adopt a "forward looking" policy and complete clarification of the Line of Actual Control. International developments also provided impetus for further improvement in Sino-Indian relations. Following the 11 September 2001 Al-Qaeda attacks on the United States, Defence Minister Fernandes, who had been the staunchest anti-China Indian official, stated that 9/11 changed the nature of the security discourse and that "the Sino-Indian relationship is to be rearranged in this altered context."[113]

In 2002, New Delhi and Beijing continued discussions over Sikkim. Annexed by India in 1975, it remained a sensitive issue because Beijing did not "recognize India's illegal annexation of Sikkim."[114] China began softening its position and moving toward recognizing Indian sovereignty over Sikkim as early as 1980, when Deng Xiaoping indicated that although China still opposed India's annexation of Sikkim, it would not allow this issue to undermine overall relations. At the same time, Deng revived the offer of a package deal to solve the boundary dispute.[115] Jiang Zemin raised the issue as well during his visit to India in November 1996. Following the visit, Minister of External Affairs Inder Kumar Gujral said that he got the impression that "there was a move in China to accept India's contention on Sikkim."[116] During Prime Minister Vajpayee's visit to China in June 2003, the first by an Indian prime minister in a decade, a Declaration of Principles for Relations and Comprehensive Cooperation was issued in which India explicitly recognized the "Tibet Autonomous Region" as part of China and Beijing agreed to allow trade between Tibet and Sikkim via the Nathu La Pass on the eastern Sikkim-Tibet border, the strategic pass traversed by the Dalai Lama in 1959 when he fled to India, and the location of a military confrontation in 1967.[117] The linkage between India's recognition of the Tibet Autonomous Region as part of the People's Republic of China and Beijing's implicit recognition of Sikkim as part of the Indian Union was clear during the negotiations.[118] The assumption that this constituted Chinese recognition of Sikkim's accession to India was refuted, however, by the Chinese Foreign Ministry's statement that "the question of Sikkim is an enduring one left over from history" that cannot be resolved "overnight," but that China would "take into consideration the reality," hinting that substantive changes were forthcoming. Vajpayee concluded: "We have started the process by which Sikkim will cease to be an issue in India-China relations."[119] China did eventually reciprocate during Premier Wen Jiabao's April 2005 visit to New Delhi, conceding that Sikkim was part of India. Wen stated that "Sikkim is no longer a problem in China-Indian relations" and presented the Indians with a Chinese map showing Sikkim as part of India.[120] Border trade officially opened in July 2006 over the fifteen-thousand-foot pass. Significantly, this settlement established a pattern of contingent recognition that set a precedent for future boundary settlements based on quid pro quo recognition of the status quo.

Vajpayee's 2003 visit also marked an important step forward in Sino-Indian relations. The prime minister noted the "compelling geographical, political and economic logic for closer relations" and recognized that "there was a period in the India-China relationship when our preoccupation with our differences prevented pragmatic understanding of the mutual benefits from cooperation." Signalling the new tack in bilateral relations, the two sides initiated high-level boundary negotiations led by "Special Representatives" that would serve as a high-level platform "to explore, from the political perspective ... the framework of a boundary settlement." Vajpayee opined that "on previous visits, we have never moved forward on the border issue as much as we have on this trip."[121] For his part, Premier Wen Jiabao said the visit had "taken the negotiations on the boundary question to a new level."[122]

At the October 2003 meeting of the Association of Southeast Asian Nations (ASEAN) in Bali, Wen made clear the larger context in which China sees the boundary dispute, telling Vajpayee that China wanted to solve the boundary dispute "in the context of the long-term strategic relations between the two countries."[123] Beijing viewed New Delhi's interest in better relations as being similarly motivated, driven by India's desire to balance its improved relations with the United States and Russia and dispel any Chinese fears over them.[124] Although continuing to insist that China was occupying Indian territory, India showed flexibility when Minister for External Affairs Digvijay Singh stated that "India and China seek a fair, reasonable and mutually acceptable settlement of the boundary question through peaceful consultations."[125]

Premier Wen's April 2005 visit to New Delhi resulted in the first negotiated agreement on "Political Parameters and Guiding Principles for the Settlement of the India-China Boundary Questions." The agreement recognized that "proceeding from the political perspective of overall bilateral relations," both sides were "seeking a political settlement of the boundary question in the context of their overall and long-term interests" and that the settlement was being "pursued as a strategic objective." The two sides pledged to "make meaningful and mutually acceptable adjustments to their respective positions ... so as to arrive at a package settlement of the boundary question." To achieve a final settlement, both sides would "take into account ... historical evidence, national sentiments, practical difficulties and reasonable concerns and sensitivities."[126] The agreement paves the way for the eventual reciprocal recognition of the status quo, leaving China controlling the Aksai Chin and India in control of the southern slope of the Himalayas that constitutes part of the state of Arunachal Pradesh. The primary barrier to such a settlement is India's inability to put behind it the trauma of 1962 and accept the status quo, but this attitude may be changing. As one Indian scholar observes, "in actuality, the border dispute has virtually ceased to exist ... China has occupied the Aksai Chin, which was never under our control, while China has tacitly accepted our rule over NEFA [Arunachal Pradesh] and the border is peaceful. China is presumably asking us to legalize this reality through a package deal. Is anything wrong with that?"[127] Beijing sees no obstacles to an early settlement if New Delhi embraces the principles of mutual understanding and mutual accommodation.[128]

However, despite the agreement to raise the level of negotiations and place the boundary dispute in a broader political context, the actual management of differences on the ground causes tensions and there is disagreement over how to interpret the 2005 "Political Parameters and Guiding Principles" document. The Line of Actual Control is not a clearly defined border, and even its actual location is disputed. To deal with the occasional spikes in tension, the Special Representatives agreed in January 2012 to establish a Working Mechanism for Consultation and Coordination on Border Affairs to "address issues and situations that may arise in the border areas that affect the maintenance of peace and tranquility."[129] In March 2013, Beijing presented a draft "Border Defence Cooperation Agreement" and negotiations are ongoing. The need for such mechanisms was demonstrated in April 2013, on the eve of Premier Li Keqiang's maiden trip to India in May. Responding to the Indian construction of permanent structures near the India-China-Pakistan trijunction in Ladakh (Tiannan River Valley), China deployed troops in the area a short distance from the Indian camp. The incident was quickly resolved "through border-related mechanisms, diplomatic channels and border defense meetings," and troops from both sides withdrew simultaneously from the disputed area.[130]

Following Li's visit, India's Special Representative travelled to Beijing in June for discussions with his counterpart. After a meeting with Premier Li, they issued a statement stressing that both sides would "manage the boundary question from a strategic and overall perspective, [and] strengthen communication to narrow the differences and work together to safeguard peace and tranquility along the border."[131] In July, the Indian defence minister visited China to continue negotiations on Beijing's proposed Border Defence Cooperation Agreement to deal with local irritants along the border. A joint statement by the two countries' defence ministers stated that "appreciating that border defense cooperation would make a significant contribution ... they agreed on an early conclusion of negotiations for a proposed agreement."[132]

Conclusion

The Sino-Indian boundary is China's only unsettled boundary in South Asia (with the minor exception of Bhutan). The Indian government has always been under intense domestic pressure not to compromise, and this pressure has not abated. Among Ministry of External Affairs officials associated with the boundary negotiations and within the military, there are "settler" and "non-settler" factions, the perceptions of which are coloured by India's humiliation and sense of betrayal in 1962.[133] However, India began to soften its views of China as an intimidating security threat in the late 1990s, and this, coupled with the normalization of relations and a boundary settlement between China and Russia, changed the strategic context. Since then, the Sino-Indian boundary settlement negotiations have been envisioned as proceeding in three stages. The first stage was the 2005 breakthrough agreement on political parameters. The second stage, which is ongoing, involves negotiating a framework for resolving the dispute in all sectors. According to India's Special Representative, National Security Adviser

Shivshankar Menon, this is the most complex stage because it will determine what will be "actually translated into the line" delineated on maps and on the ground in the third and final stage of negotiations.[134]

Inexorably, India and China are becoming economically complementary. China is now India's largest trading partner and two-way trade reached US$60 billion in 2012, with a target of US$100 billion by 2015. The need to deal with each other's growing power in the region is an additional strategic factor. As China and India increasingly share economic interests and common political and strategic objectives in global governance, they have greater incentive to resolve the boundary dispute and reduce the potential for future conflict.[135] Even George Fernandes, formerly a strong critic of China, has changed his views, commenting in February 2003 that "the Sino-Indian relationship is to be rearranged in this altered context."[136] For its part, China is motivated to push for a settlement because of the rapidly improving US-India relationship.

Bilateral relations have continued to improve in other areas but boundary negotiations have made little substantive progress. The current approach appears to be to consider the border in its entirety instead of as individual sectors, and attempt to translate the Line of Actual Control into a delimited boundary. There has been an enormous change in the approach to the dispute, with both sides agreeing to joint investigation and consultation. China has accepted Sikkim's accession to India and it continues to press for a compromise boundary settlement, but Indian public opinion remains strongly opposed to a territorial swap. Beyond some minor technical adjustments in the Line of Actual Control, however, Beijing can offer little more than the package deal it has already put on the table. According to one Chinese boundary expert, "China and India have envisaged a political settlement ... [but it] will take a prolonged period of time and will be an arduous task."[137] It will take a bold political move by Indian leaders to overcome domestic opposition to a compromise settlement.

Before the 1962 border war with India, China had already begun pursuing boundary settlements with its other South Asian neighbours. As Sino-Indian tensions grew and the likelihood of a boundary settlement faded, China concluded a boundary treaty with Burma in January 1960 and similar treaties with Nepal, Pakistan, and Afghanistan in the ensuing years. Because of the timing of these settlements, they have been commonly explained as a Chinese ploy to gain leverage by appearing flexible and willing to compromise while India appeared rigid and uncompromising.[138] China may have been conscious of this advantage, but the timing, negotiating records, and settlements exhibit a pattern that is more fully explained by placing the boundary settlements within the context of China's deteriorating relations with Moscow and trepidation over growing US involvement in the region, as well as deteriorating relations with India. China surely took tactical advantage of the settlements with its other South Asian neighbours to pressure India to compromise, but a full explanation of the fundamental strategic impetus for China's behaviour is achieved only by placing it in the larger strategic context. The boundary settlements should be seen as an effort to reduce tensions with neighbouring states and thereby adjust to the shift in the balance of power and ensure China's overall security.

The attempt to settle the boundary dispute with India was only one of several efforts undertaken by China in response to the systemic changes at the time. In the following chapters, China's boundary settlements with its other South Asian neighbours will be analyzed in the context not only of Sino-Indian relations but also of the broader and structurally more deterministic shift in China's overall strategic environment.

3 The Sino-Burmese Boundary Settlement

In the midst of growing confrontation with India over the boundary and the general deterioration in China's strategic environment, especially with the Sino-Soviet split and concerns about the growing influence of the United States in Southeast Asia, China concluded the first in a series of boundary agreements with neighbouring states on 28 January 1960. After years of refusing to negotiate and then prolonging the negotiations by modifying its position, Beijing concluded an agreement with Rangoon after five days of intense negotiations. The Sino-Burmese boundary treaty is significant not only because it was the first such agreement but also, more importantly, because of the pattern it established (see Map 4). The treaty set an important precedent, as the Chinese were eager to point out. The *Renmin ribao* editorial published the day the treaty was signed stressed:

> The key to the solution of the question is whether or not the two sides with the boundary concerned have the sincerity to abide faithfully by the Five Principles of Peaceful Coexistence, to adopt a stand of mutual understanding and mutual accommodation *[huliang hurang]* on the basis of equality and mutual benefit, and to solve the question through friendly consultations. If the two sides have such sincerity, it would not be difficult to settle the boundary question or other disputes.

The most notable point was China's flexibility and willingness to settle outstanding boundary disputes quickly.

Historical Background

Historically, Chinese viewed Burma as a vassal state following the expansion into South Asia of the Yuan Dynasty (1279-1368). After a military confrontation in 1790, China signed a treaty with local tribal chiefs that stipulated that the Burmese would return prisoners and territory and send tribute

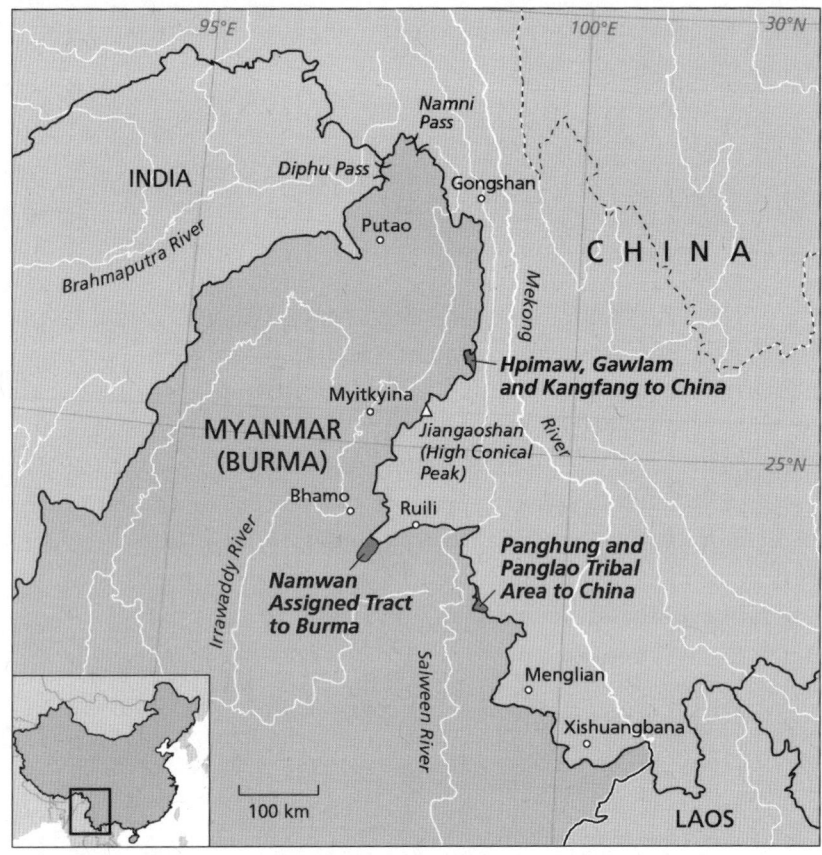

Map 4 Burma

missions to Beijing every ten years. Burmese kings were thereafter vested with authority by Qing court nobility.[1]

With the decline of the Qing court and the British domination of Burma, changes occurred along the Sino-Burmese frontier. In 1886, China claimed the territory north of Bhamo in the Kachin region. Britain rejected the claim but allowed China to retain control of the region. The British later annexed Upper Burma in response to the growing French domination of Indochina. Although Britain and China negotiated boundary conventions in 1894 and 1897, many parts of the border were left unresolved because of their inaccessibility and lack of strategic importance at the time.[2] The issue of sovereignty remained unclear because of the divided loyalties of the various tribal chiefs. With British approval, some of these chiefs continued to send decennial tribute missions to the Qing court.[3]

With the rise of the Chinese Nationalists after 1927 and a growing sense of Chinese nationalism, resolution of border problems did not become any easier. Sovereignty over the region north of Myitkyina, an area of approximately 77,000 square miles, was disputed. The Nationalists asserted that the boundary should run along the Irrawaddy River in the north. Along the southern sector of the boundary, disagreements that had gone unsettled since 1897 were submitted to a League of Nations boundary commission in 1935. The Iselin Commission presented its findings in 1937; the Nationalist government accepted the commission's report in 1941 and agreed to the so-called Iselin Line or "1941 Line."[4] It is likely that the Nationalists concluded the treaty because of the Japanese invasion of China and a desire to enlist British support, but the boundary was never demarcated. The Union of Burma gained independence on 4 January 1948, nearly two years before the establishment of the People's Republic of China (PRC). Both governments inherited an unsettled 1,500-mile boundary that traverses rugged terrain. The two newly independent states were left to settle a boundary dispute that the British authorities, the Qing court, and the Nationalist government had all failed to settle for over half a century. The PRC considered the boundary unsettled but accepted the 1941 Line in practice as an obligation inherited from the Nationalist government. Beijing argued, however, that the agreement had been forced on China after China was weakened by the Japanese invasion, and was therefore no different from the earlier treaties that Britain had forced on the crumbling Qing Dynasty.[5] Given the circumstances surrounding the agreement, this was a view that Burmese Prime Minister U Nu was "inclined to share."[6]

Early PRC-Burma Relations

Eager to establish good relations with the PRC, Burma was the first non-communist country to recognize the new government. Burma was historically sensitive to Chinese expansionism and, anxious to settle the border problems, it sought to continue the boundary discussions initiated with the Nationalists.[7] It feared that a newly united and hypernationalistic China might be expansionist, and had taken note of Chinese maps that included territory claimed by Burma.[8] According to U Nu, "our tiny nation cannot have the effrontery to quarrel with any power. And least, among these, could Burma afford to quarrel with new China."[9] A more immediate problem, however, was the approximately ten thousand Nationalist troops that had crossed the border into Burma as they fled the communist advance, and that continued to be supplied by the Nationalists from Taiwan. Rangoon was concerned about a potential conflict if People's Liberation Army troops crossed the border in pursuit of these Nationalist remnants. Rangoon assured Beijing that the Nationalists were not welcome in Burma and that it was taking every measure to have them removed.[10] Beijing, still concerned with pockets of Nationalist resistance and other problems, and eventually at war in Korea, did not respond to the Burmese overtures to discuss the boundary.[11]

Instead, it adopted a two-track policy. Although China had more pressing concerns than the unsettled boundary with Burma, it had ideological reasons for not responding to the Burmese initiatives. Mao had supported Burma's independence as early as 1945, but after it was achieved, Burma adopted a non-aligned policy and did not take a strident anti-imperialist position; as a result, Beijing criticized Rangoon for "bourgeois appeasement toward imperialism." The Chinese called for a "hard, long struggle" for "national liberation" because Burma was still a "miserable colony" of the imperialists.[12] At the outset, China made it clear that it was not seeking close ties with Burma and that Rangoon had been forced to recognize the People's Republic of China because "the victory of the Chinese people has been so overwhelming and decisive that they are left with no alternative."[13] In November 1949, even before Burma recognized the new Chinese government, Liu Shaoqi expressed the view of Beijing when he stated that "the wars of national liberation in Burma are now developing" and that the "fighters of the national liberation wars ... have acted entirely correctly."[14] The PRC continued to support the insurgent Burmese Communist Party through their base areas in northern Burma. U Nu characterized the period thus: "Our relations with the new Chinese regime remained uncertain for a number of years ... The new Chinese government seemed inclined to give our communists their moral support, apparently regarding us as stooges of the West."[15]

Besides supporting communist insurgents, the PRC continued to encourage political change in Burma in various ways. There was already a growing secessionist movement among the frontier minorities of Burma, and Burma's constitution allowed states to secede beginning in 1957. A Chinese atlas published in 1953 noted the boundary questions, but stated that "these problems await the establishment of a People's Burma ... then they can receive complete and reasonable solution."[16] By 1955, China had established five autonomous areas along the Sino-Burmese border, and reports indicated that the Chinese government was issuing identity cards to Kachins who lived in the disputed area and was supplying them with food and medical assistance. The PRC also showed support for a "greater Kachin state" that would include parts of Assam, Yunnan, and northwestern Burma. These policies all heightened Rangoon's fear that China still hoped to eventually control the Kachin and Shan states.[17] Despite its support of Burmese insurgents, however, China did not ignore other options and was careful not to jeopardize its influence with the government in Rangoon.

China's two-track policy paid off. Although Burma voted to condemn North Korean aggression in 1950, in 1951 it voted against the US-sponsored resolution condemning the PRC for aggression. Burma did not attend the San Francisco Peace Conference and consistently supported the PRC as the legitimate government of China at the UN. In May 1953, it refused US aid to protest US support for the Chinese Nationalist insurgents on the China-Burma border, and in April 1954, it signed a three-year trade agreement with the PRC. Despite these developments, however, China did not end its support for insurgency movements or compromise on territorial issues.

Surrounded by regional powers that in turn were backed by one of the two superpowers, U Nu adopted a realist view of Burma's security predicament:

> We are hemmed in like a tender gourd among the cactus. We cannot move an inch. If we act irresponsibly like some half-baked politicians who have picked up their world politics from one or two books and thrust the Union of Burma into the arms of one bloc, the other will not be content to look on with folded arms. Oh no![18]

U Nu believed that a boundary settlement with China was fundamental to Burma's national security and concluded:

> In the circumstances of today, when distance and barriers no longer make for inaccessibility, it is of the utmost importance that even the best of neighbors ... should know where the territory of one ends and the other begins so as to be in a position to apply faithfully the principle of respect for each other's sovereignty and territorial integrity.[19]

However, despite Burma's desire to settle the boundary question and eliminate problems resulting from an undefined border, China continued to resist any initiatives.

Border Problems

The dispute surfaced in 1950 with the publication of a map showing the PRC's claim to large areas of territory also claimed by Burma. The largest area was in the Kachin state north of Myitkyina, the same area that the Nationalists had claimed earlier. The boundary was shown as undelimited in the northern sector, and areas west of the 1941 Line (Iselin Line) were also claimed. When Burma protested, Chinese officials claimed that the maps were reproductions of old maps, but insisted that these areas were unsettled in any case.[20] As early as 1953, Burma also became aware that People's Liberation Army troops had moved into the area China claimed west of the 1941 Line, in the Wa region of the Shan States.[21]

Three areas were disputed (see Map 4). The early Sino-British treaty had not settled one sector in the Wa region. This sector was settled by the Iselin Commission in 1937, but was disputed by Beijing, and China continued to claim territory west of the line. The second problematic area was at the confluence of the Namwan and Shewli Rivers, commonly known as the "Namwan Assigned Tract." Although the area was recognized as Chinese territory in the 1894 boundary convention, the British built a road through it to connect Bhamo and Namwan. This became the major road connecting the Kachin state with the Shan States. In the 1897 boundary convention, Britain leased the area in perpetuity from the Qing Dynasty court for one thousand rupees annually. This fee was paid until 1948, when the Chinese Nationalist government refused to accept the payment from the government of the new Union of Burma, rejecting the perpetual lease as a violation of its sovereignty and territorial integrity and therefore an unequal treaty. The third contested area was in the Kachin region north of High Conical Peak *(Jiangaoshan* or *Manang Bum)*. This disputed region was never settled; it was the same area the Nationalists had claimed, and the boundary was described as undelimited on PRC maps. Three villages – Hpimaw, Kangfang, and Gawlum – were under Burmese administration, but Beijing pointed out that the British had acknowledged the villages as Chinese in 1911.[22]

Burma did not want the border situation to adversely affect Sino-Burmese relations; thus, despite the maps, U Nu declared that China did not show any irredentist ambitions, and accepted the Chinese explanation of the recently published maps and assurances from Beijing that "China has no territorial ambitions."[23]

In the mid-1950s, Beijing began to pursue better relations with its non-communist neighbours and the non-aligned movement generally, something that India strongly encouraged. Zhou Enlai attended the April 1955 Non-Aligned Movement conference of Asian and African countries in Bandung, Indonesia. This shift in Beijing's foreign policy led to early boundary negotiations with Rangoon because maintaining Burma's non-aligned policy was strategically important to China. However, no settlement was reached until larger strategic concerns over India, the Soviet Union, and the growing influence of the United States in Southeast Asia forced Beijing to pursue a quick settlement with Burma in order to eliminate the boundary as a major cause of friction and improve relations with Rangoon.

In the wake of the Bandung Conference, China set aside its earlier reservations about Burma's non-aligned policies and began to stress peaceful coexistence. This new policy was made clear when Zhou Enlai visited Rangoon in June 1954. The joint communiqué emphasized the Five Principles of Peaceful Coexistence and mutual respect for different social systems, and Zhou stated during a press conference that revolution could not be exported.[24]

Chinese troops that had occupied disputed areas were withdrawn at Rangoon's request, but China pointed out that this should not prejudice the outcome of future boundary negotiations. U Nu travelled to Beijing in December 1954 and broached the boundary issue. Zhou pleaded that China needed time to study the issue and pledged that it "would not behave unfairly when the time came" for a settlement. Although encouraged by some officials to press Beijing for a boundary settlement, U Nu believed that "80 percent of the border problem would be solved" if China was first confident of Burma's friendship. He therefore assured the Chinese that Burma would not become a base for military action against China. The joint communiqué issued at the conclusion of the summit stated: "In view of the incomplete delimitation of the boundary line between China and Burma the two Premiers held it necessary to settle this question in a friendly spirit at an appropriate time through normal diplomatic channels."[25]

Groundwork began to be laid for boundary negotiations, but was interrupted when an armed confrontation in November 1955 led to strained bilateral relations for several months. Minor border incidents had occurred previously, but this incident involved approximately five thousand PLA troops. A Burmese column on a flag march was forced to retreat. Chinese troops destroyed boundary markers along a five-hundred-mile stretch of the border and constructed permanent outposts in the occupied area. Beijing rejected Burma's protest on the grounds that the 1941 Line was not legitimate and that China had maintained effective control of the disputed territory, as proved by the military encounter.[26] Chinese troops continued to move into disputed areas, especially the region north of Myitkyina that had never been settled but had been controlled by the British. China implied that Burma was also occupying disputed territory. Border clashes occurred intermittently until the final boundary settlement in 1960.[27]

The 1955 incident demonstrated China's ability to occupy territory and its willingness to use force to assert sovereignty over as much as 77,000 square miles of territory claimed on published maps. It also underscored China's rejection of Burma's claims based on British agreements imposed on a weak and declining Qing Dynasty. Burma feared that this was only the beginning of expansionist pressure from China, and sought India's help toward an early resolution.[28] Larger strategic concerns motivated Beijing to seek a compromise settlement, however. It worried that Burma would be drawn into the Southeast Asia Treaty Organization (SEATO) following the deterioration of relations after the armed confrontation. Even the Soviet Union detected Burma's more sanguine view of SEATO and noted that an "about face in their political orientation" had taken place. As early as 1956, Burma began negotiating with the United States, which extended Burma $42 million dollars in development assistance in 1957.

The clash and subsequent developments provided the impetus for Beijing to seek a settlement.[29] Following the confrontation, Song Qingling (Sun Yat-sen's widow and vice chair of the Standing Committee of the National People's Congress) travelled to Rangoon in January 1956 and stressed China's intent to work for the improvement of Sino-Burmese relations based on the Five Principles of Peaceful Coexistence. Significantly, she added that the boundary could be settled on the basis of mutual benefit. Soon after, a joint boundary commission was established to consider questions regarding the boundary "left over by history." However, Beijing regarded the question of the so-called 1941 Line to be an issue of principle and not a question that a joint boundary commission could settle. This issue required high-level negotiations because it involved the question of the validity of treaties signed by previous Chinese governments with "imperialist powers." It was not simply a matter of demarcating the boundary based on earlier treaties signed by those previous governments.[30] This established a pattern for China's negotiating behaviour in other boundary disputes and settlements.

Boundary Negotiations

Events surrounding the clash in 1955 and further PLA activities in the disputed areas were reported in a series of sensational articles published by the Burmese newspaper *Nation* on 13-14 February 1956 and again on 31 July. Some have argued that this was a ploy by Burma to use public pressure against China to gain leverage in boundary negotiations.[31] In the wake of the *Nation* stories, China moved quickly to prevent the deterioration of Sino-Burmese relations. Beijing responded in a 5 August *Renmin ribao* editorial titled "Vigilance against the Saboteurs of Sino-Burmese Relations." The editorial denied that PLA troops had crossed the "border," since no settled boundary existed and Chinese troops had always been in the area. Beijing implied that the Burmese were also occupying disputed territory and called for mutual withdrawal and negotiations.[32] Negotiations on a boundary settlement continued between 1956 and 1959, but China remained quite inflexible despite Burma's willingness to forgo many of its demands. Even a Chinese "package deal" offered in 1957 was acceptable to Burma, but China demanded further boundary modifications at the last minute.[33]

China's Package Deal

Although U Nu had been replaced as prime minister by U Ba Swe, he travelled to Beijing in September 1956 and was joined by leaders from the Kachin state in meetings with Zhou Enlai. U Nu clarified the Burmese position, asserting that based on Sino-British agreements between 1894 and 1941, the boundary should be the Iselin Line in the Wa region and the McMahon Line in the north. He agreed that the "Namwan Assigned Tract" was Chinese territory and should be returned to China.[34] Zhou conceded that "the Chinese people are not happy about the '1941 Line,' which Britain created by taking advantage of China's difficult position ... Nevertheless, the Chinese side is ready to affirm this line even though the Kuomintang [Nationalist] government agreed to it under British pressure."[35]

After two weeks of negotiations, China offered a tentative settlement: the Iselin Line would be recognized except for the three villages of Hpimaw, Gawlum, and Kangfang located on the Burmese side of the line but recognized as Chinese territory even by the British in previous agreements. Along the northernmost border with Tibet, Beijing would accept the "traditional customary line" (China's term for the McMahon Line). Furthermore, the perpetual lease of the Namwan Assigned Tract would be abrogated, although China would be mindful of its logistical importance to Burma. China also offered an interim agreement to withdraw Chinese troops west of the 1941 Line (Iselin Line) within one month. Although each sector of the boundary was addressed separately, Beijing considered this a package deal and Zhou indicated that no aspect of the proposal was negotiable. The National People's Congress (NPC) approved the offer on 5 November 1956, the day U Nu left to return to Rangoon.[36] U Nu agreed in principle, but local Kachin leaders resisted recognition of the three villages as Chinese territory.

Zhou travelled to Rangoon in mid-December to continue negotiations. His public speeches downplayed the boundary dispute, stressing that the problems were historical and could be settled peacefully, while also underscoring China's willingness to be patient and seek "mutual understanding." During negotiations to clarify the tentative agreement, at U Ba Swe's suggestion, Zhou agreed to cede the Namwan area to Burma if Rangoon would compensate China with an equivalent piece of territory west of the 1941 Line. Opposition to the package deal continued in Burma, mostly from Kachin leaders with ties to the three villages, but an agreement was eventually reached to resettle the inhabitants of these villages.[37]

Other problems arose regarding the specific details of the package deal. In February 1957, U Ba Swe wrote to Zhou to clarify the proposal. He stated his understanding that Burma would transfer to China 56 square miles around the three villages; in exchange, China would transfer the Namwan Assigned Tract to Burma and the traditional customary line would follow the watershed (McMahon Line). U Nu returned as prime minister before China formally responded to U Ba Swe's letter. During negotiations in Kunming in March 1957, Zhou flatly rejected Burma's interpretation of the package deal as nothing more than an exchange of Chinese territory for Chinese territory. China maintained that the three villages were Chinese territory and encompassed 186 square miles, and proposed the exchange of a comparable tract in the Wa region west of the 1941 Line for the Namwan Assigned Tract. Beijing also claimed that the traditional customary line was different from the McMahon Line, which followed the watershed and included on the Burmese side of Rangoon's proposed boundary Tibetan monasteries and medicinal herb-producing areas that China considered part of Tibet. Zhou told U Nu that Burma's position failed to consider the basis of

China's proposal: although it dealt with three distinct areas, the offer had to be considered as a package. Zhou specifically stated that the area inhabited by the Panghung and Panglao tribes in the Wa region west of the 1941 Line would be acceptable compensation for the Namwan Assigned Tract. There was a historical precedent for transferring this tribal area to China: at the time of the Iselin Commission investigation in 1935, this area was claimed by the Nationalists but was awarded to Burma.

On 9 July 1957, Zhou told the National People's Congress that China's position on the boundary was "based on a desire to protect our national interests as well as promote Sino-Burmese friendship." He stated that China should honour all valid agreements concluded by previous governments, but he was cognizant of the historical background of the boundary and sought appropriate adjustments. The resolution adopted by the NPC on 15 July asserted China's sovereignty over the three villages and the Namwan Assigned Tract, but supported a "fair and reasonable solution of the Sino-Burmese boundary question."[38]

On 26 July, China responded formally to U Ba Swe's February proposal. The reply took into account Zhou's discussions with U Nu in March. Beijing argued that the three villages in the Kachin state should be returned to China unconditionally, and that if China ceded the Namwan Assigned Tract, it should be compensated with the two tribal areas mentioned by Zhou during the March discussions with U Nu. Using the watershed principle to delimit the northern sector of the border was not acceptable, but Zhou indicated Beijing's willingness to consider it.[39]

U Ba Swe returned to Beijing to continue negotiations in December 1957, and Burma accepted the package deal in principle if China would accept the 56 square miles around Hpimaw, Gawlum, and Kangfang in exchange for the Namwan Assigned Tract. China would not compromise on the three parts of the package deal, and in fact increased its demands to include additional areas along the northern border. Negotiations were deadlocked. In March 1958, Burma rejected the new Chinese demands, stating that there should be no adjustments to the McMahon Line except around the three villages. China rejected this position in July.[40]

The negotiations foundered over the package deal and China's new demands. At the same time, U Nu's party (the Anti-Fascist People's Freedom League) experienced a domestic political crisis that eventually led to his resignation as prime minister. In September 1958, a military caretaker government led by General Ne Win took power at U Nu's request. China's declining relations with India, the crisis in Sino-Soviet relations, and growing US involvement in Southeast Asia provided the larger strategic context within which Beijing subsequently adopted a more flexible position and moved quickly to reach a compromise boundary settlement.

The Boundary Settlement

In June 1959, Ne Win offered to transfer sixty-two square miles along the Iselin Line in exchange for the Namwan Assigned Tract. He proposed an immediate meeting in Beijing to sign a treaty based on this offer, and rejected China's counter-proposal that it be considered in conjunction with the package deal as a basis for renewed negotiations.[41] China responded positively and on 22 December invited Ne Win to Beijing to continue negotiations. On 23 January 1960, Ne Win and U Nu arrived in Beijing. The Chinese were much more conciliatory and flexible, and the parties reached an agreement five days later. The agreement was similar to earlier British treaties, except that fifty-nine square miles encompassing the three villages in the northern sector and seventy-three square miles west of the 1941 Line in the Panghung and Panglao tribal areas of the Wa state were exchanged for the Namwan Assigned Tract. It closely mirrored U Nu's position on the package deal and Ne Win's proposal the previous June. China had given up its claim to larger areas while Burma had made only minor concessions to offset China's transfer of the Namwan Assigned Tract.[42] Eager to reach agreement, Beijing accepted the McMahon Line as the basis for a new boundary treaty and ceded the Namwan Assigned Tract, which both states had always recognized as China's territory. These Chinese concessions were offset by a token Burmese concession west of the 1941 Line.[43] The Sino-Indian boundary dispute played a part in the final agreement: the India-China-Burma trijunction was left undefined, and U Nu explained this as an "intentional omission" because the "Sino-Burmese boundary must naturally be the point where the three international boundaries of China, Burma and India meet."[44] U Nu pointed out that Burma had achieved a long-term objective: "We have now got the frontier which we have claimed all along, and with Chinese agreement ... I believe that Burmese interests have been well served by the conclusion of this Agreement. For the first time in history we shall have a well-defined mutually agreed boundary between Burma and China."[45]

China conceded a great deal in the final negotiations but retained control over strategically important areas. The three villages control the southernmost pass connecting the Salween and Irrawaddy valleys and are strategically important for troop movement in the area because they provide access to eastern Tibet and India's northeastern region, an area disputed by China and India. This was an important staging area during the suppression of the Tibetan revolt in 1959 and later in the 1962 war with India.[46] In the final negotiations, China also gave up its 49 percent participation rights in the Lufang mines in Burma, with the understanding that Burma would not allow a third party to be involved in their operation.[47] Also, and perhaps more significant, was the signing of a "Treaty of Friendship and Mutual Non-aggression."

A boundary commission was quickly established and work to demarcate the boundary proceeded with no significant hitches.[48] On 1 October 1960, the formal signing of the treaties took place with great fanfare in Beijing. Emphasizing congruent interests in his speech at the ceremony, U Nu dismissed any criticism that the treaty was one-sided: "It would be ridiculous for anyone to suggest that this treaty was imposed by Burma on an unwilling China. It would be equally ridiculous for anyone to suggest that the treaty was imposed by China on Burma. When we sign today, we do so freely on the basis of absolute equality."[49]

China's Grand Strategy and the Boundary Treaty

The timing of the boundary treaty was significant. Fundamental strategic considerations motivated China's greater flexibility and readiness to settle boundary disputes quickly. After years of avoiding negotiations and then delaying a settlement once they began, Beijing accepted a boundary with Burma that corresponded with the treaties signed by the British and the Qing Dynasty in the 1890s and with the Nationalists in 1941. This acceptance came at a time when the balance of power was shifting against China, requiring Beijing to improve relations with Burma. The boundary settlement can be explained in the context of China's broader regional and strategic considerations. China's strategic situation deteriorated in the late 1950s. The disastrous Great Leap Forward devastated its domestic economy. Beijing had trade problems with Japan and tense relations with Indonesia regarding overseas Chinese, and the 1958 offshore islands crisis in the Taiwan Strait brought the United States and China to the brink of war. After a period of effusive friendship, friction with India was growing. Beijing's increased assistance to insurgency groups in Southeast Asia had alarmed China's neighbours. Rangoon responded by signing a ten-year military assistance agreement with the United States in 1958 and obtaining a US$37 million economic assistance package the following year.[50]

China was concerned over the increased friction with neighbouring states. In 1959, it renewed efforts to reduce tensions and signalled a retreat from the domestic and foreign policy radicalism of the Great Leap Forward period of 1958-60.[51] It used the treaty with Burma to publicize its willingness to conduct relations with other states amicably despite a difference in social systems. Zhou Enlai emphasized China's readiness to settle outstanding issues with other neighbours. In April 1960, he told the National People's Congress: "We firmly believe that no matter what complex questions may have been left over from history ... reasonable solutions can be found for them all, so long as friendly consultations are conducted in accordance with the Five Principles of Peaceful Coexistence."[52]

The significance of the treaty with Burma went beyond a mere boundary settlement, as Beijing used it as evidence of its willingness to settle boundary problems with other neighbours. The day the treaty was signed, a *Renmin ribao* editorial declared:

The key to the solution of the question is whether or not the two sides with the boundary concerned have sincerity to abide faithfully by the Five Principles of Peaceful Coexistence, to adopt a stand of mutual understanding and mutual accommodation on the basis of equality and mutual benefit, and to solve the question through friendly consultations. If the two sides have such sincerity, it would not be difficult to settle the boundary question or other disputes.[53]

In the wake of the domestic economic failure of the Great Leap Forward and increasing international isolation resulting from a strident foreign policy during the same period, China felt compelled to seek rapprochement with its neighbours in an attempt to counterbalance growing friction with India, Soviet hostility, and growing US influence in the region. China feared that "neutralist" states such as Burma would gravitate toward a US or Soviet alignment, and took steps to prevent such a shift.

Faced with deteriorating relations with Burma and the possibility that Burma would abandon its policy of neutrality, China sought rapprochement. Beijing concluded that the Burmese communists could never become a significant force, and rather than continue to support them, it opted to try to tilt Burmese neutrality in China's favour.[54] The end of Chinese support for Burmese communist insurgents and the settlement of the boundary question greatly alleviated Burma's fears of China and advanced Beijing's foreign policy objective of developing better relations with neighbouring states.

Of the two agreements reached in January 1960, the non-aggression treaty was more important to China in terms of national security, whereas the boundary treaty paved the way for achievement of China's real objective: having Burma as a buffer against direct and indirect Indian, Soviet, or US threats in the region. Article III of the non-aggression treaty stated: "Each Contracting Party undertakes not to carry out acts of aggression against the other and not to take part in any military alliance directed against the other Contracting Party." This gave China some assurance that Burma would not become a base from which a third power could threaten China. Burma was thus effectively neutralized in terms of the Sino-Indian and Sino-Soviet disputes and the US-dominated Southeast Asia Treaty Organization.

The non-aggression treaty was a significant security gain for the PRC. It was the first such treaty Burma had signed and the first between China and a non-communist state. Beijing made the most of this, and a *Renmin ribao* editorial touted the treaty as a "new example of friendship and solidarity among Asian countries." It called for unity, sympathy, and support between China and its neighbours in the face of "cunning aggressors" who sought to "sow discord" between them and "enslave" them.[55] Beijing had not conceded everything in order to achieve this larger objective, however. China did gain strategically and militarily significant territorial concessions from Burma. These concessions facilitated many road- and bridge-building projects that enhanced the PRC's logistical flexibility vis-à-vis India and Tibet.

The non-aggression treaty led to closer cooperation between Burma and China, and this in turn diminished the influence of the Soviet Union and the United States.[56] Article IV stated that the "Contracting Parties declare that they will develop and strengthen the economic and cultural ties between the two states." Following the conclusion of the agreements, China increased economic assistance to Burma, and two-way trade and cultural exchanges grew. On the one hand, China derived desperately needed benefits, becoming one of Burma's biggest customers for rice. On the other hand, Beijing offered Burma an $84 million interest-free loan and agreed to supply Burma with factory equipment and technical advisers, using such economic incentives to draw Burma closer. Burma was frank about the leverage China began to exert: "We have rice to sell and we must sell it if we are to survive ... It may take time before we can ... go into the motives of our customers."[57]

Burma also provided rhetorical support for China's opposition to US policy in Vietnam. Although Rangoon maintained cordial relations with the United States and the Soviet Union, after 1960 many concluded that Burma was abandoning its non-aligned policy.[58]

By 1959, Mao and Zhou were increasingly anxious about China's deteriorating relations with its neighbours and the growing Soviet and American threat. Strategic factors made Beijing want closer relations with Burma. It therefore sought a boundary settlement with Burma to improve relations with Rangoon and other neighbouring states in order to enhance China's security. China also needed to settle its boundary issues amicably to publicize its new foreign policy during a time of concern over increasing isolation.[59] National security interests took precedence over deeply held images of control over peripheral territory, and Beijing was now willing to make concessions despite legitimate historical claims. The Burma settlement demonstrated that although China rejects treaties made by previous governments, negotiations, when dictated by political circumstances, can proceed using the earlier treaties as the basis for a settlement.

Conclusion

Although the boundary treaty closely followed previous agreements negotiated between the British and the Qing court or the Nationalists, the new boundary treaty is, in the view of the PRC, different. The present boundary settlement is acceptable because it was negotiated by two independent states on the basis of equality. Thus, terms such as the "McMahon Line" are not cited as the basis for the treaty, whereas the "traditional customary line" is. The eventual "concession" of territory and acceptance of the earlier British boundary was justified as a necessary compromise between two states that were dealing with each other on the basis of equality and mutual benefit based on "mutual understanding and mutual accommodation." Thus, the present boundary is legitimate while the former was not.

More importantly, however, the boundary agreement and the non-aggression treaty, as well as the economic and cultural agreements that followed, improved China's overall strategic situation and gave China the ability to exert greater influence over Rangoon's foreign policy. China emerged as the "top power" in Burma, overshadowing the Soviet Union and the United States.[60] Burma also became cautious and refused to become involved in the Sino-Soviet dispute or Sino-Indian confrontation.[61] It received some military assistance from the United States in 1963, but this was part of the ten-year military assistance agreement concluded in 1958. West Germany also supplied Burma with arms; visiting Rangoon in 1964, Zhou Enlai sought an "explanation" of Burma's understanding of Article III of the non-aggression treaty and protested these military assistance relationships.[62] Bowing to Chinese pressure, Burma scrapped a US-funded highway project linking Rangoon to Mandalay in 1964.

China valued a stable boundary more than the return of territory that it considered China's historically. Persisting with these historical claims would only have led to more tension and instability at a time when China needed to ensure the friendship of neighbouring states in the face of perceived threats from India, the Soviet Union, and the United States. Still, China could not just simply accept the previous treaties. A new boundary agreement was necessary to nullify old treaties tainted by echoes of inequality and imperialism. This sent a clear message to other countries that had boundary disputes with China: to pave the way for rapprochement, China was flexible and was willing to adopt prior treaties as a basis for negotiations, and even to relinquish territory in order to reach an agreement. This new approach to boundary settlements was dictated by the larger strategic context and China's growing security concerns.

4 Boundary Settlements with Nepal, Sikkim, and Bhutan

On 21 March 1960, two months after concluding the boundary treaty with Burma, China reached a similar agreement with Nepal, the second in a series of such treaties negotiated by China over a three-year period. A boundary treaty with Sikkim (now recognized as part of India by China) was negotiated by the Qing court with Great Britain in the 1890s and there was no indication that the boundary was disputed by China. India closed the road linking Tibet and Sikkim following the Sino-Indian border war in 1962, and it remained closed until 2006, when the Nathu La Pass was reopened. Boundary negotiations with Bhutan have continued for many years without reaching a conclusion.

The Sino-Nepali Boundary Settlement

Significance of the Settlement

Although the Sino-Nepali boundary question was much less complicated than the dispute with Burma, its settlement followed a similar pattern. Most importantly, it exemplifies China's use of boundary settlements to reduce friction with neighbouring states. Relations between India and Nepal were historically closer than Indo-Burmese relations, and this settlement illustrates more clearly how deteriorating relations with India influenced China's efforts to improve its relations with Nepal. Specifically, this settlement was an attempt to establish a friendly buffer state between India and China, something that became increasingly important because of the Tibetan insurgency, growing Soviet influence in the region as well as Indo-Soviet cooperation, and the fact that Nepal was a staging area for covert activities by the United States in Tibet.

Historical Background

Relations between China and Nepal date from the Tang Dynasty (618-907). From early times, China considered Nepal a vassal state. Even after the

Map 5 Nepal

Gurkhas came to power in the 1760s, Nepal continued to send tribute missions to the court in Beijing. A 1792 peace treaty between Nepal and the Qing court stipulated quinquennial tribute missions, and tributary relations continued until the fall of the Manchus in 1911. As Qing control over China's periphery declined in the 1850s, however, Nepal asserted itself in Tibet. An 1856 treaty established extraterritorial status for Nepali traders in Tibet and even exacted tribute from Lhasa.

For hundreds of years, Tibet and Nepal recognized a customary boundary that was never formally demarcated. The 1792 treaty mentioned only a common border between the two states. Delimitation of a common boundary was agreed to in the 1856 Nepal-Tibet treaty, but no formal boundary treaty was ever concluded.[1] Both the People's Republic of China and Nepal accepted the Himalayan peaks as the legitimate boundary between the two countries, forming an "existing, customary, traditional line."[2] (See Map 5.)

Shortly after the communists assumed power in China, the Rana family oligarchy was overthrown and a constitutional monarchy led by King Tribhuvana was established in Nepal. King Tribhuvana favoured normalization of relations with the PRC, but domestic issues and ultimately his death delayed this until his son, King Mahendra, assumed the throne in 1955. King Mahendra ended the "special relationship" with India and pursued a more balanced relationship with India and China. China responded positively to this new direction in Nepal's foreign policy, and within a few months, normalized relations with Nepal based on the Five Principles of Peaceful Coexistence.[3] This set the tone for future Sino-Nepali relations.

A 1956 trade agreement abrogated all earlier Nepali-Tibetan treaties or agreements concluded by previous Chinese governments and ended Nepal's extraterritorial and other privileges in Tibet granted in the treaty of 1856.[4] During Zhou Enlai's visit to Kathmandu in early 1957, the Nepalis raised the question of negotiating a boundary treaty again, but Zhou was noncommittal. China responded coolly to subsequent overtures by Nepal, leading one Nepali official to conclude that Beijing was not ready to solve the border problem.[5] Nepali concern over the boundary issue intensified in 1959 because of the large number of People's Liberation Army troops deployed along the Sino-Nepali border while suppressing the Tibetan rebellion.

Boundary Negotiations and Settlement

After its initial coolness, larger strategic concerns motivated China to seek a boundary settlement. The China-Nepal boundary did not present the challenges that the Sino-Burmese boundary had. With no previous boundary agreements, there was no troublesome legacy of "unequal treaties" to complicate a settlement. Even by extreme estimates, the area actually in dispute comprised less than one thousand square miles.[6] Mount Everest was a major sticking point, however, as both China and Nepal claimed the entire peak.

Meeting with a visiting Nepali delegation in October 1959, Zhou indicated China's willingness to negotiate a boundary settlement.[7] At China's invitation, Prime Minister B.P. Koirala travelled to Beijing in February 1960 to open negotiations.[8] Koirala made it clear, however, that Nepal would not make any concessions and that he expected China to compromise: "Notwithstanding its size or might, if any power attempts to occupy or control even an inch of territory of another Asian country, such attempts will definitely disrupt peace in the world."[9] China wanted to reach an early agreement and, since disagreements were not substantial, proposed the establishment of a joint commission to demarcate the boundary.[10]

In an effort to resolve the explosive issue of Mount Everest, Mao Zedong personally decided China's position. Meeting with Mao on 18 March, Koirala stated that several differences existed that were issues of "prestige" for Nepal, and a cause for concern. Mao asserted that China did not want "one inch" of Nepali territory. Koirala pointed out the differences over the "emotional" issue of Mount Everest, claiming the mountain belonged to Nepal, while Zhou maintained that it was on the Chinese side of the boundary. Mao responded: "This can be solved by dividing it in half ... And the peak is also divided ... If it cannot be solved, then it is all right to delay settlement ... We cannot emotionally accept conceding the entire mountain to you, and you cannot emotionally bear conceding the entire mountain to us." On other disputed points, Mao told Koirala "not to discuss them with him, but rather discuss them with Premier Zhou."[11]

An agreement to respect the traditional customary boundary until a formal boundary treaty was negotiated was signed on 21 March 1960.[12] China also proposed that a non-aggression treaty be concluded, but Koirala was unwilling to go that far. China then settled for a generally worded peace and friendship treaty, which was signed in Kathmandu the following month.[13]

A joint committee used maps provided by both sides to investigate the boundary and resolve any disputes. The "customary, traditional line" was the basis for the boundary, and any problems were resolved using accepted watershed principles and other boundary-delimiting norms while considering mutual benefit and accommodation. The areas that the joint committee investigated included those where a different line was claimed by both parties but administrative control was not contested, and those where both the boundary line and administrative control were contested. The governments agreed that no military patrols would enter the disputed areas.[14]

The final agreement was not reached without problems, however. China's maps, more detailed and historically more accurate than Nepal's, placed Mount Everest about five miles inside China; Nepalese maps showed the mountain on the border, but the entire peak was within Nepal. Zhou pointed this out to Koirala during the latter's stay in Beijing in March 1960.[15] At a news conference only two days after he returned to Kathmandu, Koirala revealed that China claimed Mount Everest, but suggested that the Chinese claim was weak and that Beijing was willing to compromise on the issue because the summit had never been climbed from the north face.[16]

Mount Everest was an emotional issue in both countries. The mountain has great nationalistic significance for Nepal, and Koirala's revelation was followed by anti-China demonstrations in Kathmandu.[17] During a four-day visit to Nepal in April 1960, Zhou moved quickly to allay Nepali fears about China's claim to Everest, stating at a press conference:

> We have never laid any territorial claim to Mount Jolmo Lungma or Sagar Matha [Tibetan and Nepali names for Everest] ever since the question was raised during the talks in Peking. During the talks in Peking the two parties just exchanged maps. The delineations on the maps of the two countries are different. The Chinese maps which are drawn on the basis of the Chinese historical situation show the mountain within Chinese territory, while the Nepalese maps which were drawn on the basis of the Nepalese historical situation show the mountain on the boundary line between the two countries.

Zhou also conceded that China was willing to accept the Nepali position that the mountain was on the boundary line between the two countries: "There is no question of dividing ... The mountain links up our two countries, and will not separate our two countries."[18] Citing Mao's proposal to draw the boundary through the middle of the peak, Zhou stated "after Chairman Mao Zedong and Prime Minister Koirala discussed the issue, the Chinese government has consistently adopted this position."[19] China actively asserted its claim to part of Mount Everest when on 25 May 1960 a Chinese expedition reached the summit from the north face. China initially denied the existence of the expedition, possibly to avoid provoking an anti-China reaction in Nepal, but later published an account of it.[20]

A second cause of increased friction between the two countries occurred on 28 June 1960. In the Mustang region of Nepal, where the location of the actual boundary had not been determined, Chinese troops killed one Nepali official and took as many as seventeen more prisoners. Kathmandu protested strongly and accused China of crossing the demilitarized zone established only a few months earlier. China was carrying out operations against the Tibetan resistance at the time, and had notified Kathmandu two days before the incident that PLA troops would be moving into the area in pursuit of Tibetan insurgents.[21] In response to Kathmandu's protest, Beijing pointed out that the incident had occurred north of the Kore Pass, in Chinese territory, whereas Nepali authorities stated that it had occurred south of the pass, in Nepali territory. Confusion over the exact location of the incident was possibly a result of poor maps, but China did not want to cause further friction and did not press the issue. Although it argued that the incident had occurred on Chinese territory, Beijing assumed responsibility and paid compensation for the dead official.[22] After the final boundary demarcation, it was determined that the location where China claimed the incident had occurred was actually on the Nepali side of the border.[23]

On 15 December 1960, King Mahendra dismissed parliament and ended the constitutional monarchy, initiating a system of direct rule. Prime Minister Koirala and other officials were arrested and detained. Despite Nepal's domestic unrest, the work of the joint committee continued without any real problems.

On 5 October 1961, King Mahendra and Liu Shaoqi signed the formal boundary treaty in Beijing.[24] Estimates vary, but Nepal gained about three hundred square miles and China received about fifty-six square miles of the disputed territory. Mount Everest was divided between the two states as suggested by Mao.[25] Conscious of Indian sensitivities, the trijunctions on the east with Sikkim and on the west with India were not settled, but the boundary agreed on does correspond to the line claimed by India. On 21 January 1963, the final boundary protocol was signed in Beijing. Even after this event, however, Nepal continued to cloud the issue of Mount Everest. In Hong Kong, en route home from Beijing, Nepal's foreign minister, Tulsi Giri, publicly declared that the entire peak was within Nepal's territory.[26]

China's Global Strategy and the Boundary Treaty

China and Nepal experienced converging interests in the 1950s. Although it had pro-India and pro-China factions, on balance Nepal wanted to assert its independence and further attenuate its special relationship with India, which was actually a continuation of the earlier colonial relationship with Britain. At the same time, China wanted improved relations with Nepal to offset greater tensions with India as well as US influence in the region. The growing unrest in Tibet only increased Nepal's strategic importance to China. Nepal's professed non-aligned policy could, if implemented in practice, help mitigate China's security concerns because Nepal would act as a buffer against India. An amicable Nepal would make outside interference more difficult, whereas a hostile Nepal could provide a staging area for anti-China forces in the region.

China's concerns over the shifting balance of power brought about by the festering Tibetan rebellion, US covert activities in the area, and the growing friction with India spurred Beijing to improve its relations with Nepal. It may have favoured a pro-China communist government in Nepal, but with such a government very unlikely, a neutral, nationalistic government was the best alternative. China's only option was to ensure that Nepal tilted toward China or was at least non-aligned, similar to Burma. China and India clearly competed for Nepal's favour. King Mahendra was somewhat pro-China in his sympathies, like the first prime minister he appointed, Tanka Prasad Acharya. Surprisingly, however, his second prime minister, K.I. Singh, formerly an opposition leader who had lived in China and entered office in 1957, advocated closer relations with India and even an invigoration of the special relationship. The first popularly elected prime minister, B.P. Koirala, who headed the pro-India Nepali Congress Party, took office in May 1959. The outbreak of the Tibetan rebellion at the same time further pushed Nepal toward India and away from its previous non-aligned policy.

In May 1959, under Koirala's leadership, the Nepali Congress Party adopted a resolution on Tibet that was very critical of the PRC. Clearly referring to China's behaviour as a dominant power in the region, the resolution stated: "It would be a reactionary step if China tries to establish its sovereignty over Tibet on the basis of old standards." It went on to state that China had violated its 1951 agreement with Tibet and that this served as a "warning" to other neighbouring states. The resolution equated China's use of force in Tibet with the Soviet use of force in Hungary in 1956, and called on Beijing to apply the "Leninist" principles of national self-determination in Tibet.[27] In January 1960, Koirala travelled to India to consult with Nehru. The leaders' speeches during the visit as well as the communiqué described Nepal-India relations as "invincible" and "indestructible," and stressed their mutual understanding on international security issues. Koirala also welcomed Nehru's statement that an attack on Nepal would be considered an attack on India.[28]

Nepal's official position was more balanced than that of the Nepali Congress Party. Kathmandu was officially non-aligned and demonstrated its official neutrality by abstaining from a United Nations resolution that condemned China's actions in Tibet. Nevertheless, King Mahendra remained concerned, and he and Koirala toured the border area extensively in the winter of 1959-60. Nepal also closely coordinated its response to the situation with India. India responded to Nepal's concerns and increased its financial aid, enabling Nepal to boost defence spending by 100 percent in 1959-60.[29]

An improvement in Sino-Nepali relations during the mid-1950s was followed in the late 1950s by deterioration in China's relations with Nepal as well as with the Soviet Union and India. During this period, China felt compelled to take steps to prevent a further decline in relations with Nepal. Its objective was to preserve the gains that had been made in relations between the two countries by adopting policies and making compromises to facilitate amicable relations, which were considered vital to China's strategic interests, and to encourage Nepal's non-aligned foreign policy.

When Prime Minister Koirala returned from China in March 1960 and publicly revealed that China claimed Mount Everest, he knew he would provoke anti-China sentiment in Nepal. A boundary treaty was important to Nepal, but Koirala did not want closer relations with China. It is possible that his strategy was to draw the Chinese into a diplomatic struggle that would lead to a treaty but leave a residue of anti-China sentiment.

Beijing responded adroitly, however, and immediately made concessions to mollify Nepali public opinion. In a news conference in April 1960, immediately following demonstrations protesting China's claim to Mount Everest, Zhou Enlai stated that China was willing to accept Nepal's position that the boundary ran through the middle of the mountain. He also stressed the fact that during the March negotiations, Mao Zedong himself had suggested that the boundary be drawn through the middle of the peak. Beijing realized that the Mount Everest issue was much more sensitive for Nepal than for China, whereas settlement of the boundary was more important to China than disputing the public statements of Nepali officials. Following conclusion of the treaty, China never challenged the vague statements by King Mahendra and others that Nepal had prevailed in the negotiations and controlled Mount Everest.[30]

China was willing to ignore ideological differences to entice Kathmandu to adopt a pro-China or at least neutral position. In December 1960, after King Mahendra dismissed the cabinet and suspended the constitution, opposition leaders fled to India, where they found support, and the Nepalese Communist Party was outlawed. Nevertheless, Beijing supported King Mahendra, even though he represented the "feudal and reactionary" elements.[31]

Another example of Beijing's eagerness for better relations is the Mustang incident. China was concerned about the Tibetan resistance and US support for it and "subversive" activities in Nepal. Nevertheless, China responded to Nepal's protests immediately and demonstrated complete willingness to resolve the issue without delay. In communications with Koirala, Zhou accepted complete responsibility for the incident and agreed to Nepal's demand for compensation.[32] Certainly one motive for China's proposal that a non-aggression pact be concluded at the same time as a boundary treaty was concern over Tibet. Koirala was opposed to this, so China was forced to settle for a generally worded peace and friendship treaty with no mention of defence issues. Under such circumstances, the agreement on at least a twenty-five-mile demilitarized zone offered China something and allayed some of its security concerns. Also, in an attempt to draw Nepal into a closer strategic relationship, and in response to India's pledge to defend Nepal, Chinese Foreign Minister Chen Yi emphasized Nepal's strategic importance to China and assured Nepal that if it was attacked, China would "stand on your side."[33]

At the same time that the boundary treaty was signed, an agreement was concluded to build a Kathmandu-Tibet Highway. This had important political and strategic implications for China. Prime Minister Acharya had first proposed building such a highway in February 1957. China was not interested at the time, for both economic and political reasons. Nevertheless, the pro-China Acharya wanted closer Sino-Nepali relations and began constructing the highway; construction continued until he resigned in mid-1957.[34] By 1960, China wanted to complete construction of the highway, but Prime Minister Koirala did not endorse the idea. China now needed the road link because access to Nepal from Tibet via Sikkim had become tenuous with the decline in Sino-Indian relations. In April 1960, at his Kathmandu press conference, Zhou publicly proposed the idea of a highway link, hoping to outflank Koirala and gain public support from the Nepalese traders who strongly favoured such a highway.[35] After assuming direct rule, King Mahendra concluded an agreement to construct the highway with economic assistance from China. Strategically, this was one of the primary benefits for China of improved relations with Nepal.

Conclusion

The boundary treaty with Nepal is a key factor in the closer, more cooperative relations that developed between China and Nepal. Given King Mahendra's pro-China disposition, his assumption of direct rule also facilitated the achievement of China's foreign policy objectives in the early 1960s.

While India criticized the suspension of democracy in Nepal, Chinese officials praised Mahendra's leadership. Beijing was conscious of Nepal's sensitivity toward India's heavy-handed approach in dealing with Nepal, and early in the development of a closer relationship with Nepal, Beijing disavowed imperial China's "hegemonic" attitude toward its neighbours.[36] At the signing of the formal boundary treaty on 5 October 1961, Liu Shaoqi admitted that China had had the tendency to "ignore" smaller states, but said that in the future it would "take meticulous care to avoid the repetition of such blunders."[37] He stated that Beijing "fully respected the independent policy of peace and nonalignment pursued by His Majesty's Government of Nepal and solemnly declared ... that China would never adopt an attitude of great nation chauvinism toward Nepal."[38] Liu also assured Nepal that China would not pressure it to take a stand in the increasingly fractious Sino-Indian relationship.

With its own security in mind, China gave Nepal economic assistance, first in 1956 and then much more significantly beginning in 1960. This corresponded with the shift in China's foreign policy. The motive behind China's economic and technical assistance was expressed by Zhou, who stated that "the prosperity and strength of Nepal ... are powerful support for our country."[39]

China achieved its objectives by drawing Kathmandu away from its long-standing special relationship with India, with Nepal becoming a buffer state along China's southwestern frontier. During the 1960s, strong economic and cultural ties between the two countries were developed, and a strategically important highway was completed. Thus, concluding the boundary treaty facilitated closer political, economic, and cultural relations with Nepal at a time when China perceived a growing threat to its national security.

Unlike other boundaries, the Sino-Nepali boundary was clearly a traditional customary boundary and not a legacy of imperialism. This made settlement much easier than in the case of the boundary accords reached earlier with Burma and later with Pakistan. In the final settlement with Nepal, China accepted the watershed principle as the basis of the boundary. This may undercut China's claims in the eastern sector dispute with India, where New Delhi claims that the McMahon Line, drawn along the watershed, is the boundary; nevertheless, acceptance of the watershed as the boundary with Nepal established a precedent and signalled to India China's willingness to accept the McMahon Line in practice if India would compromise in the Aksai Chin region.

China's larger strategic interests were what ultimately motivated Beijing to seek a boundary settlement and influenced the timing of the agreement. The role of Nepal in China's security strategy had changed and disputed territory was an irritant in an otherwise good relationship. The Mount Everest issue and the Mustang incident were not allowed to prevent a quick settlement. Beijing did not want the boundary issue to hinder relations in other areas of strategic interest.

A full explanation of the Sino-Nepali boundary settlement and China's behaviour is possible only if they are placed in the broader context of Beijing's grand strategy at the time. Beijing was willing to compromise to reach a quick settlement after years of delay, and was willing to wink at Nepal's obfuscation on the issue of Mount Everest. In this way, China ensured closer Sino-Nepali relations as well as Nepal's neutrality, which enhanced China's security along its southern border. This created a more favourable balance of power for China at a time when it felt threatened not only by India but also by growing Soviet-Indian cooperation and US involvement in the region.

The China-Sikkim Boundary

On 5 December 1950, after the departure of the British from India, India and Sikkim signed a treaty by which Sikkim continued to be a "protectorate" of India and New Delhi took control of Sikkim's defence and foreign policy. As was the case with other South Asian countries, as Sino-Indian relations declined, Beijing attempted to develop closer relations with Sikkim at the expense of India, but was unsuccessful. A boundary settlement was not a factor in these efforts, however. As tensions grew along the Sino-Indian border in the late 1950s, the Sikkim-Tibet border remained relatively calm, despite the activities of Tibetan insurgents and the fact that the Dalai Lama fled to India via Sikkim in 1959. That year, Zhou Enlai stated that "the boundary between China and Sikkim has long been formally delimited and there is neither any discrepancy between the maps nor any disputes in practice."[40] Located between Nepal and Bhutan, the 140-mile China-Sikkim boundary was the only section of the long frontier negotiated by British India and China not contested by the People's Republic of China.[41]

Sikkim was ruled by a hereditary Tibetan king from 1642, and even Britain considered it a feudal dependency of Lhasa before taking control. After Sikkim became a British protectorate in 1861, the boundary issue became important due to the historical relations between Lhasa and Sikkim. China accepted British control in Sikkim but raised the issue of boundary de-limitation in 1889. The boundary was established along the watershed by treaty in 1890, the first boundary treaty signed by British Indian author-ities and the Qing court, over the objections of the Tibetans, after a British military expedition defeated Tibetan forces. China accepted the British proposal to demarcate the boundary to avoid any border incidents, and this was eventually completed in 1903. Demarcation proceeded with difficulty, however, and Tibetans continued to resist a final settlement, complaining that the border was fixed by the Chinese and British without consulting the Tibetan government and was unilaterally imposed on Tibet. The treaty also formally recognized Sikkim as a British protectorate. In the end, Tibetan authorities accepted the boundary after a British military exped-ition fought its way to Lhasa in 1904.[42] The boundary, based on the watershed that divides Sikkim and Tibet, corresponds to the boundary concluded with Nepal in 1961.

Between Two Giants

Despite Zhou Enlai's 1959 statement, Beijing has described the treaty as "unequal"; the mere fact that the treaty was negotiated between the declining Qing Dynasty and an imperialist power made it unequal in Chinese eyes.[43] However, the PRC never challenged the fact that the boundary line was for-mally delimited based on a traditional customary line recognized by both Tibet and Sikkim, and in practice the PRC has always respected the boundary. After 1950, India controlled Sikkim's defence and foreign relations but it was an independent state.[44] In 1959, Zhou wrote to Nehru stating that the bound-ary with Sikkim "does not fall within the scope" of the Sino-Indian boundary question, and in a later note stated that the "China-Sikkim boundary has long been formally delimited and its location is very clear."[45] Nevertheless, as China and India slipped toward war, and despite Sikkim's lack of concern, Nehru pledged to defend Sikkim if China attacked.[46] On several occasions in 1960, China protested Indian incursions at Nathu La Pass, the main route connecting Sikkim with Tibet, and New Delhi protested the crossing of Chinese patrols into Sikkim near Jelepla Pass.[47]

After the Sino-Indian border war in 1962, China accused India of building military installations on the Chinese side of the China-Sikkim boundary and demanded their withdrawal. Again in the midst of the 1965 Indo-Pakistani war, Beijing claimed that India was violating the China-Sikkim boundary by constructing military facilities on the Chinese side of the boundary in the strategically important passes leading from Sikkim into the Chumbi Valley of Tibet. Beijing protested these boundary violations and demanded India's immediate withdrawal. Eventually, on 21 September 1965, Indian troops withdrew from the area.[48]

India annexed Sikkim in 1975, which made the question of a China-Sikkim boundary moot. Beijing protested "India's illegal annexation of Sikkim" and reinforced its troops along the border. For three decades, it refused to recognize India's annexation until Sino-Indian relations improved, but it began inching toward softening its position and recognizing Indian sovereignty over Sikkim as early as 1980, when Deng Xiaoping indicated that while China still opposed India's annexation of Sikkim, it would not allow this issue to undermine overall relations.[49] In 1996 Jiang Zemin again raised the issue during his November visit to India. After the visit, Minister of External Affairs Inder Kumar Gujral said he got the impression that "there was a move in China to accept India's contention on Sikkim."[50]

During Atal Bihari Vajpayee's visit to China in June 2003, the first by an Indian prime minister in a decade, a Declaration of Principles for Relations and Comprehensive Cooperation was issued in which India explicitly recognized the Tibet Autonomous Region as part of China and Beijing agreed to allow trade between Tibet and Sikkim via the Nathu La Pass, the strategic pass traversed by the Dalai Lama in 1959 when he fled to India and the location of a military confrontation in 1967. The linkage of India's recognition of the Tibet Autonomous Region as part of the PRC to China's implicit recognition of Sikkim as part of India was made clear during the negotiations.[51] However, the notion that this constituted Chinese recognition of Sikkim's accession to India was refuted by a Chinese Foreign Ministry statement that "the question of Sikkim is an enduring one left over from history" that cannot be resolved "overnight," but that China would "take into consideration the reality," hinting that substantive changes were forthcoming. Vajpayee asserted that "we have started the process by which Sikkim will cease to be an issue in India-China relations."[52]

China did eventually reciprocate during Premier Wen Jiabao's April 2005 visit to New Delhi, when he stated that "Sikkim is no longer a problem in China-Indian relations" and presented the Indians with a Chinese map showing Sikkim as part of India.[53] Border trade was officially opened in July 2006 over the fifteen-thousand-foot Nathu La Pass. This has reopened the historical Lhasa-Kalimpong trade route that connects Tibet with Kolkata, and links Tibet with Paro in western Bhutan, a route that is one-third shorter than the Lhasa-Kathmandu route. This has generated new wealth in Tibet and the surrounding region as trade has developed.

Apparently, a new boundary treaty does not need to be negotiated and no boundary adjustments are needed. Beijing has stated on several occasions that the boundary is "clearly delimited" and there are no outstanding issues in this sector of the Sino-Indian boundary.

The Sino-Bhutanese Boundary

China's relations with Bhutan are paradoxical. Despite the intimate historical and ethnic connections that Bhutan shares with Tibet, since 1960, when the 470-kilometre boundary was sealed, there have been no cross-border relations between Bhutan and Tibet, and the PRC and Bhutan have yet to establish formal diplomatic relations. Momentum in Sino-Bhutanese relations and the boundary settlements itself are subordinated to overall Sino-Indian relations and progress toward settling the Sino-Indian boundary. Thus, despite holding annual meetings to discuss the boundary since 1984, Beijing and Thimphu have not achieved a final settlement (see Map 6).

Historical Relations

Bhutan is geographically isolated from India but connected to Tibet by trade as well as ethnic and religious affinities; travel to Bhutan from India requires passing through Sikkim and the Chumbi Valley of Tibet. The British East India Company sent explorers to Bhutan in the 1770s to open trade routes to Tibet. Military conflict between Britain and Bhutan ended with the 1865 Treaty of Sinchula, by which Bhutan ceded territory to Britain and, in return, Britain paid Bhutan an annual allowance. Because Bhutan borders the narrow Siliguri corridor that controls access to northeastern India and is linked to Tibet by fourteen mountain passes, it is strategically important to India's defence of its northeastern frontier and China's access to the southern slopes of the Himalayas. As China asserted its influence over Tibet, Britain maintained Bhutan as a buffer state between India and China, and Bhutan gave the British complete control over its external relations in the 1910 Treaty of Punakha, Article 8 of which stated: "On its part, the Bhutanese government agrees to be guided by the advice of the British Government in regards to its external relations."[54] After India gained its independence, Bhutan was apprehensive about India's ambitions in the Himalayas and protested the new government's assertion that Bhutan was a "protectorate" of India.[55] Shortly thereafter, however, it signed the Perpetual Peace and Friendship

Map 6　Bhutan

Agreement, and India took control of Bhutan's foreign relations; Article 2 of the 1949 treaty replicates the language used in the Treaty of Punakha except that Bhutan was required to follow New Delhi's advice in its foreign relations.[56] In 1971, Bhutan finally established a ministry of foreign affairs after joining the United Nations. India continued to assert a great deal of influence over Bhutan and its foreign relations, insisting that Bhutan was "obligated" to follow its advice, whereas the government in Thimphu maintained that it needed only to "seek and consider" India's guidance. According to Prime Minister Jigme Dorji, the architect of Bhutan's foreign policy in the early 1960s, Bhutan was "guided by the advice of India in matters of her external relations, but ... can conduct her own external relations."[57] In February 2007, India and Bhutan signed a Friendship Treaty that made no mention of New Delhi's oversight of Bhutan's foreign policy.

Historically, China's relationship with Bhutan dates from the 1720s, when Manchu officials travelled to Tibet and had contact with Bhutanese officials residing in Lhasa. Bhutan maintained a representative in Lhasa until 1959 but never established a tributary relationship with China. The Chinese claimed, however, that the Tibetan ruler Polhane had established suzerainty over Bhutan in 1731, and China asserted "residual" suzerainty over Bhutan. The Qing court protested the 1910 Treaty of Punakha, but China has made no official claims to Bhutan since then.[58] Nevertheless, in the 1939 Chinese Communist Party publication *The Chinese Revolution and the Chinese Communist Party*, Bhutan is classified as a "vassal state" *(fan)* of China that was occupied by England, and *A Brief History of China*, published in 1954, included a map showing Bhutan as a former Chinese vassal state. This alarmed the Bhutanese, who feared that Bhutan could suffer the same fate as Tibet.[59] But Beijing has not involved itself in Bhutan's internal affairs and has consistently affirmed its respect for Bhutan's monarchy.[60]

To prevent any Sino-Bhutanese relationship from developing following Zhou Enlai's 1957 visit to Kathmandu, Nehru travelled to Bhutan by horseback in September 1958 and encouraged it to end its self-imposed isolation and establish closer ties with India. Bhutan maintained its isolation until it became alarmed by the Tibetan uprising and the flight of the Dalai Lama to India in 1959. Following the uprising, Chinese troops were deployed along the ill-defined Sino-Bhutanese boundary and occupied eight historically Bhutanese enclaves (approximately three hundred square kilometres) in Tibet that Bhutan had administered since the seventeenth century by agreement with Tibetan authorities.[61] China also blocked Bhutanese access to the Chumbi Valley, effectively cutting off the only road connecting Bhutan with India. Despite King Jigme Dorji Wangchuk's profession that Bhutan did not want to be "either friend or enemy of China," he sealed the borders with Tibet in 1960 and withdrew Bhutan's representative in Lhasa.[62]

Beginning in 1961, Bhutan ended its historical isolation and began cooperating with India on military and defence issues, accepting Indian assistance in training military personnel, and developing closer economic ties.[63] As Sino-Indian relations deteriorated over the boundary dispute, Nehru assured Thimphu that if China attacked Bhutan, India would come to its defense.[64] Roads directly linking India and Bhutan were completed in the early 1960s and became Bhutan's economic lifeline.[65] The precipitate end of Bhutan's isolationism and its degree of dependence on India has "few parallels in modern history, but was clearly motivated by events beyond the Himalayas."[66]

Boundary Negotiations

No boundary was ever formally negotiated between Bhutan and Tibet. A historical customary boundary for areas around major mountain passes is recognized, but there is uncertainty as to the location of the boundary along much of the frontier. Early maps had discrepancies but this did not become a significant issue until 1958, when a detailed map published in *China Pictorial* claimed a large portion of Bhutan. Through India, King Wangchuk protested the Chinese claim to Bhutanese territory. Concern also grew after Chinese military incursions into Bhutan in 1959 and as China built roads in the vicinity of the border. Conflict between Tibetan and Bhutanese herders was common in traditional grazing areas in the Chumbi Valley, along the northwestern border. Bhutan communicated its concerns directly to Beijing in 1959, but India intervened. New Delhi protested, but Beijing rebuffed India's representations and refused to discuss issues concerning Bhutan.[67] Zhou Enlai asserted:

> The boundary between China and Bhutan ... does not fall within the scope of our present discussion. I would like, however, to take this opportunity to make clear once again that China is willing to live together in friendship with Sikkim and Bhutan, without committing aggression against each other, and has always respected the proper relations between them and India.

In a subsequent communication, Zhou stated: "There is only a certain discrepancy between the delineations on the maps of the two sides ... But it has always been tranquil along the border between the two countries."[68]

As with the other Himalayan states, China's objective was to woo Bhutan away from its close relationship with India and establish it as a neutral buffer state. In December 1960, Beijing began exploring the possibility of establishing formal ties with Bhutan. In an attempt to develop better relations with Thimphu, Beijing offered Bhutan economic and technical assistance; it expressed interest in discussing the boundary issue but refused Indian mediation.[69] Prime Minister Dorji viewed this as a Chinese attempt to encourage Bhutan "in enlightened self-interest" to "bypass India and start direct negotiations."[70] Although not responding to China's call for direct negotiations, Dorji asked to participate in Sino-Indian negotiations regarding Bhutan's border. Nehru, however, refused to include Bhutanese representatives in any boundary negotiations.[71]

At a January 1961 press conference in India, King Wangchuk confirmed the recent Chinese overtures. He said that "private persons" had approached the government proposing direct talks on a boundary settlement, and Bhutan showed some inclination to respond positively. Because of pressure from Nehru, the king said publicly that such issues should be handled by New Delhi and Bhutan declined direct negotiations with Beijing, but Bhutan clearly desired a multilateral foreign policy.[72] At the press conference, King Wangchuk also stated that "we do not want to be either friends or enemies with China," but made it clear that Bhutan would maintain the status quo and await the settlement of Sino-Indian differences.[73]

In London in 1962, Prime Minister Dorji revealed that Beijing had approached Bhutan about establishing a "Confederation of Himalayan States," but he opposed such a policy.[74] Evidence suggests, however, that China's overtures struck a responsive chord among some of Bhutan's elite, some of whom felt that Bhutan should pursue a more even-handed policy toward China and India, much as Nepal had successfully done.[75] Beijing took advantage of these pro-China sentiments but, failing to establish formal diplomatic relations, tried in other ways to eliminate friction with Bhutan.

Redrawing maps required only minor territorial concessions but would eliminate a major source of tension between the two states. Beginning in 1962, maps published by China more closely reflected the boundary claimed by Bhutan.[76] This led some scholars to conclude that despite the lack of official diplomatic relations and Indian opposition, China and Bhutan had concluded a "secret" boundary treaty in 1961 and that Bhutan had agreed to allow Chinese troops to transit its territory; however, later developments confirmed that there had been no secret agreements.[77]

With the outbreak of hostilities between India and China, Nehru publicly assured Bhutan that India would defend it against any foreign aggression. King Wangchuk stated publicly, however, that the 1949 Indo-Bhutanese treaty made no reference to any Indian defence commitment.[78] Beijing sought to reassure Bhutan by issuing a statement that it would respect Bhutan's territorial integrity as Chinese troops advanced toward the Sino-Indian frontier east of Bhutan.[79] This apparently reassured Bhutan, which during the border war tried to maintain "formal neutrality" by not allowing Indian troops access to Bhutanese territory and was relieved by the ceasefire.[80] Although China's conciliatory policy of the early 1960s was unsuccessful and Bhutan continued to resist any boundary settlement, the policy did bear fruit beginning in the 1970s, when Bhutan began to seek greater independence in its foreign policy. Bhutan became a member of the United Nations in September 1971 and voted to seat Beijing as the representative of China the following month. Thimphu has consistently supported China on human rights and Taiwan issues. Despite its historical ties to Tibet, Bhutan has no contact with the Dalai Lama's government-in-exile in Dharamsala, India, and does not, in spite of cultural affinities with Tibet, involve itself in the Tibetan independence movement.[81]

In 1974, China was one of only six countries invited to send a representative to the coronation of King Jigme Singye Wangchuk, a clear indication that Bhutan desired closer ties with China but was still waiting for progress in Sino-Indian boundary negotiations before undertaking to settle its own boundary with China. During discussions with China's chargé d'affaires in New Delhi, who represented China at the coronation, Bhutanese Foreign Minister Dawa Tsering acknowledged the outstanding border questions but recognized a basis for a settlement, stating that "China and Bhutan have no conflicting views, but only a similar perspective." The new king also acknowledged the benign nature of the boundary differences, saying that Sino-Bhutanese relations had "always been peaceful."[82]

In 1979, in response to improving Sino-Indian relations and in an effort to manage the friction caused by Tibetan herders' increasing encroachment into Bhutanese territory, members of Bhutan's national assembly considered normalizing relations with China and urged direct dialogue with that country.[83] In March 1981, Bhutan directly approached the Chinese representative in New Delhi about initiating boundary negotiations, but only after consultations with New Delhi, and in June Thimphu announced its intent to open direct boundary negotiations with Beijing.[84] In mid-April 1984, Bhutan's ambassador to India travelled to China for the first official round of negotiations, the first visit of a Bhutanese official to Beijing. After several days of discussion, a joint communiqué on 20 April announced an agreement to hold further negotiations.

Based on China's 1958 map, it appeared that the major dispute was over a 600-square-kilometre tract located along the northeastern boundary (McMahon Line) and the Tibetan enclaves that were administered by Bhutan, but the exact extent of territorial claims was vague. As negotiations got underway, however, it became clearer that the dispute centred on 269 square kilometres lying along the northwestern boundary of Bhutan and the

Chumbi Valley, which the Chinese claimed based on historical and customary Tibetan use. Subsequent rounds of negotiations, conducted by officials at ambassadorial and vice foreign minister levels, have taken place annually, alternating between Thimphu and Beijing. In 1988, agreement was reached on "guiding principles" for the settlement of the boundary. During late October and early November 1989, Bhutan's foreign minister travelled to Beijing for the sixth round of negotiations. Meeting the Bhutanese delegation, President Yang Shangkun said that despite the absence of official diplomatic relations, mutual exchanges had increased and the two countries did not have any basic conflict of interest.

China continued to press for an agreement but Bhutan hesitated. During the tenth round of negotiations, held in Beijing in November 1996, China proposed to exchange 495 square kilometres along the northern central boundary for the 269-square-kilometre tract along the Bhutan-China boundary in the Chumbi Valley. A preliminary agreement was reached based on this "package deal" offered by the Chinese, which recognized Bhutan's sovereignty along the northern boundary in exchange for Chinese claims in the northwest, and also included agreements on diplomatic relations, bilateral trade, and the road linking Bhutan and Tibet.[85] If accepted, the northwestern border along the Chumbi Valley would be pushed further south; this alarmed India because of the security implications of this strategically important region, but Bhutan responded positively.[86] Despite China's continued logging and road construction in disputed areas, during the twelfth round in 1998, Thimphu consented to an interim agreement. In the December 1998 agreement on the "Maintenance of Peace and Tranquility Along the Sino-Bhutanese Border Area," Beijing "reiterate[d] its position to fully respect the independence, sovereignty, and territorial integrity of Bhutan."[87] The two sides acknowledged that they had "reached consensus on the guiding principles on the settlement of the boundary issues and narrowed their differences on the boundary issues," and "agreed that prior to the ultimate solution of the boundary issues, peace and tranquility along the border should be maintained and the status quo of the boundary prior to March 1959 should be upheld."[88] This first official agreement between Thimphu and Beijing appeared to establish the basis for an eventual formal boundary treaty.

However, Bhutan's Council of Ministers questioned the tentative agreement on a package deal, arguing that some changes had to be made. During the fourteenth round in 2000, Bhutan pushed its claim along the northwestern

Chumbi Valley boundary beyond China's initial offer, arguing that "the earlier agreement was not acceptable and ... some changes had to be made in the claims" based on an exchange of maps that showed significant differences in the respective claims. Beijing complained that "Bhutan was raising new issues after many years of talks," but was nevertheless "willing to consider some in the demarcation of the border but their adjustment was not limitless." It is clear that Beijing was "keen to go beyond Bhutan's setback," proving its eagerness to reach a settlement and normalize relations with Thimphu. The following year, the Chinese said that the "boundary issue had, by and large, been resolved," and both sides agreed that "discussion was close to a final solution."[89]

In 2004, however, Thimphu was again alarmed by Chinese road-building projects that it claimed even crossed Bhutan's "traditional boundary claim line." Bhutanese representatives raised the issue several times with the Chinese embassy in New Delhi, protesting that road projects violated the 1998 agreement to refrain from "unilateral action to alter the status quo of the border." The issue was again raised with the Chinese foreign minister at the United Nations in September that year, and Bhutan was assured that road-work would stop. Chinese Foreign Minister Li Zhaoxing "conveyed the Chinese government's commitment to settle the issue amicably and through friendly negotiations," but argued that the roads were only improving the infrastructure in Tibet and had not entered Bhutanese territory. Nevertheless, he stated that "in view of the close relationship between the two countries, China had decided to stop construction work in the disputed area although it did not mean a change in China's position on the disputed areas."[90]

The Bhutanese national assembly urged the government to move faster toward a settlement but no final boundary has been agreed to. China wants to achieve an early settlement and its road building may be a tactic to encourage domestic pressure on a reluctant Bhutanese government to break the impasse and conclude a boundary treaty despite the failure of India and China to achieve a settlement. It is possible that Beijing may show more flexibility to achieve this goal.[91]

Conclusion

The Sino-Bhutanese boundary negotiations are distinguished by the delay in beginning talks despite the outward appearance of friendly relations, and by how long negotiations have continued with no settlement. We can safely assume that the basic reason it took so long to even initiate negotiations for a Sino-Bhutanese boundary treaty is India's domination of Bhutan's foreign affairs. India is especially sensitive about China's demands in the Chumbi Valley because of the valley's strategic significance to India, near the so-called chicken's neck that connects India with its northeastern frontier, Sikkim and Bhutan.[92] Even after negotiations got underway beginning in the early 1980s, it has been difficult to reach final agreement. This is due to the historically intimate and complex relationship between Tibet and Bhutan and to current sensitivities over China's domination of Tibet, as well as to the fact that Bhutan's foreign relations are dominated by India. No doubt the Indian factor will continue to be a key element in any future settlement. Although not linked in a formal sense, a Sino-Bhutanese boundary settlement is nevertheless linked politically to Sino-Indian relations.[93]

5 The Sino-Pakistani Boundary Settlement

On 26 December 1962, two months after the Sino-Indian border war began, China and Pakistan agreed to settle their mutual boundary. This treaty is "provisional," pending the resolution of the Indo-Pakistani dispute over Kashmir. It clearly highlights how the shifting balance of power influenced China's perceptions of strategic imperatives in the early 1960s, and how this in turn influenced Beijing's policy toward Pakistan. The *entente cordiale* between Pakistan and China was the result of congruent national interests and geopolitics, despite competing social systems and alliances.[1]

Following the 1955 Bandung Conference, Sino-Pakistani relations began to improve, with visits to Pakistan by Vice Chair of the Standing Committee of the National People's Congress Song Qingling in October 1956 and Prime Minister Zhou Enlai in December. Beijing recognized that despite the different political systems and conflicting views on many issues, congruent geostrategic interests facilitated close bilateral relations.[2] Initially, cultural and economic relations were the primary means of contact, and political relations were not close. A major wedge preventing closer Sino-Pakistani relations was the United States–Pakistan military alliance.

The Sino-Pakistani *entente cordiale* became a strategic imperative in 1960 when the balance of power in the region began to shift as Sino-Soviet and Sino-Indian relations deteriorated, and US-Pakistan relations were strained. India drew closer to the Soviet Union and the United States, thereby gaining support against China and Pakistan. The Sino-Pakistani boundary settlement is therefore a good example of the influence of strategic considerations on China's foreign policy and on its handling of boundary disputes.

Historical Background

China's relations with present-day Pakistan began even before the establishment of the legendary Silk Road that passed through the Sino-Pakistani border regions of Ladakh and Gilgit. Buddhism and Islam also brought people of the two areas into contact. Tribal leaders in Eastern Turkistan (Xinjiang) considered the Hunza region of northern Pakistan a tributary state and required payment of an annual tribute. The Qing court claimed Hunza as a vassal state as well, and as late as 1936 the Mir of Hunza paid tribute to Chinese authorities against British advice.[3]

The area of Kashmir currently under Pakistan's control was a frontier region with no clearly delimited boundaries during British domination over India. The various kingdoms, only nominally subject to British control, were recognized as separate from British India. In the 1870s, the British began to assert some political control over the region as the expansion of the Russian empire threatened to encroach into the area.[4] Fearful that Russia might eventually dominate Eastern Turkistan, British officials approached the Chinese in 1899 seeking to establish a common boundary in the Kashmir region along the Karakoram mountain range. Qing authorities considered it a fair proposal, and because the Karakoram watershed formed a clear boundary, no demarcation was negotiated.[5] These unsettled boundaries resulted in a volatile situation after the partition of India in 1947, however, and in 1949 the People's Republic of China inherited an undelimited boundary between Xinjiang and the Kashmir region contested by Pakistan and India.

In December 1949, Pakistan, along with the United States and other countries, sponsored a United Nations resolution criticizing the Chinese Communists' revolution and supporting the Chinese people's right to "choose freely their political institutions and maintain a government independent of foreign control."[6] Although Pakistan recognized the People's Republic of China in January 1950, it still participated in the San Francisco peace conference in 1951. The PRC was initially ambiguous about Pakistan and did not immediately respond to its recognition. The Chinese Communist Party had favoured a federation of Muslim and Hindi states rather than partition, and when Beijing asserted control over western China, Pakistan became uneasy; it complained about PRC troop movements along the border and took measures to prevent violations.[7]

Despite these tensions in their political relations, China came to Pakistan's assistance when India stopped supplying Pakistan with necessary coal; a barter agreement facilitated trade of Chinese coal for jute and cotton.[8] Pakistan initially supported the seating of the Beijing government as the legitimate representative of China at the United Nations, and abstained from voting on the US-sponsored UN resolution condemning the PRC for aggression in Korea. Pakistan also declined to send troops to support UN forces in Korea. Despite this initial amity with Beijing, however, Pakistan began developing closer relations with the West for strategic reasons.

Pakistan became a member of the Southeast Asia Treaty Organization (SEATO) in 1954 and the Central Treaty Organization (CENTO/Baghdad Pact) the following year. Beijing strongly opposed SEATO, viewing it as a US attempt to encircle China. Pakistan insisted that the treaties were defensive and were not directed against China, and that Pakistan would not participate in actions against China. To a degree, China accepted Pakistan's membership in SEATO as defensive, especially after Zhou Enlai and Prime Minister Mohammed Ali Bogra met at the Bandung Conference in 1955. Zhou made Beijing's views clear in a report to the Chinese People's Political Consultative Conference in March 1957:

> As everybody knows we differ on certain questions. Take the Manila Treaty (SEATO) and the Baghdad Pact (CENTO). Pakistan is, since 1954, a party to both whereas we oppose these treaties. Nevertheless we expressed a common desire to promote the cause of world peace and further develop existing friendly relations between China and Pakistan.[9]

Other aspects of Pakistan's foreign policy irritated Beijing, too. In 1956, Pakistan supported the British during the Suez Crisis and opposed the Soviet invasion of Hungary; in addition, although Pakistan claimed that it supported Beijing as the legitimate representative of China at the UN, it cast negative votes whenever the question of supplanting the Republic of China with the PRC arose after the mid-1950s.

Beijing did not openly criticize Pakistan's participation in military pacts, but stressed its desire for Pakistan to develop an "independent" policy.[10] And despite Pakistan's military alliances with the West and other irritants in bilateral relations, Sino-Pakistani relations remained cordial. Even during the high point of Sino-Indian friendship, Beijing was neutral regarding the Indo-Pakistani dispute over Kashmir. China favoured direct negotiation between India and Pakistan as called for by India, but opposed UN involvement, which Pakistan favoured.

Thus, the mid-1950s was marked by uneven relations between China and Pakistan. By the late 1950s, their outwardly cordial relations began to deteriorate. Two important developments led to this. First, China built the Xinjiang-Tibet Highway in 1956-57 and this concerned Pakistan for security reasons.[11] Then in 1958, General Muhammad Ayub Khan, a proponent of Pakistan's pro-Western security arrangements, led a military coup and began pursuing even closer ties with the West. China reacted strongly to this new direction in Pakistan's foreign policy, criticizing Ayub for "bringing the wolf into the house in an attempt to rely upon American power to maintain their unstable control and suppress the struggle waged by the people."[12]

The Tibetan rebellion heightened tension and Pakistan became increasingly concerned about security. It joined the UN criticism of Chinese suppression of the rebellion, whereas India did not take a strong stand. Pakistan also hosted a Muslim hajj delegation from Taiwan, eliciting strong criticism from Beijing.[13] In March 1959, the United States and Pakistan concluded a joint defence agreement, and, concerned about the threat from the "north," Ayub sought to establish a joint defence agreement with India as well, arguing:

> As a student of war and strategy, I can see quite clearly the inexorable push of the north in the direction of the warm waters of the Indian Ocean. This push is bound to increase if India and Pakistan go on squabbling with each other. If, on the other hand, we resolve our problems and disengage our armed forces from facing inwards as they do today, and face them outwards, I feel we shall have a good chance of preventing a recurrence of the history of the past, which was that whenever this subcontinent was divided – and often it was divided – someone or other invited an outsider to step in.[14]

India rejected Pakistan's proposal even though Sino-Indian relations were also deteriorating. Beijing criticized Pakistan's defence agreement with the United States and its proposal for a joint defence agreement with India as an attempt to sow "discord in the relations between China and India," and also accused Pakistan of "adopting an extremely unfriendly attitude toward China."[15]

Despite the increased tension with Pakistan, with the beginning of the Sino-Soviet dispute, the deterioration in Sino-Indian relations, and concerns over growing US involvement in the region, Pakistan seemed less threatening to Beijing, and a potential ally according to China's united front doctrine. As both China and Pakistan felt threatened and isolated, and because of congruent strategic interests, the stage was set for them to seek mutual accommodation. A boundary settlement played a central role in eliminating

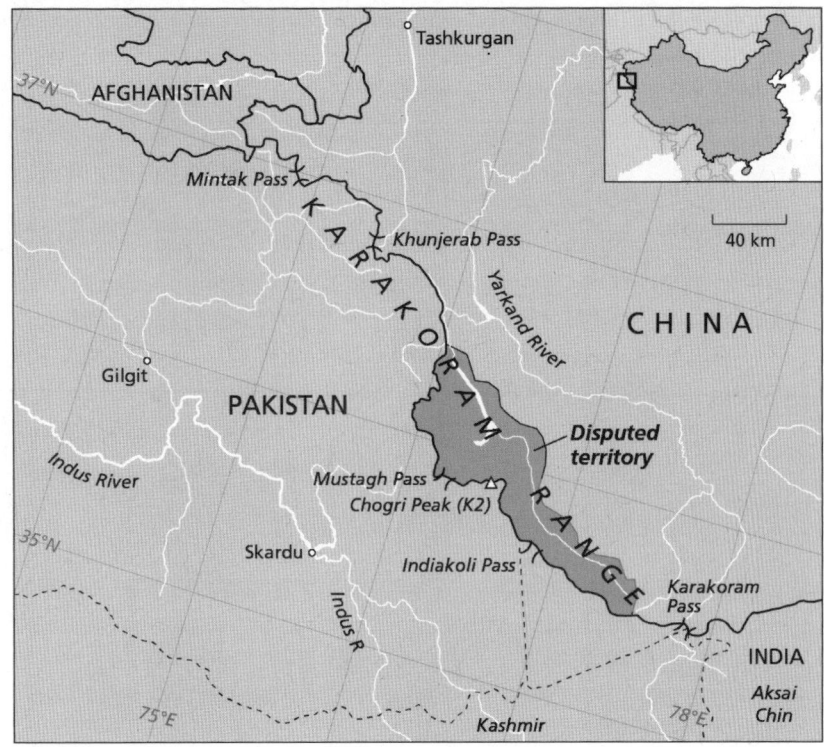

Map 7 Pakistan

residual friction and paved the way for improved relations. Ayub observed: "This agreement on border demarcation was the first step in the evolution of relations between Pakistan and China. Its sole purpose was to eliminate a possible cause of conflict in the future."[16]

Boundary Negotiations and Settlement

The China-Pakistan boundary extends 325 miles along the Karakoram mountains (following the McMahon Line), dividing Pakistani-controlled Kashmir and Xinjiang between the trijunction with Afghanistan and the Karakoram Pass (see Map 7).[17] From the Sino-Indian boundary negotiations in 1959, Pakistan learned that some Chinese maps included territory in Hunza and Gilgit as part of the PRC.[18] Although Pakistan raised the issue with Beijing and attempted to handle the boundary dispute calmly, it adopted a firm position against Chinese claims. An editorial in *Dawn*, a leading paper in Pakistan, warned:

Chinese maps ... have shown a part of the extreme northern region of our country as Chinese territory, [and] we feel it our duty to tell the comrades in Peking that, as far as Pakistan is concerned, there will be no yielding of any kind at any time. The sanctity of the McMahon Line must be preserved and maps or no maps, we will not countenance the loss of even a single inch of our territory.[19]

Ayub called China a "hovering giant" casting its shadow over Pakistan, and warned that if Beijing pushed its claims in Kashmir, "dire consequences" would result.[20] He also asserted that India and Pakistan enjoyed a "complete understanding ... in the wake of the danger developing on the northern and northwestern frontiers of the sub-continent."[21]

Beginning in 1959, minor skirmishes were reported along the border. China perceived the new direction of Pakistan's foreign policy under Ayub as a threat to its security and began to raise the territorial issue: "Should the Pakistani side continue to ... commit acts injurious to China's sovereignty and territorial integrity ... the Pakistani government must bear full responsibility for all damage thus done to Sino-Pakistani relations."[22] Concerned about a military confrontation with China, Pakistan increased its military forces in the area and eventually closed the border.[23] No formal boundary had ever been demarcated and, unlike India, Pakistan held that the boundary with China was undetermined, despite the official references to the McMahon Line. Pakistan was also motivated to settle the boundary because it was concerned that India might pre-empt Pakistan's claims in Kashmir through an agreement with China.[24]

To reduce tension along the border, Pakistan sought to discuss the boundary with China, and in October 1959 Ayub announced that it would seek a boundary settlement. What prompted him to do so was the opinion expressed by a Burmese delegate at the United Nations to Zulfikar Ali Bhutto that the Chinese had been "entirely reasonable and often, indeed, magnanimous in their dealings with Rangoon over the border."[25] However, fairly substantive Sino-Indian discussions were already underway and China delayed a reply until January 1961; even then, it did not push for a settlement because Beijing wanted to avoid derailing a possible Sino-Indian boundary settlement. In March 1961, Pakistan's ambassador in Beijing pressed the issue but Beijing hesitated to proceed with any boundary negotiation, not wanting to complicate Sino-Indian relations. By February 1962, however, Beijing had concluded that a settlement with India was unlikely, and it proposed a "temporary agreement" until "the relevant sovereign authorities will renegotiate with the Chinese Government ... a formal boundary treaty" after India and Pakistan settle the Kashmir issue. [26] This was followed by a formal proposal by Pakistan to China on 28 March, and on 3 May Beijing announced the initiation of Sino-Pakistani boundary negotiations:

> The Government of the People's Republic of China and the Government of Pakistan, after an exchange of views, affirm that the boundary between China's Xinjiang and the contiguous areas, the defense of which is under the actual control of Pakistan, has never been formally delimited and demarcated in history. With the view of ensuring tranquility along the border and growth of good neighborly relations between the two countries, they have agreed to conduct negotiations so as to obtain an agreed understanding of the location and alignment of the boundary and to sign on this basis an agreement of a provisional nature. They have also agreed that after the settlement of the dispute over Kashmir between Pakistan and India, the sovereign authorities concerned shall reopen negotiations with the Chinese Government regarding the boundary of Kashmir so as to sign a formal boundary to replace the provisional agreement. [27]

The total area disputed was approximately 3,400 square miles. Negotiations began on 12 October 1962, just one week before China attacked Indian forces; two months later, on 28 December, an agreement on the principles for settling the boundary was announced. The boundary settlement generally corresponded to Pakistan's initial claims, following the watershed of the Karakoram Mountains (the McMahon Line). At one point, the boundary deviated from the watershed to include on the Pakistan side of the line an area controlled by the PRC but claimed by Pakistan. This 750-square-mile area included salt mines that were important to the inhabitants of Pakistan's Hunza region. The settlement also divided control over the mountain peak K-2, the second highest after Mount Everest; this was the same solution adopted in the Sino-Nepali boundary settlement regarding Mount Everest. [28]

The treaty was signed in Beijing on 2 March 1963. [29] This provisional agreement explicitly deferred a formal treaty until after the settlement of the Indo-Pakistani dispute over Kashmir. India claimed that the treaty was invalid because Pakistan illegally occupied Kashmir. India also claimed that the treaty ceded 1,300 square miles of Indian territory to China. Pakistan pointed out, however, that the boundary corresponded to the boundary sought by Britain in 1899 and coincided with British claims as recent as 1939.[30] Although New Delhi criticized the agreement, Nehru indicated privately that he felt it was a good agreement.[31] It took until 1965 for demarcation to be completed, and the final boundary protocol was signed in Rawalpindi on 26 March.

China's Global Strategy and the Boundary Settlement

China's ambivalence toward and lukewarm relations with Pakistan during the early 1950s resulted primarily from Beijing's view of Pakistan's leaders as bourgeois nationalists and its pursuit of a "lean to one side" policy of aligning with Soviet bloc countries.[32] In the mid-1950s, China's opening to the Non-Aligned Movement excluded Pakistan because it was aligned with the West as a member of SEATO and CENTO. Thus, the improvement in Sino-Pakistani relations in the early 1960s is an excellent example of how strategic imperatives influenced China's relations with its non-communist (and even pro-Western) neighbours. More than any other single factor, Pakistan's role in ensuring China's national security influenced Beijing's rapprochement during this period. The boundary settlement was a necessary step in the process, eliminating a major irritant in bilateral relations and facilitating an *entente cordiale*.

When Ayub came to power in 1958, he set out to strengthen US-Pakistan military ties and proposed a joint defence agreement with India against the threat from the north. Because of his anti-communist sentiments, he also arrested many pro-China politicians and Sino-Pakistani relations deteriorated dramatically. With the growing Sino-Soviet conflict and Sino-Indian dispute, China needed to cultivate Pakistan as an ally to counter the growing cooperation between the Soviet Union and India that was dramatically shifting the regional balance of power and to allay concerns about growing US involvement in the region.

China's reaction to Pakistan's new policies was low-key so as not to increase friction. It did not openly protest Ayub's overtures to the United States and India, and it refused to include the area of Kashmir under Pakistan's control in its negotiations with India.[33] Eventually international developments shifted the situation in China's favour: India rejected Ayub's joint defence proposal, the Soviet Union's downing of the American U-2 spy plane based in Pakistan in May 1960 brought threats from the Soviet Union, and relations between Pakistan and Afghanistan deteriorated, as did Pakistan's relations with the United States. Ayub realized that his policies had backfired: "The whole pattern of our relations with others required fundamental re-thinking. Some of the essential elements in our geographical situation had not been recognized, nor was there a clear concept of the nature of the political compulsions to which we would be subjected." He concluded: "I think it was the force of events which compelled us to undertake this exercise."[34]

Pakistan found itself surrounded by hostile and alienated neighbours, and Beijing wanted closer relations with Pakistan. Pakistan was deeply concerned about India's ambitions regarding Kashmir and felt that the SEATO and CENTO pacts alone would not deter India. Pakistan wanted closer relations with China to counter the threat from India. An article in *Dawn* argued: "Let us fool ourselves no more that any power, however well meaning, will eventually rush to our aid from across the oceans if we are in peril. An alliance nearer home against a common enemy is far more logical."[35] And China now viewed Pakistan's participation in the US-led military alliances as benign; Liu Shaoqi stated that China was "convinced that your [Pakistan's] participation in SEATO is only against India and not against China at all."[36]

China's interest in better relations with Pakistan was motivated by the larger strategic situation and the shift in the regional balance of power. This shift set the stage for Sino-Pakistani rapprochement.[37] China was concerned about growing tensions along the border with the Soviet Union in Xinjiang, even as Pakistan's concerns over China were overshadowed by the threat from India, the Soviet Union, and Afghanistan.[38] Thus, complementary strategic interests opened the way for closer relations. China used the boundary treaty with Pakistan primarily to facilitate improving relations by removing a major source of friction.[39]

By October 1959, Pakistan had already signalled its desire for a settlement. A boundary settlement would facilitate rapprochement with Pakistan, but there were several possible reasons for China's delayed response. Even if China was interested in a boundary settlement, negotiations with Burma were beginning around the same time, and negotiations with Nepal and Mongolia quickly followed the settlement with Burma. The delay in commencing negotiations with Pakistan may have simply been due to Beijing's inability to handle so many sensitive diplomatic initiatives at once. A second possible reason is that at this point in its negotiations with New Delhi, Beijing was still hoping for a settlement with India and was therefore reluctant to discuss the boundary question with Pakistan. Discussions with India were at a sensitive stage and opening negotiations with Pakistan would have exacerbated Sino-Indian relations and entangled China in the Indo-Pakistani dispute over Kashmir. At the time, Beijing felt that any Sino-Pakistani negotiations should be preceded by an Indo-Pakistani settlement of the Kashmir issue. China recognized the existence of a legitimate territorial dispute over Kashmir and tried to remain neutral.

In the late 1950s, China also did not feel an acute need for closer relations with Pakistan. It considered Pakistan as a potential ally, but first Pakistan would have to abandon policies that were inimical to China.[40] A clear shift in Pakistan's foreign policy occurred in 1961, when Ayub indicated that Pakistan would support Beijing as China's representative at the United Nations. China responded by expressing its willingness to be "reasonable" regarding a boundary settlement if Pakistan would act similarly on issues that affected China.[41] The following year, China agreed to begin boundary negotiations. There is clear evidence that these developments are all related; Ayub had even discussed a quid pro quo with the Chinese ambassador.[42]

China was interested not only in a boundary settlement but also in broader strategic cooperation. A boundary settlement would be just the first step in achieving its more important strategic objectives. As in the earlier negotiations with Burma and Nepal, China raised the question of concluding a non-aggression treaty at the same time as the boundary agreement. Although China did not make Pakistan's withdrawal from its military pacts a precondition for this, Pakistan hinted that it was willing to leave the alliances.[43] Some Pakistanis favoured cutting ties with the West and developing relations with China as a more credible deterrent against India.[44]

Although there is evidence that Pakistan rejected China's offer to conclude a non-aggression pact, several statements deliberately left the impression that such an understanding had been reached secretly.[45] For example, Foreign Minister Zulfikar Ali Bhutto stated: "This ... cannot be regarded as inconsistent with our alliances with the West. Our alliances are for self-defense. A nonaggression pact further reinforces the defensive character of those alliances."[46] Despite such statements, Bhutto claimed that there were no secret agreements when the boundary treaty was concluded, and other scholars concur.[47] However, Bhutto hinted at the possibility of China's becoming involved in an Indo-Pakistani war when he stated:

> That conflict would not involve Pakistan only ... An attack by India on Pakistan would also involve the security and territorial integrity of the largest state in

Asia. This new factor that has arisen is a very important one. I would not, at this stage wish to elucidate it any further ... From that point of view ... I think I can confidently say that everything is being done to see that our national interests and territorial integrity are safeguarded and protected.[48]

China also gave assurances to Pakistan: "The US, UK and USSR have to consider that if they help India, China would support Pakistan. This is a big point that has to be considered by their policy-makers."[49] Even into the 1980s, when Beijing's relations with New Delhi had improved, China continued to pledge explicitly to defend Pakistan. Visiting Pakistan in July 1983, Chinese Foreign Minister Wu Xueqian stated that "Pakistan is China's exceptionally friendly neighbor. If there is a war and Pakistan suffers foreign armed attack, the Chinese government and people will, of course, stand on the side of Pakistan."[50]

In the context of China's desire for reconciliation with neighbouring states to ensure its strategic objectives, the timing of the boundary agreement is significant. The delay in China's response to Pakistan's earlier overtures is not so curious when we consider China's more fundamental strategic concerns. Beyond the boundary settlement, China wanted to draw Pakistan into a strategic partnership. It was careful to ensure that Pakistan was not just feigning rapprochement to gain leverage against India. In 1961, China had approached Pakistan about supporting its UN representation bid, but Ayub had said that such support was contingent on China's willingness to settle the boundary.[51] Pakistan's October 1962 vote in favour of seating Beijing at the United Nations was an important step, and China reciprocated by quickly agreeing to move forward with a boundary settlement. One Pakistani newspaper concluded that "the trend of recent events may induce China to proceed with demarcation talks. Pakistan's recent vote for the admission of China into the United Nations may be an important factor in the process."[52] However, while this may be true, Beijing had larger security concerns that made rapprochement with Pakistan even more imperative.

The start of the negotiations and the announcement of an agreement corresponded with other events in Sino-Indian relations that should not be considered coincidental. By mid-1962, Beijing knew that a boundary settlement with India was unlikely and was anticipating armed conflict in the near future. At this point, China was willing to risk greater friction with India to improve relations with Pakistan. Negotiations began in mid-October and preceded China's attack on India by one week; once the war began, China pushed for an early agreement.

By the outset of the Sino-Indian border war, China had not accepted several Pakistani conditions. It is possible that this influenced Pakistan's neutral attitude during the war, which may also have been prompted by Pakistan's desire for further Chinese concessions. In late 1962, on the eve of Indo-Pakistani negotiations on Kashmir, China unexpectedly accepted all of Pakistan's conditions. This surprised Pakistan because of Beijing's prior resistance to Pakistan's demand for control over salt mines and grazing areas beyond the Shimshal Pass, which China claimed. Suddenly and without consulting local residents, Beijing accepted Pakistan's claims.[53] Clearly, once Pakistan had met China's basic conditions for a settlement, Beijing moved rapidly to seal the Sino-Pakistani *entente cordiale* and forestall a possible Indo-Pakistani rapprochement.

Conclusion

Although there were specific political factors and general ideological issues that caused friction between China and Pakistan, Beijing was compelled to seek accommodation because of larger strategic considerations that ultimately required it to set aside lesser issues to facilitate closer relations. More than any other factor, this led to the improvement in Sino-Pakistani relations in the early 1960s. The settlement of the boundary dispute removed a major source of tension in the relationship. Under Ayub, Pakistan initially moved closer to the United States and even attempted to engage India in a joint defence agreement. China, facing growing threats from the Soviet Union, conflict with India, and a growing threat from the United States, adopted a policy of reconciliation with Pakistan despite differing ideological views and the latter's political affiliations.

Pakistan is strategically important to China for several reasons. Pakistan could give China access to the Indian Ocean, and is one of the "back doors" into China. Construction of the 1,300-kilometre Karakoram Highway connecting Xinjiang with Pakistan over the 4,800-metre Khunjerab Pass began a few years after the boundary settlement. Moreover, Pakistan borders China on the western approaches to the Aksai Chin region, and the boundary settlement helped secure the southwestern border near the strategic Xinjiang-Tibet Highway. China was concerned about US military bases and apprehensive about encirclement by the Soviet Union or Soviet-dominated states in the region.[54] A closer strategic relationship with Pakistan would be tactically beneficial in case of a second border war with India. East Pakistan (until 1971) could have played an important logistical role along the narrow choke point (chicken's neck) connecting India to the North-East Frontier Agency (Arunachal Pradesh after 1986).

China's relationship with Pakistan was strategically important for Beijing's foreign policy objectives. To allay any Pakistani fears that it was being used as a pawn in the Sino-Indian dispute, Liu Shaoqi told Ayub that "on China's part, friendship with Pakistan is a long-term policy. It is not a matter of expediency."[55] However, the agreement also benefited China in its boundary dispute with India. Whereas New Delhi had always insisted that there was no question that the location of the boundary that it claimed had been entirely settled historically, the Sino-Pakistani agreement explicitly recognized that the boundary had "never been formally delimited and demarcated in history." This implied Pakistan's support for China's position in its dispute with India. The agreement also frustrated the attempts of both the Soviet Union and the United States to encourage rapprochement between Pakistan and India in order to bolster the subcontinent as a counterweight to China, or to strengthen the containment of China along its southern flank.

Sino-Pakistani relations flourished in all areas and China's leaders became the "most welcome" visitors in Pakistan. China adapted its position on Kashmir to provide Pakistan with unequivocal support for the next two decades. When Zhou Enlai visited Pakistan in February 1964, the joint communiqué stated that the Kashmir dispute should be "resolved in accordance with the wishes of the people of Kashmir," a clear reference to Pakistan's call for self-determination, a position rejected by India.[56] Pakistan opposed Soviet attempts to establish an Asian security zone aimed at containing China, and refused to support the US military escalation in Vietnam.[57] Although Pakistan maintained its commitments to SEATO, it argued that there was no conflict of interest between closer ties with China and its treaty obligations.[58] China benefited from improved relations with Pakistan, as increased friction between the United States and Pakistan reduced US military and economic assistance to Islamabad, an important strategic gain for China.

Other areas of Sino-Pakistani relations strengthened. A 1963 agreement initiated air service between the two countries. This was China's first air link with a non-communist country and it proved to be an important conduit between China and Western countries. Important road links through the

Karakoram Mountains were also eventually reopened. In 1964, China extended a $60 million interest-free loan to Pakistan to finance imports from China. A most-favoured nation agreement caused Pakistan's exports to China to double in the next six years, while China's exports to Pakistan increased eight times in the same period. China eventually became Pakistan's biggest cotton customer, and Pakistan turned to China for help in financing $1.2 billion in development anticipated during the five-year plan for 1965-70.

Rapprochement with Pakistan was an important part of China's attempt to improve its deteriorating strategic environment. The boundary settlement played an important role in making closer relations possible. China was seeking better relations with all of its neighbours for larger strategic reasons, not just seeking short-term allies or negotiating leverage against India. Very concerned about the threat from the Soviet Union and the United States, China was keenly aware of Pakistan's geopolitical significance in the global strategic picture.[59] This is a more compelling strategic explanation of Beijing's motives in seeking a boundary settlement with Pakistan.

The Sino-Pakistan *entente cordiale* has proven to be very strong over the decades since it first took root in the mid-1960s. Even as Sino-Indian relations began to improve in the 1980s and the balance of power shifted significantly after the Cold War, China's policy toward Pakistan remained very supportive, perhaps the only significant change being China's adoption of a policy of neutrality regarding Kashmir. In 1980, to boost Sino-Indian relations, China shifted its position on the Kashmir dispute, which it began characterizing as "bilateral," dropping its previous support for Kashmir's right to self-determination. During the 1990 Kashmir crisis, Beijing remained neutral, no doubt influenced by Sino-Indian rapprochement.

Any future change in the status of the Sino-Pakistan boundary depends on the settlement of the Sino-Indian boundary dispute and the dispute over Kashmir. Although China is eager to conclude a boundary settlement with India by legitimizing the status quo, the future of Kashmir will be determined by Islamabad and New Delhi, and Beijing has carefully avoided becoming entangled in this dispute.

6 The Sino-Afghan Boundary Settlement

The boundary agreement with Afghanistan was the last in a series of settlements that China concluded with its South Asian neighbours in the early 1960s. The present configuration of the border is the legacy of the "Great Game" played by two expanding empires, Russia and Britain, at the end of the nineteenth century. The Wakhan (Vakhan) Valley, which forms the Afghan panhandle and creates a narrow buffer between Eurasia and Pakistan, is an extremely narrow corridor connecting China to Afghanistan through the Wakhjir Pass, which is closed by snow except during the summer months. This case is significant because one question in the Sino-Soviet and, after 1991, the Sino-Tajik boundary dispute involves the "Pamir Knot" – formed by the South and Central Asian mountain ranges, the Karakoram, the Hindu Kush, and the Pamir – at the trijunction of Tajikistan, Afghanistan, and China (see Map 8).

Historical Background

As early as 139 BC, the Han Dynasty sought a military alliance with Afghan tribes against the Xiongnu, who at the time presented the greatest threat to China. Afghanistan later became an important centre for Buddhism, to which Chinese were drawn, and Islam came to China via Afghanistan. At the time, a major branch of the Silk Road passed through Afghanistan and was a primary conduit for trade and communication between China and the West. During the Tang Dynasty, the emperor dispatched troops from Kashgar through the Wakhan Valley to set up a military garrison, and during the Mongol Yuan Dynasty Afghanistan was sacked and occupied. The Ming court maintained trade and tributary relations that continued during the Qing Dynasty, and regional tribal leaders sent many missions to China.

In 1759, the Emperor Qianlong sent a military expedition to the Pamirs and erected a marker recording the event. The Qing court claimed suzerainty but did not directly control the region. Between 1878 and 1889, as the Russian empire expanded into Central Asia, the Qing court established border posts and garrisoned troops in the Pamirs. In 1884, China signed the Sino-Russian Kashgar Boundary Treaty, which established a boundary with Russia west of the Pamir plateau but did not delimit the border. After Russian troops occupied the area in the early 1890s, the Qing court sought in vain to negotiate a boundary treaty, and in 1894 China sent Russia a note stating that it retained its claim to the region despite the fact that it did not maintain a garrison.[1]

The unique feature of the Sino-Afghan boundary is the eastern salient of Afghanistan, the Wakhan Valley, which forms the conduit connecting the two countries. This valley was historically a rugged section of the Silk Road through which Marco Polo passed in 1271 on his way to the court of Kublai Khan. As Britain became concerned about the threat of Russian expansion toward India in the late 1800s, it encouraged China to assert greater control in the Pamirs, but China, exhausted by the Taiping Rebellion and in decline, was defeated by both Afghan and Russian forces and its ability to control the region slipped away. In 1891, Britain persuaded the ruler of Afghanistan to take control of the Wakhan region, and Britain sought to engage both Russia and China in negotiations to establish a boundary. The Great Game between Russia and Great Britain in Central Asia ended in 1895 when the two empires negotiated a treaty that established the Oxus (Amu Darya) River as Afghanistan's northern boundary and extended the boundary eastward along the Wakhan Valley. Although invited to join the negotiations, the Qing Dynasty demurred, having just been defeated by Japan. Afghan leaders did not participate in the negotiations either, nor did they seek control over the Wakhan Valley. Russia and Britain agreed on a boundary but, because of the rugged terrain, its description was not precise. The treaty stipulated that this would "enable the two Governments to come to an agreement with the Chinese Government as to the limits of Chinese territory in the vicinity of the line," but "somewhere in that wild unknown country it would meet the western limits of the Chinese Empire."[2] Subsequent governments of China have maintained that this was a secret treaty, and Chinese maps continued to show the boundary in the Pamirs as undetermined.[3] Fraser-Tytler concludes that "it seems in fact certain had the Chinese taken part in the Commission, they would have asserted a claim to possession of the Taghdumbash Pamir, from Bayik [the Manchu outpost] for 40 miles westward up to the watershed on the Wakhjir Pass ... and I do not suppose anyone would have contested their claim, however shadowy their authority might be."[4] After 1950, Beijing effectively asserted control over the Taghdumbash

Map 8 Afghanistan

Pamir and, according to Prescott, "to anyone examining the physical and political geography of this area there appears to be a measure of geographical inevitability about this line" that was accepted by both China and Afghanistan in 1963 (see Map 8).[5]

Afghanistan became an independent kingdom after the First World War. Although it recognized the People's Republic of China in early 1950, China did not reciprocate, mainly because of Afghanistan's relations with the United States. China was critical of Afghanistan for accepting US military assistance when, to offset Soviet influence, the United States assumed Britain's role in Afghanistan after the Second World War.

China showed increased interest in Afghanistan beginning in the mid-1950s. Diplomatic relations were established in January 1955 and ushered in a period of closer cultural and economic cooperation. The Chinese press reported in some detail the visits of Soviet leaders to Kabul and the Soviet-Afghan non-aggression treaty that was signed in 1955.[6] In the late 1950s, however, China began to fear US-Soviet "collusion" in Afghanistan because of their cooperation on development projects.[7] This led to a renewal of the historical Sino-Russian rivalry in the region.

Sino-Afghan relations grew closer in January 1957, when Premier Zhou Enlai made a five-day visit to Kabul. Zhou stressed China and Afghanistan's common experiences of colonialism, imperialist domination, and struggle for independence. He also referred to the "common border" the two countries shared. In his farewell speech, he stressed the importance of direct contacts to enhance cooperation.[8] China considered closer Sino-Afghan relations strategically important as a hedge against growing threats to China's security from Central Asia.[9]

While developing closer relations with Afghanistan, China was careful to minimize the friction this caused with other countries. It did not support Afghanistan's call for an independent "Pakhtunistan," an issue that caused significant tension between Pakistan and Afghanistan.[10] India and the Soviet Union both supported Afghanistan on this issue. Visiting Kabul in 1960, Foreign Minister Chen Yi only alluded to the dispute and indicated China's unwillingness to become involved. He stated that Afghanistan's "just demands which accord with the Bandung Spirit will gain the sympathy of the Chinese people." He also emphasized that such problems were "rooted in history" and "can be solved by peaceful means." This, no doubt, was also a signal to Afghanistan regarding China's attitude toward boundary disputes with its neighbours.[11]

Closer Relations and the Mutual Non-Aggression Treaty

Reciprocating Zhou's January 1957 visit to Kabul, Afghan Prime Minister Mohammed Daoud Khan travelled to Beijing at the end of the year. However, Afghanistan continued to pursue a non-aligned policy on regional issues, abstaining when the Tibet issue came to a vote at the United Nations in 1959. Despite this lack of support on Tibet and Afghanistan's even-handed policy toward Sino-Indian differences, relations slowly improved. Real progress in developing closer relations began in 1959 when Afghanistan's foreign minister visited China and discussed issues of "major significance."[12] This probably included mutual security concerns such as the March 1959 Pakistan-United States mutual security agreement and Pakistan's proposed joint defence agreement with India. Friction between Afghanistan and Pakistan over "Pakhtunistan" was also building and eventually resulted in the closure of the border between the two countries in 1961.

Sino-Afghan discussions of mutual security concerns culminated in the signing of a non-aggression treaty in Kabul on 26 August 1960. A *Renmin ribao* editorial characterized the treaty as the opening of a new silk road, and in his farewell speech, Foreign Minister Chen Yi stated that the treaty symbolized the "crystallization" of Sino-Afghan friendship. He also alluded to the growing Sino-Indian conflict and thanked Afghanistan for supporting China's struggle in defence of its sovereignty and territorial integrity, even as he praised Afghan neutrality and emphasized the need for a peaceful international environment.[13] Despite this improvement in relations, Afghanistan went to great lengths to remain neutral during the Sino-Indian border war in 1962. The *Kabul Times* did not publish any reports of the outbreak of hostilities until a week later, and even then all news was based on Beijing and New Delhi dispatches, with no editorial comment except to welcome the ceasefire in November 1962.

Clearly, the impetus for the Sino-Afghan non-aggression treaty was the confluence of growing security concerns. The treaty was China's response to the growing Soviet and American influence in Afghanistan, coupled with concern about the rupture in Sino-Soviet relations. China also felt threatened by US-Pakistani military ties, which a *Renmin ribao* editorial characterized as "directed not only against the socialist countries but are, in the first place, a threat to such nationally independent countries as ... Afghanistan."[14]

The conclusion of the non-aggression treaty paved the way for closer economic relations and a boundary treaty. It is important to point out that unlike China's non-aggression treaty with Burma, the Sino-Afghan non-aggression treaty *preceded* the boundary treaty. The boundary issue was discussed in 1959 along with the non-aggression treaty, but it was not a big impediment to closer bilateral cooperation, as was the case with other countries.[15] As a *Renmin ribao* editorial put it, no "conflict of basic interests" existed and "certain problems left over by history ... can be solved entirely by means of peaceful consultations."[16]

Boundary Negotiations and Settlement

Eighteen months after the conclusion of the non-aggression treaty, Beijing and Kabul announced negotiations on a boundary treaty on the same day, 2 March 1963, that the Sino-Pakistan boundary protocol was signed in Beijing. The announcement said that although the "boundary was a boundary of peace and friendship," to ensure continued peace and friendship the two countries would "conduct negotiations for the purpose of formally de-limiting the boundary existing between the two countries and signing a boundary treaty."[17]

Both Afghanistan and China recognized the existing boundary with only a few differences. Beijing's position had evolved from one that included the Wakhan Valley as part of China to an acceptance of the boundary negotiated between Britain and Russia in 1895. Early maps produced by the People's Republic of China were reproductions of pre-1949 maps and included most of the Pamir plateau within Xinjiang Province. At the end of 1953, these maps were amended to show the Wakhan corridor as part of Afghanistan.[18] As early as 1957, Beijing recognized the least expansive border with Afghanistan, stating that it was only about forty-five miles long; Afghan sources at the time maintained that it was seventy-five miles long.[19]

There were no significant hurdles when negotiations began in Kabul on 17 June 1963. China had already accepted the boundary established in 1895 by the Russians and the British and did not push for the more expansive boundary claimed on earlier maps.[20] Some delay in reaching complete agreement may have been due to a related issue, however. China wanted to refer to Kashmir as part of Pakistan, a position that Afghanistan rejected.[21] However, after Premier Zhou Enlai discussed the issue with King Mohammed Zahir Shah, a boundary agreement was concluded on 1 August and the final treaty was signed in Beijing on 22 November 1963.[22] The watershed principle was applied to delimit the boundary, which corresponded to the 1895 Russo-British boundary.[23] In an official diplomatic history of the People's Republic of China, Chinese authors take a philosophical and magnanimous view of China's "concessions" to Afghanistan: "The Chinese Government decided to give due regard to Afghanistan by delimiting the boundary on the basis of the state of actual jurisdiction by each side, while declaring that this would in no way affect the Sino-Soviet boundary questions."[24]

The Sino-Afghan boundary corresponded to the Pamir boundary claimed by the Soviet Union (and after 1991 by Tajikistan).[25] While Beijing did not vigorously assert its claims in the Pamir region when negotiating with Kabul, the China-Afghanistan boundary treaty did make it clear "that this would in no way affect the Sino-Soviet Boundary question." Nevertheless, the Sino-Afghan settlement was de facto recognition by Beijing of the border claimed by the Soviet Union at the time and later by Tajikistan, and indicated Beijing's willingness to compromise to reach a settlement.

Conclusion

The China-Afghanistan boundary treaty illustrates the influence of both the Soviet Union and India on China's behaviour: it was negotiated after the Sino-Indian border war the previous year and before open acknowledgment of China's border dispute with the Soviet Union. Beijing wanted a boundary settlement for two reasons: to enhance its prestige among non-aligned neighbours, and to bolster Afghan neutrality in Sino-Soviet-Indian relations. China capitalized on the propaganda value of the Afghanistan settlement just as it had with previous settlements, asserting that agreements were possible if the "countries involved were willing to discuss the matter in a friendly and reasonable manner."[26] This was no doubt directed toward India, but the fact that China also had the Soviet Union in mind was made clear by the publication, within a week of the announcement of the Sino-Afghan negotiations, of a *Renmin ribao* article on China's boundary dispute with Russia, the first public acknowledgment of such a territorial dispute.[27]

As the Sino-Soviet dispute grew increasingly bitter, one of China's objectives was to reduce Soviet influence among China's other neighbouring states. In the mid-1950s, the Soviet Union began asserting greater influence in Kabul, which led to competition for Kabul's favour. Of course, China could not match the Soviet Union's economic or military assistance. In 1955, when relations between Afghanistan and Pakistan were poor and Sino-Pakistani relations were entering a period of difficulty after the rise of General Muhammad Ayub Khan, China responded by establishing diplomatic relations with Kabul and initiating economic and cultural exchanges. When Afghan-Pakistani relations reached a crisis, the Soviet Union conducted a massive airlift to save the Afghan economy, which was severely affected by the closure of the border with Pakistan.[28] Obviously, China could not compete for Kabul's favour on such a massive scale, but it bolstered relations with Kabul by concluding the Sino-Afghan non-aggression treaty.

Because of the open break in Sino-Soviet relations and the border war with India, a boundary agreement was strategically significant. Both the non-aggression treaty and the boundary agreement were attempts by China to preserve Afghanistan's non-alignment in the face of historical and increasing Soviet and Indian influence. China feared that Afghanistan might become a hostile neighbour with Soviet and Indian support. Thus, the boundary treaty was its way of discouraging closer Soviet-Indian-Afghan relations and securing one corner of its southwestern frontier.

China had to manage its rapprochement with Afghanistan adroitly. The boundary settlement with Pakistan had worsened relations with India and could have led to the same result with Afghanistan because of the "Pakhtunistan" issue. The Soviet Union supported both Afghanistan and India in their territorial disputes with Pakistan, whereas China remained neutral. The Sino-Pakistani boundary treaty was quickly followed by a settlement of the China-Afghanistan boundary, and China did not press for the boundary it had claimed historically.

China achieved its limited objectives in Afghanistan. King Zahir Shah was committed to maintaining Afghanistan's traditional neutrality and non-aligned foreign policy, and in 1963 he dismissed Prime Minister Daoud, who was responsible for closer relations with the Soviet Union and India beginning in the mid-1950s. This resulted in more amicable relations with Pakistan and further development in relations with China. Zahir Shah visited China in 1964, and during this visit the final boundary protocol was signed and economic and cultural agreements were reached. An air link agreement had been negotiated earlier.[29] Various speeches reiterated the significance of the non-aggression treaty and boundary settlement. Liu Shaoqi made Beijing's objective in Afghanistan clear when he praised that country's foreign policy:

> The Kingdom of Afghanistan has consistently pursued a nonalignment policy of peace and neutrality, stood for peaceful coexistence between countries with different social systems, persisted in maintaining friendship with the socialist countries and actively upheld the Bandung spirit ... The Afghan Government's independent foreign policy not only is in the interests of the Afghan people but also is conducive to the lofty cause of ... world peace.[30]

For China, the boundary treaty with Afghanistan signed shortly after the Sino-Indian border war was at least a reminder to India that, with the exception of India and Bhutan, China had now settled all its boundary disputes with its South Asian neighbours. India was sensitive to the implications of this; in fact, after the March 1963 announcement that China and Afghanistan would negotiate a boundary treaty, Nehru travelled to Kabul to convince Afghan leaders of India's desire for a negotiated settlement with China.[31] More significant for China was the fact that Kabul did not respond to the Soviet call for a collective security arrangement in South Asia, clearly demonstrating that Beijing had achieved one of its major strategic objectives in the region.

PART 3
The Sino-Soviet/Russian Dimension

7 Sino-Soviet/Russian Relations and the Boundary Settlement

The Sino-Soviet/Russian boundary dispute is complicated because it is only one aspect of the larger conflict that led to the Sino-Soviet split in 1960 that soured relations for nearly three decades. Historically, China and Russia had a tenuous relationship that was made more difficult by their long and poorly demarcated boundary. While territorial issues were a major issue in the Sino-Soviet dispute, the larger strategic context defined the relationship and the boundary issue was exacerbated by the broader political and ideological context within which it was embedded.[1]

Historical Background

Long before the Chinese Communists came to power, the seeds of the boundary dispute were germinating. The expansion of Czarist Russia into regions claimed by the Manchu rulers in Beijing eventually led to confrontation along the Far Eastern frontier. The Treaty of Nerchinsk, concluded in August 1689, delimited a portion of the Far Eastern Sino-Russian boundary in order to avoid further conflict. The 1727 Treaty of Khiakhta (Burinsk) delimited the middle sector (roughly the current Mongolia-Russia boundary). During the continued decline of the Qing (Manchu) Dynasty following China's defeat in the First Opium War of 1839-42, Russia continued to advance into the Far East. The Czar's representatives reopened the Far Eastern boundary issue while the Qing court was facing additional challenges from other Western powers. The 1858 Treaty of Aigun redrew the boundary along the Amur and Ussuri Rivers, but it left territory east of the rivers in "joint possession" pending future negotiations. Two years later, while allegedly mediating an end to the occupation of Beijing by Great Britain and France during the Second Opium War, Russia prevailed on China to negotiate the 1860 Treaty of Beijing. This treaty granted the territory between the Amur and Ussuri Rivers and the Sea of Japan to Russia. During this period of domestic unrest in China, Russia also advanced into the Ili region of Xinjiang.

Map 9 Russia

In 1864, the Chuguchak Protocol delimited the Central Asia–Xinjiang boundary.[2] China eventually quelled the rebellions in the region and re-asserted control over Xinjiang, but when it demanded that Russia evacuate the Ili Valley, Russia refused unless an acceptable settlement was reached regarding trade and other issues. The Treaty of St. Petersburg (Treaty of Ili) was concluded in 1881. Russia received territorial "compensation" for returning the Ili region, and received trade and other rights in Xinjiang.

Following the 1881 treaty, many boundary commissions worked to delimit the Sino-Russian boundary in Central Asia. This was completed except for one sector in the Pamir Mountains that was delineated in 1884 by the

Protocol on the Sino-Russian Boundary in the Kashgar Region but never demarcated. Russian troops occupied the area in the early 1890s, and in 1894 the Qing court sought in vain to negotiate a boundary treaty. China then sent Russia a note stating that it retained its claim to the region despite not maintaining a garrison.[3] The boundary in the Pamir region was further complicated by the Anglo-Russian factor. Eventually Great Britain and Russia negotiated a settlement that established Afghanistan's boundaries, but China was not a party to the agreement.

The Chinese also accuse the Russians of encroaching further into Chinese territory during the final weeks of the Qing Dynasty. Just days before the fall of the Qing court, China was forced to sign the Qiqihar Treaty of 1911, which ceded to Moscow several hundred square miles near the eastern trijunction of Russia, Mongolia, and China.

Following the Bolshevik Revolution, the new Soviet government issued the Karakhan Manifestos of 1919 and 1920, renouncing "all the treaties concluded by the former Government of Russia and China ... [and] all the annexations of Chinese territory."[4] During negotiations in 1924 to implement the declarations, the Soviet Union and the Republic of China agreed that while a new boundary treaty was being negotiated, the earlier treaties would be observed but considered "invalid."[5] A new boundary treaty was not a high priority during subsequent negotiations; the boundary question was overshadowed by the issues of Mongolia and the Chinese Eastern Railway, and a new treaty was never concluded. Initially, the new government of the People's Republic of China (PRC) considered the 1689 treaty an "equal treaty." However, although the PRC considered all subsequent treaties unequal, the Soviets changed their position to argue that the 1689 treaty was unequal whereas subsequent treaties were equal.[6]

The Boundary Dispute

Before the breakup of the Soviet Union, the Sino-Soviet boundary extended more than 4,000 miles from Afghanistan in Central Eurasia to the Sea of Japan in Northeast Asia. Bisected by the Mongolian People's Republic (MPR), the boundary can be divided into the Eurasian sector and the Northeast Asian sector. The boundary dispute involved two major areas. Ownership of hundreds of islands in the Amur and Ussuri Rivers was contested because of disagreement over the location of the riparian boundary. Initially, Moscow claimed the Chinese bank of the rivers as the international boundary, but Beijing maintained that, according to international practice, the thalweg, or main channel, was the boundary. The Soviets eventually accepted China's position on the riverine boundary and settlement of the Northeast Asian sector was concluded in 1991 with the exception of a few islands. Ownership of Heixiazi and Yinlong (Bolshoi Ussuriysky and Tarabarov) Islands (approximately 375 square kilometres), located at the confluence of the Amur and Ussuri Rivers, and Abagaitu (Bolshoi) Island in the Argun River was eventually resolved and a supplementary boundary treaty was signed in November 2004 (see Map 9).

The second area of dispute was in Central Eurasia and the Pamir Mountains, an area never delimited before the breakup of the Soviet Union (see Map 16 in Chapter 11). After 1991, Tajikistan, Kyrgyzstan, and Kazakhstan, as newly independent states depending on the technical assistance of Moscow, conducted joint boundary negotiations with Beijing. Boundary agreements were concluded with Kazakhstan and Kyrgyzstan without significant difficulty. In the case of Tajikistan, however, progress toward a settlement was slow due to a rather complex boundary and domestic political issues.[7] By 1997, negotiators had only reached an agreement "confirming the undecided boundary" and a final settlement was not reached until 2002.[8]

Problems Left Over by History

The Soviet Union assumed that it was not responsible for the historical controversies in pre-1917 Sino-Russian relations, and that a new page had been turned in its relations with China, based on socialism and class solidarity. China, however, remained haunted by its past colonial domination and claimed that through the various unequal treaties, it had been forced to cede more than 1.5 million square kilometres of territory to Russia. To support its argument that the old treaties were unequal and invalid, Beijing cited both the Karakhan Manifestos that renounced Czarist treaties with China and Moscow's agreement in 1924 to "re-demarcate" the boundary. The Soviets argued that the boundaries had been historically established and that Beijing misinterpreted the earlier Soviet declarations, and accused China of being historically expansionist.

Even before 1949, the Chinese Communists' irredentist views regarding territory along the Sino-Soviet border were clear and concerned the Russians. Moscow made inquiries and on 10 March 1949 Mao stated: "Concerning the establishment of the border signs on the Amur River, we agree with your opinion and ask that you send technicians ... The signs will be on both banks, and we promise to abide by the appropriate rules." This was the first Chinese

Communist Party and Soviet communication on boundary delimitation.[9] Later it became obvious that serious differences over the boundary existed, but it was not until several years after the Sino-Soviet split that this became public. On several occasions, China approached the Soviet Union quietly to seek a resolution of the boundary question, but to no avail. Even after tensions began to hamper their relationship, China continued to quietly seek a negotiated settlement while at the same time adopting rather pragmatic and conciliatory positions in its negotiation of new boundary treaties with other neighbouring states. The boundary dispute was first mentioned publicly by Zhou Enlai in 1961 in response to a question he was asked at a press conference in Kathmandu, where he had gone to exchange documents ratifying the Sino-Nepali boundary treaty. Zhou dismissed the Sino-Soviet boundary dispute as "a very small discrepancy on maps and ... very easy to settle."[10] In 1962, following the outbreak of the Sino-Indian border war and Soviet support of India, China did not raise the Sino-Soviet boundary issue as a polemical cudgel against the Soviet Union. It was not until after the conclusion of the boundary treaty with Afghanistan in 1963, the last of the treaties negotiated in the early 1960s, that Beijing publicly mentioned the "unequal" treaties that the Qing Dynasty had signed with Czarist Russia.[11]

Beijing repeatedly stated, however, that it was willing to accept the boundary established by the unequal treaties, with some minor adjustments:

> Considering the fact that the areas involved have long been inhabited by Soviet working people and proceeding from a desire to maintain friendship between the Chinese and Soviet peoples, the Chinese Government is ready to let the entire alignment of the boundary line between the two countries be determined on the basis of those unequal treaties.[12]

But Beijing insisted that Soviet Russia had occupied additional territory even in violation of the unequal treaties.[13] Speaking before the United Nations General Assembly in 1973, Deng Xiaoping stated that China only sought the return of some "few square kilometers here and there."[14] This included 20,000 square kilometres in the Pamir Mountains, 140 square kilometres along the Russian bank of the Amur River in the Blagoveshchensk area that encompassed sixty-four Chinese villages, and 375 square kilometres near Manzhouli (Mongolia-PRC-Russia trijunction) ceded in 1911 by the Treaty of Qiqihar two weeks before the fall of the Qing Dynasty. Numerous disputed islands in the Amur and Ussuri Rivers (approximately 1,500 square kilometres) were a very sensitive issue. The rivers were delimited as the border at the end of the nineteenth century, but in 1930 Stalin unilaterally asserted that the Chinese bank of the rivers was the international boundary.[15] The sum total of "lost" territory China claimed was approximately 33,000 square kilometres.

Territorial Issues in Sino-Soviet Relations

Mao Zedong raised the territorial issues in early 1950 while he was in Moscow negotiating the Sino-Soviet alliance. During the Mao/Stalin negotiations, the status of Mongolia was also discussed and Mao expressed his desire for the eventual "reunion" of the Mongolian People's Republic with China. It was clear long before this, however, that Mao dreamed of eventually regaining Chinese sovereignty over Outer Mongolia, since he had raised the issue of Mongolia in the 1940s. Mao and Stalin discussed other boundary issues as well, but Mao did not allow the territorial questions to get in the way of a Sino-Soviet treaty.[16] The MPR and the Soviet Union were apprehensive about China's territorial ambitions and Stalin insisted on a declaration that acknowledged the MPR's independence.

In early 1951, the underlying boundary questions did not preclude a Border Rivers Navigation Agreement.[17] Given Chinese dependence on Soviet assistance, however, China acquiesced to Soviet control of the Amur and Ussuri Rivers that required Soviet authorization before Chinese could use the rivers and the hundreds of islands along the border. Although this may have implied that the Chinese accepted the existing boundary, Zhou Enlai raised the boundary issue in October 1954, while Nikita Khrushchev was in Beijing concluding agreements on liquidating Soviet interest in joint stock companies in China. According to Soviet reports, Khrushchev refused to discuss the matter.[18] China raised the Sino-Soviet boundary question a third time in January 1957, when Zhou mentioned the issue to Khrushchev in Moscow. According to Zhou's account of the meeting:

> At the interview with Premier Khrushchev ... I requested that the USSR make proper arrangements for the territorial issues covering ... China. I could not get a satisfactory answer from him then, but the announcement of the issue was kept secret because the Sino-Soviet dispute was not public at that time.[19]

In Moscow in 1960, Liu Shaoqi again attempted to discuss boundary questions, but he was rebuffed.[20]

As ideological and political tensions escalated, the boundary issue moved closer to the surface. When questioned about it, Zhou continued to minimize the dispute, stating that "there is a very small discrepancy on maps and it is easy to settle," but these historically sensitive territorial issues fuelled Sino-Soviet tensions.[21] Although not publicized until after relations had deteriorated further, border incidents began to occur as early as 1959.[22] In early 1962, many people from Xinjiang began to cross the border into the Soviet Union, which increased tensions along the boundary. Beijing and Moscow also traded accusations regarding repatriation when many refused to return to China.[23]

The public tit-for-tat polemics on territorial issues began when, in a speech to the Supreme Soviet in December 1962, Khrushchev obliquely chided China for tolerating colonialism by accepting the status quo in Hong Kong and Macao. He praised India as an example of anti-imperialism in action; the previous year, India had dislodged the Portuguese from their colonial enclave in Goa.[24] Hong Kong and Macao were very sensitive issues for China, and a *Renmin ribao* editorial on 8 March 1963 responded to Khrushchev's remarks by enumerating the unequal treaties that the Soviets had refused to disavow, and asking: "In raising questions of this kind, do you intend to raise all the questions of unequal treaties and have a general settlement?"[25] The Soviets no longer viewed the Czarist Russia-Manchu boundary treaties as unequal and, surprised by the Chinese reaction to Khrushchev's statement, retorted that no boundary dispute existed with China and tried to deflect the issue with a warning:

> The artificial creation, in our time, of any territorial problems, especially between socialist countries, would amount to entering on a very dangerous path. If, today, countries began making territorial claims on one another, using as arguments certain ancient data and the graves of their forefathers, [and] if they start fighting to revise the historically developed frontiers, this will lead to no good ... The Soviet Union has no frontier conflict with any of her neighboring states.[26]

Khrushchev believed that the "theory of historical borders is nonsense," a "dead issue," and he correctly surmised that, if raised, the border issue would result in a "hopeless tangle of historical confusion and political quarrels."[27] By early 1963, as tensions grew, the Chinese and Soviets escalated the public accusations that eventually provoked border incidents.

The Soviets were no doubt concerned that the boundary question was becoming such a salient issue in relations with China. In May 1963, they proposed boundary "consultations." At the talks, which began in February 1964, according to some accounts, Liu Shaoqi and Khrushchev were making progress toward an agreement, but Mao made this impossible for the Soviets when he accused Moscow of defending Czarist "expansionism."[28] In a 10 July 1964 interview with members of the Japan Socialist Party, Mao enumerated examples of such expansionism at the expense of China and stated ominously: "This list is too long and we have not presented our bill for this yet."[29] This statement alarmed and angered the Soviets, who took it as a sincere revanchist claim on 1.5 million square kilometres of Soviet territory.[30] *Pravda* accused China of having gone too far in the "cold war" against the Soviet Union. In talks with members of Japan's Diet, Khrushchev accused China of being historically expansionist, especially in Mongolia, Xinjiang, and Tibet.[31] Beijing retorted that during the Czarist period, China had ceded more territory to Russia than to any other imperialist country. Beijing insisted that it sought only Russian recognition of this historical fact in principle, and not any major readjustment of the current boundary. Moscow rejected this assertion and responded inflexibly. Beijing reacted by characterizing the Soviet leadership as the "new czars." The Soviets began to view the Chinese as reincarnated "Tartars" of the "Middle Kingdom" determined to re-establish their historical empire. Later, Mao claimed that he was "firing empty cannons" and had no intention of reclaiming territory taken by unequal treaties, and Foreign Minister Chen Yi tried to minimize Mao's "cannon shot" by blaming the flare-up on the "very confused" foreign press and characterizing the issue as really "only a struggle by pen." Nevertheless, this outburst derailed negotiations until after the 1969 Zhenbao Island confrontation.[32]

A lull followed this spike in boundary tensions until the late 1960s, when the issue flared up again during the Cultural Revolution. The dramatic increase in tension along the border was preceded by the conclusion of a Soviet-Mongolian security treaty in January 1966 and the stationing of several Soviet divisions in the Mongolian People's Republic. China began to enforce strict rules of navigation along the Amur and Ussuri Rivers, and the Soviet Union responded by enforcing what it maintained was the international boundary – the Chinese bank of the rivers.

In March 1969, a military confrontation at Zhenbao (Damansky) Island in the Ussuri River proved that the boundary dispute could very well ignite a larger conflagration.[33] In the wake of the March clashes, tensions also arose along the border in Xinjiang, and in August 1969 several incidents culminated in military confrontation in the region. Moscow was alarmed and even contemplated a pre-emptive strike against China's nuclear facilities.[34] China became deeply concerned over the deterioration in its relations with the Soviet Union, tensions along the border, and the real possibility of escalation, and sought renewed boundary negotiations.

Early Initiative to Settle the Boundary

In late 1960, before the boundary dispute dissolved into polemics following the Sino-Soviet split, China attempted to initiate a discussion of outstanding boundary issues with Moscow. This initiative on the part of Beijing conforms to the Chinese pattern of behaviour toward its South and Southeast Asian neighbours at the time – an effort motivated by Beijing's larger strategic concern over growing tensions with the Soviet Union, India, and the United States at a time when China was also facing a very difficult domestic economic situation in the wake of the Great Leap Forward calamity.

China approached the Soviets quietly through diplomatic channels, requesting negotiations to settle "pending issues regarding ... boundary delineation."[35] The Soviets argued that the boundary was delimited and "firmly fixed" by treaty and historical fact. They insisted on the legitimacy of the nineteenth-century treaties and contended that reconsidering the boundary line was impossible. Moscow asserted that during the Qing Dynasty, "China's state frontier on the north, for example, was marked ... by the Great Wall of China."[36] Zhou Enlai responded by wondering aloud: "Must China give away all the territory north of the Great Wall to the Soviet revisionists in order to show that we favor relaxation of world tension and are willing to improve Sino-Soviet relations?"[37]

Moscow rejected China's contention that there was a boundary dispute, and obviously wanted to downplay what they considered to be only minor questions regarding territorial issues. Nevertheless, after initially resisting China's attempts to negotiate the boundary, Moscow took measures to defuse the dispute once it became public. Following the 1962-63 public exchanges, the Soviets proposed "consultations" on the boundary question on 17 May 1963. Negotiations began in Beijing on 25 February 1964, but broke down in August after the Mao/Khrushchev exchange via the Japanese. From the beginning, the negotiating atmosphere was highly charged due to the earlier bitter exchanges between Russia and China.[38]

At the outset of negotiations in 1964, Beijing proposed to maintain the status quo and to take measures to avoid conflict pending an overall settlement. It insisted, however, that issues of "principle" be discussed first. China expected Russia to recognize the unequal nature of the nineteenth-century boundary treaties, and was willing to negotiate a new boundary agreement using these earlier treaties as the basis for establishing the boundary:

> The rights and wrongs of history should be assessed by affirming that the treaties relating to the Sino-Soviet boundary signed by the Government of China's Qing Dynasty and Tsarist Russia were unequal treaties ... Nevertheless, ... China is willing to take these treaties as the basis for an overall settlement of the Sino-Soviet boundary question and would not ask for the return of the more than 1.5 million square kilometers of Chinese territory seized by Tsarist Russia by means of the unequal treaties. The territory of one side occupied by the other in violation of these treaties should, in principle, be returned unconditionally to the other side.[39]

From the outset, Moscow was unwilling to negotiate a new boundary treaty, arguing that adequate treaties already existed and that only minor technical adjustments were necessary:

> The Soviet Government has taken the initiative in proposing consultations to clarify the frontier line between the USSR and the People's Republic of China at certain points. In so doing, we are proceeding on the assumption that there are no territorial differences between the USSR and the People's Republic of China; that the Soviet-Chinese frontier was formed historically; and that it can only be a matter of clarifying the frontier at certain points where this is necessary.[40]

Following this early initiative, no further discussions took place until after the March 1969 Zhenbao/Damansky Island incident. Obviously, the positions on issues of principle and conflicting objectives made any resolution very difficult. Still, China made it clear that it wanted to avoid conflict along the border and that there was no reason to go to war over the boundary dispute.[41] In fact, the armed clash on Zhenbao Island, left Moscow "nothing less than stunned over the fact that the Chinese had departed from the long-established practice of resolving border violations short of firefights."[42]

In the wake of this incident, the situation along the boundary remained tense and minor armed conflicts continued throughout the summer. In one such incident, Moscow used regular military forces and easily defeated Chinese border guards. Moscow's willingness to risk escalation signalled its resolve to Beijing. China continued to call for recognition of the unequal nature of the old treaties, Soviet acceptance of the thalweg principle for delimiting river boundaries, and an end to provocations and armed threats.[43] Moscow rejected these "preconditions" and accused Beijing of attempting to "substantiate its claim to 1.5 million square kilometers of land that properly belongs to the Soviet Union" by using a "far-fetched pretext of righting the 'injustices' of past centuries."[44]

Boundary Negotiations

Alarmed by the growing number of military confrontations, Moscow took steps to renew negotiations. Zhou unexpectedly agreed to an airport summit with Premier Alexei Kosygin on 11 September 1969, a meeting, however, that later became a point of dispute.[45] Returning from the funeral of North Vietnamese president Ho Chi Minh, Kosygin made an unplanned stop in Beijing and met with Zhou at the airport. China later asserted that Kosygin had not been welcome but had the "gall to insist on coming." Beijing maintained that the two had reached "verbal agreement" on procedural issues. According to China, they agreed: (1) that the issue was a "historical" one; (2) to maintain the status quo pending an overall agreement; (3) to withdraw troops from the contested areas; and (4) to convene negotiations. China claimed, however, that the Soviets later "went back on their word."[46]

The Soviets gave a very different account of the agreement. They asserted that the discussions were about more general bilateral concerns and that there was no agreement on the boundary question. Russian scholars now admit that Kosygin's last-minute detour to Beijing was a mistake and created misconceptions that eventually were one cause of a breakdown in the negotiations.[47] The sudden nature of Kosygin's visit meant that he had received no advance briefing and was not accompanied by technical experts. He was not skilful in such situations and misunderstood Chinese intentions. He mistakenly used the term "disputed territory," and suggested that Russia was willing to discuss the matter. China interpreted this misstatement as an indication that Moscow was prepared to enter regular boundary negotiations. There was also disagreement over various nuances in terminology. China insisted on recognition of "boundary problems" *(bianjie wenti)*, but the Soviet Union insisted on recognizing only "questions on the border" *(bianjieshang de wenti)*. The Soviets were willing to consider "re-demarcation" (implying simply reconfirming the existing boundary), but translated the term into Chinese as *chongxin huading* (delimit anew), whereas the Chinese translated it as *chongxin dingli* (define anew), giving the nuance of "re-establishing" a boundary (according to the historical boundary agreed to by treaty, despite the unequal nature of these treaties). As a result, the Soviets became increasingly skeptical of China's motives.[48] This ill-fated renewal of boundary negotiations overshadowed talks for the next decade.

Nevertheless, talks were held on 20 October 1969 and continued until June 1978. Conducted at the deputy foreign minister level, each round lasted for several months. They achieved no breakthroughs, however, and a short round held in 1979 also ended in deadlock. China tabled a five-point proposal at the outset of the negotiations.[49] The proposal called for the discussion of issues of principle first: the old treaties must be recognized as "unequal" and "imposed" on China, but used as the basis for delimiting the present boundary, not the return of territory "annexed" by Czarist Russia. However, territory occupied in violation of these treaties must be returned and any "necessary adjustments" should be made through consultation, followed by the conclusion of a new "equal" treaty and the demarcation of the boundary. The final point called for a disengagement of troops from the border area and maintenance of the status quo pending negotiation of a new treaty.

Beijing argued that if Moscow would first consider issues of principle such as the recognition of unequal treaties, and even the violation of these treaties in some cases, China was willing to make necessary adjustments along the boundary to make the boundary more manageable and to correspond to natural features. The issues of principle were, in China's view, only preconditions for discussing specific questions. Beijing was concerned about many issues, such as the militarization of the border, but considering the consistent pattern in China's negotiating behaviour in other cases, it is clear that it viewed moving beyond this problem "left over by history" and negotiating a legitimate boundary as a major element in improving Sino-Soviet relations. Beijing made this clear by stating: "It is really quite simple. If the Soviet revisionists genuinely desire an improvement of Sino-Soviet relations and a solution to the border question, then why not just ... negotiate a status quo agreement?"[50]

The Soviets were truly apprehensive of Chinese irredentism, and the Chinese delegation exacerbated this fear by refusing to disavow Mao's July 1964 statement on Czarist expansionism, arguing that since it was not part of any official government statement, it should not be an issue in the negotiations. Moscow feared, however, that this would allow China to press for territorial concessions.[51] Negotiations were deadlocked from the outset because Beijing insisted on first addressing issues of principle whereas the Soviets maintained that an agreement to normalize relations first was necessary, before specific technical questions could be addressed. The impasse was primarily due to very different interpretations of the Zhou/Kosygin meeting: China believed that Moscow was reneging on commitments made by Kosygin to Zhou.[52]

Despite this deadlock, negotiations continued because Beijing wanted to continue the dialogue in hopes of lessening tensions along the boundary:

> The Chinese government has never covered up the fact that there exists irreconcilable differences of principle between China and the Soviet Union and that the struggle of principle between them will continue for a long period of time. But this should not prevent China and the Soviet Union from maintaining normal state relations on the basis of the Five Principles of Peaceful Coexistence.[53]

Although they reached no settlement, China and the Soviet Union achieved some meeting of the minds on at least one substantive issue. The Soviets initially rejected the thalweg principle, contending that "there exists no norms that automatically establishes the border on border rivers as passing through the middle of the river's main stream."[54] In 1970-71, the Soviets suggested their willingness to accept the thalweg principle, in effect acknowledging China's ownership of hundreds of islands in the Amur and Ussuri Rivers, but serious discussion of this substantive compromise was blocked by China's insistence on Soviet recognition of unequal treaties and Soviet objections to including the islands at the confluence of the Amur and Ussuri Rivers.[55] A short round of negotiations held in 1979 ended when the Soviet Union invaded Afghanistan.

Boundary Settlement

Despite continued resistance within the Soviet Foreign Ministry, where some high-ranking officials insisted that "our two countries are geopolitical enemies and this factor will never go away," relations did begin to improve.[56] The Soviets paved the way with speeches by Leonid Brezhnev, one in Tashkent in March 1982 followed by one in Baku in September in which he appealed for improved relations.[57] Boundary negotiations resumed in October 1982, and a major stumbling block was removed in 1983 when China stopped insisting that the Soviet Union acknowledge the unequal character of the nineteenth-century treaties.[58] A compromise agreement began to take shape and several areas where compromise was most likely were identified.[59] Beijing stood firm on the boundary in the Pamir Mountains, but compromise was possible, as indicated by the fact that the Sino-Afghan boundary was delimited to correspond with the boundary claimed by the Soviet Union. Its seemingly inflexible stand on the Pamir boundary could very well have been a bargaining chip that Beijing was willing to give up for a possible Soviet concession in the very complicated task of delimitating the riparian boundary at the confluence of the Amur and Ussuri Rivers near Khabarovsk.

By 1982, leaders in Beijing had decided to seek better relations with Moscow, both as part of China's new independent foreign policy and because of deteriorating relations with the United States over the Taiwan issue following the election of Ronald Reagan. Beijing concluded that its strategic interests were better served by striking a balance in its relations with the two superpowers. In line with this, Deng Xiaoping turned the focus from ideological differences to substantive issues in Sino-Soviet relations. On the eve of the Twelfth Party Congress in September, the Chinese Communist Party decided to "distance China from the US and relax relations with the Soviet Union" *(dui Meiguo lakai juli, dui Sulian songdong guanxi).*[60] In November, Foreign Minister Huang Hua attended Brezhnev's funeral in Moscow and met his counterpart, Andrei Gromyko, the first such high-level meeting in twenty years.

Soviet thinking also was undergoing transformation. Premier Li Peng attended General Secretary Konstantin Chernenko's funeral in March 1985, and Igor Rogachev, a pro-China high-level Russian sinologist who became deputy foreign minister over Asian affairs in early 1987, acted as translator for Li and Mikhail Gorbachev. Although others continued to oppose concessions to China in boundary negotiations, Gorbachev wanted Sino-Soviet relations freed from the albatross of the twenty-five-year-long boundary dispute and took the initiative in these discussions on the sidelines of Chernenko's funeral. This was an important turning point on the road toward an eventual boundary agreement. Resistance came primarily from Foreign Minister Gromyko; Deputy Foreign Minister Mikhail Kapitsa, who oversaw Asian affairs; and Central Committee China policy czar Oleg B. Rakhmanin, who argued that any concession to China would weaken Soviet control of the border and require a change in the Russian interpretation of nineteenth-century treaties. Nevertheless, Gorbachev accepted the thalweg principle as customary international law when redrawing the eastern riverine boundary. His rationale was that the Soviet Union was simply accepting international legal principles in agreeing to delimit the boundary along the thalweg, thereby deflecting the criticism that he was "capitulating" to Chinese demands. This "new thinking" was possible because the emerging Russian leadership moderated their "attitudes toward the Chinese version of the history of Sino-Russian relations and even to the historical ownership of some disputed regions," focusing more on the possibility of "non-confrontational ... consensus on sensitive questions" like the boundary.[61]

Gorbachev's re-examination of Soviet ideology and his personal leadership were crucial in paving the way for rapprochement.[62] A significant breakthrough occurred in Vladivostok in July 1986, when, publicly for the first time, Gorbachev stated that Moscow was willing to delimit the eastern boundary using the main channel of the Amur and Ussuri Rivers. At a press conference on 8 August, the Chinese Foreign Ministry spokesperson spoke of Beijing's recognition that Gorbachev had offered new ideas on improving Sino-Soviet relations and settling the boundary question, and on 13 August 1986, Foreign Minister Wu Xueqian met with Soviet embassy officials in Beijing and signalled China's desire to reopen boundary negotiations.[63]

Gorbachev pushed aside the hard-line Sinophobes and agreed to restart the negotiations.[64] After a nine-year hiatus, negotiations resumed in February 1987. Both sides agreed to use the old treaties as the basis for determining the entire border and, according to internationally accepted principles of international law, re-delimit the boundary beginning with the eastern sector. During a session that ran from 20 to 31 October 1988, they reached general agreement on the alignment of the boundary in the eastern sector; subsequently, a group was organized to work on demarcation issues. From 20 February to 9 March 1989, negotiations on the western sector made significant progress. According to the joint communiqué issued during Gorbachev's May 1989 trip to Beijing, the two countries agreed to settle the dispute "on the basis of the treaties concerning the present Sino-Soviet boundary," which implied Chinese acceptance of the boundary established by the historical treaties, but with the obvious adjustments based on contemporary international practices. Negotiations proceeded rapidly, and in June 1990 both sides decided to sign a treaty covering areas where agreement had been reached and to begin the work of surveying and demarcating the boundary. Work on a draft treaty covering the eastern sector was completed in March 1991, and the treaty was signed when Jiang Zemin travelled to Moscow in May.[65] During Jiang's September 1994 trip to Moscow, a treaty delimiting the short fifty-three-kilometre boundary to the west of Mongolia was concluded. The following month, China, Mongolia, and Russia jointly drafted a protocol and map of the eastern and western boundary junctures.[66]

After achieving an agreement on principles, the boundary negotiations became more of a technical question of demarcation for the Chinese, and the political atmosphere did not dictate progress. During this final stage, Chinese negotiators were straightforward and flexible.[67] Nevertheless, a pivotal issue arose to complicate a final agreement. The dispute centred on Heixiazi and Yinlong (Bolshoi Ussuriyskyy and Tarabarov) Islands, located in the confluence of the Amur and Ussuri Rivers. An island in the Argun River, Abagaitu (Bolshoi) Island, was also disputed. Although the thalweg principle was the basis for demarcating the riparian boundary, Beijing and Moscow disagreed over which channel around the islands was the main channel of the Amur River. This outstanding issue was further complicated by questions of historical occupation. Beijing contended that according to the 1858 Treaty of Aigun and the subsequent 1860 Treaty of Beijing, Moscow had recognized that the islands at the Ussuri-Amur confluence were Chinese territory, and that in 1927 Soviet officials also acknowledged this boundary. As Japan expanded into Manchuria in the early 1930s, however, the Soviets took control of the islands for security reasons.[68] Foreign Minister Eduard Shevardnadze favoured recognition of China's historical claims in order to settle the boundary. The minister of defense and Prime Minister Nikolay Ryzhkov strongly opposed this concession, arguing that it was strategically unwise because of the islands' proximity to Khabarovsk and because it would set a dangerous precedent in the dispute with Japan over the Kuril Islands. In Beijing in May 1989, Gorbachev explained to Deng Xiaoping that domestic political constraints made it impossible for him to accept China's claim to these islands. Deng appreciated the situation and suggested postponing a final settlement of this particular issue so that all other issues could be settled.[69]

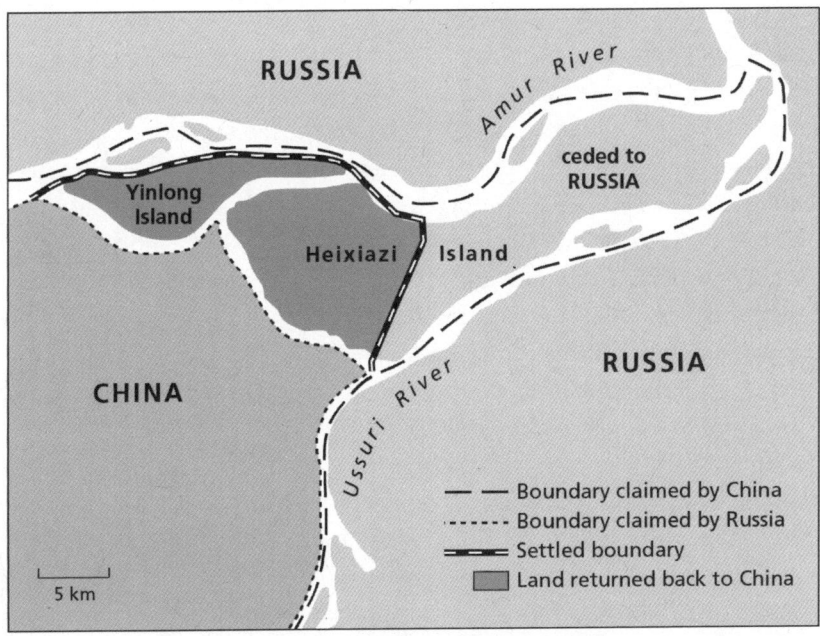

Map 10 Heixiazi and Yinlong Islands

China had stood firm on the river boundary for thirty years. This stance proved to be successful and in 1991, before the breakup of the Soviet Union, Moscow and Beijing reached an agreement that settled the Amur and Ussuri River boundary, an agreement made possible by Deng's willingness to shelve the issue of the few remaining islands during the final stages of negotiations (see Map 10). Besides islands in the Amur and Ussuri Rivers that were transferred to Chinese sovereignty, Beijing also pushed for the transfer of fifteen square kilometres of territory near the mouth of the Tumen River, at the China-Korea-Russia trijunction, to provide China with access to the Sea of Japan (see Map 11). China claimed that this territory had been taken by Russia through the unequal 1860 Treaty of Beijing.[70] Despite the fact that Chinese territory no longer extended to the Sea of Japan, China's right to navigate the Tumen River to the Sea of Japan was recognized by Russia in an 1886 treaty settling this section of the eastern boundary. However, this right was rescinded in 1938 after the occupation of northern China by Japan, and was never restored by the Soviet Union after the Second World War. China was only asserting a historically recognized right, but was willing to compromise to reach the boundary agreement.[71]

According to some Chinese sources, Jiang Zemin actually offered to recognize Russian sovereignty over Heixiazi Island in exchange for a Russian concession of this territory along the Tumen River, but Russia rejected the proposal.[72] Beijing's failure to recover this territorially small but strategically important tract of "lost territory" at the mouth of the Tumen River infuriated Chinese nationalists, who accused the government of capitulating and trading acceptance of the humiliating and unequal nineteenth-century treaties for minor economic and strategic benefits. The newly established Supreme Soviet of the Russian Federation ratified the treaty on 3 February 1992, and the Standing Committee of the National People's Congress ratified it on 25 February.[73] The protocol on the trijunction of the boundary between Russia, China, and North Korea was signed in 2002.[74]

Opposition to the treaty was strong among conservative nationalists. Fuelling suspicions about Russian concessions to China was the fact that local officials in the Russian Far East and China experts had not been consulted about the proposed territorial concessions and the details of the treaty had not been publicized. Evgenii Nazdratenko, the governor of Primoria, publicly stated that he would refuse to comply with the border agreement and would block the transfer of any territory to Chinese control.[75] At a news conference in May 1994, the governor of Khabarovsk, Viktor Ishaev, called the boundary treaty "unfair and an infringement of Russian interests"; as late as October 1999, he was asserting that the few remaining islands that were yet to be settled "always will be Russian land." He complained that according to the boundary treaty, the territory transferred to China could amount to as much as ten thousand square kilometres of fertile pastureland.[76] Vladimir Podoprigora, chair of the Federation Council International Affairs Committee, argued that regional interests should not have been neglected by Moscow when determining Russia's China policy, and underlined the fact that border-area residents opposed transferring land to China as Moscow had agreed. Russian nationalists called for a review of the treaty even though it had already been ratified.[77]

Actual demarcation of the boundary presented significant challenges. Following the collapse of the Soviet Union in December 1991, Sino-Russian relations entered a brief period of uncertainty. China worried that Moscow would adopt an anti-China policy based on its new democratic paradigm. China was also ranked below the West and Japan in importance in Russia's foreign policy. Moreover, after the exacerbation of Sino-Russian relations due to a sudden and alarming influx of Chinese traders in the Russian Far

East, local governments resisted any territorial concessions during the process of demarcation. However, an uptick in tension between Russia and the West set the stage for a quick return to cooperative Sino-Russian relations. Encouraged by pro-China foreign policy advisers such as Sergei N. Goncharov, President Boris Yeltsin began to adjust Russia's pro-Western foreign policy. To "overcome the legacy of ... confrontation and to dismantle the confrontational structures" required a quick conclusion of the boundary demarcation process to prevent historical suspicions and animosity from bubbling up and turning back the clock on the improved relations with China initiated by Gorbachev before the collapse of the Soviet Union.[78]

In the Russian Far East, local opposition continued as Moscow's territorial concessions became known to local political leaders, who complained that improved relations with China were being pursued at the expense of local interests. This complicated the demarcation process. Major General Valery Rozov, leader of the Russian demarcation commission, resigned in protest over what he alleged was the transfer of "several strategically important Russian lands to a rival power," arguing that documents could "indisputably prove Russia's right to the lands around the Tumen River, which China is eager to get."[79] Beijing demanded that demarcation proceed according to the 1991 agreements, and Yeltsin urged local authorities to stop dragging their feet. In Beijing in March 1995, Russian Foreign Minister Kozyrev made it clear that Moscow "held the decision-making power" and would fully implement the boundary accord.[80] Nonetheless, to appease local leaders during a stopover in Khabarovsk on his way to the April 1996 Beijing summit, Yeltsin said that "there are instances in which we agree to no compromise ... With regard to this our position remains firm: the border should be where it lies now." He denied that demarcation was an insurmountable problem, and issued a decree to accelerate the process.[81] Possibly in an attempt to mollify local opposition in Russia and pave the way for an eventual compromise, the two sides agreed to initiate parallel negotiations for "joint economic exploitation of the individual border areas incorporated into the other side after the boundary survey."[82] Moreover, perhaps to appease the Chinese over the delays in demarcation, Yeltsin proposed, on the eve of summit, the establishment of a Sino-Russian "strategic partnership."[83] Nevertheless, during demarcation China was compelled to make some minor concessions because it dreaded an acrimonious boundary dispute if the 1991 settlement was not finalized. Russia's regional politics would create new hurdles if renegotiation became necessary.[84]

Despite the complications of domestic politics in Russia, demarcation of the eastern sector was completed in November 1997 and demarcation of the short western sector in November 1998. The entire 4,300-kilometre Sino-Russian boundary was finally demarcated (except for the confluence of the Amur and Ussuri Rivers), and the protocols were exchanged in April 1999.[85] Following final demarcation, of the 2,444 disputed islands, 1,281 were determined to be Chinese and 1,163 Russian, but a five-year joint-use agreement was appended that allowed Russians to continue using some islands transferred to China; approximately 14 square kilometres of territory in Primorskii Krai was transferred to China, but Beijing agreed to Russian retention of approximately 1.5 square kilometres of land in the Khasanski district along the Tumen River that was a Russian military cemetery dating from Russo-Japanese conflict in 1938 (but had been Chinese territory ceded to Russia by the 1860 Treaty of Beijing); 2,084 boundary markers were erected, and the detailed maps and comprehensive documentation weighed over one hundred pounds.[86] An additional agreement dealt with cooperation to resolve the dispute over the few remaining islands.

After the signing of a treaty of friendship and cooperation in 2001, work on the unsettled islands gained momentum. The ownership of these islands – Heixiazi and Yinlong (Bolshoi Ussuriysky and Tarabarov) Islands in the Amur River and Abagaitu (Bolshoi) Island in the Argun River – was finally resolved and a supplementary treaty was signed in November 2004 (see Map 10). This agreement on the Eastern Section of the China-Russia Boundary divided the islands, with China establishing sovereignty over all of Yinlong Island and about half (174 square kilometres) of Heixiazi Island, and gaining control of 337 square kilometres of the disputed territory.[87] A joint statement by Presidents Hu Jintao and Vladimir Putin called the agreement a "balanced and rational plan for the political win-win" that would promote the "development of China-Russia strategic partnership of cooperation." No doubt in a hint to India, the Chinese embassy in New Delhi issued a statement saying that "the experience of the two sides demonstrate [sic] that the correct and effective way in settling complicated and sensitive issues like border issues lies in peaceful dialogue, fairness, equal consultations, mutual understanding and concessions and balance in each other's interests."[88] After ratification by the Russian and Chinese parliaments, the final treaty was exchanged on 2 June 2005, during the Russia-China-India trilateral summit in Vladivostok – a less than subtle jab at the Indians.

Russian Foreign Minister Sergei Lavrov stated that the settlement removed "serious irritants in bilateral relations" and was possible because bilateral relations were on "a level of strategic partnership."[89] The final concession by Russia – ceding sovereignty over islands that border the strategic city of Khabarovsk – eliminated the long drawn out territorial irritant in Sino-Russian relations. According to one Chinese scholar, the Chinese also appreciated the domestic political difficulty of the Russian concession and realized that "resolving minor issues [when implementing the treaty] will test the level of mutual trust, openness, and understanding of mutual benefit."[90] However, Chinese nationalists chastised the government for trading territory for "good neighborly relations," calling the settlement a "meaningless and symbolic" treaty to buy Russian friendship at the expense of Chinese territory.[91] China assumed formal control of the disputed islands in October 2008, when the newly established boundary markers were unveiled.[92]

The present boundary may be more favourable to China than the agreement nearly concluded in 1964, before Mao's outburst, but is not significantly different. The Russians were apprehensive that Deng willingly shelved the issue of the three outstanding islands because he believed that time was on China's side and that Beijing would raise the issue in the future, when China was even stronger and could extract additional territorial concessions from Russia.[93] And despite President Yeltsin's April 1996 assurance to residents of Khabarovsk that the islands would never be surrendered to China, in reality the final settlement required Russia to surrender to Chinese control a large portion of the disputed islands.[94]

Despite the boundary agreements, Russian nationalists still harbour a deep paranoia that in Chinese minds the present boundary agreement is only a provisional settlement, and that once China is a strong world power, it will reassert its "historical claims." According to one veteran Russian sinologist:

Chinese border policy has to this day remained an essential means whereby China puts pressure to bear on neighboring states, Russia included. Existing in mass conscience and sustained by pertinent publications are the ideas of "Russia's historical territorial debt to China." Mao Zedong skillfully played that card in the 1960's and the 1970's. And there are no guarantees that a similar problem will never recur and this presents the most sensitive historical problem which may affect the relations between Russia and China for many years to come.[95]

China has unwittingly fuelled such fears because of its own internalized historical image of Chinese geography, which requires a ritualistic representation of the "history of China's lost territory" at the hands of imperialism. Deng's comments to Gorbachev at the historic May 1989 summit leading to the final boundary settlement exemplify this:

> In the past, the great powers have divided and humiliated China ... The Czarist Empire and the Soviet Union – during a certain time – had taken great advantage [of China's weakness]. Through inequitable treaties, including the understanding at Yalta and the treaties with the Kuomintang, the Russians took from China ... about three million square km [including Mongolia].

In *The Selected Works of Deng Xiaoping*, published in 1993, which recounts this conversation, a footnote is added that glosses the various "unequal treaties" by which "Czarist Russia occupied over 1.5 million square kilometers of Chinese territory."[96] From Russia's perspective, a boundary treaty put an end to these vast territorial claims.[97]

Conclusion

The fundamental change that made the eventual settlement of the Sino-Russian border possible was the shifting strategic context of the bilateral relationship that both Gorbachev and Deng understood so well. Despite the friction caused by the controversies over the final demarcation, as Moscow and Beijing's relations with Washington became strained, a "strategic reassessment" required better relations between China and Russia, and this became a key component of both countries' foreign policy.[98] A "strategic partnership" was in the interests of both countries.[99]

Beijing's shift to an independent foreign policy in 1982 was an important factor in generating momentum toward a boundary settlement. With the collapse of the Soviet Union and the end of the Cold War, it faced a new international system dominated by the lone superpower, the United States. This sudden and fundamental shift in the global balance of power made it imperative for China to develop closer relations with Russia and the newly independent Eurasian states in order to, in the words of one Chinese scholar, "change the disadvantageous geostrategic situation."[100] Beijing's view of the importance of a boundary treaty in facilitating closer relations with Russia was clear when the communiqué issued after the signing of the boundary treaty criticized "hegemonism of whatever form in international politics" and a *Renmin ribao* editorial stated that Moscow and Beijing had "opened up a new prospect for strengthening Sino-Soviet friendship."[101]

The pattern followed by China in its dispute with Russia is strikingly similar to the pattern it followed with other states, except that China took the initiative and raised the issue early with the Soviets, whereas it resisted discussing the issue with other states until its strategic environment changed in 1960. In the Russian case, it was China that was seeking redress; in the other cases, China's neighbours were asking for concessions. As in other cases, China made it clear that it expected acknowledgment of the unequal nature of the nineteenth-century treaties and would not accept them as legitimate, although China agreed that these treaties corresponded to a "historical and customary" boundary and formed a basis for the negotiation of new treaties.[102] The Soviet Union rejected this position, as India continues to do today.

Following the Sino-Soviet split, and particularly after the 1969 border incidents, Beijing was clearly concerned by the direct security threat presented by general tensions, but was still unwilling to drop its demand that a discussion of the historical question of unequal treaties precede any negotiation of technical questions. As Sino-Soviet tensions diminished in the 1980s, however, Deng Xiaoping downplayed ideological issues, the strategic context changed, and negotiations to solve the boundary dispute along the Amur and Ussuri Rivers made significant progress. The second major Sino-Soviet boundary issue involved the Pamir Mountains in Tajikistan. By the late 1980s, Moscow was willing to accept the watershed principle and establish the boundary, but both sides agreed to leave the issue until after the eastern sector had been settled. With the collapse of the Soviet Union, the venue for negotiations over the Pamir boundary changed, and China eventually came to an agreement with the newly independent and nationalistic Tajikistan.

With the new strategic context and imperatives, China no longer insisted on recognition of the "unequal treaties" as a "principled precondition" and negotiations moved directly to the consideration of specific geographic issues and the conclusion of a new boundary treaty with Russia.

Sino-Korean Boundary Questions
Before considering other settlements that fall within the Sino-Soviet/Russian dimension, a brief discussion of the Sino-Korean boundary is appropriate.

Although data are scarce, fragmentary evidence does make some conclusions possible. In fact, in the twelve-volume compendium on boundary affairs and treaties published by China in 2004-5, an introductory "survey of the boundary" is included in each country volume, with the exception of the Korea volume. The only published boundary treaties are the 1998 and 2002 agreements regarding the China-Russia-Korea Trijunction along the Tumen River.[103]

The modern Sino-Korean boundary is complicated by the contemporary esoteric debate over the ancient Korean kingdom of Koguryo (37 BC – 668 AD) that extended into Manchuria, China's northeastern region. Koguryo's ancient capital of Guonei was along the Yalu River but moved to Pyongyang in 427 AD. Koguryo rivalled China as a culturally sophisticated and politically well organized empire on the periphery of China. The attempt of the Sui Dynasty (581-618) to conquer Koguryo so weakened the Sui court that this military misadventure led to its downfall. The Tang Dynasty (618-907) did eventually defeat Koguryo and for a few years dominated Korea before the kingdom of Silla unified the entire Korean peninsula under its rule in 668 AD and eventually drove Chinese troops out of Korea. The successor Korean kingdom of Parhae (Balhae) (698-926) emerged as a powerful entity incorporating the area of Manchuria previously controlled by Koguryo and, though fiercely independent of the Tang Dynasty, did adopt Tang culture and political institutions.

The contemporary debate between Chinese and Koreans is over whether Koguryo and Parhae were independent kingdoms and hence imply an ancient historical claim to northeastern China by Korea, or were vassals of Chinese dynasties, as Chinese historians argue. North Korea asserts that "Koguryo was a sovereign state without doubt, far from ... a tributary of any state power" and "firmly maintained its national independence ... crushing any attempts to trespass on its sovereignty." China's building of the Great Wall "proves that Koguryo ... posed a grave threat to China from the beginning."[104] But even this historical narrative oversimplifies the ethnic history of the region. Until the eighteenth century, Khitan and Jurchen/Manchu nomads inhabited the Yalu-Tumen frontier and were not yet subject to Korean or Chinese conquest.[105]

Such historiographical issues continue to be contentious in Sino-Korean relations and overshadow the debate over historical boundaries. The present Korea-China boundary demarcation remains an issue fraught with strong irredentist discontent in Korea, and many Koreans believe they should

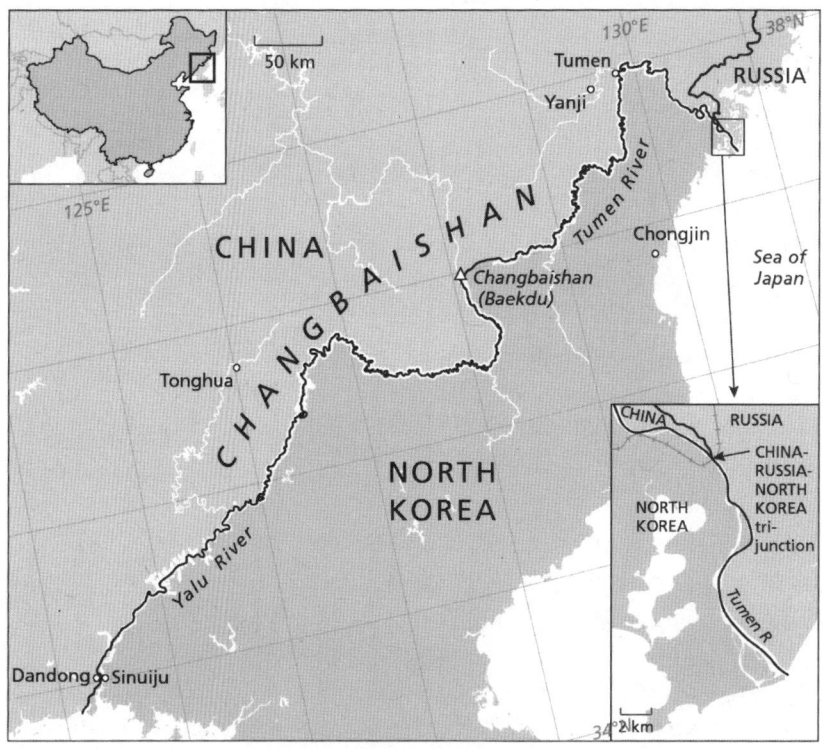

Map 11 Korea

reclaim this "lost former territory" as well as territory on the north bank of the Tumen River that Japan ceded to China as recently as 1909.[106]

Along the 880-mile border dividing China and Korea, the Yalu and Tumen Rivers mark the border for all but a 20-mile segment (see Map 11). Certain islands remained a source of friction, but during the Qing Dynasty, the natural riverine boundary was generally undisputed, although an approximately 600-square-mile triangular area between the headwaters of the Yalu and Tumen Rivers, including Mount Changbai *(Paektu/Baekdu)* and the crater lake Tianchi *(Ch'onji)* continued to be a source of tension between China and Korea. Chinese and Koreans both claimed Mount Changbai and Tianchi, nationalistic symbols for Koreans and a sacred place for the Manchus. Following an expedition to the headwaters of the Yalu and Tumen Rivers in 1712 ordered by Emperor Kangxi, a marker was erected just south of Mount Changbai to demarcate the boundary between China and Korea in that area.[107] According to an account of the expedition by a Korean interpreter, the Manchu envoy stated: "I have come here on the order of the emperor ... You say your country's border is there, but has this been brought before the emperor and decided by him?" The Korean responded: "Our small country has of old taken this to be the border; the children all know it. How could it be brought before the emperor and what need is there for documents as proof?" At the time, Korean officials were worried about Qing expansionism: "The large empty space south of Paektu-san is not filled with people of our country: if they designate this region as being within their border, there are no written documents with which to refute their claim."[108] These 1712 negotiations essentially established the modern Sino-Korean boundary, but some sectors were not clearly demarcated. As Koreans began settling north of the Tumen River, a joint Qing-Korean survey of the region in 1887 demarcated the boundary east of Mount Changbai in the Dong Jiandao *(Kando)* region and pushed the boundary north of the Tumen River. However, China entered into negotiations with Japan, then the colonial power in Korea, in 1909, and Tokyo accepted the Tumen River as the international boundary.[109]

Despite these early boundary settlements in the remote area between the Yalu and Tumen Rivers, this border continued to plague the People's Republic of China and the Democratic People's Republic of Korea. Initially, in the early 1950s, China rebuffed Pyongyang's appeal to discuss the boundary.[110] The Beijing/Pyongyang dispute was rooted in differing interpretations of the historical treaties. Early PRC maps showed Mount Changbai and Tianchi within Chinese territory. In early 1961, China surveyed the area, and in October published a map that placed the boundary about thirty kilometres south of the mountain. In August 1961, Pyongyang published material describing the mountain and lake as Korean territory. Beijing then published a map with a short article in the November issue of *Zhongguo huabao* claiming the area as Chinese territory.[111] In addition to the Mount Changbai dispute, several islands in the Yalu and Tumen Rivers were inhabited by Korean farmers who, China claimed, had displaced Chinese settlers during the Japanese occupation of Korea and Manchuria. Despite these differences, thirty agreements on boundary issues were signed between 1954 and 2002. The earliest published document specifically regarding the boundary was the 8 June 1955 "Minutes from the Meeting Resolving Issues along the Contiguous Boundary," which primarily dealt with cross-border relations and controls, implying that there was some understanding on the location of the border.[112]

In early 1960, as the Sino-Soviet dispute unfolded, Beijing decided, "in light of developing circumstances," to reduce friction in Sino-Korean relations. One issue that was clearly a bone of contention involved overlapping claims to the sacred mountain and lake. While Kim Il-sung was in Beijing to sign a treaty of friendship and cooperation in July 1961 Premier Zhou Enlai took the opportunity to raise the boundary issue and proposed dividing sovereignty over Mount Changbai and Tianchi. North Korea was reluctant to discuss the boundary dispute but responded positively to Zhou's proposal and agreed to begin substantive negotiations.[113]

Although documentation is sparse, a clear pattern is evident. As in earlier boundary disputes, China sought a boundary settlement with North Korea in order to improve bilateral relations in response to an unfavourable shift in the balance of power. Zhou instructed Chinese negotiators "to be sympathetic and accommodating because of the overriding importance of the burgeoning Sino-Soviet dispute." Formal negotiations began in the Chinese border town of Dandong in April 1962, but soon hit a snag. They settled the division of Tianchi without any problem, but disagreement over the land boundary in the Changbaishan region created tension. China proposed that the boundary run through the peak of Mount Changbai (2,744 metres), but Korea responded angrily, accusing China of still dealing with Korea with a "national chauvinistic attitude like the Manchu" *(Qingchao de daguo taidu)*. Zhou recalled the Chinese delegation led by Deputy Foreign Ministry Ji Pengfei and elevated the level of the negotiations, instructing Peng Zhen, who was in Pyongyang at the time, to raise the boundary issue directly with Kim Il-sung, who agreed to continue negotiations according to the original principle of dividing overlapping claims.

Zhou personally presented Beijing's proposal for a comprehensive boundary settlement to a Korean delegation that travelled to Beijing in June 1962. The proposal divided Tianchi (DPRK controls approximately 60 percent) and accepted Korea's claim to the peak of Mount Changbai out of "consideration" *(zhaogu)* for Korean national sentiments. The riverine boundary was complicated by the islands in the Yalu and Tumen Rivers inhabited by Korean and Chinese farmers, but China agreed to recognize these islands as Korean territory "based on the principle of respect for historical reality" *(genju zunzhong lishi xianzhuang yuanze)*. Neither the thalweg principle nor the mid-channel could be used to delimit the rivers due to complications this would create, since many islands were on the Chinese side of the main channel of the river. China proposed a solution of "mutual sovereignty, mutual control, and mutual use."

Shortly after Zhou's personal intervention, Pyongyang accepted China's proposed boundary settlement. In September, Ji Pengfei returned to Pyongyang for a final round of negotiations that concluded on 3 October 1962. On 12 October, Zhou and Kim signed the China-Korea boundary treaty. Following a boundary investigation, demarcation, and mapping, the final protocol was signed in March 1964. The Yalu River and Tumen Rivers have 468 islands; these were allocated not according to the thalweg principle but rather by determining the dominant ethnic group inhabiting each island at the time of the treaty. North Korea received 280 islands and China 187 (one island at the mouth of the Tumen belongs to Russia). Two of the largest islands in the Yalu River, Hwanggumpyong *(Huangjinping Dao)* and Bidan, are actually adjacent to the Chinese bank of the river and the Chinese border town of Dandong. At the time of the 1962 treaty, a narrow flow of the Yalu River divided the Chinese bank from the islands, but sediment has reduced this to a very small flow.[114] This delimitation resulted in the DPRK's control of approximately 90 percent of the Yalu estuary. They agreed not to publicize the treaty, but maps were changed to reflect the new boundary. According to one analysis, Chinese concessions were so significant that officials from the bordering provinces of Jilin and Liaoning protested the settlement.[115]

Initially, North Korea leaned toward China following the Sino-Soviet split in 1960 and supported China in the Sino-Indian boundary war in 1962.[116] Beginning in 1964, however, after the fall of Khrushchev, Pyongyang began to pursue closer relations with Moscow. Sino-Korean relations deteriorated and tension increased along the border. A North Korean diplomat in Moscow suggested that Mao raised the territorial issue anew and demanded that North Korea recognize Beijing's claims, justifying the demand for 250 square kilometres of territory around Mount Changbai as "compensation" for the support given to North Korea during the Korean War.[117] As relations declined further during the Cultural Revolution, Sino-Korean cultural exchanges were almost entirely discontinued and Kim Il-sung lamented China's proclivity for "big-power chauvinism." Several People's Liberation Army divisions were stationed along the Yalu River and border incidents occurred as China continued to assert its territorial claims.[118] According to one account, Zhou travelled to Pyongyang in 1966 and again raised the issue of sovereignty over

Mount Changbai. Armed confrontations continued and North Korea eventually closed the border. Kim even turned to Moscow for support in resolving the issue.[119]

In response to the growing Soviet threat, Beijing made conciliatory moves toward North Korea after 1969. Zhou travelled to Pyongyang in April 1970 to repair relations, the first high-level visit in many years. Beijing dropped its demands and one of the issues discussed during Zhou's visit was a final settlement of the boundary dispute.[120] A treaty on navigation of the Yalu and Tumen Rivers was concluded and, according to "reliable intelligence reports," a final boundary settlement was reached in October. Maps reflected this agreement beginning in 1970.[121]

Accounts of the boundary settlement are contradictory but generally corroborate the foregoing version. Deep feelings about the boundary demarcation remain, however. A North Korean representative attending a conference in Bandung, Indonesia, in April 1985 said that North Korea "mistakenly decided to split Mt. Paektu with China." In South Korea in October 1985, a North Korean Red Cross representative said that Mount Paektu was divided between China and North Korea, and that this was the "result of the courageous political decision made by Kim Il-sung." A North Korean map published in 1977 shows the boundary running through the peak of Mount Changbai, and a PRC map published in 1998 draws the boundary through Tianchi.[122] In fact, the problem may be the scale of the maps, which makes it difficult to determine with any accuracy exactly where the line runs.

In any case, suspicions persist, and in 1979, following China's invasion of Vietnam, North Korea fortified the border in the Mount Changbai area, suggesting lingering concern about China's intentions.[123] The border was reopened in the mid-1980s and treaties on cross-border trade and travel were renewed. Some further details of the boundary were resolved by a 1998 agreement on the boundary line in the Tumen River dividing China, Russia, and North Korea, a 2001 agreement on joint management of border ports, and a June 2002 protocol on the alignment of the eastern trijunction along the Tumen River between Russia, China, and North Korea.[124]

The timing of various phases of the Sino-Korean boundary negotiations and settlement are significant. As in the other cases, China took steps in the early 1960s to reach a settlement and reduce tensions along its border with Korea. This was both a response to deteriorating relations with the Soviet Union and, more generally, a reaction to the overall shift in the strategic environment. As relations with North Korea deteriorated in the mid-1960s following Pyongyang's tilt toward Moscow, China again raised the boundary issue, possibly to chastise Pyongyang and exact a price for its changing policy toward the two feuding communist giants. In 1970, however, after the Soviet Union emerged as China's primary security threat, Beijing again took steps to cultivate better relations with Pyongyang and concluded boundary agreements.

Unification of the Korean peninsula may precipitate a new border dispute. Seoul was not a participant in the negotiations, and by many indications does not support the accords between Beijing and Pyongyang. As early as 1978, some South Koreans began to claim that Yanbian, a Chinese-Korean autonomous area, was part of the ancient Korean kingdom of Koguryo, and in 1991 a *Chosen ilbo* article urged the reassertion of Korean control over Yanbian. In 1983, a proposal to affirm that Mount Paektu *(Baitoushan)* was Korean territory was introduced in the South Korean national assembly, and in August 1992, three days after South Korea normalized relations with China, South Korean newspapers raised the territorial issue. As recently as 2004, a bipartisan group of legislators in the South Korean national assembly introduced a bill to nullify the 1909 Sino-Japanese agreement that recognized Chinese sovereignty north of the Tumen River.[125] Despite the formal settlement of the boundary, the Sino-Korean border remains contested, at least in some academic, popular, and even political circles. The 2014 Russian annexation of Crimea and the lack of a muscular international opposition to Russian expansion touched a nerve for many Koreans, raising concerns over Chinese irredentism in Korea.[126]

8 The Sino-Mongolian Boundary Settlement

One of the deeply rooted historical causes of the Sino-Soviet schism was China's revanchist claims to Mongolia. Despite Mao Zedong's early statements supporting self-determination, he sought ultimately to restore the multi-ethnic Chinese empire of the Qing, and these ambitions exacerbated Russian and Mongolian fears of Chinese irredentism.[1] By establishing a de jure boundary between China and Mongolia for the first time in history with the 1962 boundary agreement, Beijing attempted to dampen what had historically been a cause of Mongolian apprehension regarding China. Because of Mongolia's geopolitical and historical relations with China, significant insights regarding China's revanchism and boundary settlements are gained by carefully studying the circumstances surrounding this dispute and its resolution. The timing of the boundary settlement fits the larger pattern. Taking place when hostilities between Beijing and Moscow were escalating and Sino-Mongolian tensions were increasing, this case clearly illustrates the thesis that Beijing's settlement of boundary disputes in the early 1960s correlates with China's deteriorating security situation and that Beijing attempted to use boundary settlements to shift the balance of power and enhance China's security.

Historical Background

The Jebtsundamba Khutukhtu (the Living Buddha of Urga), leader of Mongolia when it declared independence from China in 1911, characterized his country as "a lonely and isolated spot, in a critical condition, like piled up eggs, in the midst of neighboring nations."[2] Since Russian expansion into the Far East ran up against the Manchu empire, Mongolia had been an arena of Sino-Russian geopolitical rivalry. Historically, whereas the Russians viewed Mongolia as a classic buffer state, the Chinese have considered it to be an integral part of China. Russia supported Mongolia's bid for full independence following the 1911 revolution and the collapse of the Manchu empire. Later, to counterbalance Chinese hegemony, the Mongolian People's Republic (MPR) allied itself closely with the Soviet Union until the end of the Cold War.

The 1911 Revolution and Mongolian Independence

Resentful of Manchu colonialism and taking advantage of the chaos in China following the October 1911 revolution, the Mongols declared the independence of Outer Mongolia in December and proclaimed the Jebtsundamba Khutukhtu leader of an independent Mongolian nation. Mongolians maintained that they had enjoyed a special relationship with the Manchu court and that Mongolia was not part of China. Because of the weakness of the new central government, the Republic of China was unable to bring about the integration of Outer Mongolia through military force.

Yuan Shikai, president of the new republic, personally appealed to the Jebtsundamba for unity. His arguments are interesting because they reveal not only his naive Han (Chinese) chauvinism but also the Urga Khutukhtu's understanding of Mongolia's precarious position and of realpolitik. After several unanswered telegrams from Yuan, the Khutukhtu responded:

> Mongolia and China differ in customs and in religion. Their written and spoken languages are entirely unlike. We are in a far corner and there is no mutual understanding of one another ... If the poor stupid Mongols were to dwell in the same house with the cultured sons of Han, there would be likelihood of feuds arising which would result in conflict ... Therefore we should establish ourselves in amity and peace as neighboring states each adhering to its own territory and preserving its integrity. As to the matters of trade and those of travel and delimitation of boundaries, it will be to our mutual advantage to invite a neighboring state to act as intermediary.

Yuan Shikai countered:

> We are men of the same race ... For many centuries our peoples have shared the same roof and have grown and become one family ... There is danger and peril to you and to us if Outer Mongolia is severed from China. Look at the territories around us and say if there be any ... which has escaped annexation after its separation from China. Verily, the relation that lies between Mongolia and China is like that of the "lips to the teeth," of the "entrance hall to the main building." Your Holiness will doubtlessly be able to perceive

where danger lurks and where safety lies. Thrust not incalculable harm on the people of Outer Mongolia.

It is earnestly hoped that you will appreciate rightly my frank and open presentation of the actual situation ...

The Living Buddha responded:

As to whether happiness or disaster shall result, will depend upon the considerate treatment of Your Excellency. If we may hope for your assistance in establishing internal government, peaceful foreign relations, a satisfactory arrangement of boundaries and in firmly laying the foundation of the states, then not only will Mongolia be preserved intact, but China herself will have no cause for anxiety on her northern borders. I, the lama, am by nature stupid, but I understand the duties of a neighbor ... Truly Outer Mongolia is a lonely and isolated spot, in a critical condition, like piled up eggs, in the midst of neighboring nations ... Thus placed between strong powers we find it alike difficult to advance or retire. If we do not maintain independence how shall we escape the fisherman's net? As the situation now stands our preservation or destruction depends upon the attitude of Your Excellency. If you hold to a course too severe, I cannot be responsible for the consequences. Will it not be driving us to desperate courses?

Yuan's final telegram appealed to the Jebtsundamba Khutukhtu to rescind Mongolia's declaration of independence:

Today when the five races are united in an effort to form a new government, I, the President, and you, Reverend Sir, are like the hand and foot of the same body, like elder and younger brother in the same family, sharing together good fortune or ill ... Why should we trouble others to meddle in the affair to the loss of sovereignty? I earnestly hope that you will with broad charity consider the general welfare and cancel the declaration of independence very soon and unite with us as a single nation. Thus the threatening danger may be averted and the foundation of the state made strong.

The Jebtsundamba Khutukhtu responded:

Your work in uniting the five races and laying the foundation of the republic has aroused the admiration of all, at home and abroad. But we of the

Mongolian Banner in this period of wrangling and contest find ourselves living on the dangerous frontier and are in circumstances quite unlike those of the other races ... With regard to your statement about "troubling others to meddle in the matter to the loss of sovereignty," although I am not intelligent, I have a general understanding of your meaning. Under the pressure of present conditions, however, no other course is open. Otherwise it is difficult to conjecture "in whose hands the deer will die."[3]

Yuan's appeal to the Jebtsundamba failed and China turned to Russia as a last resort. Moscow's objective was to preserve Mongolia's autonomy, much as Britain had done in Tibet, but it was willing to sacrifice Mongolia's complete independence in order to ensure Russia's commercial and other rights, which had been granted earlier by the Manchu government.

Sino-Russian negotiations on the status of Mongolia began in November 1912. China sought recognition of its "sovereignty" over Outer Mongolia. Russia insisted on three conditions: no Chinese occupation, administration, or colonization in Outer Mongolia. An agreement was reached after nearly a year of difficult negotiations and bitter debate among the Chinese. Russia recognized Chinese "suzerainty" over Outer Mongolia in exchange for Beijing's recognition of Mongolian "autonomy." They also agreed that Russia would facilitate the establishment of relations between Urga and Beijing and that the boundaries of Outer Mongolia would be negotiated at an early date.[4] In 1913, Beijing did agree to delimit the boundary, but this was never done.

Whereas China was disgruntled with the agreement, Mongolia felt betrayed. Its prime minister sent a protest to Beijing stating that the Mongolian government considered "relations with China severed forever."[5] Nevertheless, a tripartite agreement was signed in June 1915 that included agreements on trade, taxes, and other matters. Although the boundary was not settled, a neutral zone between Outer and Inner Mongolia was established. The political conditions surrounding this agreement changed dramatically two years later, after the overthrow of the Czar and the October Revolution in Russia.

Beijing made its intentions clear when it dismissed the tripartite agreement as "nothing but a diplomatic trick of a temporary character" and eventually reasserted control over Outer Mongolia.[6] Russia's new Bolshevik government was unable to help Mongolia. Under tremendous pressure from Beijing, the Jebtsundamba Khutukhtu "petitioned" for the abolition of

Mongolia's autonomy in November 1919, and China gladly "complied." China's renewed hegemony did not last long, however. Mongolia became a battlefield of the Russian civil war, and in 1921 the Chinese were driven from Urga by the White Russians, who in turn were soon defeated by the Bolsheviks.

Establishment of the Mongolian People's Republic

Mongolian Marxists Sukhe Baatar and Choybalsan, with the blessings of the Jebtsundamba and the support of the Soviet Union, established a communist regime in Urga in 1921. Nevertheless, the Soviet Union, like Czarist Russia, still used Mongolia as a bargaining chip in its relations with China. In May 1924, it recognized China's full sovereignty over Outer Mongolia, but a month later, following the death of the Jebtsundamba Khutukhtu, Mongolia declared its independence as the Mongolian People's Republic (MPR). The capital, Urga, was renamed Ulaanbaatar (Red Hero) and Choybalsan eventually became premier. China's internal problems prevented it from reasserting control; the most it could do was protest Soviet-Mongolian agreements.[7]

The independence of the MPR was ensured two decades later at the Yalta Conference. The Soviet Union, the United States, and Great Britain agreed that the status quo in Mongolia should be preserved after the Second World War. The Nationalist Chinese government concluded a Treaty of Friendship and Alliance between the Republic of China and the USSR in August 1945; the treaty stipulated: "In view of the desire repeatedly expressed by the people of Outer Mongolia for their independence, the Chinese Government declares that after the defeat of Japan should a plebiscite of the Outer Mongolian people confirm this desire, the Chinese Government will recognize the independence of Outer Mongolia with the existing boundary as its boundary." Held on 20 October 1945, the vote for independence was virtually unanimous. The Republic of China officially recognized the Mongolian People's Republic within the "existing boundary" the following January, but no boundary settlement was negotiated by the two governments.[8]

China Attempts to Reassert Its Power

Even the Chinese Communists, reluctant to accept the independence of Mongolia, harboured irredentist sentiments. In an interview with Edgar Snow in 1936, Mao expressed the view that "when the people's revolution has been victorious in China the Outer Mongolian republic will automatically become part of the Chinese federation, at their own will."[9] Even before establishing a new regime, Mao raised the issue of Mongolia with his Soviet interlocutors. He seemed to assume that the 1945 recognition of Mongolian independence was simply a short-lived phase that would end with the collapse of the Republic of China, when Stalin would agree to the "reunification" of Mongolia with the People's Republic of China. In January and February 1949, Stalin sent a high-level delegation to Xibaipo, the interim headquarters of the Chinese Communist Party (CCP) in Hebei, to discuss Soviet assistance. Anastas Mikoyan, one of Stalin's closest advisers and a member of the Politburo and vice chair of the Council of Ministers, and Ivan V. Kovalev, Stalin's personal liaison with Mao, met with Mao, Zhou Enlai, and other top CCP leaders. Mikoyan reported:

> Mao Zedong himself raised the question of our attitude towards the unification of Outer and Inner Mongolia. I replied that we did not support such unification since it would lead to the loss of considerable Chinese territory. Mao Zedong said that he was of the opinion that Outer and Inner Mongolia could unite and become part of the Chinese Republic ... In connection with this information, Stalin sent me a telegram to give to Mao Zedong, which stated:
>
> > "The leaders of Outer Mongolia support the unification of all of the Mongolian regions of China with Outer Mongolia to form an independent and united Mongolian state ... We do not think that Outer Mongolia would agree to surrender its independence in favour of autonomy within the Chinese state, even if all the Mongolian regions were united in one autonomous entity. Clearly the final word on this issue belongs to Outer Mongolia itself."[10]

According to Kovalev, Mao asked him in early 1949: "But why shouldn't we unite Inner and Outer Mongolia into an autonomous entity and incorporate it into the People's Republic of China?" Kovalev dismissed the query, saying he was not authorized to discuss the question because "this was an internal matter of the Mongolian People's Republic, and that the Mongolian people would hardly be in favor of such an arrangement."[11]

Mongolia was again discussed during Liu Shaoqi's visit to Moscow in July 1949, but the Chinese were careful not to provoke Stalin and conceded the

MPR's independence. Liu gave Stalin a "Report of the CCP Central Committee Delegation" dated 4 July 1949. The document stated:

> Some persons from democratic parties, students and workers raised the issue
> ... about the independence of Mongolia ... We said that the Mongolian people,
> in keeping with the principle of national self-determination, had demanded
> independence and thus we ought to recognize Mongolia's independence. But
> if the MPR wishes to join China, we would welcome that. It is the Mongolian
> people alone that have the right to decide this issue ... Are these explanations
> of ours correct?

Stalin wrote "yes" in the margin. The document hints at the reasons for the
CCP's change of mind: "The strong friendship between the great peoples
of the USSR and China is of paramount importance ... It is crucial particularly for the independence of China and its constructive development. The
CPC [CCP] Central Committee is fully awake to the importance of this
matter." Continuing to push the issue of Mongolia only heightened tensions
between the CCP and the Soviet Union, and the CCP conceded that it "submits to the decisions of the Soviet Communist Party."[12]

Despite these discussions of the Mongolia question, Mao again raised
the issue with Stalin during his historic trip to Moscow from December 1949
to February 1950 to negotiate the Sino-Soviet alliance. Although little has
been written, Mao clearly expressed his desire for the eventual reunion of
Mongolia with China, but did not allow his irredentist dreams to prevent
the conclusion of a Sino-Soviet treaty. According to Russian documents,
although Stalin anticipated that Mao would push for Mongolia's unification
with China, the Russians were surprised when Zhou broached the issue but
indicated that the PRC recognized the independence of the MPR. That the
MPR and the Soviet Union were apprehensive about China's revanchist
attitude toward Mongolia was shown by Stalin's insistence on a declaration
that acknowledged the MPR's independence.[13] At the conclusion of the negotiations on 14 February, a communiqué announced the exchange of "notes
to the effect that ... both Governments affirm a full guarantee of the independent position of the Mongolian People's Republic."[14]

Sensitive to popular Chinese feelings regarding the status of Outer
Mongolia, the CCP published a statement explaining the rationale for the
agreement:

To each and every truly patriotic Chinese, our recognition of Mongolia as an independent state was a right and proper act, but to the reactionary bloc of the Kuomintang, which was somewhat compelled to accord recognition to Mongolia, it has always been a bitter memory ... "The independence of Mongolia is the loss of Chinese territory," they said. Among our people, there are some who are not familiar with the actual conditions and who have been contaminated with the sentiments of "suzerainty," and they think the map of China appears out of shape and unreal without Mongolia. These are the people who have been intoxicated by the poison of "Hanism." While the various ethnical [sic] groups within China were still under the oppression of both imperialism and feudalism and while their liberation was still very far off, Mongolia found rightful assistance from a socialist country – the Soviet Union – and by its own hard struggle achieved liberation and independence. Such liberation and independence we Chinese should hail, and we should express our respect to the Mongolian people. We should learn from them, we should not oppose their independence, we should not drag them to share our suffering. They attained liberation twenty-eight years ago and now march forward to socialism; as for us, we have just liberated ourselves ... Therefore, our attitude should be one recognizing its independence and not one pulling them back to our fold and making them follow us again.

In regard to Inner Mongolia, Tibet, and other ethnical groups [sic], the present question is not how to divide ourselves and each try to become independent, but to unite our efforts to build a strong, new, democratic China since we all have been liberated more or less during the same period.[15]

Despite this official declaration affirming Mongolia's independence, China raised the issue again after Stalin's death. The first time was in October 1954, during Khrushchev's first trip to Beijing. One Chinese account indicates that Zhou Enlai resisted raising the question because he understood the strategic importance of the MPR to the Soviet Union, but under intense pressure from Mao, he reluctantly broached the issue. According to Khrushchev's memoirs, Zhou queried: "What would you think if Mongolia became part of the Chinese state?" Khrushchev claims he declined to speak for Mongolia but did not voice strong opposition.[16] According to other Soviet accounts of the meeting, Khrushchev insisted that the status of Mongolia was not negotiable. *Pravda* reported:

The existence of an independent Mongolian state which maintains friendly relations with the USSR and other countries of socialism does not suit the Chinese leaders. They would like to deprive the Mongolian People's Republic of independence, to make it a Chinese province. The CPR [PRC] leaders proposed to N.S. Khrushchev ... that they "reach agreement" on just this.[17]

However, according to Mao's interpreter, Shi Zhe, "Nikolai Bulganin proposed that Mongolia be returned to China," and in Khrushchev's memoirs, "he did not tell the truth and said that it was we who raised the issue."[18] But Khrushchev's rebuff of Mao, if in fact that was the case, did not end Mao's persistent efforts to reopen the Mongolian question. Khrushchev claims that as he departed China, Mao, holding up one finger, remarked that "one question remained unsolved – Mongolia," thus setting the stage for future discussions of Mongolia's status.[19]

The next time the Chinese raised the issue (according to Soviet sources) was in April 1956, while Mikoyan was in Beijing. Zhou Enlai recalled the 1949 Xibaipo meeting at which Mongolia's relationship with China was first discussed, and asked whether the Soviet refusal to reconsider Mongolia's independence was "one of Stalin's mistakes." Liu Shaoqi commented that the Chinese people were "very deeply pained by the fact of Mongolia's secession from China," and said that the Chinese "consider Mongolia, like Taiwan, a part of their territory." Liu and Zhou hedged by saying that "they are not raising the question of reuniting Mongolia with the PRC, this could be done later [!], but they considered it expedient to express 'the opinion of the Chinese people on the question.'" Mikoyan rejected the argument that Mongolia was equivalent to Taiwan, saying that Mongolia was a "completely different nation" and that Mongolians would not surrender their independence.[20]

Following Choybalsan's death, the new Mongolian leader, Umjagin Tsedenbal, met with Zhou and, with Moscow's tacit agreement, ushered in an era of cooperation.[21] During the mid-1950s, the PRC and Mongolia concluded more than twenty-five agreements on all aspects of bilateral relations. A rapid increase in Chinese aid to Mongolia followed. A 1955 agreement for Chinese labourers to work in the MPR even gave them the option of permanent settlement and citizenship along with their families.[22] "Tens of thousands" of Chinese labourers reportedly went to the MPR.[23] In

1956, additional agreements provided increased economic and technical assistance. One allowed the mutual use of grasslands by herders in both Mongolia and the Inner Mongolian Autonomous Region (IMAR) of China.[24]

At the same time, Soviet aid and trade decreased. Between 1952 and 1957, trade between China and Mongolia grew nearly fiftyfold, whereas trade between the Soviet Union and Mongolia decreased by about 20 percent.[25] If China had continued at that rate, the Soviets' dominance would have been threatened. An article in the *Far Eastern Economic Review* quoted an Asian diplomat in Ulaanbaatar who characterized the situation: "The momentum of Chinese initiative is so great, the attractive force of Chinese dynamism so overpowering, that it is hard to see how, in the long run, Russia can maintain her position here."[26]

During the mid-1950s, the Mongolian domestic political situation also became more favourable for China. A pro-Beijing leadership began to emerge in Ulaanbaatar.[27] Jargalsaihen, the first ambassador to China, became foreign minister; other individuals who favoured a balanced or pro-China position also began to gain influence. At the Twelfth Party Congress of the Mongolian People's Revolutionary Party (MPRP) in 1954, the Chinese representative, Ulanfu, an ethnic Mongolian, emphasized closer Sino-Mongolian ties. In 1956, Soviet soldiers stationed in the MPR withdrew completely, and civilian advisers also returned home.[28] Later, as the Soviet Union wavered in its support of China during the 1958 Quemoy-Matsu crisis, the Mongolian Minister of the Army and Public Security travelled to Beijing and "supported the firm measures adopted by the Peking Government over Quemoy." Ulaanbaatar issued a statement that "aggression against China is aggression against Mongolia."[29]

China also encouraged pan-Mongolian nationalism. Beijing offered to help the MPR write a history of Mongolia and undertake archaeological excavations. A Chinggis Khan mausoleum was constructed in Inner Mongolia although his birthplace was in Outer Mongolia. The Cyrillic alphabet was adopted in Inner Mongolia to ease communication with the MPR; under pressure from Moscow, the Cyrillic alphabet had been adopted by the MPR in 1941, replacing Mongolian script.

As Sino-Soviet relations deteriorated in the late 1950s, however, Soviet complacency turned into alarm over Chinese ambitions in Mongolia. Bulganin and Tsedenbal issued a joint statement in May 1957 that signalled the reassertion of Soviet domination in the MPR.[30] Khrushchev allegedly commented to a Vietnamese delegation in Moscow that China's assistance to Mongolia, and especially its encouragement of the revival of Chinggis Khan, smacks of the "yellow peril." The Soviets responded to the Chinese challenge and would not be outbid: "Soviet generosity seemed to increase in direct proportion to analogous Chinese efforts."[31] The Soviets proved their ability to outbid the Chinese by seeing and then raising the Chinese offers of aid to the MPR. The bidding war peaked by the end of 1958, and in 1962 Mongolia became the first Asian state to be made a full member of the Council on Mutual Economic Assistance (COMECON).[32]

Mongolia was caught in the middle of an escalating dispute between the Soviet Union and China. Its initial wish was to remain neutral because it had benefited greatly from the Sino-Soviet competition for several years, but its precarious geopolitical circumstances made it impossible to remain neutral for long. Following the open split between the Soviet Union and China after the Twenty-Second Congress of the Communist Party of the Soviet Union in October 1961, Mongolia adopted a pro-Soviet position.[33]

Boundary Dispute and Settlement

In the wake of the escalating Sino-Soviet dispute, Beijing announced on 16 December 1962 that Zhou Enlai had invited Tsedenbal to Beijing to sign a boundary treaty. Two days later, Tsedenbal agreed to travel to Beijing and on 26 December China and Mongolia signed a boundary treaty.[34] This was the first public acknowledgment of Sino-Mongolian boundary negotiations. As with its other international boundaries, throughout the 1950s, China was reluctant to settle this boundary quickly because of inadequate knowledge of the geography of the region and confusion concerning the boundary's historical location. Irredentist sentiments also kept Beijing from negotiating a boundary treaty earlier. However, with the deterioration in Sino-Soviet relations, an increasing number of boundary incidents, and clear concern over the general deterioration of China's security, Beijing moved to settle the boundary.

That a Sino-Mongolian boundary dispute existed first became widely known in 1957 when Beijing rejected Mongolia's assertion that the boundary had been delimited in 1945.[35] According to Mongolian maps, the boundary was clearly established and demarcated. The basis for this claim was a boundary settlement regarding Manchuria, Inner Mongolia, and the MPR negotiated with Japan after the conclusion of the 1941 Soviet-Japanese Neutrality Pact, and the Republic of China's recognition of the MPR in 1945, including the current boundary of the MPR.

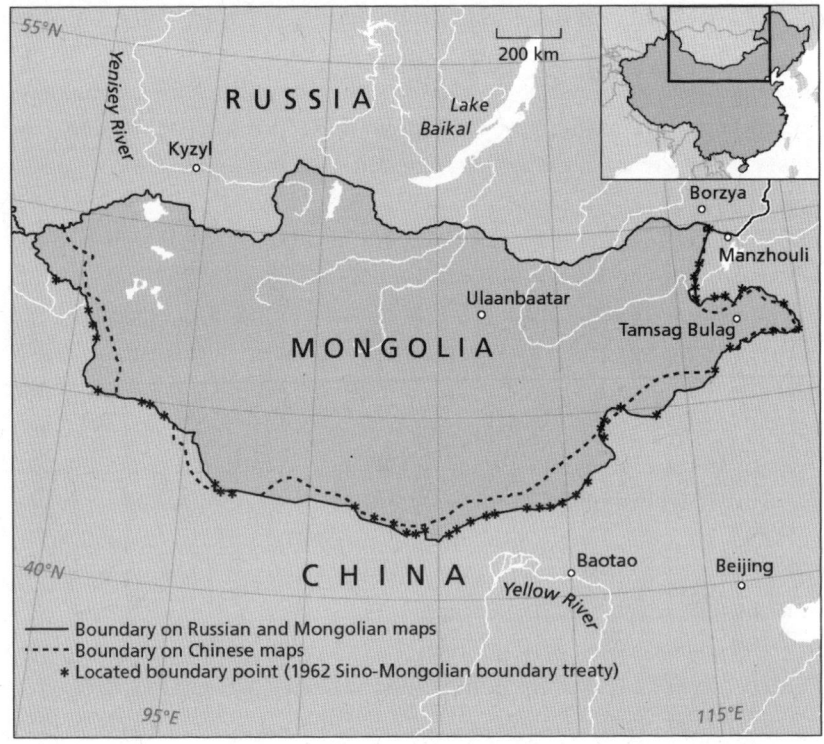

Map 12 Mongolia

Disagreement over the boundary was not publicly debated, but discrepancies on published maps made it undeniable (see Map 12). Chinese, Mongolian, and other maps showed significant differences, and Beijing considered the boundary a "complex question left over by history" that had "never been formally delimited."[36] Nevertheless, officials on both sides referred to the discrepancies as "alleged boundary differences," refusing to call the issue a boundary dispute.

Chinese maps showed the approximate location of the boundary with the notation "undemarcated." More than 1,000 miles of the 2,900-mile border was delineated differently on the two countries' maps. The boundary overlapped as much as 100 miles in places, and Mongolia claimed that Chinese maps incorporated as much as 12 percent of Mongolian territory. Of the approximately 44,000 square miles of disputed territory, much was uninhabitable desert, but a great deal included valuable grasslands. Most of the disputed territory was in the eastern sector, which was important to China's livestock industry.[37] Differences had always existed, but it is important to note that the discrepancies diminished when China's claims were adjusted between 1951 and 1960, the period of increased Chinese influence in Mongolia.

Several incidents resulted from the discrepancies during the 1950s, but there were no serious confrontations. In 1957, Mongolia sought to initiate boundary negotiations but was rebuffed by Beijing. As Sino-Mongolian relations deteriorated, however, the scope and the seriousness of incidents escalated, especially during early 1962.[38]

On 13 April that year, Beijing initiated boundary talks with Ulaanbaatar. At the same time, it suggested that in the "spirit of proletarian internationalism," measures be taken to avoid confrontations along the boundary. On 12 October, negotiations began quietly in Ulaanbaatar, and agreement on all outstanding issues was reached on 13 November, with a memorandum of the negotiations being signed on 17 November. A treaty was drafted in Beijing from 10 to 23 December, and was completed just before the arrival of Tsedenbal.[39]

At the signing ceremony, Liu Shaoqi told Tsedenbal that China had settled the boundary in a "spirit of mutual understanding and mutual accommodation," and "hopes to settle its boundary with other socialist countries on the basis of the same principles." Editorials pointed out that the settlement marked "a further consolidation and growth" of Sino-Mongolian ties and that it was "an important contribution to the strengthening of the unity of the socialist camp." Beijing stressed that this also "set a good example for the socialist countries in the handling of their mutual relations," and proved the ability of "fraternal socialist countries" to settle disputes peacefully. This was a clear signal to Moscow that China was willing to settle their boundary dispute (which was not yet publicly acknowledged). In his speech at Tsedenbal's farewell banquet, Zhou said that China had solved "complicated boundary questions with other countries, including Burma and Nepal." He mentioned the "agreement in principle" reached between China and Pakistan that same day and, in a clear reference to India, went on to say that "it has been repeatedly proved by facts that, given sincerity on both sides, the differences in social systems does not in any way hinder the peaceful settlement of issues." Zhou told Tsedenbal that the "reasonable settlement of the border question between China and Mongolia will be an example and an encouragement for border negotiations with other countries." In the midst of the Sino-Indian border war, this was a clear message to New Delhi that Beijing wanted to reach a boundary settlement.[40]

Liu Shaoqi signed the treaty on 8 March 1963 and the exchange of the instruments of ratification took place in Ulaanbaatar on 23 March.[41] A joint commission was created to survey the boundary and establish permanent markers. The commission met several times over eighteen months, but work slowed as Sino-Mongolian relations deteriorated further. Despite this, the final demarcation of the boundary was completed and documents were signed in Ulaanbaatar on 2 July 1964.[42] Mongolia received approximately 31,000 square miles of the disputed territory. According to a Mongolian scholar, China accepted almost all of the Mongolian claims, settling the boundary dispute in a way "highly favorable to Mongolia."[43] Neither country has raised questions regarding the final settlement.[44]

As Sino-Mongolian relations deteriorated and polemics became sharper, Mongolia reminded China of its historical irredentism. In 1967, the Mongolian Communist Party newspaper, *Unen*, linked the PRC with other modern Chinese regimes, arguing that the "Maoists inherited their venomous intentions and vain ambitions from the Manchu conquerors and the reactionary Chiang Kai-shek clique. This has been repeatedly confirmed by the public pronouncements of Mao Tse-tung himself and his supporters with regard to the state sovereignty and national independence of the Mongolian People's Republic."[45] A Mongolian scholar continued this line of reasoning, arguing that:

> Underlying the foreign policy doctrine of the Maoists were temporarily veiled hegemonistic and chauvinistic designs ... Although the Chinese leaders had time and again declared their respect for Mongolia's independence and integrity ... Mao Tse-tung questioned Mongolia's independence almost as soon as he took over the leadership of the CPC [CCP] ... As time passed, it became quite obvious that Mao Tse-tung was in effect pursuing towards People's Mongolia the traditional policy that had been enforced after the revolution of 1911-1912 by China's landowner-bourgeois rulers. They sought to decide the destiny of Mongolia's independence behind the backs of the Mongolian people and reduce the country to the status of a colony.[46]

China's Grand Strategy and the Boundary Settlement

The broader strategic context and the pattern the settlement followed illustrate Beijing's efforts to counterbalance the growing Soviet threat and alliance with Mongolia by salvaging deteriorating Sino-Mongolian relations. One Russian concluded as much, arguing that a "more important reason for China to sign a border treaty with Mongolia was to use it as a lever in winning Ulaanbaatar's support for the Chinese position in the Sino-Soviet quarrel."[47] This settlement follows the clear pattern in China's policy toward boundary settlements at the time that viewed them as part of a grand strategy.

As late as 1957, relations between Beijing and Ulaanbaatar showed no sign of deteriorating, although the Soviet Union had begun to reassert its influence in Mongolia. In the May 1957 Bulganin-Tsedenbal joint statement, the PRC was mentioned in a positive context: "Relations among the USSR, the CPR [PRC]and the MPR have created even more favorable conditions for the building of socialism in the Mongolian People's Republic and for the peaceful development of the country. Both the great fraternal neighboring states ensure peace and tranquility on the MPR borders."[48] As the Sino-Soviet dispute intensified, however, it became clear that the MPR was tilting toward Moscow and that Ulaanbaatar was beginning to abandon its even-handed policies of the mid-1950s.[49] During the initial stages of the Sino-Indian boundary dispute, Mongolia followed the Soviet Union in obliquely criticizing China, and in September 1959, Tsedenbal made a timely and significant state visit to India.[50]

The preamble to the new Mongolian constitution adopted on 6 July 1960 stated that "the Mongolian People's Republic grew and gained strength with the fraternal socialist aid of the Soviet Union." It did not mention China's assistance but alluded to the Sino-Soviet debate and indicated its own position in Article 89: "It is the duty of ... the MPR ... to promote the unity and solidarity of the peoples of the socialist camp, headed by the Soviet Union, to struggle with determination against all manifestations detrimental to the sacred friendship and unity."[51]

Military developments in the MPR also alarmed China. After 1960, a regular exchange of military delegations began and Soviet military advisers and troops returned to the MPR. The Mongolians "repeatedly stated that the [Soviet] troops were present at their request as a measure against China's aggressive territorial ambitions."[52] In January 1966, a new treaty included "military measures" to defend Mongolia, and secret agreements permitted Soviet missile bases in Mongolia.

China was unable to compete with Moscow for Ulaanbaatar's favour. After its unsuccessful bid to enhance its influence in Mongolia through aid and trade agreements, and in the wake of the acrimonious Sino-Soviet split, China's recognition of a delimited boundary dividing China and Mongolia was Beijing's last card. Thus, any irredentist claims China may have asserted in the past would be renounced and a major cause of bilateral friction removed in an attempt to maintain amicable relations with the MPR. No doubt China hoped that a flexible approach to the boundary dispute would induce Mongolia to at least take a more neutral position in the Sino-Soviet dispute.[53] The Chinese repeatedly expressed the hope that the boundary treaty would improve Sino-Mongolian relations. A *Renmin ribao* editorial published on 25 December 1962, the day Tsedenbal arrived in Beijing to sign the treaty, stressed the intimacy of their friendship and then stated: "We are convinced that ... the signing of the Sino-Mongolian Boundary Treaty will be a positive contribution to the strengthening of fraternal friendship and solidarity between the Chinese and Mongolian peoples."[54] Zhou Enlai's speeches, both at the signing ceremony and afterwards, emphasized the same theme.[55] Mao did not participate in the signing ceremonies or banquets. Even Tsedenbal did not meet with Mao when he was in Beijing. This may indicate how personally painful it was for Mao to recognize Mongolia's independence. Whatever the case may have been, no boundary treaty could have been concluded without Mao's personal approval.

Conclusion
The Sino-Mongolian boundary treaty is unique because of China's long history of dominating Mongolia. Clearly, even the Chinese Communists, despite their earlier rhetoric supporting self-determination and independence for the various nationalities that inhabit the frontiers of China, harboured a desire to recover areas once controlled by China's imperial dynasties. Nevertheless, the Communists were willing to trade territory for an illusory alliance, just as the Nationalists did in 1945. China's desire to recover "lost territory" was left unfulfilled because of the strategic imperatives to which it was forced to respond – in this case, by playing its boundary settlement card once again.[56] The boundary treaty was a desperate, unsuccessful attempt by China to win favour with Mongolia and encourage Mongolian neutrality in the Sino-Soviet dispute. Even as Tsedenbal was in Beijing to sign the treaty, while the Chinese used terms such as "intimate," "unbreakable," and "traditional, profound friendship" to describe Sino-Mongolian relations, he fully supported the Soviet position on peaceful coexistence and in the Cuban Missile Crisis, and lauded Soviet actions to avoid nuclear war. He emphasized the fact that Mongolia was the first Asian member of COMECON. Referring to the ongoing Sino-Indian border war, he supported India and indirectly criticized China by stressing that such disputes "should be settled only by

peaceful means – that is, through negotiations."[57] At a Conference on the Question of Ideological Work held in Ulaanbaatar in January 1963, just two weeks after the signing of the boundary treaty, the Chinese did not participate and Tsedenbal used his keynote address to criticize China:

> It must be forcefully emphasized that dogmatism and left opportunism are becoming an ever-greater danger in the world Communist movement. It is impossible not to see that, hiding behind ultra-revolutionary phrases and taking into its arsenal the ideology of nationalism and left opportunism [China] tries to attack the ... line of the world Communist movement on all important questions.[58]

His pride in Mongolia's "senior" status over China among socialist countries was evident, and he pointed out that Mongolia was "the first in the Far East to break away from colonial rule and build socialism." He reminded the Chinese of their past domination over Mongolia, which was ended with Russian assistance, making it possible for Mongolians to realize their "dreams of freedom, independence and happiness."[59]

Strong criticism of China continued. Tsedenbal openly and directly criticized China as "wrong and extremely destructive," and accused Beijing of "conducting schismatic subversive activities in the Communist movement." In October 1963, the second secretary of the Mongolian People's Revolutionary Party and chair of the Great Khural (national assembly) stated bluntly: "We believe that the recent lying statements of the Chinese leaders constitute an attack on Mongolia, as well as on our best friend, the Soviet Union."[60]

Beijing responded that such statements would be "an item on the account."[61] Mao personally responded on 10 July 1964, just a week after the ratification of the boundary treaty. He said that under the guise of helping Mongolia gain independence, the Soviets had in fact begun to dominate the MPR.[62]

Economic relations between China and Mongolia also deteriorated. Air service between Beijing and Ulaanbaatar was suspended by the Mongolians in January 1963.[63] Relations became so tense that street fights between Chinese workers and local Mongolians broke out in Ulaanbaatar, and the Chinese workers were asked to leave in April 1964. The following month, China banned the transit of goods across China to Mongolia. This meant that Mongolia's only access to the world was through the Soviet Union, which increased costs and made trade with other nations much more difficult. Very little was being shipped to China from the Soviet Union through Mongolia, but Mongolia had relied on the transit fees paid by China to finance its importation of essential goods from the PRC. This made it significantly harder for Mongolia to pay for imports from China. This was Beijing's first act of economic retaliation against the Mongolians for supporting Moscow in its dispute with China.

The Mongolians issued a statement that they depended on the Soviet Union "to protect it from the 'sinister schemes by the Chinese.'" The Soviets sent five thousand workers to help them finish the projects left incomplete by the Chinese, and as the Sino-Mongolian border grew tense, Moscow and Ulaanbaatar negotiated closer military cooperation and a larger Soviet military presence in Mongolia. At a special, first-ever observance of the 1939 battle in which Mongolian troops, with the aid of the Soviet Union, defeated the Japanese army at Nomonhan (Khalkhin-Gol), speeches emphasized Soviet-Mongolian solidarity in the face of a Chinese threat.[64]

Beijing did attempt to reduce bilateral friction. In March 1964, despite Mongolian criticism of China, Zhou Enlai offered ten tons of corn and 200,000 yuan to Mongolia following a crop failure, and the Chinese Red Cross sent medicine. In mid-June, an agreement on cultural cooperation was signed despite the release one week earlier of a lengthy MPRP Central Committee resolution that condemned China in the strongest terms to date.[65]

Despite the passage of time since the boundary settlement, both China and Mongolia remain extremely sensitive about their historical relationship, and China continues to exhibit latent irredentism. During the historic May 1989 Sino-Soviet summit in Beijing, Deng Xiaoping couldn't resist resurrecting China's historic obsession with territorial issues. He told Gorbachev that "in the past great powers have divided and humiliated China ... the Czarist Empire and the Soviet Union – during a certain time – had taken great advantage [of China's weakness]. Through inequitable treaties, including the understanding at Yalta ... the Russians took from China ... the present day Popular Republic of Mongolia, territory which is [rightfully] China's."[66] In 1992, the State Security Ministry also gave voice to China's historical irredentism: "As of now, the Mongolian region comprises three parts that belong to three countries" – the Russian republic of Buryatia, Mongolia, and China's Inner Mongolia Autonomous Region – but "the Mongolian region has from ancient times been Chinese territory."[67] Following Mongolia's transition to democracy, Beijing has also become very sensitive to the possibility that Ulaanbaatar will emerge as an advocate of reinvigorated pan-Mongol nationalism. In 1992, Chinese Defense Minister Qin Jiwei called for a strengthening of defences against "international hostile forces" along the border between Inner Mongolia and Mongolia. Among Chinese, there is growing concern that the democratic movement in Mongolia could spill over into Inner Mongolia, inflaming anti-Chinese nationalist sentiments among China's ethnic Mongolian population.[68] Clearly, although the PRC has recognized Mongolia and negotiated a boundary treaty, the legacy of the Chinese empire lingers in popular sentiment and in the minds of China's elite. And despite the assertions of Chinese officials that historical questions have all been resolved, Mongolian suspicions of Chinese expansionist ambitions persist to this day.

9 The Sino-Japanese Senkaku/Diaoyu Islands Dispute

To understand China's approach to the dispute over the Senkaku Islands ("Diaoyu" in Chinese), it must be placed within the larger context of the change in China's grand strategy between 1969 and 1978.[1] This makes it possible to explain why a flotilla of armed Chinese fishing boats sailed to the Senkakus in April 1978 during a crucial juncture in negotiations on the Sino-Japanese Treaty of Peace and Friendship. It will also illustrate how this dispute follows a pattern similar to the other territorial disputes, demonstrating the importance of strategic calculations in China's behaviour. Although the spike in tensions over the islands beginning in 2010 raises some new questions about Beijing's policy, the general strategic patterns in China's behaviour remain consistent.

Following the Second World War, Sino-Japanese relations were negligible during the 1950s due to Japan's support of the US effort to isolate the People's Republic of China. During this period, only small-scale nongovernmental trade relations were established and agreements were negotiated for other programs, such as repatriating Chinese and Japanese and cultural exchanges. Beijing viewed Japan's China policy as derivative of US China policy. Zhou Enlai told a delegation of visiting Japanese that "China cannot but suspect that Prime Minister [Nobusuke] Kishi is deliberately creating difficulties for China and cursing China to please the United States."[2] In 1957, Mao Zedong told a Japan Socialist Party delegation that "if Japan would only cancel the US-Japan security treaty and close American military bases in Japan ... then it would be possible to revise the clause on preventing the reemergence of Japanese militarism or a third country taking advantage of Japanese militarism in the Sino-Soviet treaty of friendship and alliance."[3]

Beginning in 1960, Tokyo sought better relations with China. Prime Minister Hayato Ikeda stated that he did "not think it necessary to adopt an attitude exactly the same as that of the United States with regard to China."[4]

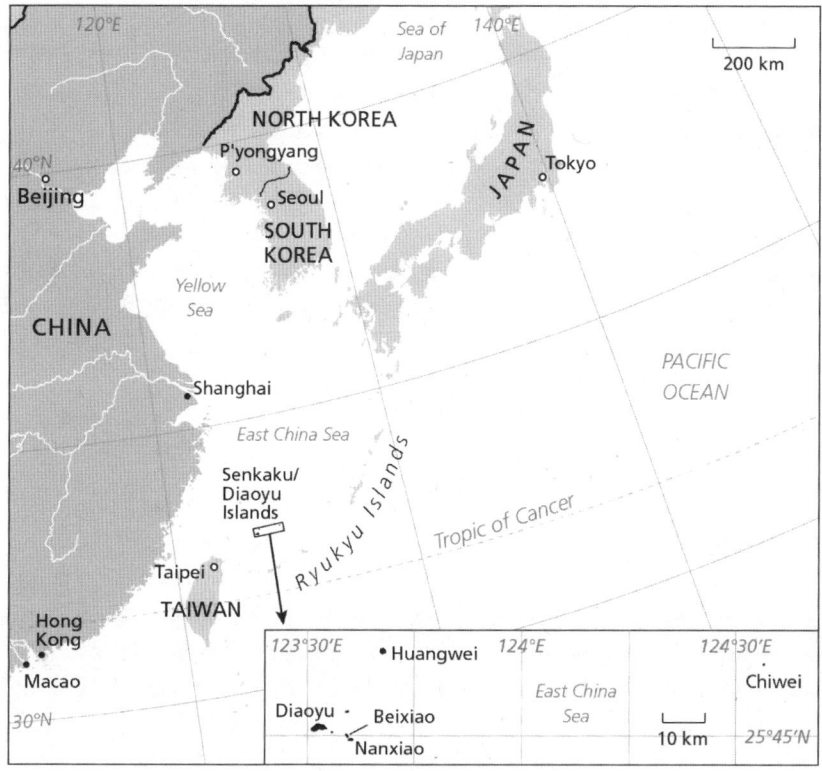

Map 13 Senkaku/Diaoyu Islands

Relations improved, but in the mid-1960s, with the onset of the Cultural Revolution and the pro-Taiwan inclinations of Eisaku Sato's government in Japan, they deteriorated once again and Beijing accused Tokyo of reviving Japanese militarism. At the height of the Cultural Revolution, Sino-Japanese relations were further exacerbated by the Senkaku Islands dispute (see Map 13).

Historical Background
In a 1953 *People's Daily* article supporting Okinawans' resistance to US bases, the Senkaku Islands (the article used the Japanese name) were included in a description of the Ryukyu chain.[5] Previously mostly ignored, the tiny islands (five uninhabited islets and three rocky outcroppings located about 120 miles northeast of Taiwan on the continental shelf) gained attention when the United Nations Economic Commission for Asia and the Pacific publicized the potential for offshore oil in the surrounding waters. This 1969 report

based on a geophysical survey of the seabed surrounding the islands concluded that "a high probability exists that the continental shelf between Taiwan and Japan may be one of the most prolific oil reservoirs in the world." Foreshadowing the intensity of the dispute that would emerge within a few years, the report went on to say: "It is also one of the few large continental shelves of the world that has remained untested by the drill, owing to military and political factors."[6]

The People's Republic of China and the Republic of China (Taiwan) began to assert claims to the Senkaku Islands. The United States was indirectly involved because Washington administered the islands as part of the Ryukyus until mid-1972, when it returned administration to Tokyo. The dispute grew when the ROC passed legislation in 1970 allowing oil exploration in waters surrounding Taiwan that included the Senkakus, and Chinese from Taiwan landed on the islands and planted the ROC flag, sparking a confrontation with Japanese authorities. In late 1970, Japan and the ROC initiated negotiations, including the Republic of Korea, in an effort to reach agreement on joint exploration in the waters bordering Japan, Taiwan, and South Korea. Beijing remained silent during the early stage of public polemics, but on 4 December it broke its silence and condemned the Taiwan/Japan/South Korea negotiations, declaring that "this 'new act of aggression committed by the ... Japanese reactionaries in league with the Seoul and Taipei regimes would provoke 'great indignation' in China and North Korea."[7]

The dispute got more attention when the United States made it clear that the Senkaku Islands would be included in the territory returned to Japanese administration under the terms of the US–Japan Okinawa reversion treaty. China asserted that the island group had been Chinese territory since ancient times and was occupied by Japan only during the 1895 Sino-Japanese War, and so should be returned to China according to the terms of the Cairo Declaration and the 1951 San Francisco Peace Treaty. Japan, on the other hand, asserted that the islets were *terra nullius* when Japan discovered them in 1884 and subsequently included them as part of its Ryukyu territories in 1895. In fact, the *Republic of China New Atlas* published in 1933 does list the Senkaku Islands as Japanese territory. Moreover, Tokyo pointed out that Beijing had never challenged Japan's claim after 1945 until the potential for resources became known and the US-Japan negotiations over the reversion of the Ryukyus to Japanese administration commenced.

Conflicting historical claims are not the only thing that complicates the dispute over these uninhabited islands; differing interpretations of the law of the sea do too. The United States administered the islands as part of Okinawa following the Second World War but, sensitive to the conflicting claims by Beijing, Taipei, and Tokyo, Washington declared that it did not intend to "prejudice any underlying claims" when it returned the islands to Japanese jurisdiction in May 1972.[8]

China issued an official statement on 30 December 1971, asserting: "Like Taiwan, they have been an inalienable part of Chinese territory since ancient times ... [The Chinese people] are determined to recover the Tiaoyu and other islands appertaining to Taiwan!"[9] China denounced the Okinawa reversion treaty as a "fraud" and an attempt to create a "pretext to carve off China's territory and plunder the sea resources belonging to China."[10] Around the time of formal reversion on 15 May 1972, China published several articles supporting its position.[11] Tokyo responded by claiming that the Okinawa agreement had settled the matter completely as far as Japan was concerned.[12]

Following the historic shift in the United States' China policy and Richard Nixon's trip to China in February 1972, Prime Minister Kakuei Tanaka moved quickly to normalize relations with the People's Republic of China. One outstanding issue was the Senkaku Islands dispute. In preliminary negotiations, Zhou made it clear that Beijing wanted to set aside the sovereignty issue and move forward with normalization. He responded to Tanaka's query about the islands by saying: "I do not want to talk about the Senkaku Islands ... It is not good to discuss this now. It became an issue because of the oil out there. If there wasn't oil, neither Taiwan nor the United States would make this an issue."[13] It was clear that normalization of relations with Japan was an important component in China's grand strategy to offset the growing Soviet threat to China. To accomplish this, according to Deng Xiaoping, the "two sides agreed not to touch upon this (Diaoyu Island) question when diplomatic relations were normalized." Beijing was willing to "seek common ground on major issues while reserving differences on minor ones" *(qiu datong cun xiaoyi)*.[14] Beginning in 2010, Tokyo has claimed that while Beijing was willing to sidestep the issue, "Japan never recognized the existence of an issue to be solved on the territorial sovereignty over the Senkaku Islands," and Japan did not make any agreement "about 'shelving' or 'maintaining the status quo' regarding the Senkaku Islands," but other accounts of the negotiations contradict this position.[15] On 29 September 1972, after over three decades of strained relations, China and Japan established normal diplomatic relations. Since there was no formal peace treaty ending the

Second World War, a communiqué that included an anti-hegemony clause called for the conclusion of a peace treaty.

Treaty of Peace and Friendship Negotiations

Negotiations on a peace treaty began on 11 November 1974, after the signing of trade, airlines, and shipping agreements earlier that year. This was the beginning of nearly four years of difficult negotiations leading to the Treaty of Peace and Friendship signed on 12 August 1978.

Disagreement over China's demand that an "anti-hegemony" clause be included resulted in an early breakdown in negotiations. Concerned that including an "anti-hegemony" clause would provoke the Soviet Union, Japan opposed it without broadening its scope and interpretation. Beijing argued that not including an anti-hegemony clause would constitute a "retreat" from the communiqué on normalization of relations.

After several years of impasse, a breakthrough appeared to be near in 1978. After coming to power in December 1976, Prime Minister Takeo Fukuda initiated high-level contacts with Beijing and indicated his willingness to observe "faithfully" the communiqué signed when diplomatic relations were established. In an important policy speech on 21 January 1978, he stated that it was time to resume negotiations and called for a Liberal Democratic Party (LDP) consensus. In July 1977, Deng Xiaoping told visiting Japanese politicians that the Sino-Soviet alliance, in which Japan was singled out as the raison d'être, had "naturally ceased to exist."[16] These important developments cleared the way for final negotiations. However, on 12 April 1978, when a breakthrough in reaching the necessary LDP consensus appeared imminent, the appearance of armed Chinese fishing boats around the Senkaku Islands surprised and shocked Japan.

China's Changing Negotiating Position

The eruption of the territorial dispute with the publication of the UN Economic Commission report in 1969 coincided with China's campaign against the re-emergence of "Japanese militarism." Japan's offer to negotiate a joint development agreement was characterized as "merely an established practice of the Japanese militarist pirates in unscrupulously plundering others," and a tactic by which "Japanese militarism will tighten its control ... while striving to realize its ambition of annexing China's territory." At the time, "postponing" a resolution of the territorial dispute was rejected as a "vicious trick" or "wicked tactic," which really meant that the "people of

China ... should surrender their sovereignty and let Japanese militarism plunder and occupy the islands and resources at will" to speed up the militarization of its economy.[17] On 29 December 1970, *Renmin ribao* quoted Mao as stating: "The Chinese people will defend their territory and sovereignty and absolutely will not permit encroachment by foreign governments."[18]

Criticism of Japan continued throughout 1971. The tone, however, was less shrill than it had been throughout 1970, and Beijing framed the sovereignty issue in the context of the legitimacy of the US-Japan Okinawa reversion agreement rather than implying a Japanese militarist motivation. China sent a formal protest to the secretary general of the United Nations protesting the inclusion of the Senkakus in this agreement. Following reversion in 1972, China began framing its position on the dispute within the context of the debate over the United Nations Convention on the Law of the Sea (UNCLOS). China supported the two-hundred-mile territorial water limit and linked this with its claim to the Senkakus.[19] But as the two countries moved quickly to establish full diplomatic relations, the Japanese public and press supported the government's stand on the Senkaku Islands dispute, and China was forced to be flexible when asserting its claim. In July 1972, Zhou Enlai indicated China's willingness to "shelve" the territorial dispute and move forward with normalization.[20] When Prime Minister Tanaka raised the sovereignty question again during the final stage of negotiations on normalization, Zhou downplayed the issue, saying: "Let's not argue over it here. They are, after all, tiny specks you can hardly spot on maps and they have become a problem just because oil was found around them."[21] In September, despite the dispute, Beijing normalized relations with Tokyo.

China's initial unyielding position changed because of Beijing's concerns over larger strategic issues such as the growing Soviet threat. Its willingness to subordinate the territorial dispute to more fundamental national security considerations, such as an *entente cordiale* with Japan, was clear when China's UN representative stated that the "Chinese people absolutely will not permit" the territorial dispute to "sow discord in the friendly relations between the Chinese and Japanese people."[22] With Beijing's changing perception of Japan's role in China's grand strategy, the "wicked tactic" of "postponing" resolution of the dispute now became a virtue of flexibility, completely acceptable when pursuing an *entente* with a former enemy, Japan, to confront a former ally, the Soviet Union, which had become the pre-eminent threat to China's security.

As the Treaty of Peace and Friendship negotiations commenced in 1974, China again expressed its willingness to sidestep the territorial issue and further strengthen relations with Japan. That October, Vice Premier Deng Xiaoping told a Japan-China Friendship Association delegation in Beijing that delaying settlement of the Senkaku sovereignty issue would be best. Later that month Hua Guofeng, who had succeeded both Mao and Zhou after their deaths in 1976, suggested that the treaty should take precedence over the territorial dispute and that the Senkaku Islands issue could be resolved gradually after conclusion of the treaty.[23] With increased anxiety over Soviet encirclement, Beijing, as in earlier cases, felt compelled to set aside the territorial dispute in order to conclude the treaty and establish closer relations with Japan.

The Fishing Boat Incident

As negotiations over the treaty came close to fruition, a flotilla of armed Chinese fishing boats appeared in the disputed waters around the Senkakus, jeopardizing both the treaty and the achievement of an important Chinese foreign policy goal. Approximately 140 boats were involved in the incident that occurred over a one-week period beginning on 12 April 1978. Fishing boats came from as far away as Qingdao and Tianjin, nearly one thousand miles north of the Senkaku Islands, but most of the boats were from Shanghai. Many were armed and carried camera crews who filmed the incident. Approximately forty boats carried large signs that read "The Diaoyu Islands are the territory of the People's Republic of China."[24]

When questioned soon after the boats first entered the disputed waters, a Chinese Foreign Ministry official refused to comment.[25] Questioned by a Japanese reporter two days later, China's ambassador to Japan, Fu Hao, said he was informed of the facts but had received no instructions from Beijing and "expected the situation ... would be clarified shortly."[26] That same day, in response to Japan's demand that China withdraw its fishing boats, Deputy Director of the Foreign Ministry Asia Bureau Wang Xiaoyun, citing the 30 December 1971 Foreign Ministry statement, asserted that the islands belonged to China but said that he would "check about the presence of Chinese fishing boats off the islands."[27]

Japan demanded an investigation and on 15 April Chinese Vice Premier Geng Biao, in the first real response to Japan's protests, stated that the incident was obviously "neither intentional nor deliberate" and that the Chinese boats were simply "chasing fish around the island at that time." He added that "we should not argue the island problem and we should resolve that problem in the future." The following day, Liao Chengzhi, who was both president of the China-Japan Friendship Association and vice chair of the Standing Committee of the National People's Congress, stated that Geng Biao's comments were a "satisfactory reply." The fishing boats withdrew that same day.[28]

Tokyo rejected Geng Biao's explanation, calling it not a "satisfactory reply." On 17 April, Japanese Foreign Minister Sonoda Sunao said, "It is regrettable that China gave its explanation in such a way while official contact was underway through the embassies in Tokyo and Peking," and the following day he "expressed strong dissatisfaction with the Chinese attitude."[29] The Japanese embassy in Beijing lodged a formal protest and asked to see the results of Beijing's promised investigation. Meanwhile, Chinese boats re-entered the disputed waters despite the presence of seven Japanese naval vessels and four planes on patrol.

Following a second Japanese protest and China's "investigation" and "official response," the incident was resolved. On 21 April, Wang Xiaoyun stated that the "final" conclusion was that the incident was an accident and China would "deal with the problem."[30] That evening in Tokyo, Sonoda said that such a response was "not unexpected" and Japan would accept China's "official explanation." Sonoda opined that this would "put an end to this incident," but added that the "government would determine how to react to China's reply after taking all factors into consideration."[31]

During discussions with Japanese officials in Beijing a few days later, Liao Chengzhi commented that "if China had planned the incident, naturally I ought to have been informed of it. But I had no knowledge of the incident"; he added: "Personally, I think the issue has already been settled."[32] Japanese Ambassador Sato Shoji and Chinese Vice Foreign Minister Han Nianlong agreed not to discuss the issue again before concluding the Treaty of Peace and Friendship. Sato told reporters that the "question ... was officially closed for the moment."[33]

Treaty negotiations resumed and a final agreement was reached on 9 August. Sonoda felt that raising the territorial issue would complicate the negotiations; nevertheless, he reluctantly broached the subject during discussions with Deng Xiaoping. Deng merely reiterated China's official position.[34] Although Sonoda would not give details of the negotiations at his news conference after signing the treaty, he did say that "much hard work occurred before the final agreement was reached" and some "very delicate issues" were settled.[35] No doubt, the Senkaku Islands issue was one of the most delicate issues, but was not allowed to delay the signing of the Treaty of Peace and Friendship. Beginning in 2010, Japan has asserted that it "never recognized the existence" of a dispute over the Senkaku Islands and it "is not true that there has been an agreement with the Chinese side about 'shelving' or 'maintaining the status quo' regarding the Senkaku Islands" during negotiations over diplomatic relations in 1972 or the Treaty of Peace and Friendship in 1978. Other accounts of the negotiations claim that there was a mutual agreement to sidestep the sovereignty issues.[36]

Although China maintained that the entire fishing boat incident was "accidental and not ordered by the Chinese Government" and Japan accepted this explanation, the veracity of Beijing's explanation is dubious. Japan's acceptance of Beijing's explanation was due to the nature of the dispute. Foreign Minister Sonoda pointed out that since Japan controlled the Senkaku Islands, the issue was quite different from the Takeshima *(Dokdo)* quarrel with South Korea and the Northern Territories dispute with Russia, where Japan did not control the disputed territory.[37]

China's Grand Strategy and the Senkaku Islands Dispute

To understand why Beijing undertook the fishing boat demonstration at such a critical juncture in the negotiations, it is necessary to place the incident within the broader strategic context and also the context of Sino-Japanese rapprochement. China's behaviour was determined by the shift in the regional balance of power and Japan's changing role in China's grand strategy. Throughout the 1970s, the Senkaku Islands dispute was a salient issue in relations between the two countries. The fishing boat incident, on the other hand, was only an acute crisis that, if not handled adroitly, could have aborted the treaty and led to greater Sino-Japanese tensions at a time Beijing was acutely concerned about the growing Soviet threat.

Between 1969 and 1978, Japan's role in China's grand strategy changed significantly. Prompted by the armed confrontation with the Soviet Union at Zhenbao Island in 1969, China began to view the Soviet Union as the greatest threat to its security. Speaking to foreign leaders in the early 1970s, Mao made it clear that the guiding principle during this period was the "Three Worlds Theory," which, using a united front strategy, called for closer relations between China and capitalist, industrialized countries, of which Japan was the primary one in East Asia, to offset the Soviet threat.[38] In the early 1970s, one of China's strategic objectives was to form an *entente* with

Japan, along with economic, political, and even strategic ties with the United States. The practical effect of China's changing grand strategy is evident in the establishment of diplomatic relations with Japan in 1972 and the signing of the Treaty of Peace and Friendship in 1978. This is a significant change in policy from one that, until the early 1970s, considered Japan, allied with the United States, as China's primary security threat.

Given China's changing perception of strategic imperatives during the 1970s and the impact this had on Beijing's foreign policy, its handling of the Senkaku Islands dispute fits a larger pattern in its security strategy. Japan was a key Second World country, and forming a united front with it against Soviet hegemony was vital to China's security, so Beijing felt an urgency to normalize relations with Japan.

The dispute over the Senkakus was a source of tension between the two countries with no simple resolution at hand. China decided to set aside the issue and move ahead with normalization despite its earlier refusal to do so, because to press its claim to sovereignty under such circumstances would have risked delaying or giving up a higher foreign policy objective – counterbalancing the growing Soviet threat.[39] During the negotiations over the Treaty of Peace and Friendship, China again indicated its desire to set aside the territorial dispute. As its fear of Soviet encirclement increased and relations with Soviet-allied Vietnam became more acrimonious, Beijing again subordinated the Senkaku sovereignty issue to the more important objective of concluding a peace treaty with Japan.

However, pro-Taiwan and anti-treaty members of Japan's Diet insisted on raising the territorial issue. Anti-treaty forces fully understood that the status quo favoured Japan, and the Foreign Ministry had determined that pressing the issue would complicate treaty negotiations.[40] Nevertheless, on 7 April 1978, while meeting with Foreign Minister Sonoda, anti-treaty politicians demanded that the territorial issue be resolved before conclusion of the treaty.[41]

The gauntlet was thrown and China could hardly overlook it without asserting its counterclaim. Following the fishing boat incident, Chinese ambassador Fu Hao stated that the situation "might have something to do with statements some Japanese were making," indicating China's concern over the anti-treaty factions' proposals regarding the islands.[42] Based on statements by Wang Xiaoyun, Sonoda concluded that it was an "act of protest ... against hawkish elements ... who have raised the Senkaku territorial dispute as a means of blocking the Japan-China peace treaty." Wang regretted that they had done this despite China's decision not to raise the issue during treaty negotiations, and suggested that it was an act of protest against Japan for bringing up the issue itself.[43] Wang also said that China recognized that the two countries' positions differed but that China had not intended to contest the issue under the circumstances; however, failure to act after the anti-treaty faction raised the question could be viewed as tacit recognition of Japan's claim.[44] At a later meeting, Wang stressed that "China had taken the necessary steps in order for the dispute to be seen in the context" of overall relations between the two countries.[45] More than a year after the incident and the conclusion of the Treaty of Peace and Friendship, Deng Xiaoping opined that Japan had exaggerated the Senkaku dispute and that the "Chinese Government was forced to make clear its views" when Japan raised the issue.[46]

The problem China faced was how to demonstrate its territorial claim without thwarting conclusion of the treaty. Boundary disputes with other countries were, no doubt, also a consideration, especially the disputes with the Soviet Union and Vietnam, both of which were reaching critical points at this time. Soviet negotiators would be returning to Beijing on 4 May 1978 to resume negotiations, and tensions along the Vietnamese border were quickly escalating. Failure to react to Japan's claims would have sent the wrong signal to both Moscow and Hanoi.

The size, duration, and logistical support for the operation indicate that it was someone like Deng Xiaoping, who controlled the military through the Central Military Commission, which orchestrated the incident.[47] This forceful demonstration of China's claim in the face of a challenge is not surprising when one recalls China's behaviour in other territorial disputes. Beijing's dilemma was how to assert its claim to the islands and then deal with the post-demonstration fallout and also conclude the Treaty of Peace and Friendship.

Still unclear about the nature of Japan's reaction, China's initial response was to reject Japan's protests and assert its own claim to sovereignty.[48] Chinese officials claimed that Japanese actions precipitated the demonstration, but, not anticipating Japan's strong, unified response, Beijing faced a quandary. It is unclear whether asserting that the incident was accidental was a contingency plan or was adopted as the "official" explanation only after Geng Biao offered it to the visiting Japanese delegation. Whatever the case, China was able to avoid cancellation of the treaty negotiations while dramatically asserting its claim to sovereignty over the islands.

The Beijing-controlled press in Hong Kong offered its view of the territorial issue in a 19 May 1978 *Xinwanbao* article arguing that China "can only wait until conditions are ripe. We cannot act recklessly." The article supported China's decision to delay the question of sovereignty because "neither side wants this problem to affect the negotiating and signing of the peace treaty ... Peking wants both the peace treaty and Tiaoyutai [the Senkakus]. China has nothing to lose in negotiating and signing the peace treaty first and then negotiating and reaffirming Tiaoyutai later."[49] No doubt echoing Beijing's views, the article underscores China's changed attitude toward the Senkakus because of the changing strategic environment and Japan's new role in China's security strategy. As for Deng's assurances to Sonoda during the final negotiations that such an incident would not be repeated, a *Xinwanbao* article argued that the assurance did not recognize Japanese sovereignty, as some Japanese politicians had argued. Rather, it asserted that the assurance had "nothing to do with giving consent to ownership of the controversial land ... As far as China's stand is concerned, it will fight for every inch of its land. This was China's stand before and is China's stand after the signing of the treaty ... Tacitness may sometimes occur (it is just impossible to shout all day long). However, tacit consent will never be given."[50]

The delicate nature of the Senkaku Islands dispute, the fishing boat incident, and Beijing's handling of these problems was influenced by China's domestic political situation. With the change in China's strategic calculations, gaining popular support for rapprochement with Japan required dropping public coverage of the territorial dispute while quietly insisting on China's claim. China was in the difficult position of being unable to assert its claim publicly because this would have inflamed public opinion and complicated subsequent compromise. Coverage given to other territorial disputes contrasts markedly with that given the Senkaku Islands at the time.

No reports of the fishing boat incident were ever published in the PRC. *Renmin ribao* reported the meeting between Geng Biao and Japanese politicians on 15 April 1978, but made no mention of the ongoing incident or Geng's explanation of it. Liao Chengzhi's meeting with a Japanese delegation the same day was also reported without mention of the fishing boat incident. The press reported the meeting between Vice Foreign Minister Han Nianlong and Ambassador Sato Shoji in mid-May (which formally concluded the incident), but did not mention the Senkaku Islands.[51] The only Chinese publication that mentioned the dispute was *Peking Review*. It published excerpts from a press conference held by Deng Xiaoping in Tokyo in October 1978, at which he stated that "when we were negotiating the Treaty of Peace and Friendship, the two sides again agreed not to touch on it" – an assertion denied by Japan – and speculated that "our generation is not wise enough to find common language on this question. Our next generation will certainly be wiser. They will surely find a solution that is acceptable to all." The report did not mention the fishing boat incident, however.[52] Not publicly pushing the territorial dispute at this time, as Beijing had in the past, made it possible for China to finesse the fishing boat demonstration and sign the peace treaty with Japan, accomplishing a major foreign policy goal.

The Continuing Dispute

With the rise of Chinese nationalism in the 1990s and the conservative turn in Japan, the Senkaku/Diaoyu Islands dispute has had a new lease on life as part of Chinese popular resentment of Japan and, in Japan, a symbol of Japan's concerns over a rising China. These developments as well as economic changes in both China and Japan have influenced the strategic calculations of both Beijing and Tokyo and changed the dynamics of this dispute. During demonstrations protesting Japanese history textbooks, the visits of Japanese officials to the Yasukuni Shrine, and other issues related to the bitter legacy of the Second World War and Japanese imperialism, the Senkaku Islands issue is a persistent Chinese irredentist grievance. Protests have become a regular occurrence and served to heighten popular awareness of the territorial dispute. Incidents involving the islets have increased significantly since 1996, exerting pressure on Beijing to go beyond the war of words and take action, but authorities have tried to stifle activists so that they do not hamper Beijing's flexibility in searching for a resolution.[53] Tokyo is also pursuing a more muscular foreign policy, and beginning in 2010, has adopted a more rigid policy toward the Senkaku Islands by denying that there was any agreement to shelve the sovereignty issue and asserting that the islands are Japan's "inherent territory" over which there "exists no issue of territorial sovereignty to be resolved."[54] This uncompromising stand makes any concession by Tokyo costly in terms of domestic politics. In September 2012, China responded with a white paper detailing its historical case and refuting Japan's claims.[55]

Tokyo's more intransigent policy was exhibited in September 2010 when a Chinese fishing vessel collided with a Japanese coast guard ship and Japan detained the Chinese crew, causing a major diplomatic crisis; in earlier incidents, Japan simply prevented Chinese fishing boats from entering waters surrounding the islands or immediately released Chinese protesters attempting to land on the islands.[56] This incident heightened China's vigilance and marked the beginning of a much more "reactive assertiveness" on the part of Beijing.

In April 2012, the nationalistic governor of Tokyo, Ishihara Shintaro, proposed that the Tokyo municipal government purchase the islands in order to enhance Japan's "effective control" over them. This forced the Democratic Party of Japan government to "nationalize" ownership of the islands by purchasing them from their private owners that September, a move that sparked a more persistent spike in tensions with China. In the view of the Japanese government, nationalization was a proactive measure "aimed at maintaining and managing the Senkaku Islands peacefully and stably on a long-term basis," to avoid complicating the dispute, and to reduce tensions with Beijing and the popular outcry following the 2010 incident.[57] However, Tokyo's increasingly intransigent language provoked government and popular opinion in China, which framed "nationalization" as a tactic by Tokyo to enhance Japan's claim to the islands. Beijing responded by increasing the frequency and duration of Chinese maritime enforcement vessels' patrols around the islands in a "tit-for-tat struggle *(zhenfeng xiangdui di zuo douzheng)* to safeguard its territorial sovereignty."[58] At the same time, however, Beijing has actively pursued crisis management at various levels.[59]

Even before the spike in tension since 2010, Beijing had pushed for negotiations and proposed joint resource development around the Senkakus in 1990, in 2006, and in 2010, shortly after the arrest of the Chinese fishing crew. In June 2008, Beijing and Tokyo reached a "Principled Consensus on the East China Sea Issue," agreeing to jointly develop the Chunxiao oil and gas fields located a few miles west of the unsettled median line and Japan's claims. The agreement was to "conduct cooperation in the transitional period prior to delimitation without prejudicing their respective legal positions." The consensus was not a legal agreement but rather a concurrent press release with no signatures, and differences over its meaning became apparent soon after it was issued.[60] The agreement raised Chinese expectations that Tokyo would agree to joint development of the Senkaku Islands' resources too, but Tokyo nixed these proposals.[61] Now, the objective of Beijing's more assertive behaviour is to undermine Japan's administrative control and to force Tokyo to recognize that there is a dispute and engage in meaningful negotiations. The *Global Times*, the populist and nationalistic newspaper published by the

Chinese Communist Party's *People's Daily*, ran an editorial in 2012 titled "Backing Off Not an Option for China," arguing that the "political dynamics surrounding the Diaoyu Islands will surely be reshaped once China routinely dispatches ships to patrol the islands ... China should seek to gather momentum ... to achieve these objectives ... China should be confident about strategically overwhelming Japan."[62]

Despite this bombast, to Beijing a satisfactory resolution would be a Japanese recognition that a dispute does exist and a settlement sometime in the future when conditions are optimal, with joint development of resources in the meantime. Beijing's new, more assertive policy toward the Senkaku Islands issue is also part of a larger goal to gain "more strategic space in the western part of the Pacific, so that American strategic weapons will not be able to pass through the ... East China Sea" and China can break through the barrier created by the chain of islands controlled by the United States and its allies between China's coast and the western Pacific Ocean.[63]

Conclusion

In the 1970s, China dropped its inflexible position on the Senkaku Islands to achieve a foreign policy goal that was motivated by larger strategic objectives. Friendly relations with Japan, a key Asian power, became a Chinese priority as the Soviet threat grew. In the late 1970s, an *entente* with Japan was sought as China's foreign policy came to rely on Japan and the United States to maintain its security so that it could pursue its ambitious economic development goals. Under the circumstances, China hoped to conclude a Treaty of Peace and Friendship that included an anti-hegemony clause, making it more politically significant as an anti-Soviet treaty. This made it necessary for China not to press its claim to the potentially resource-rich Senkaku Islands and the surrounding seabed. When its claim to sovereignty was openly challenged, however, Beijing felt unable to brush aside the issue as it had in 1972, when relations between China and Japan were normalized, and again in 1974, when the peace treaty negotiations commenced.

Allowing Japan to maintain control of the islands in practice while not recognizing its sovereignty in principle became impossible once anti-treaty Diet members linked the issue to the conclusion of the Treaty of Peace and Friendship. The fishing boat demonstration reminded Tokyo of China's claim to sovereignty and possibly served as a signal to other countries that Beijing would not back down if its sovereignty claims were challenged. Beijing did not overplay its hand and signed the much-desired treaty, which included the anti-hegemony clause, but it also asserted its claim to the Senkaku Islands. A "premeditated accident" helped China accomplish these two conflicting goals.

Although separated from the earlier territorial disputes and settlements by over a decade, the influence of Beijing's fundamental strategic imperatives on the handling of this territorial dispute is evident. That this dispute fits within the context of China's global strategy at the time is clear from the following Chinese statement: "At the time of normalization of the diplomatic relations between China and Japan and the conclusion of the peace and friendship treaty, the two sides, *taking the whole situation of Sino-Japanese friendship into account,* had agreed to settle the question in the future."[64]

The Senkaku Islands dispute remains unsettled and continues to be an irritant in relations between the two countries. It flared up in 1990, when the Japanese Maritime Safety Agency announced that it would formally recognize the lighthouse, originally built in 1978 by a right-wing group, as a "navigation mark." This triggered a Chinese protest and Beijing asserted that "we have always made it clear that China and Japan should place their overall interests above everything else and handle the Diaoyu Islands issues prudently, thus preventing it from affecting bilateral relations."[65] Two years later, CCP General Secretary Jiang Zemin's April 1992 visit to Tokyo was complicated by the February promulgation of a new law on Chinese territorial waters by the National People's Congress; the law reasserted China's claim and authorized the use of military force to prevent foreign occupation of the islands. The Foreign Ministry opposed the law, arguing that specific mention of the Senkaku Islands would cause unwanted diplomatic friction with Tokyo, but the military prevailed when it insisted that it would strengthen Beijing's hand in future negotiations.[66] A year earlier, Foreign Minister Qian Qichen had stated that China and Japan had "reached an understanding that this issue should be set aside for the time being." And despite the new law, Beijing made it clear that it was still willing to be flexible and delay final settlement to achieve more pressing and vital foreign policy objectives. In Tokyo, Jiang Zemin reiterated China's policy, stating that "Comrade Deng Xiaoping thoroughly explained the Chinese government's position and stand on the Diaoyu Islands' issue. This position and stand have not changed."[67] In 1993, Beijing agreed to let Japanese oil companies participate in developing offshore oil fields in the East China Sea, but only after Japan recognized the area as Chinese territory. Tokyo agreed to these conditions, but differences soon surfaced over the interpretation of the agreement. However, in June 2008, following Hu Jintao's visit to Japan the previous month, the first by a Chinese president in a decade, the two countries finally concluded a joint development agreement for the gas fields near the median line of the overlapping exclusive economic zones. This establishes the precedent that Beijing will agree to joint development if the territory in question is first recognized as Chinese territory. A similar scenario in the South China Sea is possible.[68]

The "nationalization" of the islands by Tokyo in 2012 pushed tensions over the islands to new heights and possibly signalled a new chapter in the ongoing dispute. Public opinion and the rise of popular nationalism in both China and Japan are relatively new factors. How these domestic political drivers, which are deeply rooted in cultural and historical conflicts, and the evolving military balance will affect any future settlement, or even an agreement facilitating joint development, is a matter of speculation, but China has restrained popular nationalism in order to prevent the dispute from damaging bilateral relations in other vital areas.[69] China and Japan do profess to have a "mutually beneficial relationship based on common strategic interests," something both governments consider key to improving their bilateral relations. In order not to hamper relations, the Senkaku/Diaoyu Islands dispute will have to be nested within the broader context of both countries' strategic and economic interests. To this end, on 7 November 2014, China and Japan concluded a "four-point principled agreement." The agreement "acknowledged that different positions exist between them regarding the tensions which have emerged in recent years over the Diaoyu Islands and some waters in the East China Sea, and agreed to prevent the situation from aggravating through dialogue and consultation and establish crisis management mechanisms to avoid contingencies."[70] Beijing's willingness to delay a resolution of the dispute raises the question of why. First, the absence of a compromise settlement is due to Japan's persistent unwillingness to recognize that in fact a dispute does exist. But China's forbearance can be attributed to three factors: (1) the "shadow of the future," or the anticipation of a more advantageous settlement in the future; (2) "cost of compromise," with possible exposure of the regime to accusations of national betrayal *(hanjian)*, a hypersensitive concern in modern Chinese history; and (3) the "benefits of compromise," which do not yet outweigh the cost of the ongoing dispute to bilateral relations.[71] A resolution of the dispute in the near term is unlikely, and China's larger strategic objectives still constrain Beijing to follow Zhou Enlai and Deng Xiaoping's earlier tactic of shelving the dispute in order to prevent it from spiralling out of control and undermining those very objectives.

10 The Sino-Vietnamese Territorial and Boundary Settlements

As was the case with India and the Soviet Union, for many years the Sino-Vietnamese boundary dispute was masked by the close cooperation between China and North Vietnam in the face of a common threat, first from France when it attempted to reassert control in Indochina after the Second World War and then from the United States after the mid-1950s. However, when Sino-Soviet tension grew in the late 1960s, the common strategic imperative that had unified China and Vietnam also changed. Beijing began to pursue rapprochement with the United States, still Hanoi's major adversary. Following the unification of Vietnam in 1975, there was a significant shift in the regional balance of power, and China witnessed the "Soviet advance into the vacuum in Southeast Asia left by the withdrawal of the U.S. ... and [the unfolding of] Vietnam's own ambitions in Indochina."[1] Vietnam began to play an important role in what China considered a Soviet attempt to encircle China. Eventually, Sino-Vietnamese tensions escalated into open hostility when China acted to frustrate Vietnam's bid for regional domination.

Although treaties between China and France concluded in the final decades of the nineteenth century defined the entire boundary, it is helpful when analyzing the dispute to divide it into three separate issues: the land boundary, the delimitation of the Gulf of Tonkin (Beibuwan), and claims to the South China Sea islands. The South China Sea disputes are considered in a separate chapter. Here, we consider the land boundary and the delimitation of the Gulf of Tonkin. Closely related to the Sino-Vietnamese land boundary dispute is the Sino-Laotian boundary, also established by the same series of treaties between China and France; this boundary settlement is considered at the end of the chapter.

As in the cases already considered, the Sino-Vietnamese boundary dispute must be framed in the broader context of China's strategic concerns and grand strategy. By the late 1970s, China's relations with Vietnam took place within the context of growing Soviet influence in Southeast Asia. The growing tension between China and Vietnam in the late 1970s after several decades of what appeared to be a close alliance culminated in a six-week border war in February and March 1979. This enmity was merely a return to the historical animosity between the two countries. The brief period of cooperation was possible only because they faced a common threat from the United States. Initially, in an attempt to reduce tensions, China quietly sought a boundary settlement with Vietnam to eliminate territorial issues as a source of friction. Failing to achieve this objective, China used the many clashes along the border as a pretext to punish Vietnam for cooperating with the Soviet Union and to "disrupt Soviet strategic calculation" and what Beijing perceived as an attempt to encircle and contain China.[2]

Historical Background

Although Vietnam was often considered part of the Chinese empire throughout the history of imperial China, Vietnamese resistance to Chinese domination was consistent. In 938, during a period of disunity in China, direct rule by China ended and Vietnam maintained its independence militarily; nevertheless, the Vietnamese court was still compelled to send tribute missions to the Chinese court three times a year. Until the French colonization of Indochina in the late nineteenth century, whenever a strong dynasty emerged in China, it attempted to reassert direct control over Vietnam. During the Ming Dynasty (1368-1644), China re-established control for a short period (1406-27), but popular resistance forced it to retreat. The last Chinese invasion, during the Qing Dynasty, was repulsed in 1789. Vietnam celebrates these anti-China wars as great nationalist movements. More recently, it has bitter memories of the post–Second World War Allied occupation of Vietnam by Chinese Nationalist forces. This historical legacy leaves Vietnam wary whenever China is unified and strong.

During Vietnam's postwar struggle for independence, the People's Republic of China extended assistance to the Vietnamese communists. Even during this period of close cooperation, however, conflicting national interests caused tension. During the Geneva Conference of 1954, China supported the proposal to partition Vietnam into North and South and pressured the Vietnamese communists to go along. According to some reports, in an attempt to bind North Vietnam to China, Ye Jianying, who led a military delegation to Hanoi in December 1961, proposed the formation of a Sino-Vietnamese military alliance, but Hanoi rejected the proposal.[3] Sino-Soviet tensions and competition had an adverse impact on Vietnam; China rejected a Soviet proposal for "united action" in Vietnam, and during the Cultural Revolution it interrupted the flow of Soviet aid to Hanoi across China.

Chinese aid to the North during the Vietnam War is estimated to have reached as high as $20 billion, making Vietnam the largest single recipient of Chinese aid. The PRC also deployed many troops across the border from 1965 to 1971, and Chinese labourers maintained communication routes during heavy American bombing.[4] Perhaps most important, China deterred the United States from a complete invasion of North Vietnam and therefore played a crucial role in the North Vietnamese war effort.[5] Vietnam acknowledges the assistance rendered by China, but also feels that China's real motive was to deter the United States, not fraternal generosity.[6]

By the early 1970s, China and Vietnam's strategic imperatives came into conflict. The Soviet Union had emerged as China's principal threat and China began seeking rapprochement with the United States and Japan. The invitation for President Nixon to visit China in 1972, while Vietnam was still fighting a war against "American imperialism," further strained Sino-Vietnamese relations. Following the Paris Peace Accords in 1973, Vietnam felt it could act more independently and no longer sought to strike a balance between the Soviet Union and China. Thus, as relations between China and Vietnam continued to deteriorate, territorial issues that had been downplayed historically began moving to the fore.

Although the territorial disputes have a long history, their re-emergence in the mid-1970s was a symptom of the underlying tension, which was rooted in regional competition, alliance politics, and bilateral issues such as the treatment of ethnic Chinese in Vietnam.[7] This was clear during the negotiations that followed the 1979 border war. Beijing often cited other issues as the cause of the conflict and made it clear that issues that were not even strictly bilateral, such as an anti-hegemony policy and Vietnam's occupation of Cambodia, had to be dealt with before the territorial issues could be settled.[8] Beijing's objective was to use a boundary settlement to improve relations with Hanoi and undercut Moscow's influence in the region.

Territorial Disputes
The territorial disputes were rooted in the interpretation of the boundary treaty signed by the Qing court and France in 1887, which delimited the land boundary (1,347 kilometres) and, according to Hanoi, the sea boundary in the Gulf of Tonkin (see Map 14). A supplementary convention negotiated

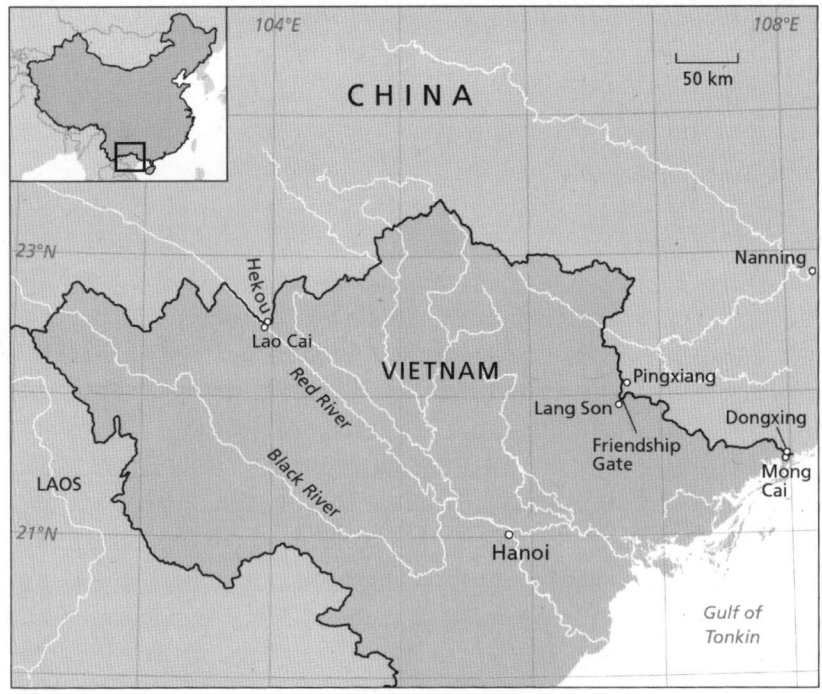

Map 14 Vietnam

in 1895 also delimited the China-Laos boundary (see the discussion of Laos below). The treaty was not subsequently challenged by China, but Beijing's reservations about the legitimacy of the treaty were announced after the boundary dispute became public in the 1970s.[9]

Vietnam maintained that the treaties established a "complete borderline which has a historical basis in the age-old political life of the two nations, a solid international legal value, and all practical elements for recognition on the terrain." At other times, however, Vietnam argued that the Sino-French conventions "are too old and cumbersome to give guidance in defining the frontier," and contended that France "cut off" several pieces of Vietnamese territory and gave them to China. A March 1979 Vietnamese statement raised French territorial concessions and claimed that China had seized additional territory prior to 1949; it accused the PRC of taking advantage of war-torn Vietnam to move border markers, encroach into areas along the border, and, in the guise of repairing the railroad, relocate the boundary 300 metres further south in 1955.[10]

Although Beijing advocated using the Sino-French conventions as the basis for a negotiated settlement, it considered them "unequal treaties." Beijing pointed out that while China was not defeated by France in 1885, the "Qing Dynasty Government accepted France's humiliating conditions and signed an unequal treaty." China countered Vietnam's assertion that France ceded Vietnamese territory with the query, "How could the Qing Dynasty Government, corrupt and submissive to foreign powers as it was, 'bring pressure to bear on France' and make the latter 'concede' land?"[11]

The dispute in the Gulf of Tonkin stemmed from the vagueness of the 1887 treaty. Article two of the treaty states:

> The islands which are east of the Paris meridian of 105°43' east (108°3' east of Greenwich), that is to say the north-south line passing through the eastern point of the island Tch'a Kou or Ouan-Chan (Tra-co), which forms the boundary, are also awarded to China. The Gotho and other islands west of this meridian belong to Annam.[12]

China maintained that this refers only to the islands and did not delimit the gulf itself, while Vietnam argued that the treaty delimited the entire gulf waters.

During a period of close cooperation between China and Vietnam in 1957, it was understood that there were differences over the boundary, but Vietnam proposed that the two countries maintain the status quo until a negotiated settlement could be reached in "accordance with the existing legal principles or with new ones defined by the two Governments." In April 1958, the Central Committee of the Chinese Communist Party accepted this proposal. Presumably as a show of good faith, Mao Zedong transferred control of Bach Long Vi (*Bailongwei* or White Dragon Tail) Island, located west of the meridian line, to Hanoi. Both Vietnam and China viewed the 1957-58 exchange of letters as being in "keeping with historical reality and international law," and constituting "the common basis for dealing with the boundary issues prior to a negotiated settlement of the boundary question."[13]

Boundary Negotiations

As Sino-Vietnamese relations deteriorated and China initiated boundary discussions in 1973, Hanoi rejected the Sino-French treaty as the basis for the boundary, arguing that it was "outmoded, too tedious, and not suitable to mark the boundary," but claimed that a "historical boundary line" existed. Hanoi also claimed that the Gulf of Tonkin had never been delimited but that a historical boundary existed. In 1974, an attempt to negotiate an agreement on the Gulf collapsed after three months of negotiations. Beijing initiated further boundary negotiations in 1975 in an attempt to stabilize relations with Vietnam. After a June 1977 meeting between Li Xiannian and Pham Van Dong, Vietnam agreed to enter formal negotiations that lasted from October 1977 until August 1978.[14]

The basic disagreement was over the Sino-French conventions and China's assertion that they were unequal treaties and therefore a new agreement must be negotiated. China accepted the earlier treaties, but only as a "problem left over by history" and not binding in the ongoing negotiations. Moreover, Beijing argued that since the original demarcation of the land boundary, the passage of time had obscured the original markers, resulting in confusion over the exact location of the boundary. Beijing would not accept Hanoi's position on the Gulf of Tonkin. Vietnam insisted that the entire border was established and was reluctant to negotiate a new treaty for fear that it would allow China to advance historical claims reaching beyond the "borderline left by history." These fundamental disagreements, especially in the context of dramatically deteriorating relations, made mutual understanding and accommodation difficult.

Nevertheless, although negotiations were hampered by a dramatic rise in tensions and although both sides maintained their basic positions, important procedural issues were settled. Beijing agreed that the alignment of the boundary should be verified and adjusted as necessary according to the Sino-French treaties, returning areas occupied beyond the boundary established by the treaty. After differences were settled, a new treaty could be concluded based on "respect for the borderline left by history" and the Sino-French treaties. This new treaty would supersede the earlier ones. Vietnam asserted that the treaties delineated the entire Sino-Vietnamese boundary, including the Gulf of Tonkin, and that it was necessary only to replace boundary markers that were destroyed or obscured.[15] Agreement was eventually reached to deal with the land boundary first because of the ongoing incidents and the real possibility of further military conflict. The Gulf of Tonkin issue was much more complex and was therefore put off until after resolution of the land boundary. The two sides agreed to a second round of negotiations, but Vietnam's treatment of overseas Chinese became the major bilateral issue and the boundary was not discussed again until 1979, after the six-week border war.

Prelude to War

As Sino-Vietnamese relations deteriorated, border incidents increased dramatically.[16] As early as 1974, China accused Vietnam of "aggravating ... tensions along the Sino-Vietnamese border" by "inciting" incidents and violating its territory. In the six months before the outbreak of hostilities in February 1979, China accused Vietnam of encroaching into Chinese territory in 162 locations, provoking 705 armed clashes, and killing or wounding more than 300 people. One of the most serious incidents occurred in August 1978, when, Beijing claimed, Vietnam attempted to force 2,000 Chinese across the border, killing 4, and attacking PRC officials. Vietnam did not deny the Chinese allegations of incursions, but also accused China of encroaching on Vietnamese territory.[17] China did not deny the Vietnamese allegations, and in fact admitted that some incidents occurred when Chinese border officials acted without government authorization.

Assuming that earlier cases demonstrate a clear pattern in China's approach toward boundary disputes, I argue that Beijing was willing to settle the boundary in order to improve relations with Hanoi in an attempt to improve its strategic environment by curtailing the growing Soviet influence in Southeast Asia, China's primary security concern at the time. Nevertheless, tensions in Sino-Vietnamese relations continued to mount as the Soviet-Vietnamese alliance became stronger. Vietnam joined the Council on Mutual Economic Assistance (COMECON) in June 1978, and China responded by cutting all economic aid and recalling its technical advisers. Hanoi accused Beijing of anti-Vietnam actions and collusion with American imperialism. China began to portray Vietnam as the "Cuba of the East." In November, Vietnam signed a treaty of friendship and cooperation with the Soviet Union. At this point, Beijing concluded that an improvement in Sino-Vietnamese relations was unlikely and that closer Soviet-Vietnamese cooperation to encircle China was inevitable.[18] Despite efforts to solve the boundary issues, Beijing concluded that any accommodation with Vietnam was impossible while Vietnam was supported by the Soviet Union. Li Xiannian, the influential first-ranking vice premier at the time, made this clear when he stated that "the Chinese people are very indignant at this. We have time and again warned the Vietnamese not to turn a deaf ear to what we have said."[19] By late 1978, China adopted a new, less conciliatory policy toward Vietnam and began to consider actions to "punish" Vietnam and thwart Soviet strategic objectives.

To prepare for such an eventuality, Beijing began to improve relations with other states in the region. It retreated from its assertion of sovereignty over the Senkaku Islands and concluded the Treaty of Peace and Friendship with Japan in August, formalizing a Sino-Japanese *entente*, and then moved quickly to normalize relations with the United States despite continued arms sales to Taiwan. In the United States in January 1979, Deng Xiaoping stated that "on questions of common interest and the current international situation ... there is much common ground between us." He also clearly indicated Beijing's intentions to "teach Vietnam a lesson."[20]

The 1979 Border War

China launched a "counterattack in self-defense" against Vietnam on 15 February 1979, deploying an estimated 160,000 troops and carrying out air strikes in Vietnam that destroyed military installations and industrial facilities in the border area as well as bridges and roads. From the outset, Beijing made its limited goals in the border war clear.[21] After penetrating deep into Vietnam, China proposed on 17 February that the two sides "speedily hold negotiations to discuss the restoration of peace and tranquility along the border and between the two countries and proceed to settle the dispute concerning the boundary and territory."[22]

Many scholars have argued that the February invasion was in retaliation for Vietnam's invasion of China's ally Cambodia in December 1978 and China's perceptions of Soviet-Vietnamese collusion to dominate Southeast Asia.[23] These considerations are significant and all the issues were intertwined as causes of the general deterioration in relations. However, placing too much emphasis on these factors ignores the boundary issue itself as an immediate cause of war, and neglects other factors such as the timing of the Chinese invasion and Vietnamese provocations along the border.[24]

These provocations occurred while Vietnam was preparing to invade Cambodia, and they provided Beijing with a pretext for invading, a dangerous gambit that is difficult to explain. Months before the February invasion, China had tried to discourage further provocation with clear warnings of possible retaliation. A September 1978 Chinese Foreign Ministry statement warned that Vietnam "must shoulder all responsibility for the consequences arising from the ... encroachment on Chinese territorial integrity and sovereignty."[25]

This indicates that, as early as then, China had begun planning for war with Vietnam as boundary incidents increased and relations deteriorated, even before Vietnam's invasion of Cambodia in late December 1978. *Renmin ribao* gave an unequivocal warning that "if it is attacked, it [China] will certainly counterattack," and concluded with the assertion that "China means what it says."[26]

If Beijing really wanted to deter Hanoi from invading Cambodia, China's "counterattack" would not have been launched after the Vietnamese invasion of Cambodia. One must consider the opportunity presented to China: with Vietnam preoccupied in Cambodia, it was an opportune time to settle a score along the border and punish Vietnam for not settling the boundary dispute earlier. That this was a major purpose of the "lesson" is demonstrated by the fact that Deng Xiaoping, when presenting the case for China's planned invasion to the United States in January, cited China's invasion of India in 1962 as a precedent.[27] The Sino-Vietnamese border war also followed the pattern set seventeen years earlier with India: if you fail to reach a compromise settlement in the boundary dispute, occupy disputed areas by military force and then call for new negotiations. After the border war with Vietnam, however, China clearly had several preconditions before the territorial issues could be settled. Besides the boundary, Beijing was very concerned about the growing Soviet-Vietnamese alliance and the direct threat to China that it presented. In Beijing's eyes, elimination of this strategic concern was of primary importance, and, after the initial attempt to settle the boundary failed, a boundary settlement became secondary.

Hanoi insisted that before negotiations could begin, China must withdraw its troops to the "other side of the historical frontier that the two sides have agreed to respect."[28] China withdrew its troops six weeks after the invasion, although Vietnam protested that they continued to occupy areas extending as far as ten to twenty kilometres inside Vietnam. China countered that it was merely maintaining the "status quo border line" and that "those places where there are Chinese troops are all on the Chinese side of the boundary and have always been under China's jurisdiction." China accused Vietnam of setting preconditions and called for the differences to be settled during negotiations.[29] Vietnam later dropped its preconditions and negotiations began in Hanoi on 18 April 1979.

Renewed Negotiations
At the first session of this second round of negotiations, Hanoi offered a three-point proposal calling for measures to secure peace along the border,

restore normal relations, and settle the boundary based on the historical status quo and the Sino-French conventions of 1887 and 1895. Beijing suggested an eight-point proposal during the following session.

China's proposal made it clear Beijing now viewed the boundary dispute in a much broader strategic context and wanted Vietnam to concede on several issues of "principle" before actually dealing with the boundary dispute. China wanted to restore relations based on the Five Principles of Peaceful Coexistence; it also wanted an agreement on an "anti-hegemony" clause that would forbid stationing troops in a foreign country or joining a military bloc.[30] China agreed that the 1887 and 1895 Sino-French agreements should be used as the basis for negotiating the land boundary, but insisted that modern principles of international law be used to delimit the Gulf of Tonkin. China also raised the South China Sea disputes and demanded that Vietnam revert to its earlier position regarding the Paracel *(Xisha)* and Spratly *(Nansha)* Islands and evacuate its troops from the latter. Previously Hanoi had not asserted claims to the South China Sea islands and had not protested when China drove South Vietnamese troops from the Paracels by force in 1974.

Clearly, Vietnam wanted to restrict the negotiations to the land boundary issue and the recent military confrontation. On the other hand, China's earlier attempts to use boundary accommodation and conciliation to dissuade Hanoi from developing closer relations with the Soviet Union had failed and unequivocal warnings had not deterred Vietnam from invading Cambodia. China was now attempting to use a possible boundary settlement to induce Vietnamese concessions on other issues of strategic concern.[31] Most important were the two issues of principle – anti-hegemony and the Five Principles of Peaceful Coexistence – that required Vietnam to abandon its new position of dominance in Indochina made possible by its alliance with the Soviet Union. To reduce the tension along the border, Hanoi would first have to curb that alliance and end its occupation of Cambodia. If successful, China would achieve two important foreign policy goals: curtail Soviet influence in Southeast Asia and stop Vietnam's growing domination of Indochina.

Despite having a basis for the settlement of the land boundary, moving forward was difficult in the poisoned political atmosphere. Disagreement over procedure caused negotiations to break down. China insisted on first discussing the principle of not seeking hegemony. Vietnam denounced this as an attempt by China to "evade its responsibility for the war of aggression against Vietnam," and accused China of "raising questions not belonging to bilateral relations between the two countries."[32] China characterized Vietnam's three-point proposal as ignoring the "major issues of principle leading to the dispute," and therefore demonstrating Vietnam's unwillingness to "improve Sino-Vietnamese relations fundamentally."[33] Beijing remained unyielding in its demand that "fundamental principles" be discussed before dealing with the border dispute.

After several months of negotiations, it was clear that the two sides were hopelessly deadlocked. At a press briefing on 28 June 1979, Han Nianlong, the head of China's delegation, rejected Vietnam's proposals as "nothing but an attempt to conceal the tense situation it continues to create along the border." In October, Hanoi published a white paper titled "Thirty Years of Sino-Vietnamese Relations." The document was so bitterly anti-China that Beijing believed there was no hope of any progress in negotiations and accused Hanoi of creating a new anti-China tide. At the thirteenth plenary session of this second round of negotiations in Beijing on 19 October, Han stated that "negotiations have reached a stalemate and it is difficult to make any progress." He reiterated that since a main cause of the poor relations was the issue of regional hegemony, the two sides must therefore begin by discussing the "Five Principles of Peaceful Coexistence and the principle of not seeking hegemony."[34] Hanoi pressed for continued negotiation, but in March 1980 Beijing accused it of being insincere and rejected a new round, asserting that Vietnam's unwillingness to first discuss fundamental principles blocked progress toward resolving the root cause of the conflict. Beijing stated that it was "willing to wait patiently" and that "as soon as an active factor in favor of talks emerges, even if it is a small one," it would be willing to begin a third round of negotiations.[35]

The negotiations broke down for political reasons, not because of disagreements regarding the Sino-French boundary conventions or the 1957-58 exchange of letters. Although China and Vietnam did not completely agree on those issues, they were a basis for future negotiations. Beijing indicated that maintaining the status quo, as had been agreed, did not mean that they would determine disputed territory according to actual control, but rather that minor adjustments should be made in a reasonable and fair manner.[36] In earlier boundary settlements with other countries, China had adopted a similar position regarding treaties it considered unequal, but in the end it had even ceded territory that had been China's historically. Technicalities or the interpretation of earlier treaties did not cause the breakdown; rather, larger and more complex strategic issues surrounding Sino-Vietnamese relations made progress toward a resolution unlikely at the time. These relations deteriorated further when, in March 1988, China wrested control of several islets in the Spratly group from Vietnam and established its first foothold in the South China Sea (Chapter 12).

Negotiating a Settlement

With the collapse of the Soviet empire and the end of the Cold War, the strategic environment changed quickly in Southeast Asia: Moscow curtailed assistance to Vietnam and international pressure on Vietnam to leave Cambodia intensified. With China's preconditions for the restoration of relations largely satisfied, conditions were favourable for mutual accommodation. Beijing moved quickly to adjust its policy toward Vietnam and take advantage of the opportunity to enhance its influence in the region. It arranged a secret summit with Vietnamese officials in Chengdu, China, in September 1990. Although disagreements on many issues remained, the meeting paved the way for a resumption of negotiations on the nettlesome boundary dispute.[37] Vietnamese Communist Party General Secretary Do Muoi and Prime Minister Vo Van Kiet travelled to Beijing in November 1991 to formalize normal relations between the two countries. At the summit, they reached an economic agreement and an agreement to resume boundary negotiations.[38] Although the South China Sea dispute caused a spike in tensions in February 1992, when China passed a law on territorial waters that asserted sovereignty over all the islands of the South China Sea, Foreign Minister Qian Qichen travelled to Hanoi that same month and the two countries agreed to renew boundary talks at the working group level in October.

Negotiations on the land and sea boundaries took place in Hanoi in February 1993 and in Beijing in August. During Foreign Minister Tang Jiaxuan's visit to Hanoi in October, preliminary agreements on principles were reached and expert-level working groups were established. Meeting in November, however, Chinese President Jiang Zemin and Vietnamese President Le Duc Anh simply reiterated historical claims to the disputed territory. The focus of the dispute was still the Sino-French treaties, both their legitimacy and interpretation. Although "positive results" were claimed, there was little indication that the two leaders made any substantive progress.

Tension along the boundary continued to abate and the border was reopened in early 1992. By early 1995, twenty-one road links had been opened and Vietnam had cleared thousands of mines along the border, allowing nearly ten thousand families to return to the area; China also cleared large minefields. In December 1995, during Do Muoi's visit to Beijing, both sides agreed in principle to re-establish rail links, and rail traffic resumed the following February, although the three hundred metres of disputed territory had not yet been resolved. Between 1992 and 1997, border trade grew from $100 million to $360 million.[39] An oral agreement was reached to shelve the South China Sea dispute for the time being, and following a second visit by Jiang Zemin in November 1994, a communiqué announced the continuation of negotiations on the land boundary and the Gulf of Tonkin. During Do Muoi's 1995 visit to China, they finalized an agreement to solve the boundary questions on the basis of international law and practice, using the Sino-French treaty as a basis for settling the land boundary but modern international law to delimit the Gulf of Tonkin.[40]

Because the differences over the land boundary were less significant, negotiations proceeded with relative ease as relations improved. In Bangkok in February 1996 for the Asia-Europe Summit Meeting, Chinese Premier Li Peng said that there was a consensus on the land boundary based on the historical customary boundary with no significant adjustments, and that negotiations on the Gulf of Tonkin would soon resume. In 1997, the two sides agreed to conclude a land boundary treaty by 2000 and accelerated the pace of negotiations, focusing on seventy specific disputed areas along the border. The Gulf of Tonkin presented more complex challenges, and so both sides agreed to put off negotiating this settlement until after the conclusion of the land boundary agreement.[41] In early 1999, the communiqué following a visit to Beijing by Vietnamese Communist Party General Secretary Le Kha Pieu stated that "international law and reality" would be the criteria for determining the final boundary. During Premier Zhu Rongji's visit to Hanoi in early December 1999, the boundary treaty was concluded, with only a few technical issues left to be resolved before Foreign Minister Tang Jiaxuan travelled to Hanoi later that month to sign the formal treaty.[42] According to Vietnamese Foreign Minister Le Cong Phung, in the end, disputed territory was divided evenly, "ensuring fairness and satisfaction for both sides."[43] Some details of the settlement were made public in 2002, including the fact that of the 87.6 square miles of disputed territory along the border, Vietnam received 43.6 square miles and China 44 square miles. A ceremony in February 2009 marked the completion of demarcation and the placement of 1,971 boundary markers along the border.[44]

Negotiations on the Gulf of Tonkin were complicated by recurring incidents such as Vietnam's seizure of Chinese fishing boats in July 1994 for "illegally" fishing in Vietnamese territorial waters and Hanoi's solicitation of foreign investment and development of gulf resources. Despite such complications, however, the working group pushed forward.[45] The major dispute was over how to treat Bach Long Vi *(Bailongwei)* Island, located midway between mainland Vietnam and Hainan Island, because the status of this island was key to determining the location of the equidistant boundary in the gulf.[46]

Meeting in Singapore in November 2000, Premier Zhu and Prime Minister Phan Van Khai agreed to accelerate negotiations and conclude a treaty before the end of the year. In December, they signed the final agreement delimiting the territorial waters, the exclusive economic zone, and the continental shelf in the Gulf of Tonkin. They also issued a joint statement declaring that outstanding issues (such as the South China Sea) would be settled "in the spirit of tackling easier issues before difficult ones" and that both countries would "not take actions to complicate or aggravate disputes. Nor will they resort to force or the threat of force."[47]

Conclusion

Despite the ongoing conflict over the South China Sea, China pushed forward with the settlement of the land boundary and the delimitation of the Gulf of Tonkin. Clearly, the changing strategic environment played a critical role. The collapse of the Soviet Union, Hanoi's only patron, was a factor, but even before this watershed, as Vietnam's relations with Southeast Asian nations began improving in the late 1980s, Beijing was anxious to eliminate sources of friction in Sino-Vietnamese relations and pushed for normalizing relations even before a resolution of the boundary and territorial issues – the same position it had advocated during the initial negotiations following the 1979 border war.[48] Moreover, China did not want to allow the South China Sea dispute with Vietnam to block the settlement of the land boundary and the demarcation of the Gulf of Tonkin. The smouldering South China Sea dispute would only alarm other countries and drive a wedge between China and the Association of Southeast Asian Nations (ASEAN). Sidestepping the complex South China Sea dispute and quickly settling other Sino-Vietnamese boundary and territorial disputes served Beijing's broader strategic interests in Southeast Asia.

As in previous boundary settlements, the historical boundary treaty provided the basis for the conclusion of a new treaty. China conceded that the nineteenth-century Sino-French treaties had established a boundary and that this boundary simply needed to be restored and a new treaty concluded, despite Beijing's assertion that it was an unequal treaty. On the other hand, China insisted that the treaty demarcating the Gulf of Tonkin was not in harmony with modern principles of international law and therefore required negotiations to establish equidistant delimitation. In both cases, it is clear that the broader international strategic context played an important role in motivating Beijing to compromise and in facilitating a settlement to eliminate causes of continuing friction.

The Sino-Laotian Border

The boundary between Laos and China should be considered in conjunction with the Sino-Vietnamese boundary because it too is based on the Sino-French treaty. Laos and China share a 260-mile boundary delimited by treaty in 1895 and later demarcated (see Map 15). In the treaty, China renounced any territorial claims to northern Laos. This treaty was a supplementary convention to the 1887 agreement that delimited the Sino-Vietnamese boundary from the Gulf of Tonkin to the Black River, near the present Laos-Vietnam border.

Following the rout of France from Indochina, China's policy was to maintain Laos as a neutral buffer state. In 1958, it became very concerned about US efforts to establish an anti-communist regime in Laos. An emerging international crisis was defused by a second Geneva agreement in 1962 that reaffirmed the neutrality of Laos, which China supported.

The People's Republic of China and Laos established diplomatic relations just before the conference held in Geneva opened in 1961, and China extended economic assistance to Laos and began building a network of roads connecting China to northern Laos.[49] Beijing's real concern was the escalating American presence in Southeast Asia, and its strategic objective at the time of the second Geneva agreement was to decrease American influence in Laos by supporting the neutralist forces. The Geneva conference established a coalition government that included the Chinese-backed neutralist faction. Beijing supported the proposal calling for Laos to "pursue a policy of neutrality and refrain from joining military blocs, and the establishment of foreign military bases on Laotian territory." While the second Geneva conference

Map 15 Laos

reaffirmed Laotian neutrality, instability continued and Laos became a theatre of the conflict in Southeast Asia for the coming decade. China became increasingly involved by supporting the Lao People's Democratic Government.[30] However, following the end of the Vietnam conflict, Laos followed Vietnam's lead in tilting toward the Soviet Union and Sino-Laotian relations deteriorated.

It is unclear why China and Laos did not negotiate a new boundary treaty in the 1960s. In other cases, China's neighbours took the initiative and Laos may very well have been satisfied with the 1895 treaty. In fact, it was the French treaty that initially established Laos's present boundaries as a unified state.[51] China did not challenge the boundary's legitimacy during the 1950s and 1960s, and although Beijing was alarmed in 1975 when the Vietnamese-backed regime came to power in Laos, it did not claim that a boundary question existed.[52] However, the Sino-Vietnamese boundary dispute, which intensified in the late 1970s, was rooted in a fundamental disagreement regarding the legitimacy of the 1887 and 1895 Sino-French boundary conventions, and this directly affected the Sino-Laotian boundary. China began questioning the boundary's legitimacy because of the supplementary Sino-French convention of 1895 that delimited the Sino-Laotian boundary, which in the eyes of the Chinese was problematic for both historical and technical reasons.[53]

Sino-Laotian relations began to improve in the mid-1980s and full diplomatic relations were restored in 1987. Laotian premier Kaysone Phomvihane visited China in October 1989 and boundary issues were discussed. Boundary negotiations were held in August and November 1990. One area of possible dispute was located near the China-Burma-Laos trijunction. The area was recognized as Chinese by Britain in 1894 but was ceded to France the following year.[54] China may have raised the issue during negotiations, but it posed no problem in reaching a settlement.[55] Premier Li Peng travelled to Vientiane in December 1990 and negotiations gained momentum.

During a third round of negotiations in September 1991, China and Laos reached agreement on a border treaty based on the 1895 Sino-French convention by "solving boundary problems through friendly consultation, in the spirit of mutual understanding and mutual accommodation, and being fair and reasonable." With little fanfare, they signed a treaty in Beijing on 24 October, and exchanged instruments of ratification in Vientiane on 21 January 1992. Inspection and demarcation proceeded with no problems except around a few villages where the boundary line was unclear, and were completed in April 1992.[56] On 8 April 1994, China, Laos, and Myanmar (Burma) signed an agreement delimiting the trijunction where their borders meet.[57]

After 1975, Laos was dominated by Vietnam and discussing the boundary question was problematic. By the late 1980s, however, the time was ripe for a settlement. The timing of the treaty, the basis for the delimitation of the boundary, and the ease with which the treaty was negotiated are all significant. As the balance of forces shifted in the region, Beijing adjusted to the new power reality by pursuing better relations with Laos. The boundary settlement led to the emergence of a pro-China tilt within the Laotian government and a significant improvement in relations.[58] Moreover, the treaty sent a clear signal to Hanoi of Beijing's willingness to solve their boundary dispute based on the earlier Sino-French treaties; this set the stage for progress toward the settlement of the Sino-Vietnamese land boundary in the coming years, and the subsequent settlement of the much more complex Gulf of Tonkin dispute.

PART 4
Contemporary Settlements and Disputes

11 Boundary Settlements with Eurasian States

As early as the Han Dynasty, China attempted to project its influence into Eurasia for strategic reasons, primarily to form alliances against the Xiongnu, who threatened China's northern frontier. Because of the importance of the historical Silk Road, Eurasia was strategically important and historically "Chinese strategy towards its Central Asian frontier was cognizant of the fact that the power of the centre was linked to its ability to project its influence along the distant periphery."[1] China's control over its western frontier waxed and waned as its dynastic reach expanded and contracted.

The collapse of the Soviet Union was a watershed in China's strategic environment. Although the People's Republic of China had extended firm control over its western border after 1949, Beijing inherited a 2,800-kilometre unsettled boundary with newly independent Kazakhstan, Kyrgyzstan, and Tajikistan in 1991 (see Map 16). Beijing's primary security concern was the power vacuum in the region and what this meant for China's security along its western boundary. It was particularly concerned about the subsequent increase in the influence of the United States in the region, perceiving Turkey, a NATO member, to be a "conduit for the expansion of US interests in the region."[2] On the other hand, China's historical legacy made the Central Eurasian states apprehensive about Beijing's ambitions in the region. In fact, "in the collective memory preserved in the oral epics of Central Asian peoples, in particular among the Kazakh and the Kyrgyz, traditionally the Middle Kingdom is presented as the historical enemy of peoples of the Steppe."[3] Quickly addressing the boundary questions left over by history was Beijing's first move to dampen any apprehension about China's historical irredentism in the region and establish a foundation for good relations with the newly independent Central Eurasian states.

There is very little detailed information available on the exact nature of China's boundary differences with these states, except for the most contentious boundary dispute, in the Pamir Mountains with Tajikistan. What were

Map 16 Central Eurasia

the "problems left over by history" and how did resolving them facilitate China's grand strategy? To answer these questions, the Sino-Eurasian boundary settlements and other economic, military, and cultural agreements must be placed in the larger strategic context of China's foreign policy toward the region.

Beijing's Grand Strategy and the Boundary Settlements

With the collapse of the Soviet Union, a new "Great Game" emerged in Eurasia. Different from the nineteenth-century strategic competition that pitted Great Britain against Czarist Russia, the major players today are the United States (and its NATO allies), China, and Russia, with the vast natural resources of the region as the prize. China seeks to establish a security perimeter in this crossroads by a "good neighbour policy" to ensure its strategic and economic security.[4] Beijing used boundary settlements to facilitate improved relations in response to changing strategic imperatives, a pattern consistent with earlier cases. Premier Li Peng made this policy clear during his April 1994 Eurasian trip. Speaking before the parliament of Uzbekistan, he stated that disputes should be settled "through peaceful negotiations, in the spirit of equal consultation, mutual understanding and mutual accommodation." However, "when conditions are not ripe, disputes can be shelved temporarily, and efforts made to seek common ground. Disputes over some issues should not hamper the development of normal nation-to-nation relations."[5] In Kazakhstan, President Jiang Zemin expressed the view that "historically boundary problems are very sensitive and complicated questions and if handled poorly, will result in conflict." But, he concluded, the "smooth resolution of this problem ... will have a positive influence on the resolution of boundary problems with other countries."[6]

China's relations with the Central Eurasian states are themselves a "problem left over from history." Long before the establishment of the People's Republic of China, Russia had asserted control over Eurasia. Boundary and other questions in the region became a subset of the larger Sino-Soviet relationship. After the collapse of the Soviet Union, Beijing faced the challenge of managing bilateral relations with the newly independent states, for which the long-smouldering boundary disputes were central concerns.

The Central Eurasian states perceived China as a potential economic and demographic threat. Many analyses of China's potential threat focus on China's dramatic population growth and energy needs and the pressure this could generate for Chinese *lebensraum*.[7] In 1989, only an estimated forty thousand people crossed the border between China and Central Asia. In 1994, an estimated 300,000 Chinese lived in Kazakhstan, and this grew to 500,000 early in the twenty-first century. A senior Kazakh military official concluded that "if we do not stop the flood coming to Kazakhstan, there is no doubt that they will overcome us in ten to fifteen years."[8] Kazakh scholars were also apprehensive because parts of present-day Kazakhstan are identified as historically part of China on some Chinese maps. Apprehension grew over Beijing's irredentist claims and the possibility of Chinese expansion. In Kyrgyzstan, Chinese traders purchased considerable amounts of real estate, alarming local officials.

Beijing took steps to allay such fears of Chinese revanchism. It too was very apprehensive about the instability that developments in Eurasia could cause in China, so it quickly uncoupled its foreign policy toward Moscow from relations with Central Eurasian states because of the region's strategic importance to China.[9] Beijing had a historic opportunity to re-establish Chinese influence in Eurasia at the expense of Russia, but also faced a potential challenge to Beijing's control over western China if ethnic unrest escalated in Xinjiang.

After establishing relations with the Eurasian states in early 1992, China signed within a short period of time over twenty agreements on economic and cultural cooperation. At the same time, it "began to discuss some issues that influenced the further development of relations" important to China's security, resulting in, for example, the September 1995 communiqué announcing a unified stand in opposition to separatism.[10]

During the 1970s, this unsettled frontier had been a potential flashpoint for Sino-Soviet military conflict. Negotiations on the reduction of military forces along the frontier began in November 1989 and, after the breakup of the Soviet Union, continued with the newly independent republics. China initiated talks in Moscow with a united delegation from Russia and the Eurasian states in late July and early August 1992. In September, China, Russia, Kazakhstan, Kyrgyzstan, and Tajikistan signed an agreement to proceed with negotiations on the mutual demobilization of forces along the frontier.[11]

Beijing was no doubt alarmed when in July 1994 the Central Eurasian states joined the US-sponsored NATO Partnership for Peace. Responding to these growing security concerns, China pressed for closer security relations with its neighbours. On 26 April 1996, Kazakhstan, Kyrgyzstan, Tajikistan, Russia, and China formed the "Shanghai Five" and signed an agreement on confidence-building measures along the border. *Xinhua* emphasized that the agreement "shows that China is an important power and a factor in safeguarding peace and stability," and is a "repudiation of the so-called 'China threat' theory spread in the world by those who have ulterior motives."[12] The Hong Kong *Wenhui bao* editorial was more explicit:

> The five nation agreement is aimed at safeguarding peace and reducing military activity, whereas the NATO ... security system was established during the Cold War period. However, instead of ending itself after the Cold War, it still operates with an overbearing air ... NATO is actively expanding itself ... NATO constitutes a new threat ... The revival of the military system of the Cold War period indicates that instead of restraining its power politics and hegemonism, the superpower [USA] is intensifying its efforts to continue to pursue them. This cannot but evoke the concern and vigilance of various countries in the Asia-Pacific region.[13]

On 24 April 1997, a second agreement was reached to withdraw military forces 100 kilometres along the 3,000-kilometre boundary. On 3 July 1998, a third agreement reaffirmed the first two agreements and emphasized cooperation to dampen ethnic unrest in the region. These three agreements were significant confidence-building measures and, for China, a reassurance of its security. The agreements were also important adjuncts in the final settlement of the boundary issues that eliminated barriers to further development of relations.

The connection between larger geostrategic concerns and boundary settlements was illustrated by a Chinese scholar, Zhang Wenmu. He argued that the United States is driven by concerns over energy security and concluded that the "trend in US foreign policy toward South and Central Asia, will have an effect upon Tibet and Xinjiang. The military power of NATO has already been extended to Central Asia, and as soon as the US forms a military alliance ... similar to the one it has with Japan, China will certainly be deeply concerned about the security of the western region of Tibet and Xinjiang." The author goes on to argue that it is very possibly a goal of the West, led by the United States, to divide western China and "use Tibet and Xinjiang to establish a political buffer between China and the oil producing countries of Central Asia and the Middle East."[14] Therefore, the author concluded, China must

> from a geopolitical perspective, recognize the strategic significance of the Tibet/Xinjiang region to China's development in the next century ... The Tibet/Xinjiang region is China's geopolitical pivot ... If Tibet and Xinjiang become independent, it will certainly cause a chain reaction, and China's western front will not only lose the natural protection of the high plateau buffer, but this also will threaten the industrial security of the southwestern region ... China must emphasize good neighborly relations with the Central Asian states and, from a geostrategic perspective, recognize the far-reaching significance of China's involvement in the development of the oil resources of Central Asia and the Middle East.[15]

This may represent an alarmist viewpoint, but the author was an analyst at the China Institutes of Contemporary International Relations, an official research institute under the State Council's Ministry of State Security, and then a professor at the Center for Strategic Studies at the Beijing University of Aeronautics and Astronautics (now *Beihang daxue*). *Strategy and Management*, in which Zhang's analysis appeared, is not an official publication but is published by the China Institute for Strategy and Management, an organization with close ties to the People's Liberation Army and strategic circles in China.

Economic Context

Eurasia quickly became an important focus of China's economic attention as part of the "Great Islamic Circle" and the revival of the "Silk Road" economy in the wake of the disintegration of the Soviet Union and economic reform in China that emphasized western China's development. In 1992, *Xinhua* promoted this new thinking, asserting that China would "boldly lay down a new strategy" by promoting economic relations with the newly independent Central Eurasian states. Chinese economic reformers in Xinjiang argued that the "geographical, human and cultural advantages" of Xinjiang's ethnic ties with other parts of Eurasia would facilitate western China's economic development due to "complementary resources and markets."[16] China promoted trade and investment in all three of the neighbouring states, with most of the investment going to the largest state, Kazakhstan, particularly its energy sector.

Border trade is an important part of the growing economic ties. In 1989, Xinjiang's trade with Soviet Central Asia amounted to only US$118.5 million. By 1994, trade through fifteen border towns totalled US$570 million, an increase of 58 percent since 1992. By one estimate, by late 1992 Kazakhstan imported 50 percent of its consumer goods from China. In 1995, total trade between China and Eurasia was an estimated US$718 million, with border trade accounting for $500 million. Trade with Kyrgyzstan grew by 85 percent in 1998, to US$200 million. With over sixty cross-border transport routes, by 2004 Xinjiang's trade volume reached US$3.7 billion, 65 percent of the region's total trade; of this total, Xinjiang-Kazakh bilateral trade was US$3.3 billion, or 73 percent of China's total. China became Kazakhstan's major trading partner, and 25 percent of Kyrgyzstan's foreign trade was with China. Trade with Tajikistan totalled only $2.7 million in 1992, but expanded rapidly to $4.4 million in the first four months of 1993. China's exports to Tajikistan as a percentage of its total imports climbed from 0.3 percent in 1999 to 4.1 percent by 2004.

Trade potential was indicated by the numerous economic cooperation agreements that were concluded. Following the boundary settlements,

China's relations with its Eurasian neighbours continued to develop rapidly, significantly displacing Russian influence in the region. In 2000, only 3.8 percent of the region's trade was with China, but by 2010 this had grown to 24.4 percent, primarily at the expense of Russia. China-Eurasian trade was only US$1 billion in 2000, but had leaped to US$459 billion by 2012, making China Central Eurasia's largest trading partner. China also became a major lender, providing US$10-15 billion for Kazakhstan and over US$603 million for Tajikistan, and setting up a US$10 billion loan facility for members of the Shanghai Cooperation Organization (formerly the Shanghai Five).[17]

By 2004, Beijing had invested approximately US$4 billion in Eurasia, not including Kazakhstan, which has been the primary target of China's investment.[18] In 2005, China pledged US$900 million to Kyrgyzstan to build a transportation network, granted Tajikistan US$6 million in unattached aid, and committed to investing over US$11 million in Gorno-Badakhshan, the remote region of Tajikistan nearest the Chinese border, with fifteen joint Tajik-Chinese projects.[19] The China-Kazakhstan rail link was completed in September 1990, and a new Central Eurasian transport artery – an Islamabad-Kashgar-Bishkek-Almaty Highway – was opened in October 2004. In subsequent years, more roads were opened connecting Tajikistan with China, such as the 700-kilometre Khorog-Karakoram Highway, which opened in May 2004. Opening roads established important economic links and is a significant part of China's strategy to connect Eurasia to itself economically and geopolitically.[20]

Oil and gas development is an important area of strategic cooperation. An oil-importing country, China has turned to the Eurasian states as a reliable source of energy. In 1994, China signed an agreement with Turkmenistan to construct a Turkmenistan-China-Japan gas pipeline.[21] In 1997, it won the bid to develop Kazakhstan's Uzen oilfield and construct a 3,000-kilometre oil pipeline from Kazakhstan's Caspian oilfields at Tengiz to Xinjiang, and then to China's eastern coast. During the bidding, China was in competition with Russia, the United States, and other Southeast Asian nations for the estimated $10 billion project.[22] Pipeline construction began in September 2004, was completed in 2011, and now carries 20 million tons of oil a year over its 3,000 kilometres. China also signed agreements with Kazakhstan to develop the Aktyubinsk oilfields along the Russian-Kazakh border, and built a 988-kilometre pipeline from Atasu to the Chinese border. Total Chinese investment in oil resource development in Kazakhstan is estimated at US$9.7 billion, equivalent to 50 percent of Kazakhstan's GNP. In 2003, a natural gas pipeline project alongside the oil pipeline was undertaken. The commitment to the two pipelines was reaffirmed in July 2005 along with the establishment of a strategic partnership. In total, China has invested approximately US$9 billion to build a network of pipelines linking the region.[23]

These agreements are a clear indication that China and Central Eurasia are developing important strategic economic links. In particular, the pipelines, which will form a "steel umbilical cord" between China and the region, will greatly influence the balance of power. By 2008, the region provided China with approximately 5 percent of its imported oil, and this is expected to rise to 10 percent when all projects are completed. China is not only seeking energy security for the future but also attempting to shift the focus of Central Eurasia's global vision toward itself and away from Russia and Turkey.[24]

Problems Left Over from History

Although the collapse of the Soviet empire created new strategic and economic realities, China and the three newly established Central Eurasian states also inherited a legacy of "unequal treaties" and territorial disputes. Beijing's stated policy toward "questions left over from history" was that "the Chinese government has taken the most prudent approach towards the boundary questions ... While both the historical background and the actual circumstance that have taken shape are to be given due regard during negotiations, necessary adjustments can be made with the consent of both parties."[25] The Sino–Central Eurasian boundary was originally established by "unequal treaties" – the 1860 Treaty of Beijing, 1864 Protocol of Tarbagatai (Chuguchak), the 1881 Treaty of Ili (St. Petersburg), and the 1884 Sino-Russian Treaty of Kashgar. According to Chinese scholars, through these treaties, China lost 440,000 square kilometres of territory south and east of Lake Balkhash, and 70,000 square kilometres east of Lake Zayson.[26] Beijing's position regarding this "lost territory" was that "it was Tsarist Russia that forced China into signing these unequal treaties ... [but] the Chinese government is ready to let the entire alignment of the boundary line ... be determined on the basis of those unequal treaties."[27] In the course of boundary negotiations with Central Eurasian states, there is no indication that China raised the issue of "unequal treaties" or "lost territory." This was certainly not the case in the earlier territorial disputes with the Soviet

Union, where China frequently asserted that over 1.5 million square kilometres of territory was "lost" to Czarist Russia by unequal treaties. According to the policy statement quoted above, however, China was willing to accept the unequal treaties as the basis for new boundary agreements, a pattern motivated by larger strategic concerns and followed in all earlier boundary settlements in an effort to develop closer relations with neighbours that had their own security considerations.

One problem in reaching new boundary agreements was that, according to Beijing, Czarist and Soviet Russia had even encroached into Chinese territory beyond the boundaries stipulated in the earlier treaties, creating many newly disputed sectors that required negotiations.[28] One oft-cited example was the 1892 Russian occupation of more than 20,000 square kilometres of Chinese territory in the Pamir region, which China insisted "must, in principle," be returned "unconditionally." Even so, China conceded that in such cases, "both sides can, considering the interests of the local inhabitants, make necessary adjustments."[29] This historical issue made the Sino-Tajik treaty the most complicated and sensitive of the three settlements.

Boundary Negotiations

Before the collapse of the Soviet Union, Sino-Soviet boundary negotiations had made significant progress. In Beijing in December 1990, the first meeting of a joint working group was held to discuss the Sino-Soviet Eurasia boundary. Before the work of this group made any significant progress, the Soviet Union collapsed and China faced three newly independent states and a different set of challenges. Beijing sought to demonstrate its benign interests in Central Eurasia by quickly initiating boundary negotiations in October 1992. Initially Russia joined the negotiations in a four-plus-one arrangement, both to provide the Eurasians with necessary expertise and to relieve fears that China would bully the three states into major territorial concessions. Initially, each government reaffirmed the principles for resolving the boundary disputes reached in previous Sino-Soviet border talks, and agreed to establish working groups to draft boundary settlements and continue negotiations on sectors that were yet to be settled.[30] In April 1993, the five states met again in Shanghai to continue discussions. They identified twenty disputed sectors comprising an estimated total disputed area of approximately 35,000 square kilometres. The largest and most complex dispute was with Tajikistan, in the Pamir Mountains.[31]

Kazakhstan

China and Kazakhstan inherited fifteen disputed sectors along their border. One report asserted that even though Kazakh officials had wanted to initiate boundary talks earlier, China would not agree to such talks. Accordingly, the conclusion at the time was that China would delay any boundary settlement and reserve irredentist claims as an option for future expansion.[32] However, during a visit to Beijing by Foreign Minister T.S. Suleymenov in August 1992, Beijing agreed to settle the boundary. Over the next two years, talks were held each month until an initial agreement was reached. Following a preliminary agreement in July 1993, Premier Li Peng signed a Sino-Kazakh boundary treaty on 26 April 1994 and the instruments of ratification were exchanged in Beijing on 13 September 1995. This initial treaty left several disputed sectors unresolved, but supplementary agreements were signed on 25 September 1997 and, in Almaty, Kazakhstan, during a visit by President Jiang Zemin, on 4 July 1998. According to *Renmin ribao*, the second supplementary boundary agreement marked the "comprehensive settlement of boundary questions between the two countries left over by history," a 1,783-kilometre border that involved approximately 2,200 square kilometres of disputed territory. China received approximately 43 percent of the disputed territory, and Beijing relinquished its claim to almost all the territory already controlled by Kazakhstan.[33]

The April 1994 boundary agreement with Kazakhstan "established basic principles for resolving the lingering historical problems" along the boundary, but did not cover three areas that remained disputed.[34] High-level leaders overcame some of these problems, and the supplementary boundary agreement signed in September 1995 settled an eleven-kilometre dispute in the Khan Tengri *(Hantenggeli)* Peak area. This was a breakthrough in settling the remaining areas of disagreement.[35] A Sino-Kazakh joint boundary commission was established, and between 29 July 1996 and 8 September 1997 it held ten meetings and resolved the principal differences. Following a survey, several points of dispute still remained, with China alleging that problems in delimiting the boundary occurred when local Kazakh governments settled people along the disputed areas and created problems over water resources. The final settlement was reached in July 1998 on the basis of historical nineteenth-century documents. Boundary delineation was completed in 2002 and demarcation in November 2003, and markers were set in place by 2005.[36]

There were minor difficulties in concluding the settlement, and many protested the fact that Kazakhstan "ceded" territory to China. Kazakh Foreign

Minister Tokayev rejected the protests, stating: "Let me emphasize right here and now: Kazakhstan did not give any lands to China. According to the delimitation agreement, the border runs along the line along which it has always run, i.e., along the guarded line. In other words, Kazakhstan did not gain or lose anything."[37]

The Sino-Kazakh boundary was an issue that, according to Chinese accounts, had "stood between the two neighbors for years."[38] Fu Quanyou, chief of the General Staff of the People's Liberation Army, characterized the boundary negotiations as "smooth" and as setting the stage for "increasing political mutual trust between the two sides" and "smooth cooperation in the Shanghai Cooperation Organization." However, some eminent scholars of China's diplomatic history continued to include a "litany of historical grievances" in books published after the boundary settlement, and other elites expressed dissatisfaction with the treaties and feared that China would concede too much in a subsequent settlement with Tajikistan.[39] Despite some popular misgivings, the border settlement removed a major source of tension in Sino-Kazakh relations and helped Beijing strengthen and solidify security relationships with increased economic ties. At the press conference following the signing ceremony for the second supplemental agreement in 1998, Jiang Zemin stated that, in a "spirit of mutual understanding and mutual accommodation, and based on considerations for mutual benefit," the two countries had established a "boundary with no problems, a boundary of peace and friendship, and a boundary that will foster the mutual prosperity of both countries."[40]

Kyrgyzstan

In April 1993, Premier Li Peng and Kyrgyzstan's president, Askar Akayev, initiated talks on a boundary settlement. A statement indicated that a settlement of the eight disputed sectors would be finalized "in the not-too-distant future." Li stated that "reaching a border agreement at an early date will be of great significance to strengthening Chinese-Kyrgyz relations. It is hoped that the border between the two countries will become a bond of peace and friendship, as well as a bridge leading to economic prosperity" and a "new silk road." It was clear that a boundary settlement was near, but that "friendly negotiations on some remaining issues should be continued."[41]

A tentative accord was reached during a July 1995 meeting of high-level officials held in Beijing, and in January 1996, topographic maps were exchanged after three years of work by a joint mapping group that "laid a solid foundation for future border surveys and demarcation work."[42] Finally, on 4 July 1996, President Jiang Zemin signed a boundary agreement, characterized by a Chinese spokesperson as "yet another important positive element ... in enhancing regional peace and stability."[43] The instruments of ratification were exchanged on 29 April 1998, settling most of the 858-kilometre Sino-Kyrgyz boundary involving approximately 3,700 square kilometres of disputed territory. The Sino-Kyrgyz joint communiqué stated that the two sides would "strictly observe" the boundary treaty and at an early date begin the process of demarcating the border using the "present boundary treaty as the basis, through consultations on the basis of the spirit of equality and mutual understanding, and according to the recognized principles of international law, [and] through negotiations proceed to determine the boundary line in the remaining sectors and comprehensively and completely settle the boundary questions."[44] In the final settlement, China received 30 percent of the disputed territories, approximately 1,270 square kilometres.[45] The Kyrgyz government recognized land in four disputed sections as Chinese territory, causing some internal dissension in Kyrgyzstan and heightening anti-Chinese sentiment among the Kyrgyz.[46]

The agreement left unresolved the sensitive Uzengi-Kuush river basin sector. The dispute was finally resolved in August 1999, and in response to domestic Kyrgyz opposition to the supplementary boundary treaty, President Akayev indicated that the negotiations had not been easy but argued that China "advocate[d] a generous policy towards Kyrgyzstan in general and border issues in particular."[47] China initially demanded 94 percent of the 3,000 square kilometres of this hotly contested sector but was willing to divide the disputed territory fifty-fifty. After further negotiations, Beijing relented and received only 30 percent (900 square kilometres) of the disputed area. Although Kyrgyzstan received 70 percent, members of parliament initially refused to ratify the supplementary treaty.[48] A trilateral agreement also signed in August 1999 established the Chinese-Kazakh-Kyrgyz boundary intersection with "sacred" Khan Tengri Peak as the conjunction. Although this settlement was controversial, with some allegations that Kazakhstan and Kyrgyzstan had surrendered territory, no historical documents identified the peak with any specific country. Akayev described the issue as "one of the most sensitive issues" in Sino-Kyrgyz bilateral relations, and described the resolution of this "burden of the past" as "a truly history-making day."[49]

Opposition to ratification led to protests in January 2002, reportedly the worst political violence to date since Kyrgyzstan became independent. Several thousand people demonstrated against the new boundary and several dozen demonstrators were arrested in front of parliament by the Kyrgyz police. Nevertheless, Akayev pushed ratification through while opposition leaders complained that this violated proper procedures for ratification, which required a two-thirds majority.[50] A Kyrgyz Foreign Ministry official characterized the boundary question as a "burden inherited from the Soviet past" and criticized those who opposed the settlement as having "no idea of how complex and delicate an issue this is," rejecting the accusation that corrupt Kyrgyz officials received side payments from China for ceding territory. The official explained that "what was at stake was an 'area on which there was no agreement' or, in normal diplomatic parlance, a 'disputed area' ... that belonged to neither side. The question had remained unresolved for over 150 years, and it was now necessary to establish the line of the state border between the Kyrgyz Republic and the People's Republic of China."[51] After years of negotiations and work on the ground, the Sino-Kyrgyz border was fully demarcated by September 2004.[52]

Tajikistan

Civil war in Tajikistan delayed negotiations and Beijing did not push to reach an early compromise settlement.[53] China had consistently asserted that, in violation of the 1884 Sino-Russian Kashgar Boundary Treaty, Czarist Russia had occupied approximately 28,000 square kilometres of Chinese territory in the Pamir Mountains in 1892.[54] Negotiations eventually got under way in October 1997, and in August 1999 an agreement settled the boundary except for one complicated sector. The agreement divided disputed mountain passes equally in the Pamirs and the Karazak Pass region. A July 2002 agreement settled the intersection of the Kyrgyzstan-China-Tajikistan boundary, and a supplementary Sino-Tajik boundary agreement in May 2002 finalized the boundary. Even before the boundary settlement, however, Beijing and Dushanbe concluded numerous agreements, including one to open a road connecting the two countries to facilitate border trade.[55]

Negotiations with Tajikistan were more difficult due to Beijing's assertion that, despite the unequal treaties, Czarist Russia had still encroached further into China's territory. Also complicating a settlement was the secondary impact on Tajikistan's relations with its other neighbours. Tajik President Emomali Rakhmanov recognized this, saying: "We are facing the heavy task of solving ... the important border issues left by history." A Tajik newspaper made the concerns more explicit, writing that "the day may come when China will raise border problems and demand its so-called historical territories from Tajikistan, and then we shall also demand our historical lands back from our neighbours." Nevertheless, the paper also indicated a realistic approach and willingness to negotiate a settlement, saying that "the opportunity of gaining independence should not be lost because of border disputes."[56]

This boundary on the eastern slope of the "Pamir Knot," in the region of Gorno-Badakhshan, was isolated, with no modern roads suitable for commerce linking Tajikistan and China.[57] Beijing turned to Kazakhstan as a "strategic partner" to act as a "consultant" in the negotiations with Tajikistan.[58] In January 1996, progress toward an eventual settlement was symbolized by the exchange of topographic maps of the disputed areas.[59] Initial boundary negotiations held from 25 to 30 October 1997 resulted in "substantial and concrete achievements." An agreement delimiting the mountain passes was signed in August 1999, during President Rakhmanov's trip to China, and instruments of ratification were exchanged the following year, but the complex Pamir question prevented further progress.[60]

Tensions between China and the United States spiked on 7 May 1999, when US warplanes accidentally bombed China's embassy in Belgrade during the NATO air war in Kosovo. This heightened China's sense of vulnerability as relations with the United States deteriorated and US relations with the Central Eurasian states improved. Despite the absence of a final boundary settlement, Beijing pushed to enhance relations with Dushanbe, symbolized by the August 1999 agreement to open a border crossing and build a road through the 4,360-metre Kulma Pass connecting Khorog (Badakhshan) in Tajikistan with Tashkurgan and Kashgar in China. This was the first genuine and only road connecting the two countries; it was completed in August 2001 but not opened to regular traffic until May 2004. A joint statement indicated that "on the basis of this [agreement] and in accordance with acknowledged international practices, the two agree to continue negotiations on the borderline that has not been settled, in the spirit of equal consultations and mutual accommodations for an early and successful solution," and in the meantime "maintain the current situation along the border until a final solution is found."[61] An agreement in May 2002 resolved the historically complicated sector involving the territory in the Pamir region, including the disputed territory occupied by Czarist Russia. Closer relations between China and Tajikistan were signified by a Chinese military delegation's visit to Tajikistan that same month, and developing bilateral security cooperation through the Shanghai Cooperation Organization (formerly the Shanghai Five). These developments reflect Beijing's efforts to blunt further American or Russian penetration of the region.[62]

Tajikistan maintained an unyielding position on the Pamir region because of the proportionally large size of the disputed territory and the implication of any compromise for disputes with its other neighbours, while China continued to push its historical claims. Both sides expressed willingness to reach a settlement when Jiang Zemin was in Dushanbe in July 2000, and issued a joint statement that "on the basis of equality, mutual understanding and mutual accommodation, the two sides shall ... take flexible positions to seek solutions acceptable to both sides as soon as possible."[63]

The terrorist attacks on New York and Washington, DC, on 11 September 2001 set off a fundamental geopolitical change in the region. A *Dagong bao* editorial expressed Beijing's concerns over the change in the strategic situation: "The demolition of the original power balance in Central Asia ... [has made] Central Asia a region with a prominently unbalanced security mechanism ... We should attach enough importance and be vigilant to this possible variable in the international security situation that has an effect on China."[64] As a hedge against the dramatic increase in attention and aid that the United States and others focused on Tajikistan, China extended Dushanbe US$970 million in military aid in 2002. Even with increased multilateral security cooperation, Beijing pushed to settle the boundary with Tajikistan in order to ensure that the dispute would not be a wedge in the bilateral relationship, and Beijing made it clear that it was willing to make significant concessions in order to settle this one remaining (but largest) territorial dispute with its Eurasian neighbours.

The final sector ran several hundred kilometres from the Uzbel Pass to the Afghanistan-China border, and included the disputed 28,000 square kilometres in the Pamir region. An initial agreement was negotiated in December 2001 and the Supplementary Agreement on the China-Tajikistan Boundary was signed on 17 May 2002, completing the boundary settlement.[65] Russian ambassador Vitaliy Vorobyev, who headed the joint delegation of Russia, Kazakhstan, and Kyrgyzstan that assisted Tajikistan during negotiations, stated that the "border line, which has been fixed by China and Tajikistan, practically reiterates what has been existing before, with slight changes" but "no revolutionary shifts of the historically established border," only "certain adjustments acceptable to both sides." According to Beijing, this treaty represented the "final and complete solution of all the boundary issues with neighboring countries in Central Asia handed down by history."[66]

In the final settlement, China relinquished its historical claim and received a mere 1,000 square kilometres, approximately 3.5 percent of the disputed area. Addressing the "concession," a Tajik statement minimized the relinquished territory as "unpopulated areas lying high in the mountains," and stated that Tajikistan was "satisfied with the agreement on the disputed territories" because "these areas are of no great value to Tajikistan." Tajik Foreign Minister Hamrohon Zarifi characterized the settlement as a "strategically crucial development of relations with China." The director of Tajikistan's Centre for Strategic Studies, Shukhrob Sharipov, pointed out that "at first China insisted on the transfer of 28,500 sq. km., and in the end, we ceded 1,100. If we hadn't decided to transfer the land (at this time), we would not have been able to resist China's pressure."[67] On the other hand, Chinese dissidents expressed anger and accused Jiang Zemin of betraying China by relinquishing Chinese territory.[68] However, Beijing had, as in earlier cases, ceded disputed territory to ensure larger strategic interests.

The Strategic Context of the Boundary Settlements

The strategic context of these boundary settlements is important. Soon after the Central Eurasian states gained their independence, Beijing moved quickly to enhance security cooperation in the region. In April 1996, while meeting in Shanghai for discussions on the boundary, China, Russia, Kazakhstan, Kyrgyzstan, and Tajikistan established the "Shanghai Five," a multilateral security community for the region that evolved into the Shanghai Cooperation Organization in 2001.

Following the final settlement of the Kazakhstan boundary, President Jiang emphasized the larger security considerations, stating that the agreement was "an important contribution to regional stability."[69] Stressing the larger strategic context, he said that "mutual understanding and trust between the peoples of our two countries has grown deeper by the day. Based on this, the boundary questions were completely and thoroughly resolved." In his toast, Kazakhstan's president, Nursultan Nazarbayev, commented that the two countries had achieved a high level of economic, scientific, and cultural cooperation since the establishment of diplomatic relations six years earlier, but that "the agreement reached on this most complicated territory and boundary is still the most important accomplishment." He added that it was a "good foundation for realizing mutual prosperity and strengthening friendship."[70]

Despite heightened anti-Chinese sentiments among the Kyrgyz resulting from their government's recognition of some disputed areas as Chinese territory, China pushed forward with negotiations in other areas critical to its security, and the two sides concluded agreements to open new border crossings and construct a rail line linking the two countries.[71] After signing the boundary treaty in July 1996, the Chinese characterized it as "yet another important positive element ... in enhancing regional peace and stability."[72] And although the Sino-Tajik boundary was the most complicated one and settlement was delayed by domestic politics in Tajikistan, even before the settlement Beijing pushed to conclude numerous agreements, including one to open a road connecting China and Tajikistan to facilitate border trade.[73]

As boundary issues were resolved, strategic relations improved, symbolized by multilateral agreements such as the Treaty on Deepening Military Trust in Border Regions and the organization of the "Shanghai Five" in April 1996, an agreement on mutual reduction of military forces in the border area in 1997, and the establishment of the Shanghai Cooperation Organization for mutual security in 2001, with Beijing as the driving force behind the organization.[74] Closer security cooperation was symbolized by the joint military exercises China held with Kyrgyzstan in 2002, the first ever for China and one of its new neighbours, and the multilateral military exercises held with Russia, Kazakhstan, Kyrgyzstan, and Tajikistan the following year. These developments underscore China's strategic calculations behind the early push to settle boundaries that had been disputed with Russia for the past century.

These agreements with China's Central Eurasian neighbours were important steps in China's grand strategy to shore up its boundaries and enhance security cooperation with countries along its western flank. Concerned about the strategic vacuum left by the collapse of the Soviet Union in 1991, Beijing moved quickly to settle its boundary disputes in order to facilitate closer relations with these important neighbours. According to a Tajik newspaper, *Leninabadskaya Pravda*, "Thus, China began hastily solving the problems of disputed sections with the Central Asian states of the CIS in order to strengthen its positions there."[75]

Conclusions

Beijing moved quickly to conclude a range of agreements with the newly independent Central Eurasian states as a hedge against growing US influence in the region or the possibility that Russia might try to reassert its power; to blunt an attempt by Turkey to re-establish its historical links to the region; to circumvent the West's efforts to exclude China from a larger economic role in the region; and to prevent foreign-inspired radical Islamic movements from fostering ethnic unrest that could destabilize Xinjiang. As one French scholar concluded: "Chinese diplomacy has focused on three objectives: to safeguard stability along the frontiers and in the hinterland ... to expand its sphere of influence in the Central Asian region, and to find new markets for Chinese products."[76] This has been accomplished by settling boundary questions "left over from history," concluding military agreements to dampen concerns about China's ambitions in the region, and developing economic relationships that tie Eurasia to China and lessen its dependence on Russia and Europe.

These boundary settlements should be understood in this larger strategic context. As with other boundary disputes and settlements, China has behaved very pragmatically in seeking to settle boundary problems that were primarily the legacy of the "Great Game" of empires. Among Central Eurasians, there was apprehension that this would not be the case. The former Kazakh ambassador to China, Murat Auezov, opined: "As a historian I'm telling you that 19th Century China, 20th Century China, and 21st Century China are three different Chinas. But what unites them is the desire to expand their territories."[77] Many assumed that the outstanding boundary issues that China and the Soviet Union had failed to settle would continue to plague China's relations with its newly independent neighbours and even erupt into military conflict. Wondering whether China would continue to pursue a policy of pragmatism in the 1990s, one scholar argued that "there is some potential within the region for the occurrence of events that would cause Beijing to deviate from this path" because there are a "range of issues on which the Chinese adamantly refuse to compromise," and "In no case would the probability of losing trade and other advantages preclude a forceful response."[78] Another scholar argued that "more ominously for Central Asia [is] Beijing's willingness to use force as an instrument of foreign policy ... The Chinese military shows no signs of military adventurism in areas outside what it considers legitimate Chinese territory. But what might its response be if opportunity arose to take back those areas lost to Russia during the 19th century?"[79]

Despite the Eurasians' concerns and speculation by scholars, China proved to be pragmatic and subordinated territorial disputes to larger strategic and economic concerns, as it had done in the 1960s and 1970s. In no earlier disputes did China insist on the return of territory seen as unjustly taken from China by unequal treaties. In fact, the unequal treaties were the basis for new treaties that correspond to the "historical and customary" boundaries established in the nineteenth century. The three Central Eurasian cases demonstrate again that China will compromise, making boundary and territorial settlements possible in order to realize more fundamental strategic and economic interests.

Popular resentment of the boundary resolutions continues among Central Eurasians, who remain anxious regarding Beijing's larger territorial ambitions and suspicious of a possible hidden agenda on the part of China.[80] Such apprehensions are fuelled by China's rapidly growing economic and cultural power in the region as its largest trading partner. Conflict over cross-border water resources continues, and development of agricultural lands by Chinese farmers triggers local opposition. In 2004, for example, Chinese farmers leased seven thousand hectares across the border in Kazakhstan, and in 2009 rented an additional one million hectares of farmland. A similar pattern occurred in Tajikistan. A 2011 agreement granted Chinese farmers control over approximately two thousand hectares for agriculture operations, and China has invested over $200 million on roads connecting China and Tajikistan. These developments fuel misgivings over China's growing influence in the region.

12 The South China Sea Territorial Disputes

The South China Sea is the geostrategic heart of Southeast Asia. Controlled by outlets in the north through the Luzon Strait and Taiwan Strait and in the south through the narrow Strait of Malacca and Singapore Strait, it is the primary seaway through which vital natural resources and merchandise are shipped to and from Southeast Asian states, China, Japan, and Korea.[1] The disputed territories involve hundreds of uninhabitable small islets, coral atolls, reefs, shoals, and submerged rocks scattered across the South China Sea that are included in four main groups of islands. China's total maritime claim encompasses approximately 3.5 million square kilometres.[2]

China and Vietnam are the major players in the South China Sea disputes, but these disputes are not just a Sino-Vietnamese issue. It is important to distinguish two separate issues: the Sino-Vietnamese dispute over the Paracel Islands *(Xisha)*, about 150 miles southwest of Hainan Island, and the multilateral dispute over the Spratly Islands *(Nansha)*. The issue of sovereignty over the Spratlys is more complex because it involves claims by the People's Republic of China, Vietnam, the Philippines, Malaysia, and Brunei, with the added complication of claims by the Republic of China on Taiwan (ROC).[3] China (and Taiwan) and Vietnam claim all islands, reefs, rocks, and other features in the Spratly archipelago and Macclesfield Bank *(Zhongsha)* group. China's dispute with the Philippines centres on various islands in the Spratlys known to Filipinos as "Kalayaan" (Freedomland) and islands in the Macclesfield Bank group. The dispute with Malaysia is over seven outcroppings known as James Shoal *(Zengmu Ansha)* off the coast of Borneo, which Malaysia claims falls within its continental shelf boundary and is the southernmost South China Sea feature claimed by China. The conflict with Brunei involves the Louisa Reef *(Nantong Jiao)*, located west of Brunei within its claimed exclusive economic zone. Taiwan controls the Pratas Islands *(Dongsha)*, which are not disputed, as well as Itu Aba *(Taiping Dao)*, the largest island in the Spratly group (see Map 17).

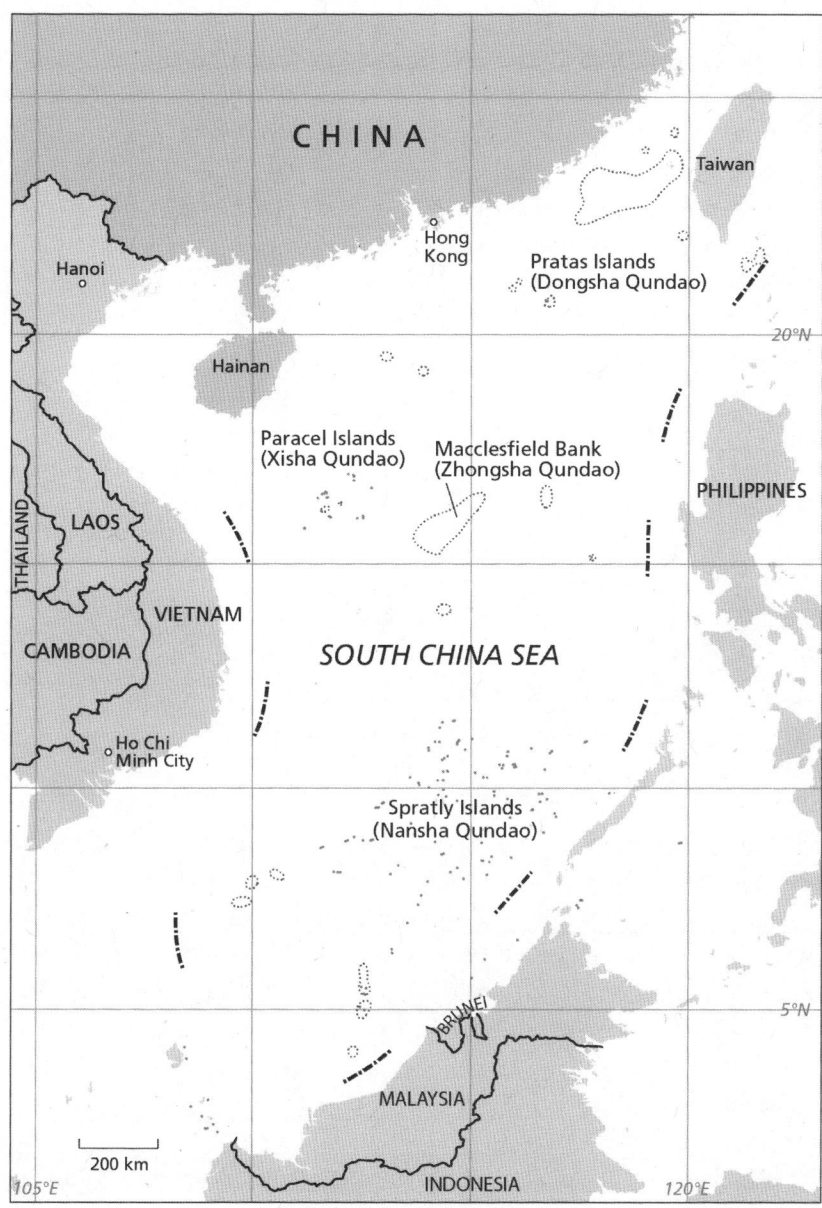

Map 17 South China Sea

The 1982 United Nations Convention on the Law of the Sea (UNCLOS) complicated the South China Sea disputes by prescribing rights that exacerbated the scramble by the littoral states to assert claims to the continental shelf and establish special economic zones. The prospect of oil and natural gas reserves and marine life resources around the islands raised the economic stakes and compounded the difficulty in finding a resolution. Although natural resources are an important factor, strategic considerations also are at the heart of the dispute.[4]

China Asserts Control

In August 1951, Premier Zhou Enlai declared the sovereignty of the People's Republic of China over the South China Sea, reflecting previous claims by the Republic of China.[5] Even before this declaration, China had occupied Woody Island *(Yongxing Dao)* in the Paracel group following the evacuation of Nationalist troops in 1950. Conflict between the PRC and South Vietnam over the Paracels flared up occasionally in subsequent years, usually over fishing boats working in the area. Finally, on 19 January 1974, Chinese forces occupied the remaining islands in the Paracel group held by the collapsing South Vietnamese regime. Hanoi did not publicly protest the action, and in fact at the time acknowledged China's claim to sovereignty over the many island groups in the South China Sea.[6] In 1950, China also occupied White Dragon Tail Island *(Bailongwei)*, located in the Gulf of Tonkin, which had been held by Nationalist troops. In 1957, however, apparently responding to protests from Hanoi, Mao ordered the transfer of this island to North Vietnam in order to eliminate it as an irritant in Sino-Vietnamese relations in the face of what he perceived as external threats to China.[7]

After the fall of South Vietnam in 1975, Hanoi began to assert claims over the Paracels and Spratlys. In April, it took possession of six islets that had been held by the Saigon regime. Beijing responded in 1976, asserting that all of the Spratly Islands

have always been part of China's territory ... The Government of the People's Republic of China has time and again declared that China has indisputable sovereignty over these islands and their adjacent sea areas ... Any foreign country's armed invasion and occupation of any of the Nansha [Spratly] Islands ... constitute encroachment on China's territorial integrity and sovereignty and are impermissible. Any foreign country's claim to sovereignty over any of the Nansha Islands is illegal and null and void.[8]

On 12 May 1977, the Foreign Ministry of Vietnam declared that Vietnam's territorial waters included the Paracel and Spratly groups, and Hanoi declared a two-hundred-mile exclusive economic zone (EEZ).[9] Beijing reacted swiftly. In a secret meeting with Vietnamese Premier Pham Van Dong in June, Chinese Vice Premier Li Xiannian challenged Vietnam's claim, pointing out that Vietnam had supported China's claims as early as 1958 and as recently as 1974. Dong rationalized Vietnam's previous position by arguing that it was a "matter of necessity" to support China's claims during the war because of the need to "place resistance to United States imperialism above everything else." Vietnam's previous position should therefore be interpreted in the "context of the historical circumstances of the time."[10] Li argued that "war could not justify a different interpretation," and furthermore, "there was no war going on in Vietnam when on September 14, 1958 Pham Van Dong ... acknowledged in his note to Premier Zhou Enlai that the Xisha and Nansha Islands are Chinese territory."[11]

By late 1977, China had begun openly accusing Hanoi of making "unreasonable claims." Li stated that from China's perspective, because of Hanoi's actions, "the Nansha and Xisha Islands, over which there never was any issue, have now become a major subject of dispute in Sino-Vietnamese relations."[12] On 26 December 1978, the Chinese Foreign Ministry issued a formal statement asserting sovereignty over the islands of the South China Sea and warned that "invasion or occupation" of any of the islands would "constitute encroachments on China's territorial integrity and sovereignty."[13] Again, on 30 January 1980, the *People's Daily* published a Foreign Ministry statement reiterating China's historical claim to the islands of the South China Sea.[14]

All of the other claimants, including Taiwan, had occupied islands in the Spratly archipelago before the PRC gained a foothold in 1988 at the expense of Vietnam. An estimated twenty-one islets, shoals, and reefs were already occupied by other claimants before Beijing wrested control of the six islets from Hanoi.

Competing Claims

China's official position is that "China possesses indisputable sovereignty over the islands in the South China Sea [within the nine-dash line] and the adjacent waters, and it enjoys sovereign rights and jurisdiction over the relevant waters as well as the seabed and subsoil thereof."[15] China maintains that its sovereignty dates to ancient times, and that in modern times these "historical claims" were clearly asserted in 1935 when the Nationalist government's China Map Verification Committee declared sovereignty over 132 islands, reefs, and shoals in the South China Sea; in addition, the committee published a map in 1947 that included a U-shaped line (eleven-dash line) encompassing the entire South China Sea.[16] Although the PRC maps retain the U-shaped line (dropping two dashes in the Gulf of Tonkin), this should be considered a "customary line" *(xiguan xian)* that was initially drawn without careful consideration and no clear understanding of its legal significance (see Map 18). It does not indicate that Beijing claims the entire South China Sea, but only the features within the nine-dash line.[17]

After decades of being incapable of physically asserting its claims, Beijing felt compelled to use "defensive" military force to affirm its "legitimate territorial entitlement," which was denied by other states through their occupation of "China's territory." Scholar Chen Jie expressed Chinese sentiments thus: "Initially taking advantage of China's turbulent domestic policies and its preoccupation with superpower threats, regional countries have occupied China's islands and reefs, carved up its sea areas, and looted its marine resources." Beijing does not view establishing a foothold in the South China Sea as "constituting territorial gains but minimizing territorial losses." A more unvarnished Chinese description characterized the situation as "a free-for-all grab-what-you-can in the South China Sea" before Beijing was able to assert itself.[18]

Following independence in 1946, Manila claimed some of the Spratlys (which the 1898 Treaty of Paris did not recognize as Filipino territory). Japan had occupied some of these islands during the Second World War, and Manila based its legal claim on the assumption that Japan enjoyed sovereignty over the islands and had abandoned them after the war, leaving them up for grabs. But Tokyo "renounced all right, title, and claim" to the Spratlys and the Paracels in the Sino-Japanese Peace Treaty (Treaty of Taipei) signed by Japan and the Republic of China in 1952, implying recognition of the Chinese claim. Manila has employed various means, such as naval inspection tours and diplomatic notes, to assert ownership. Decades after making its claim, the Philippines began actively asserting control over some islets. In 1971, a brief conflict with ROC forces occurred when Philippine troops attempted to land on Itu Aba Island *(Taiping Dao)* but were repelled. In 1974, however, the Philippine navy took control of five islands and a 1978 presidential decree declared the "Kalayaan Islands" an integral part of the Philippines and strategically important for national defence.

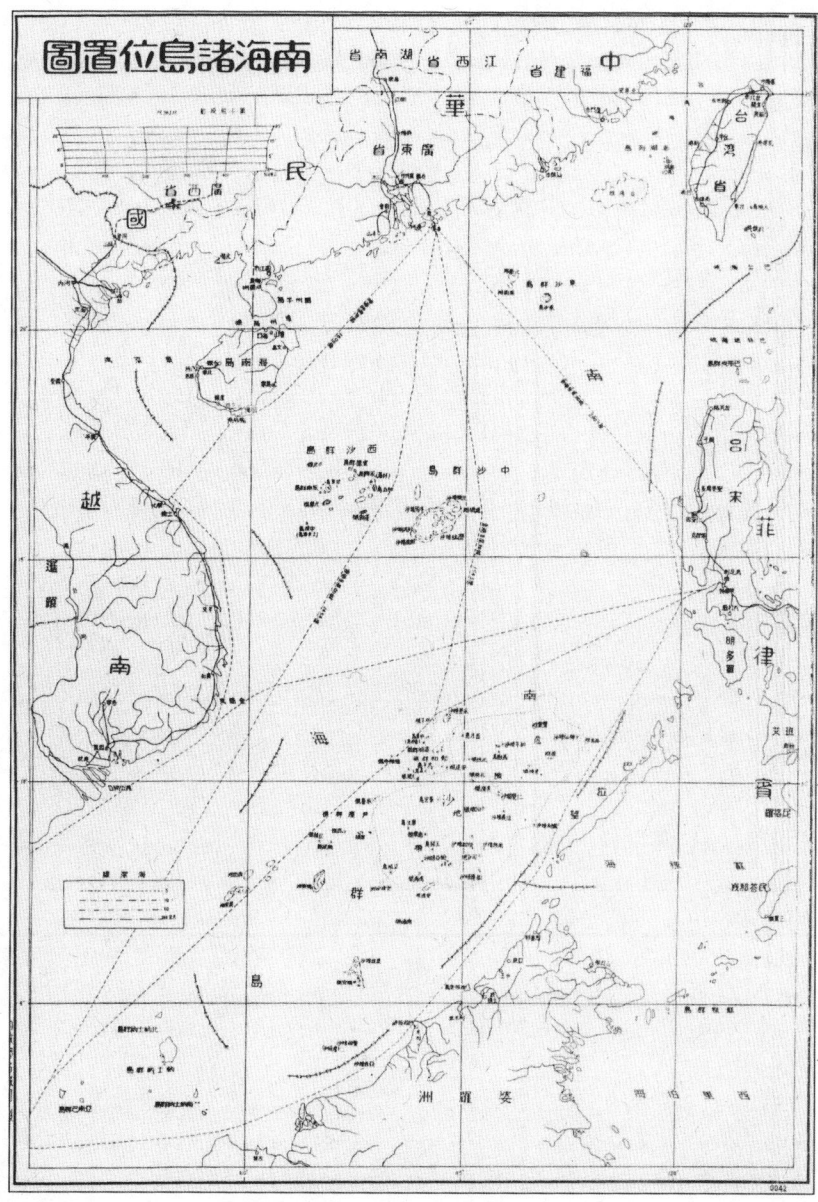

Map 18 South China Sea 1947 map

In late 1994, the PRC began construction on Mischief Reef *(Meiji Jiao)*, which provoked tension with Manila when it was discovered in early 1995. Beijing claimed that the construction was to provide refuge for fishermen and offered to share the facilities with Filipino fishermen, but Manila rejected the offer, reasserting its claim to the reef. For several months, tit-for-tat actions occurred, with Chinese detaining Filipino fishermen near Mischief Reef and the Philippine navy detaining five Chinese fishing boats and arresting sixty-two Chinese fishermen for "illegal entry" and "poaching." Manila strengthened its forces by sending additional patrol boats, and increased air surveillance by fighter interceptors in the area. In late February 1995, Philippines President Fidel Ramos declared: "I will not allow any slackening in our defense capabilities ... If there be any intruders into our territory or exclusive economic zone, we shall ask them to depart and leave us in peace." After negotiations in Beijing in March 1995 and in Manila in August, the two governments issued a joint statement, agreeing to refrain from "provocative actions" and to settle disputes "in accordance with the recognized principles of international law and the UN Convention on the Law of the Sea."[19]

In 1998, Manila complained when China reinforced its facilities on the reef, and Beijing accused Manila of making irresponsible statements by claiming the island as Philippine territory. On the sidelines of the November 1998 Asia Pacific Economic Cooperation (APEC) summit, however, Jiang Zemin and President Joseph Estrada endorsed a proposal to establish an expert group and explore joint use of the disputed territory.[20] In mid-1999, a second dispute erupted over an island in the Pratas *(Dongsha)* group (actually occupied by Taiwan), and in 2012 a dispute erupted over Scarborough Shoal *(Huangyen Dao)* located between the Macclesfield Bank and the Philippine island of Luzon, when the Philippine navy confronted Chinese fishing boats.[21]

Malaysia asserted a claim to the continental shelf in 1979 and established an exclusive economic zone adjacent to Borneo in 1980. As a result, Kuala Lumpur claims several islands in the Spratly group and actually occupies three atolls included in James Shoal *(Zengmu Ansha)*. This contrasts with the claims of others, which are all premised on prior occupation or discovery. Because Malaysia's claim is historically the weakest, Kuala Lumpur is reluctant to accept any third-party involvement in settling the dispute, and "Malaysia does not intend to be a mere bystander in the scramble for territorial possessions in the South China Sea."[22] In March 1995, Malaysian patrol boats opened fire on a Chinese trawler off the coast of Sarawak, injuring several Chinese fishermen. Kuala Lumpur asserted that "we had to stop them. They were trying to run into regional waters."[23] While Kuala Lumpur has vigorously asserted its claims, it has generally avoided any confrontation with China and did not attempt to prevent the Chinese navy from conducting exercises around James Shoal in January 2014 involving China's newly launched aircraft carrier.[24] On the other hand, Malaysia has extracted more resources with its deep-water developments in the South China Sea than other claimants. Brunei's involvement in the dispute stems from its claim over the continental shelf off its coast, which includes the Louisa Reef.

Strategic Roots of the South China Sea Disputes

Although the South China Sea territorial disputes have a long history, their re-emergence in the mid-1970s was symptomatic of the underlying tensions rooted in regional competition, alliance politics, and bilateral issues associated with the end of the Vietnam War, such as Sino-American rapprochement and increasing discord in Sino-Vietnamese relations. As the latter deteriorated rapidly in the mid-1970s, Beijing became more assertive over territorial issues in the South China Sea.

Throughout the Cold War, the rivalry between the United States and the Soviet Union in Southeast Asia was a stabilizing influence on the balance of power in the region. As this balance began to shift in the 1980s, with Vietnam bogged down in Cambodia and suffering international isolation, and Mikhail Gorbachev reducing Moscow's support of Hanoi, China began actively asserting its claim to islands in the South China Sea. At the same time, however, in order to allay the fears of Southeast Asian nations, Beijing also indicated its willingness to compromise. In 1984, even before China physically controlled any islands in the Spratly archipelago, Deng Xiaoping proposed setting aside the question of sovereignty *(butan zhuquan)* while pursuing joint development and "seeking a new road to a resolution."[25] Spending New Year's Day 1986 with troops stationed on the Paracel Islands, Chinese Communist Party General Secretary Hu Yaobang said that "we do not want even one inch of another country's territory, but we will not allow another country to occupy one inch of our great motherland."[26] In late 1987, China began regular patrols of the Spratly Islands and asserted control over disputed waters. The Chinese Foreign Ministry issued a statement warning Hanoi that if Vietnam interfered with these patrols, it would be held responsible for the consequences. On 14 March 1988, following a skirmish with

Vietnamese forces, China wrested control of several islets in the western Spratlys from Hanoi, the first islands in the Spratly group to be held by Beijing. China has used its military to block Vietnam's oil exploration but has held "friendly consultations" with Hanoi, holding out the possibility of shelving the sovereignty dispute and jointly developing the region's resources.[27]

With the end of the Cold War, Southeast Asian nations experienced new concerns. Many began to fear that Beijing intended to establish the South China Sea as a "Chinese lake." Domination of the South China Sea "heartland" would give the Chinese great political, economic, and military clout over the "rim land" states. Such an eventuality had never been considered possible until the Russian navy, with facilities in Vietnam, and the US Navy, based in the Philippines, withdrew from the region after the Cold War and the Chinese navy began developing the capability to project force far beyond China's coastal waters. China's emergence as the dominant regional military power caused insecurity in the region. No combination of Southeast Asian nations can defeat the Chinese military, which has embarked on a significant modernization drive and reoriented its naval forces to fight short and intense conflicts over disputed territory and distant islands in the South China Sea. In response, since 2010 the United States has strengthened its naval presence in the region and tightened cooperation, especially with Vietnam and the Philippines. In July 2010, Secretary of State Hillary Clinton asserted that the United States "has a national interest" in the region; a year later she stated that "the United States is concerned that recent incidents in the South China Sea threaten the peace and stability" and "oppose the threat or use of force by any claimant in the South China Sea to advance its claims or interfere with legitimate economic activity."[28]

Future Conflict and Cooperation

The South China Sea disputes have received renewed attention in recent years because they are now seen as the most likely crucible of regional conflict and cooperation. During the 1970s and 1980s, any desire to resolve the disputes was complicated by the Indochina conflicts. Opposition to Vietnam's occupation of Cambodia provided common ground for China and the Association of Southeast Asian Nations (ASEAN), but with the settlement of the Cambodian issue in 1991, regional attention turned to territorial disputes and tensions arose between China and ASEAN. Vietnam became a member of ASEAN in 1995, further complicating matters. Although efforts to seek a resolution have gradually gained momentum, and a resolution may be possible in the future because of the much-improved political atmosphere in the region, incidents such as the flare-ups between China and Vietnam in May 2011 and between China and the Philippines in April 2012 make guarded optimism sensible. A negotiated settlement of the disputes is now even more important because of the lack of a security regime in Southeast Asia. China and the Southeast Asian states have all grown more self-confident as their national strength and nationalism have increased. This change in the power equation could cause conflict given the lack of a regional security regime; at the same time, however, it could give the different countries the self-confidence to seek a negotiated settlement. In any case, a settlement will require difficult multilateral negotiations and mutual accommodation. China prefers a bilateral approach to each dispute, but Beijing has warmed to the idea of multilateral cooperation.

The approach Beijing has adopted toward the South China Sea disputes follows the same tack taken in earlier cases. Over the course of this particular dispute, China has used military force to occupy disputed territory and has, since 1991, stationed naval forces on Woody Island *(Yongxing Dao)*, the largest island in the Paracel group, where it has built a 2,600-metre runway.[29] A government publication, *Military Secrets*, declared that "it is a top priority for China to have air support for the possible battle in the Spratly Islands."[30] Beijing has deployed an aircraft carrier and other assets that enable it to project force into the region.

Beijing initially resisted formal negotiations, believing that these might in fact heighten tensions in the region. At the same time, however, it showed a willingness to seek a peaceful settlement and participated in conferences that have explored alternative solutions, including joint development of the region's natural resources. A step in this direction came in August 1990, when Premier Li Peng again raised the possibility of joint exploitation of South China Sea resources, but only if the sovereignty issue was shelved. In Singapore, he stated that "China is ready to join efforts ... to develop [the Spratly] islands, while putting aside for the time being the question of sovereignty." During a five-nation Southeast Asian tour in 1993, National People's Congress (NPC) Standing Committee chair Qiao Shi reiterated this general position, and in his report to the NPC, he recommended shelving the dispute *(gezhi zhengyi)* and did not mention the contention over sovereignty *(zhuquan zhengyi)*.[31] In May 1994, Li Peng told Malaysian Prime Minister Mahathir Mohamad that "we will discuss the [Spratlys] by putting aside disputes and seeking joint exploration as proposed by Chinese leader Deng Xiaoping [in 1984]." Following Jiang Zemin's visit to Vietnam in late 1994, Beijing and Hanoi reached an agreement to establish an expert group to discuss the South China Sea dispute.[32] However, China is holding fast to its sovereignty claim and continues to develop its military capabilities, and in June 2012, it established Sansha as a prefecture-level city in the Paracel Islands group to administer all of the islands of the South China Sea. In the words of an official Chinese publication, the endgame is to engage in some type of cooperative development, but shelving the question of sovereignty and pursuing joint development of the region's resources "would be cosmetic without a stronger navy."[33]

China's military buildup in the South China Sea does not necessarily suggest that Beijing will use force to occupy more islands, but rather that Beijing is seeking to maintain the status quo by enhancing its military presence, and to increase its leverage in future negotiations. China's behaviour in the South China Sea case is similar to that in earlier cases, inasmuch as China shows no real willingness to move quickly to settle the dispute because strategic concerns are not sufficiently acute at this time. This mirrors the pattern followed in the unsettled dispute with Japan over the Senkaku/Diaoyu Islands; Beijing stridently asserted an unwillingness to negotiate with Japan but, as strategic imperatives changed, quickly sought a compromise settlement. Given the established pattern in earlier cases, we can assume with some confidence that events will unfold in a similar way in the South China Sea, and that progress toward a settlement will take place when larger strategic concerns motivate Beijing to adopt a pragmatic policy and a more flexible approach.

China's relations with Southeast Asian countries improved rapidly in the early 1990s. However, the territorial disputes remain a significant cause of concern and are a major foreign policy challenge for China, which needs to reassure its Southeast Asian neighbours that it will work to resolve the disputes peacefully. Given China's desire to establish itself as a regional leader, it is unlikely that Beijing will block a settlement if the other parties are all willing to compromise or participate in a joint development agreement while putting off settlement of the sovereignty question. A rationale for this was laid out in an influential Chinese policy journal in 1995. The author argued that because of the possibility of armed conflict if "obstinate exploration and development activity" is undertaken unilaterally, commercial development is no longer viable. Therefore, joint development is in China's interest because it will be "compensated by greater political and economic benefit" with improved relations between China and the ASEAN states. From this perspective, "joint development is not a purely economic activity but a serious political struggle." By "uphold[ing] the dignity of ... national sovereignty, but also partly yield[ing] a portion of sovereignty rights ... this can prevent disputes from developing to extremes and so is advantageous to national stability and relations between neighboring countries."[34]

Indonesia stepped forward as an honest broker and, beginning in 1990, hosted a series of "Workshops on Managing Potential Conflicts in the South China Sea." China insisted that the meetings be limited to an "exchange of views among scholars" and not be official negotiations. At the Bandung workshop held in July 1991, Indonesia suggested including Japan, the United States, and Russia, but Beijing opposed the inclusion of outside powers, arguing that it would only complicate the situation.[35] This position has not changed, and Beijing reacted strongly to US expressions of concern about freedom of navigation in the South China Sea and encouragement of a multilateral resolution of the disputes. In response to Secretary of State Hillary Clinton's July 2010 statement that the United States had a "national interest in ... the South China Sea," China asserted that this "seemingly impartial talk was actually an attack on China."[36]

At the 1991 workshop, all claimants agreed to halt independent development and renounced the use of force to settle the disputes. In February 1992, however, before the third workshop, which was to be held in June, the National People's Congress promulgated a "Law of the People's Republic of China on the Territorial Sea and Contiguous Zone" that asserted China's claims to the Dongsha (Pratas) Islands, the Xisha (Paracel) Islands, the Zhongsha (Macclesfield Bank) Islands and the Nansha (Spratly) Islands, and authorized the use of military force to prevent other states from occupying the islands. A Malaysian scholar who directed strategic and security studies at a Malaysian university responded to Beijing's move thus: "Don't forget, they have a track record of using force in that part of the world."[37] Beijing rejected any criticism that this move demonstrated a hardening of China's position or complicated the issue and increased tensions in the area, but argued that it instead "clarified" China's position through domestic legislation. China also dismissed arguments that this new legislation was directly linked to Beijing's future approach toward settling territorial disputes, asserting that it was simply a clear statement of China's claims and did not alter China's willingness to "shelve the dispute" *(gezhi zhengyi)* and move forward with joint development negotiations.[38] ASEAN states were not reassured. B.A. Hamzah, then assistant director of the Malaysian Institute of Strategic and International Studies, opined: "China's intentions in the South China Sea are very much more than settling old scores with Vietnam. Beijing's recent actions strongly suggest that its ultimate aim is to replace the US and Russia in the region."[39]

In response, the ASEAN states issued their "Declaration on the South China Sea" on 22 July 1992. The declaration called for "all parties concerned to exercise restraint with a view to creating a positive climate for the eventual resolution of all disputes." It emphasized the importance of efforts to "resolve all sovereignty and jurisdictional issues pertaining to the South China Sea by peaceful means, without resort to force." ASEAN also urged cooperation for maritime safety, search and rescue, environmental protection, and combating piracy and drug trafficking. Beijing did not sign the declaration and reiterated its position that it was not prepared to enter formal negotiations over the conflicting claims.[40]

Beijing has taken other controversial steps to enhance its claims. In May 1993, it signed a contract with an American company to explore for oil and gas and pledged the use of its navy to protect the company. In July 1993, it awarded a second contract to an American company to cooperate in the development of South China Sea oil fields.[41] At the time, despite its commitment not to take unilateral action, China felt it could not stand idly by while Vietnam moved forward to develop oil resources in disputed areas.[42] China's unilateral moves were condemned by the other parties to the dispute, and other states began to assert their claims more aggressively.[43] Also in May 1993, Philippine President Fidel Ramos ordered the expansion of military facilities on the "Kalayaan Islands" to enable civilian and military planes to use the runway. China responded by building facilities for "protecting the lives and labor of Chinese Fishermen," which Ramos claimed were sophisticated military structures. Beijing made it clear that it believed the Philippines had "ulterior motives" in protesting Beijing's actions, which it said were "in accordance with international law."[44] Ramos contended that "no country should dominate the Spratly group ... Internationally recognized and guaranteed sea lanes cut across the area, making it to everyone's interest that no single power should exercise hegemony over the Spratlys."[45] The Southeast Asian states also took measures to undercut the legitimacy of China's claims; ASEAN called for a name change of the South China Sea to eliminate "any connotation of Chinese ownership over that body of water."[46]

China's Strategic Concerns and the South China Sea Disputes

China's approach toward the South China Sea disputes is determined by larger strategic considerations. For example, after Manila's attempt to occupy islands in the Spratlys in 1971, Beijing responded:

> The Nansha Islands and the Hsisha [Xisha] Islands have always been China's territory. The People's Republic of China has indisputable sovereignty over these islands and absolutely allows no country to encroach upon this sovereignty right under whatever pretext and in whatever form. The Philippine government must immediately stop its encroachment upon China's territory and withdraw all its personnel from the Nansha Islands.[47]

In the mid-1970s, however, as the strategic environment changed following the US exit from Vietnam and the rise in Soviet influence in the region, Beijing changed its approach in order to facilitate rapprochement with the Philippines. Although Manila had by then actually occupied several islands claimed by China, diplomatic relations with the Philippines were established in June 1975. When President Ferdinand Marcos travelled to Beijing for this purpose, the dispute over the islands was sidestepped and, as with Sino-Japanese rapprochement several years earlier, the sovereignty issue was not allowed to interfere with a more important strategic objective – establishing a united front with Southeast Asian nations in the face of the growing Soviet-Vietnamese alliance; the communiqué included the standard "anti-hegemony" clause. This approach reflected Beijing's perception of the growing importance of the ASEAN states (of which Vietnam was not yet a member) in the regional balance of power. This shift illustrates Beijing's willingness to downplay territorial disputes in order to improve political relations in response to a changing strategic environment.

During the late 1970s and 1980s, China's approach to the dispute with Malaysia followed a pattern similar to that with the Philippines. After Malaysia claimed several islands in the Spratlys in 1979, Beijing's response was very low-key and was sent through diplomatic channels. No public reference to the Sino-Malaysian dispute was made until 1983, and even then it was made indirectly, couched in a general statement of China's claim to all of the Spratly Islands.[48]

In contrast, when Vietnamese leader Le Duan went to Beijing in September 1975, China asserted that its claim was "indisputable" and that sovereignty was "nonnegotiable."[49] From the late 1970s to the early 1990s, China adopted a very inflexible approach toward Vietnam on the South China Sea disputes, but with the end of the Soviet-Vietnamese alliance, Beijing reestablished relations with Hanoi in 1991, softened its rhetoric, and adopted a policy promoting cooperation in the South China Sea by establishing an expert group.

However, despite its softer rhetoric, Beijing remained vigilant and this did heighten ASEAN fears of China.[50] For example, in July 1994 tensions spiked when Vietnam began drilling in an area 280 miles off its southern coast. China dispatched warships to blockade the area and protested that Vietnamese drilling activities seriously "encroached upon China's sovereignty and maritime interests."[51] The following year, the dispute with the Philippines over Mischief Reef *(Meiji Jiao)* flared up. Manila viewed China's occupation of Mischief Reef in early 1995 as another step in Beijing's "quiet but ... relentless advance into the South China Sea."[52] ASEAN states protested China's actions and were disturbed by Beijing's disregard for the 1992 ASEAN Declaration on the South China Sea, which called on disputants to exercise self-restraint and eschew the use of force when settling territorial claims. China's vigilance is not unlike the behaviour of the other disputants, however, and does not necessarily foreshadow aggressive action to assert control over all of the South China Sea. Philippine Chief of Staff General Angelo Reyes considered China's actions in the Spratlys "very, very, measured," but warned that if Beijing "goes overboard and fiercely and aggressively asserts its claim over disputed areas, there will be a backlash."[53]

By the late 1990s, all islets large enough to sustain some kind of permanent military presence were occupied, thus creating a stalemate unless one state was willing and able to challenge another one over a particular islet. Given China's naval capabilities, it probably could dislodge other states from the various islands but has not done so; this is at least an indication that China is exercising self-restraint and is willing to negotiate joint development of the resources of the South China Sea.

Following the Established Pattern
The South China Sea disputes differ from earlier territorial disputes and settlements in which China has been involved because of their multilateral nature; all the others were bilateral. This does complicate things greatly, but China's general behaviour follows the common pattern in its approach to territorial and boundary disputes.

Like other territorial disputes, this dispute is complicated by the "Chinese national psyche," which believes that the South China Sea has been part of the "motherland's territory since ancient times."[54] Painstaking efforts are made to uncover archaeological evidence and document early historical accounts of Chinese expeditions to the islands to substantiate China's historical claims.[55] China bases its claim to sovereignty on prior discovery during the pre-modern era. In other territorial disputes in the 1950s and 1960s, similar historical arguments were advanced by China, causing a great deal of alarm among its neighbours over Chinese revanchist claims. One major difference is that the South China Sea cases have no legacy of "unequal treaties." Their economic significance lies in the resource potential of the South China Sea, and concerns over freedom of navigation are a complicating factor. The vital sea lanes of communication running through the South China Sea make it an "umbilical cord" that is vital to the economic survival of other Asian nations and US allies in the region.

Beijing's more assertive policy of physically occupying islands in the South China Sea was a response to the dramatically reduced US presence and the waning Soviet influence in Southeast Asia; Vietnam's occupation of Cambodia was also an important factor. This created a situation in which Beijing could physically assert its claims without too much concern that it would provoke direct conflict with the United States or other powers in the region; in other words, the counterbalancing effect of the Soviet Union and United States in the 1970s and 1980s had diminished, and Beijing could act more confidently. Even before the end of the Cold War, the Chinese move against the Paracels in 1974 reflected the initial shift in the regional balance of power, and the confrontation with Vietnam in 1988 and face-off with the Philippines over Mischief Reef in 1995 showed the impact of the ongoing changes in the region on Beijing's behaviour. The US pivot to Asia, including the assertion of national interests in the South China Sea and rhetorical support for allies and friends against China beginning in 2010 has again changed the strategic context of the disputes.

Beijing understands that a more aggressive policy will alienate Southeast Asian nations if they perceive that China is seeking hegemony in the region, and this would only aggravate China's security concerns.[56] The US rebalancing toward Asia is a clear sign that China's more assertive policy has already provoked a strategic response by the United States. Still, although Beijing has become more assertive, it has proven to be pragmatic and sensitive to the response of other states, and has demonstrated its willingness to cooperate in seeking a resolution of the disputes. Likewise, Beijing's military buildup and more assertive behaviour does not necessarily suggest a shift from the conciliatory approach it had adopted in earlier territorial settlements. Although its occupation of South China Sea islets has alarmed many, one Chinese scholar argues that China was simply taking measures to "stay in the game" because, in Beijing's eyes, "initially taking advantage of China's ... preoccupation with superpower threats, regional countries have occupied China's islands and reefs, carved up its sea areas, and looted its marine resources." Beijing's "occupation of an increasing number of islands and reefs in the archipelago" should not be viewed as "constituting territorial gains but minimizing territorial losses."[57]

The pattern Beijing established in earlier settlements is unfolding in the South China Sea. After adopting a very defiant position throughout the 1970s and 1980s, China signalled its new flexibility in the 1990s. In Kuala Lumpur in May 1993, the Chinese defence minister, Chi Haotian, ruled out the use of force to settle the disputes. Beijing's professed willingness to shelve the sovereignty question, forswear the use of force, and move ahead with joint development contrasted sharply with Foreign Minister Huang Hua's 1977 statement that "when the time comes ... we will retrieve those islands. There will be no need then to negotiate at all."[58] Thus, it is clear that China's policy is determined by its larger strategic considerations and its assessment of the role of other parties to the dispute.

After occupying islands in the Spratlys in 1988, Beijing quickly moved to assuage the fears of ASEAN states and prevent the conflict from damaging relations with them. Writing in 1990, B.A. Hamzah, then director-general of the Malaysian Institute of Maritime Affairs, asked: "Will the PRC continue to resort to arms as an instrument of national policy in pursuit of what others have long feared, a hegemonic scheme in the South China Sea?"[59] Li Peng's 1990 statement supporting joint development of resources was clearly intended to allay such fears. At the United Nations in April 1995, Foreign Minister Qian Qichen also gave assurances that Beijing did not intend to settle the South China Sea disputes by military means.[60] These reassurances led the Malaysian defence minister, Syed Hamid Albar, to conclude in 1996:

> But we in Southeast Asia generally feel that China has so far been a sober and responsible regional player. Its advocacy of joint exploitation of the South China Sea resources ... and its recent indication of a readiness to abide by

international law in resolving the Spratly issue have made us feel that it wants to coexist in peace with its neighbors.[61]

In December 1997, a joint statement issued after a China-ASEAN meeting in Kuala Lumpur called on all parties to maintain the status quo and resolve the South China Sea disputes by peaceful means. Beijing also made it clear, however, that it would go only so far. Despite China's willingness to cooperate in jointly developing resources around the Spratlys, a senior Chinese military official insisted that Beijing would not negotiate with Hanoi a similar joint development scheme for the Paracels, which China has controlled since 1974.[62]

Although China has made some missteps, it has continued to undertake confidence-building measures with ASEAN through participation in unofficial workshops and conferences on marine science research and other mutual interests. At the 1994 workshop, China proposed sharing marine data and establishing an oceanographic research centre. Following the Mischief Reef incident in February 1995, China hosted a China-ASEAN meeting in Hangzhou in April, and to reassure ASEAN, it agreed to hold annual meetings at the vice minister level to continue discussions of the issues.[63] Prompted by ASEAN solidarity over the Mischief Reef incident and the imminent accession of Vietnam as an ASEAN member, this Chinese concession was a marked shift in Beijing's policy in order to facilitate China's primary strategic interests: economic cooperation and "good-neighborly relations."[64] With Beijing's acquiescence, the South China Sea dispute was placed, for the first time, on the formal agenda of the ASEAN Regional Forum (ARF) held in August 1995 in Brunei, where Foreign Minister Qian committed China to seeking a settlement consistent with the UN Law of the Sea; Qian also stated that China's claims did not bar the right of safe passage and freedom of navigation through the South China Sea.[65] In November 2002, a Declaration on the Conduct of Parties in the South China Sea (DOC) was signed by all ASEAN members and China. Recognizing the "need to promote a peaceful, friendly and harmonious environment in the South China Sea ... for the enhancement of peace, stability, economic growth and prosperity in the region," the declaration explicitly commits all parties to the dispute "to resolve their territorial and jurisdictional disputes by peaceful means, without resorting to the threat or use of force, through friendly consultations and negotiations by sovereign states directly concerned."[66]

However, Beijing remains opposed to involving states outside the region or "institutionalizing" a multilateral process of dispute resolution, preferring a bilateral approach as conflicts arise. Following US statements urging multilateral negotiations, Chinese Foreign Minister Yang Jiechi criticized US involvement, asking, "What will be the consequences if this issue is turned into an international or multilateral one?" His answer: "It will only make matters worse and the resolution more difficult."[67]

China's renewed assertiveness in recent years has been driven by many factors. Following Deng Xiaoping's decision to shelve the controversy and pursue cooperative development, China did not unilaterally pursue oil or other resource development in disputed areas of the South China Sea, whereas other states did, especially Malaysia and Vietnam. Chinese officials began to feel that China was "snookered" *(chiqui)*, and they urged a more assertive policy. Some Foreign Ministry officials argued for upgrading the South China Sea to a "core interest" (and even hinted at this idea when talking with US officials), but the People's Liberation Army, despite its strident public position, argued against such a policy change because putting the South China Sea on par with Taiwan, Tibet, and Xinjiang would require it to assume a more aggressive military stance to protect such an interest and signal an unwillingness to compromise, which is not Beijing's official policy toward the territorial dispute in the South China Sea.[68]

This debate is reflected in the Chinese press. According to *China Daily:*

> For a long time, China showed restraint in the disputes over the South China Sea. However, China's stance in a peaceful resolution of territory disputes seems to be misinterpreted ... If China's constant diplomatic claims won't work anymore, it must consider effective alternatives.[69]

The populist and nationalistic *Global Times* was more explicit:

> Some of China's neighboring countries have been exploiting China's mild diplomatic stance, making it their golden opportunity to expand their regional interests ... Hard-line response will cause trouble for China, but if the problems and "pains" these countries bring exceed the risk China has to endure to change its policies and strategies, then a "counter-attack" is likely ... If a situation turns ugly, some military action is necessary ... We need to be ready for that, as it may be the only way for the disputes in the sea to be resolved.[70]

A Foreign Ministry spokesperson responded to a question about whether the *Global Times* "view [is] official to some extent? Is it also held by the Chinese Government?" by stating: "The media has the right to edit and comment. It is believed that they will report in a truthful, objective and responsible manner ... We hold that it is imperative that relevant countries earnestly implement the Declaration on the Conduct of Parties in the South China Sea, which is vital to safeguarding and enhancing mutual trust between the countries. We maintain a smooth channel of communication and consultation with countries directly involved in the South China Sea dispute."[71]

A more assertive position also was advanced by a scholar at the International Strategy Division, Institute of World Economics and Politics of the Chinese Academy of Social Sciences, who argued:

China must reassess its South China Sea strategy ... China must firmly possess the ability to occupy islands and ensure an active occupancy of islands and reefs rather than symbolic possession ... China has put aside the resolution of disputes in favor of seeking common development. However, this misreads Deng Xiaoping's fundamental principle of territorial integrity. In China's border security issues, the country must seek to resolve issues in a timely fashion to avoid conflicts later on.[72]

Wang Jisi, a leading Chinese international relations scholar and adviser to top Chinese Communist Party officials rejected this sharp rhetoric, asserting that "reckless statements, made with no official authorization created a great deal of confusion," and Chinese diplomats warned that "such a move might fan the flames of the 'China threat' theory in Southeast Asian countries, not to mention the United States."[73]

This public debate reflected a debate within the government and CCP over how to deal with what was perceived as China's loss of negotiating leverage in the South China Sea. The voices of pragmatism won out. China has not elevated the South China Sea to a "core interest." Careful research has turned up no official PRC government statement or document that explicitly identified the South China Sea as such. One *Xinhua* report in August 2011 stated that "China has always made itself loud and clear that it has indisputable sovereignty over the sea's islands and surrounding waters, which is part of China's core interests."[74] However, public acknowledgment of this is problematic. Zhu Feng, an international relations scholar at Peking University, observed that while it is "not Chinese policy to declare the South China Sea as a core interest … the problem is that a public denial will be some sort of chicken action on the part of Chinese leaders. So the government also doesn't want to inflame the Chinese people."[75]

Nevertheless, China's increased assertiveness had an impact. The Philippines responded by strengthening its security cooperation with the United States under the 1951 US-Philippines Mutual Security Treaty and filed a petition for arbitration of the Sino-Philippine dispute under UNCLOS. Vietnam, too, initiated increased security cooperation with the United States. Beijing responded by adjusting its tactics in an effort to dampen the spike in anti-China sentiment among some ASEAN nations and curb the growth of US involvement in the South China Sea dispute. This change in policy was signalled by the July 2011 China-ASEAN agreement on "Guidelines for the Implementation of the Declaration on the Conduct of Parties in the South China Sea." This agreement was the result of years of negotiation and compromise. In 2004, a Joint Working Group was created to negotiate specific measures to implement the DOC. China rejected ASEAN's policy of "continu[ing] its … practice of consulting among themselves before meeting with China" and insisted that disputes should be resolved through bilateral negotiations. Finally, ASEAN dropped the statement on consultation and China agreed to the set of guidelines; this was a diplomatic breakthrough but it was a rather toothless set of guidelines.[76] In October 2011, China concluded with Vietnam an "agreement on the basic principles guiding the resolution of maritime issues."[77] While being more assertive, China has in fact not changed its fundamental policy of seeking a compromise solution, fully aware that changing this policy would only trigger strong reaction from ASEAN and invite a more active role for the United States, something not in China's strategic interest. To deal with the consequences of China's more assertive policy, Zha Daojiong, a professor at Peking University's School of International Studies, suggested that "China needs to learn a diplomatic lesson from the South China Sea issue. It is time to rethink and repair relations with those countries involved to deal with their affiliation with the US."[78]

As scenarios for resolving the disputes are considered, a possible complicating factor is the involvement of the Republic of China on Taiwan. After briefly abandoning its foothold in the Spratlys following its retreat to Taiwan, the Nationalist government has occupied Itu Aba Island *(Taiping Dao)*, the largest island in the Spratly group, and the Pratas group *(Dongsha)* since

1956. In 2009, Taipei submitted claims to the United Nations on the Outer Limits of the Continental Shelf that matched Beijing's claims to the South China Sea, and added that Taiwan supported "joint exploration and resources-sharing."[79]

At a government-sponsored "seminar" on the South China Sea held in Taipei in September 1993, a plan to enhance Taiwan's military and civilian presence in the region was announced, and preparations were initiated to increase sea patrols around the Pratas and the Spratlys. Characterized as a "symbolic move" to signal the Southeast Asian states that Taiwan was "indispensable" in resolving the disputes, Taipei pointedly did not challenge Beijing's position. Participants agreed that Taipei and Beijing should exchange official documents jointly affirming Chinese sovereignty over the islands, and that Taipei should sponsor cross-strait meetings on the issue.[80] As cross-strait relations improved, a fisheries agreement was negotiated in September 1990 that specifically mentioned cooperation in the Spratlys, and with improving cooperation, in early 1995 the Chinese Petroleum Corporation (Taipei) and China National Offshore Oil Corporation (Beijing) established a joint venture to explore for oil in the South China Sea.[81] A tacit Beijing-Taipei "united front" supporting "China's" claims has clearly developed.

Taipei responds without fail to statements and actions by any other party to the dispute but does not challenge Beijing's claims, and both parties have avoided any military confrontation over islands that the "other China" occupies. Taipei did not criticize Beijing's use of force to wrest control of the Paracels and some Spratly islands from Vietnam. In fact, Nationalist troops watched passively as the PLA routed Vietnamese troops in the March 1988 battle, and Taiwan's defence minister suggested that Taipei would, if necessary, help Beijing defend its position on the islands.[82]

This Beijing-Taipei united front approach conforms to Beijing's behaviour in other disputes – that is, subordination of territorial differences to more fundamental strategic interests. Beijing does not want to allow Southeast Asian states to use PRC-ROC conflict over other sovereignty to breach their unity on China's historical claims to the islands in the South China Sea. After the election of the independence-minded Democratic Progressive Party in 2000, relations between the two Chinas soured dramatically but there was no indication of substantive change in the tacit united front regarding islands in the South China Sea.[83] Since the Nationalist Party regained power in March 2008, the government in Taipei has vigorously defended "China's" claim to sovereignty over all island groups in the South China Sea, and has strengthened its ability to defend these claims militarily.

Conclusions

The approach China took in earlier settlements has emerged in the South China Sea disputes as well. Beijing was initially reluctant to enter formal negotiations, but ASEAN went ahead with steps at the official level and at its 1992 Ministerial Meeting issued a South China Sea Declaration that called for military restraint and joint development while leaving open the question of sovereignty. Beijing did not criticize this step and supported the general principles of the declaration.[84] In the mid-1990s, China indicated a willingness to examine the disputes according to international law based on the 1982 United Nations Convention on the Law of the Sea. China signed the Declaration on the Conduct of Parties in the South China Sea in November 2002, the first formal China-ASEAN agreement on that issue, committing Beijing to resolve disputes by peaceful means and to show self-restraint. Premier Zhu Rongji characterized the declaration as marking "a higher level of political trust" between China and the ASEAN states.[85] In 2003, China became a signatory of the 1976 Treaty of Amity and Cooperation in Southeast Asia, pledging to settle disputes through direct negotiations or refer the dispute to some type of third-party arbitration.[86] In July 2011, within weeks after tensions flared up between China and Vietnam, all parties concluded an agreement on guidelines for the implementation of the Declaration on the Conduct of Parties in the South China Sea. China's assistant foreign minister characterized this agreement as "an important milestone document for cooperation among China and ASEAN countries."[87]

Thus, Beijing has shifted to a more conciliatory position, determined by larger strategic considerations. Chinese scholars believe that whereas in the past "historical influences limited Chinese flexibility in the South China Sea," Beijing now is more willing to compromise because "accumulating international prestige and being accepted as part of international society" has become more important in China's grand strategy and in relations with its ASEAN neighbours.[88] Therefore, although the South China Sea disputes will not be settled in the foreseeable future, Beijing's policy has changed to accommodate the emerging strategic imperatives in Southeast Asia – compromising to achieve broader security and economic objectives.[89]

If nothing occurs to threaten Beijing's security interests in the South China Sea, the status quo could continue indefinitely. We can expect Beijing to continue participating in track II diplomacy through "workshops" and "seminars," as well as more official settings such as the ASEAN Regional Forum, but to resist involving outside powers in the region, as was demonstrated by its angry reaction to the US statement on national interests in the South China Sea and support for a multilateral settlement.

If the past offers any insights into the future, we can assume that if a sufficiently acute external threat emerges, China will show flexibility in resolving disputes in order to reduce friction with other states and develop alliances to counter the perceived threat. The US pivot to Southeast Asia has resulted in Chinese countermoves, such as quick dampening of spikes in tensions to reduce the incentive of other states to seek a greater US presence and closer cooperation with the United States to prevent Chinese domination. The increased focus of the United States on the South China Sea since 2010 has alarmed China and likely provided the impetus for it to sign the agreement on steps to implement the Declaration on the Conduct of Parties in 2011, which the parties had wrestled with for six years. Beijing has also shown a greater willingness to negotiate a code of conduct, something ASEAN states have advocated for some time. After initially dragging its feet, China began supporting a code of conduct in 2010 in response to the more active engagement of the United States in the South China Sea dispute. China's strategic calculation is that engaging the other parties in negotiations over a code of conduct will dampen their efforts, especially those of Vietnam and the Philippines, to draw the US into the dispute.

If ASEAN progresses toward some mode of formal cooperation for resource development, China should not be expected to remain on the sidelines as a bystander. The possibility of such an eventuality is demonstrated by the 1992 agreement between Kuala Lumpur and Hanoi to develop areas jointly where their claims overlap.[90] An ASEAN agreement to move forward with joint development of the South China Sea resources would force China to seek a multilateral settlement. In any case, these scenarios support the conclusion that China will move to prevent any anti-China coalitions by seeking to settle these disputes. The scenarios illustrate various conditions under which China's approach to the South China Sea disputes could become more flexible and follow the pattern established in earlier boundary settlements.

The particular characteristics of the South China Sea disputes must be considered too. In terms of sovereignty, this is a multilateral zero-sum game and, from the perspective of economic cooperation and development, it is a classic prisoners' dilemma. Given China's attitude since the end of the Cold War, we can see the emergence of a pattern of behaviour particular to this multilateral dispute. Beijing appears willing to cooperate with the other states in joint development when China does not control the territory in question. Li Peng's 1990 Singapore statement and the Indonesian-sponsored workshops initiated in 1990 that China has participated in make this clear. However, if Beijing controls the disputed territory, participating in any joint development scheme is less likely. Beijing has expressed its willingness to cooperate in the Spratlys, where it controls only a few islands, but has refused any such cooperation in the Paracels, where it has complete control. The agreement with Japan to develop resources in the East China Sea shows China's willingness to cooperate in a joint development project if other parties first concede Chinese sovereignty over the disputed territory, as Tokyo did before joint development was undertaken. More generally, it illustrates China's policy of setting aside disputes to pursue joint development, which reflects the fact that, for China, fashioning settlements based on international law is less important than finding a resolution "reflecting thinking and calculations about what serves China's national interests."[91]

A concern that many have is that as China's military power and ability to project force into the South China Sea grows, Beijing will become more aggressive and less willing to compromise. Some scholars have concluded that China has adopted a strategy of delaying settlement "at least until the balance of power changes substantially in favor of China," and that at some point irredentist claims "in some cases *might* be pursued in more concerted form if favorable changes take place in the future regional balance of power." Therefore, "down the line [these territorial disputes can be resolved] to China's advantage by any means of its own choosing if its national capabilities are allowed to grow rapidly and undisturbed in the interim."[92] One Chinese analyst concludes, however, that Beijing's strategic rivalries in the region will "constrain China from becoming openly confrontational" because an "overly assertive posture ... will only further generate suspicion in many regional states toward China." Chinese scholars, Foreign Ministry officials, and PLA officers generally support this view. Thus, a "combination of non-confrontation and assertiveness is likely to dominate China's behavior" in the future.[93] The more assertive and nationalistic Chinese public may complicate Beijing's ability to negotiate compromise over these historically sensitive territorial claims, but recent scholarship concludes that "the rise of popular nationalism in reform-era China has not correlated with a rise in military aggression" and a "foolhardy, overly aggressive foreign policy."[94] This, we can conclude, is due to the fact that the CCP central leadership has decided "to pursue a non-coercive approach toward ... territorial disputes."[95]

An example of this non-confrontational but assertive approach is the May 2012 crisis over Scarborough Shoal *(Huangyan Dao)* involving the Philippines and China. The PLA newspaper *Liberation Army Daily (Jiefangjun bao)* published a strong editorial against any compromise, asserting "not only the Chinese government will not agree, neither will the Chinese people, and the Chinese Army will disagree even more."[96] However, despite popular calls for a more aggressive policy, Beijing, as in previous such incidents, moved quickly to calm the waters and craft a diplomatic resolution.[97] This pragmatism is reflected by Zhao Minghao, a research fellow at the China Center for Contemporary World Studies under the International Department of the CCP Central Committee, who argues that China must "avoid strategic myopia" and "maintain a strategic restraint over the coming years in light of its territorial disputes with neighboring countries, rising nationalism and growing diversity in foreign policy making." This requires Beijing to adopt "policies to handle its growing power capabilities and curb its imperialistic impulses."[98] Motivating this more moderate approach is China's larger grand strategy.

Although complex historical and legal questions complicate any resolution of the South China Sea, as in other territorial disputes Beijing can be expected to behave pragmatically, taking into consideration larger strategic and economic concerns. China will probably eventually seek a compromise settlement in the South China Sea to maintain good relations with its ASEAN neighbours, and to ease cooperation on fundamental economic and security issues where military force has little or no utility and runs counter to China's long-term strategic interests in the region. Beijing responded to the growing concerns of other Southeast Asian states in a *Global Times* editorial recognizing that

> clearly stating China's intention and easing the concerns of other countries remains a challenge ... As the largest country in the region, China has the responsibility to reduce the divergence and build a consensus. Disagreements may be hard to put aside but China should find ways to push forward joint developments, through which reciprocating ventures can be formed to reduce

conflicts. It takes time to solve this conflict, a historical issue, but through joint efforts and mutual understanding, common ground can be reached. Clashes are not destined in the South China Sea conflict, and one must break this expectation.[99]

Foreign Minister Wang Yi, addressing the Chinese People's Institute of Foreign Affairs Second World Peace Forum in Beijing in June 2013, reiterated China's policy regarding disputed territory: "China maintains that proper solutions must be sought through dialogue and negotiation on the basis of fully respecting historical facts and international law ... Pending the settlement of disputes over maritime rights and interests, parties could shelve differences and engage in joint development."[100] Again at the United Nations General Assembly in September 2013, he stressed the continuity in China's policy toward the unresolved disputes, stating that

> with regard to China's disputes with some countries over territorial sover-
> eignty and maritime rights and interests, we sincerely hope to properly resolve
> them through negotiation and consultation with countries directly involved
> ... This is our consistent position and practice. On the other hand, we will,
> under whatever circumstances, firmly safeguard China's sovereignty and
> territorial integrity and resolutely uphold China's legitimate and lawful rights
> and interests.[101]

At a press conference on the sidelines of the 2014 annual National People's Congress (no doubt targeted at the domestic audience), he used a stronger tone, asserting that China will "never bully smaller countries," but "we will defend every inch of territory that belongs to us" and "will not accept unreasonable denounce [sic] from smaller countries" either.[102]

Compared with the other boundary and territorial disputes that China has settled, the South China Sea disputes are more complex and will be the most difficult to resolve. Unlike earlier disputes, they involve potentially resource-rich and strategically important islands and sea lanes. A multilateral solution must be reached, but China has been reluctant to engage in multilateral negotiations. It is likely that the status quo of no solution but no large-scale military conflict will persist into the foreseeable future.

Conclusion

The correlation between China's territorial disputes and settlements and its strategic environment has been the main analytical thread throughout this book. China's boundary disputes and settlements were analyzed within the context of its global strategy as determined by strategic imperatives: the deteriorating strategic environment in the 1960s, especially the Sino-Soviet split in 1960, the Sino-Indian border war in 1962, and the escalating US war in Vietnam; escalating Sino-Soviet tensions in the 1970s; and the end of the Cold War in the 1990s. The case studies were divided into groups and placed in this larger strategic context: those within the Sino-Indian dimension, those within the Sino-Soviet/Russian dimension, and contemporary cases. There is also a chronological pattern: during the first period, boundary disputes were settled with Burma in 1960, with Nepal in 1961, with Mongolia in 1962, and with Pakistan and Afghanistan in 1963. China fought a border war with India in 1962 after failing to achieve a boundary settlement. The boundary dispute with the Soviet Union became public in 1963, and after smouldering for years with acrimonious exchanges, a border war erupted in 1969. This escalation of tensions in Sino-Soviet relations set the context for the second period in the 1970s. In September 1972, Beijing sidestepped the Senkaku/Diaoyu Islands disputes and normalized relations with Tokyo, and then in August 1978, it shelved the territorial dispute with Japan in order to conclude the Treaty of Peace and Friendship before engaging Vietnam in a border war the following February. The third shift in China's strategic environment – the end of the Cold War – set the stage for the third period and the settlements with the Central Eurasian states in the 1990s. Reflecting Beijing's post–Cold War strategic calculations, China's behaviour follows the same pattern in the ongoing disputes in the South China Sea. Despite the separation of each set of cases based on Beijing's larger strategic concerns, the same systemic structural constraints were considered when analyzing China's behaviour. Each case study provided an island of knowledge about China's approach to boundary disputes and settlements. The task now is to build bridges between these islands and synthesize the findings with the objective of generalizing Beijing's pattern of behaviour across cases and time periods.

Historical Legacy and Boundary Settlements

The Chinese have a clear image of China's historical frontiers supported by impressive historical evidence. This image even transcends different ideological affinities from one regime to the next. Traditionally, China endeavoured to maintain a system of buffer states beyond its borders. The objective was to establish a defensive parameter of suzerain or tributary states controlled by the central court or government that were unable or unwilling to challenge China's hegemony. The strategic motivation was defence of the heartland against the nomads of inner Asia, the pirates of the East and South China Seas, and the threats to China's underbelly from South Asia. One legacy of this traditional grand strategy is that in many cases China's borders were not defined by clearly delimited boundaries, but by the extent to which the particular dynasty in power controlled the outer regions. Boundaries drawn by treaty were for the most part established only in the wake of European colonialism and China's dynastic decline. Consequently, China views these early treaties concluded under the shadow of imperialism as illegitimate. This legacy of "unequal treaties" haunted all of China's boundary disputes and settlements. It is a truism that history matters, but these case studies make clear that this historical legacy is a complicating aspect of China's boundary disputes and settlements.

Nevertheless, this study makes clear that while rejecting the early treaties in principle, China has in fact accepted them as the basis for new treaties. Beijing proved willing to surmount "problems left over by history" and did not demand the return of "lost" territory considered historically part of the Chinese empire. Beijing was satisfied when its neighbours tacitly recognized China's territorial victimization by European imperialism. This recognition is symbolized by the abolition of the unequal treaties. It is also evident that ceding territory that was historically considered China's, despite previous treaties, is acceptable if it is based on an equal treaty negotiated by two independent sovereign states. Beijing has therefore demonstrated that while being rigid on issues of "principle," it has been flexible and accommodating when larger strategic considerations dictated. This is especially important when contemplating the smouldering disputes in the East and

South China Seas and with India, the one major land boundary that remains unsettled. Based on the treaties concluded, it is clear that Beijing accepts the norms and principles of international law regarding objective determinants of boundaries, such as watersheds in mountainous areas, the thalweg for rivers, and straight baseline and equidistance principles for maritime boundaries.

A legacy of the early Chinese tributary system (which also served as a "boundary maintenance system") and traditional grand strategy is China's desire to establish a system of buffer states to ensure the security of the Chinese heartland, demonstrated by the fact that Beijing attempted to link mutual non-aggression treaties to the conclusion of the boundary treaties of the early 1960s.

China's Global Strategy and Boundary Disputes

China's changing relations with other states in the region determined the balance of power and provided the strategic context within which China formulated its policy toward particular boundary disputes and settlements. It is clear that decisions were made by Mao Zedong personally before his death in 1976, and by Deng Xiaoping during subsequent years until the early 1990s. Mao exercised almost complete control over foreign affairs during the early 1960s, when most disputes were settled, as did Deng in the late 1970s during the Senkaku Islands dispute and early 1990s, when settlements were negotiated with Vietnam and the Central Eurasian states. The ideological affinities and nationalism of Mao and Deng were constrained by broader strategic imperatives, and both exhibited a defensive realist approach to boundary settlements, emphasizing the maintenance of a favourable balance of power, and security over expansion and territorial aggrandizement. China's policy was only marginally affected, if at all, by domestic politics or elite factionalism. The very centralized decision-making process facilitated Beijing's capacity to compromise and make territorial concessions when necessary. Based on the evidence examined, it is therefore possible to conclude that how Beijing handled the various disputes was determined not so much by domestic politics or the preferences of individual leaders but by broader strategic imperatives.

In the early 1960s, China's relations with India and the Soviet Union were deteriorating whereas Soviet-Indian relations were improving, and the US threat in Southeast Asia was growing. In response to this shift in the balance of power, Beijing adopted a flexible boundary policy to eliminate boundary disputes as an irritant in relations with countries that could play a role as buffer states and balancers. Beijing's primary consideration was its broader strategic interests – it was willing to compromise on narrow secondary considerations if necessary. China proved that it could be very accommodating to settle a boundary dispute (or willingly delay settlement, as with Japan and Russia regarding Heixiazi Island) when strategically necessary. In other words, boundary dispute settlements were driven by larger strategic considerations that required compromise to achieve a settlement.

I have argued that China used boundary settlements to eliminate friction in bilateral relations and foster allies to offset the threat from the Soviet Union, India, and the United States in the 1960s. In the case of Mongolia, China's objective was to encourage Ulaanbaatar to adopt a more neutral policy. To accomplish this, China was even willing to appease Mongolian nationalism. Unfortunately for China, Beijing miscalculated Mongolia's fear of Chinese irredentism and the boundary settlement did not diminish this apprehension. That China failed to achieve its objectives in this case underscored its inability to either compete with the Soviet Union or otherwise provide sufficient inducements to Soviet allies to win their support. In the other cases, countries made certain accommodations and China was in return generous in the final settlements. In the Senkaku/Diaoyu Islands case, China did not enforce its assertion of sovereignty over the islands, and Japan agreed to include an "anti-hegemony" clause in the two nations' Treaty of Peace and Friendship; mutual accommodation made conclusion of the treaty possible. Other boundary treaties facilitated non-aggression pacts that enhanced China's security.

Explaining China's Behaviour

In the 1960s, China sought boundary settlements with India, the Soviet Union, and Vietnam, but these three countries were unwilling to make any compromises. As the strategic context began to change in the late 1980s, Russia and China moved to settle the boundary in a manner notable for the absence of polemics, and in the 1990s, after the collapse of the Soviet Union and the fundamental change in the international environment, China and Vietnam moved quickly to conclude boundary treaties. Even in the case of India (and Bhutan), the lone unsettled land boundary, there has been important progress in recent years toward an eventual resolution of the issue; in the meantime, a stable status quo prevails.

In some cases Beijing has used military force to occupy disputed territory and then called for negotiations to settle the dispute. This was the pattern followed with India in 1962 and Vietnam in 1979. In both cases, China withdrew from the occupied territory before the renewal of boundary talks, surrendering any leverage gained by occupying disputed territory. It is not clear that China was attempting to occupy territory that it was disputing with the Soviet Union in 1969, or whether this border skirmish was triggered by the high level of tension at the time, caused by the Cultural Revolution. In the fishing boat incident around the Senkaku/Diaoyu Islands in 1978, China clearly did not contemplate occupation of the islands in the face of Japan's refusal to compromise on the sovereignty issue. Small-scale skirmishes occurred along the Sino-Burmese and Sino-Nepali borders as settlements were being concluded, but there is no evidence that China was attempting to occupy territory to force compromise. In fact, these cases show that China has not used force to compel other states to make concessions before a settlement. China's behaviour in the South China Sea is more problematic. China occupied the Paracel Islands by force in 1974, but did not occupy any islands in the Spratly group until 1988, when it used military force to gain a foothold at the expense of Vietnam. China has since agreed to a Declaration of Conduct (DOC) and supported a negotiated resolution of these disputes. A cautionary note is necessary, however. China has used force in over half of the disputes over islands in the South China Sea to "strengthen its position," especially if it did not occupy the contested territory.[1] This pattern does not bode well for the unresolved disputes in the East and South China Seas, where tensions have been escalating in recent years.

The most often asked question is why, since China was willing to compromise in so many cases to achieve a settlement, is it unable to resolve the remaining disputes with India and Japan and in the South China Sea. Some scholars of China's grand strategy conclude that China has adopted a strategy of delaying the resolution of the remaining boundary disputes "at least until the balance of power changes substantially in favor of China," and in the future irredentist claims "in some cases *might* be pursued." Therefore, "down the line [these territorial disputes can be resolved] to China's advantage by any means of its own choosing if its national capabilities are allowed to grow rapidly and undisturbed in the interim."[2]

The response to this conclusion has several dimensions and underscores one fact common to all the boundary settlements – they are a function of

Beijing's larger strategic considerations and grand strategy. Unsettled cases can be divided into two general categories. First, the territorial disputes with Japan and the other states that border the East and South China Seas are characterized by conflicting historical claims to hundreds of mostly uninhabited small islands, coral reefs, or atolls. The multilateral disputes are even more complicated. No treaties have ever determined sovereignty over the islands of the East and South China Seas. Negotiating a compromise settlement is further complicated by disagreement regarding international legal criteria on questions such as discovery and delimitation of the continental shelf and increased demand for natural resources. If a compromise settlement is not possible, Beijing will delay settlement to facilitate better relations in the face of larger strategic concerns. In the case of Japan, the Senkaku/Diaoyu Islands dispute has proven to be so intractable that China adopted a policy of "tactically" subordinating it to achieve more important strategic objectives. This also is the case with Russia and the resolution of disputed islands at the confluence of the Amur and Ussuri rivers near Khabarovsk, which was deferred so a boundary treaty could be concluded in 1991. The South China Sea is in the same category, where final settlement is delayed while larger strategic interests are pursued.

In the second category, which includes India and, until recently, Vietnam and Russia, China rejects the legitimacy of earlier boundary treaties while India insists that these are valid international treaties and refuses to negotiate new ones. China has consistently insisted on negotiating new treaties, but it is also willing to take into consideration the earlier "unequal treaties" when negotiating new ones. Russia and Vietnam eventually relented on the old treaties and achieved settlements with relative ease. In every settlement, possibly including Korea, one common and important feature was Beijing's insistence on negotiating new treaties to replace the unequal treaties of the past. There is no evidence that China ever insisted that its vast irredentist claims be satisfied when negotiating these new treaties. Rather, Beijing has insisted only that the other countries recognize that the boundaries are legacies of imperialism. The major obstacle that has prevented a settlement with India is New Delhi's insistence on the legitimacy of treaties concluded by previous governments from a bygone era.

Trends and Prospects

The paradigm developed in this study makes it possible to anticipate the pattern that a settlement with India and resolution of the disputes in the

East and South China Seas will follow. This pattern became clear in the 1991 settlement of the Sino-Russian boundary and subsequent settlements with China's Eurasian neighbours. The threat that China felt from the Soviet Union abated and in May 1989 Sino-Soviet rapprochement was symbolized by Mikhail Gorbachev's trip to China. In the new strategic environment, the Sino-Russian boundary dispute was a source of friction in an otherwise cordial relationship. Under this new set of strategic imperatives, Beijing no longer insisted on the settlement of all issues of "principle," such as recognition of the older treaties as unequal, and Russia was less concerned about strategic considerations and Chinese irredentism, so a settlement was achieved with relative ease. The one sticking point regarding a few islands was set aside and not allowed to delay an agreement, but even this minor dispute (involving less than two percent of the entire border) was settled in November 2004 with virtually no acrimony. The Eurasian settlements followed a similar pattern, as did the settlement with Vietnam in the latter 1990s. With the collapse of the Soviet Union, support for Vietnam, its proxy in Southeast Asia, evaporated. In this new strategic contest, China and Vietnam agreed on procedural issues for a boundary settlement and soon signed new treaties based on the "historical customary line" established by the Sino-French treaties.

The conclusion of the Sino-Russian and Sino-Vietnamese boundary treaties has increased the pressure on India to be more flexible and has increased China's leverage in those negotiations. With the post–Cold War evolution of the balance of power, Sino-Indian relations have already improved significantly. Rajiv Gandhi travelled to Beijing in December 1988, just six months before Gorbachev's historic visit to Beijing, and placed Sino-Indian relations on a new path. And, as demonstrated in other cases, China is willing to be accommodating when negotiating a boundary settlement. If India can gracefully retreat from its own uncompromising position and find the necessary political will, a settlement is possible.

The strategic importance of the East and South China Seas, the potential for oil, and the multilateral nature in the case of the South China Sea make these the most complex of all of China's territorial disputes. For the foreseeable future, the Senkaku/Diaoyu Islands will hamper Tokyo-Beijing diplomacy and the South China Sea dispute will continue to be a source of friction in China-ASEAN relations. Moreover, the "strident turn" in Chinese foreign policy since 2008 will potentially complicate attempts to resolve these disputes. Popular nationalism now has much more influence on China's foreign policy and, given the historical sensitivities over territorial issues, in combination with state nationalism, has compelled Beijing to adopt a much more assertive policy, which makes a compromise settlement politically more difficult to pursue.[3] In the past, Beijing stressed Deng Xiaoping's emphasis on delaying the resolution of these difficult disputes, but rhetoric shifted after 2008 and Deng was again used, but now to justify an uncompromising policy: "The Chinese people will never turn a blind eye to those who are working to undermine China's territorial integrity, national unification and dignity. Comrade Deng Xiaoping said: One should never expect the Chinese to swallow the bitter pill which harms their benefits. Of course, we don't want to see that happen, but if it does happen, then we will respond to make those relative countries realize this point."[4] This more nationalistic sentiment was reflected by Assistant Minister of Foreign Affairs Le Yucheng in more specific terms when he asserted that "as the situation develops, we will give them tit for tat and take effective measures to safeguard our territorial sovereignty resolutely."[5] Despite this more uncompromising rhetoric, since 2012 Beijing has moved to moderate its policy and stem the tide of growing concern over Chinese assertive behaviour. As this book has shown, China has behaved pragmatically in pursuing resolutions of its land boundary disputes. As other studies have argued, there is little likelihood that China will pursue territorial expansion in the seas surrounding China, especially the South China Sea.[6]

The geopolitical significance of the region will not change, and Beijing has perceived a shift in the strategic context – such as a renewed assertion of US influence in the region – and as the pressure to develop new sources of oil increases, the incentive for mutual compromise and joint development will grow. All the parties to this dispute are caught in a prisoner's dilemma – mutual cooperation would benefit all, whereas unilateral defection would be costly in terms of resource development and possibly even war. Because of the high stakes, once strategic and economic incentives are great enough and political conditions permit, Beijing will pursue a negotiated settlement.

The pattern followed in the settlement of China's boundary disputes is clear. Ernest R. May has argued that a state's foreign policy can be characterized as either "calculated" or "axiomatic."[7] A calculated foreign policy is a more explicit strategy based on considerations of ends and means, whereas the roots of an axiomatic foreign policy are more historical and run deep.

While China's historical experience – both pre-modern and contemporary – provides the substance of its axiomatic policies, strategic imperatives drive Beijing's calculated foreign policy. Axiomatic policies and calculated policies may at times appear to contradict each other, but although *a posteriori* axioms drive China's world view, general strategic parameters and realities have determined Beijing's calculations. The interplay of historical and strategic considerations is central to understanding the pattern of Beijing's behaviour when dealing with boundary disputes and settlements. This analytical conceptualization is helpful in explaining China's behaviour.

Notes

Introduction

1 Paul K. Huth, *Standing Your Ground: Territorial Disputes and International Conflict* (Ann Arbor: University of Michigan Press, 1996), 4.
2 John A. Vasquez, *The War Puzzle* (Cambridge: Cambridge University Press, 1993), 123-24.
3 Allen Carlson, *Unifying China, Integrating with the World: Securing China's Sovereignty in the Reform Era* (Stanford, CA: Stanford University Press, 2005); Chien-peng Chung, *Domestic Politics, International Bargaining and China's Territorial Disputes* (New York: RoutledgeCurzon, 2004); M. Taylor Fravel, *Strong Borders, Secure Nation: Cooperation and Conflict in China's Territorial Disputes* (Princeton, NJ: Princeton University Press, 2008).
4 Francis Watson, *The Frontiers of China* (New York: Praeger, 1966), 92.
5 Douglas M. Gibler, "Alliances that Never Balance: The Territorial-Settlement Treaty," in *A Road Map to War: Territorial Dimensions of International Conflict,* ed. Paul F. Diehl (Nashville: Vanderbilt University Press, 1999), 183.
6 Lowell Dittmer, "The Strategic Triangle: An Elementary Game-Theoretical Analysis," *World Politics* 33, 4 (July 1981): 487.
7 Carlson, *Unifying China, Integrating with the World,* 3, 50, 90-91.
8 Chung, *Domestic Politics, International Bargaining and China's Territorial Disputes,* 163.
9 M. Taylor Fravel, "Regime Insecurity and International Cooperation: Explaining China's Compromises in Territorial Disputes," *International Security* 3, 2 (Fall 2005): 49-50, 62.
10 Quincy Wright, *A Study of War* (Chicago: University of Chicago Press, 1965), 130.
11 Jiang Junzhang, *Zhongguo bianjiang yu guofang* [China's frontiers and national defence] (Taipei: Liming wenhua 1979), 2-7.
12 Kenneth N. Waltz, *Theory of International Politics* (Reading, MA: Addison-Wesley, 1979), 65.
13 John Gittings, *The World and China, 1922-1972* (New York: Harper and Row, 1974), 267.
14 Allen S. Whiting, "Forecasting Chinese Foreign Policy: IR Theory vs. the Fortune Cookie," in *Chinese Foreign Policy: Theory and Practice,* ed. Thomas W. Robinson and David Shambaugh (Oxford: Clarendon Press, 1994), 506, 521.
15 Wang Jisi, "International Relations Theory and the Study of Chinese Foreign Policy: A Chinese Perspective" in Robinson and Shambaugh, ibid., 489-90.
16 David M. Lampton, "China: Outward Bound but Inner-Directed," *SAISPHERE 2006,* http://www.sais-jhu.edu/.
17 Paul K. Huth, "Enduring Rivalries and Territorial Disputes, 1950-1990," *Conflict Management and Peace Science* 15, 1 (1996): 14-15.
18 Fravel, "Regime Insecurity and International Cooperation," Table 1.
19 Waltz, *Theory of International Politics,* 68.

20 A. Doak Barnett, *The Making of Foreign Policy in China: Structure and Process* (Boulder, CO: Westview Press, 1985), 7-8.
21 Qingmin Zhang, "Towards an Integrated Theory of Chinese Foreign Policy: Bringing Leadership Personality Back In," *Journal of Contemporary China* 23, 89 (2014): 908.
22 Carol Lee Hamrin and Suisheng Zhao, eds., *Decision-Making in Deng's China: Perspectives from Insiders* (Armonk, NY: M.E. Sharpe, 1995), xxiv, 91-92.
23 Zhang, "Towards an Integrated Theory of Chinese Foreign Policy."
24 Alice Miller, "Dilemmas of Globalization and Governance," in *The Politics of China: Sixty Years of the People's Republic of China*, 3rd ed., ed. Roderick MacFarquhar (Oxford: Cambridge University Press, 2011), 561-64.
25 Michael D. Swaine, "China's Assertive Behavior Part Three: The Role of the Military in Foreign Policy," *China Leadership Monitor* 36 (Winter 2012): 4-5, 10.
26 James Reilly, *Strong Society, Smart State: The Rise of Public Opinion in China's Japan Policy* (New York: Columbia University Press, 2012), 17.
27 Ibid., 24, 46-47, 49, 131.
28 Feng Zhaokui, "Dui zhong-ri guanxi 'zhengleng jingre' de zai sikao" [Rethinking "cold politics, hot economics" in China-Japan relations], quoted in Reilly, ibid., 49.
29 Allen S. Whiting, "Leaping the Great Wall between Security Studies and China Studies," *Security Studies* 6, 4 (Summer 1997): 188-89.
30 Tian Zengpei, ed., *Gaige kaifang yilai de Zhongguo waijiao* [Chinese foreign policy since opening up and reform] (Beijing: Shijie zhishi chubanshe, 1993), 628.
31 Huth, *Standing Your Ground: Territorial Disputes and International Conflict*, 19-22. I do not consider the Taiwan, Hong Kong, or Macao cases because they do not constitute cases of "boundary disputes" but rather sovereignty disputes over colonial enclaves or, in the case of Taiwan, two rival governments that claim to be the legitimate government of China.
32 Carol Lee Hamrin, "Elite Politics and the Development of China's Foreign Relations," in Robinson and Shambaugh, *Chinese Foreign Policy*, 80-82.
33 Waltz, *Theory of International Politics*, 127.
34 John J. Mearsheimer, *The Tragedy of Great Power Politics* (New York: W.W. Norton, 2001), 164-65.
35 See Yuan-Kang Wang, *Harmony and War: Confucian Culture and Chinese Power Politics* (New York: Columbia University Press, 2011); Huiyun Feng, *Chinese Strategic Culture and Foreign Policy Decision-Making: Confucianism, Leadership and War* (New York: Routledge, 2007), 44, 59, 121.
36 Shiping Tang, "From Offensive to Defensive Realism: A Social Evolutionary Interpretation of China's Security Strategy," in *China's Ascent: Power, Security, and the Future of International Politics*, ed. Robert Ross and Zhu Feng (Ithaca, NY: Cornell University Press, 2008); Vidya Prakash Dutt, *China and the World: An Analysis of Communist China's Foreign Policy* (New York: Praeger, 1964), 100; David P. Mozingo, "Communist China: Its Southern Border Lands," *SAIS Review* 12, 2 (Winter 1968): 43-54.
37 Malcolm Anderson, *Frontiers: Territory and State Formation in the Modern World* (Cambridge: Polity Press, 1996), 30-31; Fravel, *Strong Borders, Secure Nation*, 58.
38 Xiaohong Liu, *Chinese Ambassadors: The Rise of Diplomatic Professionalism since 1949* (Seattle: University of Washington Press, 2001), 56-57.
39 Government of India, Ministry of External Affairs, *White Paper* 1 (New Delhi: External Publicity Division, Ministry of External Affairs, 1959), 76.
40 *Renmin ribao*, 19 April 1959, 4.
41 Liu Shaoqi, *Collected Works of Liu Shao-ch'i, 1958-1967* (Hong Kong: Union Research Institute, 1968), 153.

42   Allen S. Whiting, *The Chinese Calculus of Deterrence: India and Indochina* (Ann Arbor: University of Michigan Press, 1975), 38-39, 48.
43   "Declaration on the Conduct of Parties in the South China Sea," signed by China and the ASEAN states on 4 November 2002 in Phnom Penh, Cambodia.
44   Michael D. Swaine and Ashley J. Tellis, *Interpreting China's Grand Strategy: Past, Present, and Future* (Santa Monica, CA: RAND, 2000), 129.
45   Robert H. Donaldson, *The Soviet-Indian Alignment: Quest for Influence* (Denver: Graduate School of International Studies, University of Denver, 1979), 4-11.
46   John W. Garver, *Protracted Contest: Sino-Indian Rivalry in the Twentieth Century* (Seattle: University of Washington Press, 2001), 29-30.
47   Huth, "Enduring Rivalries and Territorial Disputes, 1950-1990."
48   Han Nianlong, ed., *Diplomacy of Contemporary China* (Hong Kong: New Horizon Press, 1990), 117-18.
49   *Wen wei po* (Hong Kong), 26 April 1996.
50   Qian Qichen, *Waijiao shiji* [Ten foreign policy events] (Beijing: Shijie zhishi chubanshe, 2003), 227; Mark Burles, *Chinese Policy toward Russia and the Central Asian Republics* (Santa Monica, CA: RAND, 1999), 5; Chien-peng Chung, "The Defense of Xinjiang," *Harvard International Review* 25, 2 (Summer 2003): 58; Niklas Swanström, "China and Central Asia: A New Great Game or Traditional Vassal Relations?" *Journal of Contemporary China* 14, 45 (November 2005): 570; Tariq Mahmud Ashraf, "Afghanistan and Chinese Strategy toward South and Central Asia," Jamestown Foundation *China Brief* 7, 10 (13 May 2008).
51   Gearóid Ó Tuathail, *Critical Geopolitics: The Politics of Writing Global Space* (Minneapolis: University of Minnesota Press, 1996), 1.
52   Henry A. Kissinger, *A World Restored: Metternich, Castlereagh and the Problems of Peace, 1812-22* (New York: Houghton Mifflin, 1957), 146-47.

Chapter 1: The Historical Legacy

1   Michael H. Hunt, "Chinese Foreign Relations in Historical Perspective," in *China's Foreign Relations in the 1980s*, ed. Harry Harding (New Haven, CT: Yale University Press, 1984), 1.
2   John K. Fairbank, "China's Foreign Policy in Historical Perspective," *Foreign Affairs* 47, 3 (April 1969): 449.
3   Herbert Franke and Denis Twitchett, "Introduction," in *The Cambridge History of China*, vol. 6, *Alien Regimes and Border States, 907-1368*, ed. Herbert Franke and Denis Twitchett (Cambridge: Cambridge University Press, 1994), 4.
4   Lian-sheng Yang, "Historical Notes on the Chinese World Order," in *The Chinese World Order: Traditional China's Foreign Relations*, ed. John King Fairbank (Cambridge, MA: Harvard University Press, 1968), 22.
5   Mark Mancall, *China at the Center: 300 Years of Foreign Policy* (New York: Free Press, 1984).
6   John Cranmer-Byng, "The Chinese View of Their Place in the World: An Historical Perspective," *China Quarterly* 53 (January-March 1973): 68.
7   Peter C. Perdue, "Boundaries, Maps, and Movement: Chinese, Russian, and Mongolian Empires in Early Modern Central Eurasia," *International History Review* 20, 2 (June 1998): 285.
8   Mark Mancall, "The Persistence of Tradition in Chinese Foreign Policy," *Annals of the American Academy of Political and Social Science* 349 (September 1963): 20.
9   Tu Wei-ming, "Cultural China: The Periphery as the Center," *Daedalus* 120, 2 (Spring 1991): 3.

10 Li Jijun, "Traditional Military Thinking and the Defensive Strategy of China," Letort Paper 1 (Carlisle, PA: Strategic Studies Institute, United States Army War College, 1997).

11 Peter C. Perdue, "Comparing Empires: Manchu Colonialism," *International History Review* 20, 2 (June 1998): 255.

12 David Curtis Wright, *From War to Diplomatic Parity in Eleventh-Century China: Sung's Foreign Relations with Kitan Liao* (Leiden, Netherlands: Brill, 2005), 28-29.

13 Malcolm Anderson, *Frontiers: Territory and State Formation in the Modern World* (Cambridge: Polity Press, 1996), 34-36.

14 Ping-Ti Ho, "The Significance of the Ch'ing Period in Chinese History," *Journal of Asian Studies* 26, 2 (February 1967): 191.

15 Chinese Ministry of Foreign Affairs, *Documents Concerning the Simla Conference*, Appendix 11, quoted in Ting-tsz Kao, *The Chinese Frontiers* (Aurora, IL: Chinese Scholarly Publishing 1980), 227.

16 Xie Bin, *Zhongguo sangdi shi* [History of China's lost territory] (Shanghai: Zhonghua shuju, 1925).

17 Ibid., 6

18 Foreign Broadcast Information Service [hereafter FBIS], *Daily Report: China* (6 June 1985): K3-K4.

19 Ibid., K4.

20 Ross Terrill, *The New Chinese Empire* (New York: Basic Books, 2003), 2, 54; Richard J. Smith, *Chinese Maps: Images of "All under Heaven"* (London: Oxford University Press, 1996), 78.

21 Lee Kuan Yew, speech given at the "1996 Architect of the New Century Dinner," Nixon Center, Washington, DC, 24 November 1996, http://www.nixoncenter.org/publications/YEW96.html.

22 Weng Tu-chien, "China's Policy on National Minorities," *People's China* 1, 7 (1 April 1950): 6.

23 G.F. Hudson, "The Nationalities of China," *St. Antony's Papers* 7 (1960): 53-54.

24 Translated in Conrad Brandt, Benjamin Schwartz, and John K. Fairbank, eds., *A Documentary History of Chinese Communism* (New York: Athenaeum, 1966), 64.

25 Ibid., 132.

26 Bela Kun, *Fundamental Laws of the Chinese Soviet Republic* (New York: International Publishers, 1934), 78-83.

27 Mao Tse-tung, *China: The March toward Unity* (New York: Workers Library Publishers, 1937), 40-41.

28 United States Senate, Committee on the Judiciary, Subcommittee to Investigate the Administration of the Internal Security Act and Other Internal Security Laws (91st Cong., 1st sess.), *The Amerasia Papers: A Clue to the Catastrophe of China* 2 (Washington, DC: Government Printing Office, 1970), 982.

29 Mao Zedong, *Zhongguo geming yu Zhongguo gongchandang* [The Chinese revolution and the Chinese Communist Party] (Zhangjiakou: Xinhua shudian, 1945), 1 (revised ed., Renmin chubanshe, 1952).

30 Harold Hinton, ed., *The People's Republic of China, 1949-1979: A Documentary Survey*, vol. 1 (Wilmington, DE: Scholarly Resources, 1980), 55.

31 Article 3, Chapter 1, Constitution of the People's Republic of China, *Documents of the First Session of the First National People's Congress of the CPR* (Peking: Foreign Language Press, 1955).

32 Chang Chih-i, *A Discussion of the National Question in the Chinese Revolution and of Actual Nationalities Policy (Draft)*, translated in George Moseley, *The Party and the National Question in China* (Cambridge, MA: MIT Press, 1966), 67-68.

33 Ho, "The Significance of the Ch'ing Period in Chinese History," 190-91.
34 Liu Peihua, *Zhongguo jindai shi* [Modern Chinese history] (Beijing: Yichang shuju, 1954), 129.
35 Ibid., 113-14.
36 *Renmin ribao,* 21 July 1962, 2; *China News Analysis* 437 (14 September 1962): 4.
37 Stuart Schram, *Mao Tse-tung* (New York: Penguin Books, 1977), 255-56.
38 Hua Di, "China's Comprehensive Strategic Doctrine," in *The Role of Technology in Meeting the Defense Challenges of the 1980s: Report of a Conference,* ed. William Perry and Hua Di (Stanford, CA: Arms Control and Disarmament Program, Stanford University, 1981), 85-86.
39 Mira Sinha Bhattacharjea, "China's Strategy for the Determination and Consolidation of Its Territorial Boundaries: A Preliminary Investigation," *China Report* 23, 4 (1987): 397-419.
40 *Zhong-Su youhao guanxi xuexi shouce* [Sino-Soviet friendly relations study handbook] (Shanghai: Zhanwang zhoukan, 1950), 57-58.
41 Hungdah Chiu, *Comparison of the Nationalist and Communist Chinese Views of Unequal Treaties,* Harvard Law School Studies in Chinese Law No. 19 (Cambridge, MA: Harvard Law School, 1972), 251-52, 258, 264.
42 Dong Wang, *China's Unequal Treaties: Narrating National History* (Lanham, MD: Lexington Books, 2005), 77.
43 See Li Jijun, "Traditional Military Thinking and the Defensive Strategy of China."
44 Wright, *From War to Diplomatic Parity,* 17.
45 Agnes Fang-Chin Chen, "Chinese Frontier Diplomacy: The Eclipse of Manchuria," *Yenching Journal of Social Studies* 5, 1 (July 1950): 118-20.
46 G.V. Ambekar and V.P. Divekar, eds., *Documents on China's Relations with South and South-East Asia (1949-1962)* (Bombay: Allied Publishers, 1964), 19.
47 *China News Analysis* 437 (14 September 1962): 6; Francis Watson, *The Frontiers of China* (New York: Praeger, 1966), 90, 63; *Renmin ribao,* 8 March 1963.
48 Chiu, "Comparison of the Nationalist and Communist Chinese Views of Unequal Treaties," 264-65; *Renmin ribao,* 8 March 1963, 1.
49 *Pravda,* 2 September 1964, in *Current Digest of the Soviet Press* 16, 34 (6 September 1964): 6-7.
50 Ouyang Yujing, Foreign Ministry, Department of Treaty and Law division director, quoted in "90% of Land Boundaries Settled," *China Youth Daily,* 5 May 2005, http://www.china.org.cn/archive/.
51 Pei Jianzhang, ed., *Yanjiu Zhou Enlai – waijiao sixiang yu shijian* (Research on Zhou Enlai: diplomatic thought and practice) (Beijing: Shijie zhishi chubanshe, 1989), 101-3.
52 Tian Zengpei, ed., *Gaige kaifang yilai de Zhongguo waijiao* [Chinese foreign policy since opening up and reform] (Beijing: Shijie zhishi chubanshe, 1993), 628.
53 See Li Jijun, "Traditional Military Thinking and the Defensive Strategy of China."

Chapter 2: Sino-Indian Relations and Boundary Disputes

1 Quoted in Han Nianlong, ed., *Diplomacy of Contemporary China* (Hong Kong: New Horizon Press, 1990), 221.
2 *Documents on the Sino-Indian Boundary Question* (Peking: Foreign Language Press, 1960), 6-7 and 88-89; Government of India, Ministry of External Affairs, *White Paper* 2 (New Delhi: External Publicity Division, Ministry of External Affairs, 1959), 39; Han, ibid., 221-22.
3 *The Times,* 8 September 1959, quoted in Xuecheng Liu, *The Sino-Indian Border Dispute and Sino-Indian Relations* (Lanham, MD: University Press of America, 1994), 57-59.

4 John Lall, *Aksaichin and Sino-Indian Conflict* (New Delhi: Allied Publishers, 1989), 254.

5 Quoted in Frank Moraes, *Witness to an Era: India, 1920 to the Present Day* (London: Weidenfeld and Nicolson, 1973), 220.

6 K.M. Panikkar, *In Two Chinas: Memoirs of a Diplomat* (London: George Allen and Unwin 1955), 101-2.

7 Krishna P.S. Menon, *Delhi-Chungking: A Travel Diary* (Bombay: Oxford University Press, 1947), 29.

8 Sarvepalli Gopal, *Jawaharlal Nehru: A Biography, Volume 2: 1947-1956* (Cambridge, MA: Harvard University Press, 1979), 105-6; Xie Yixian, *Zhongguo waijiao shi: Zhonghua Renmin Gongheguo shiqi 1949-1979* [A diplomatic history of China: the period of the People's Republic of China, 1949-1979] (Zhengzhou: Henan renmin chubanshe, 1988), 22-23.

9 Steven A. Hoffman, *India and the China Crisis* (Berkeley: University of California Press, 1990), 32.

10 *Zhonghua Renmin Gongheguo bianjie shiwu tiaoyueji: ZhongYin ZhongBu juan* [The People's Republic of China boundary affairs treaty collection: China-India China-Bhutan volume] (Beijing: Shijie zhishi chubanshe, 2004); Government of India, Ministry of External Affairs, *White Paper* 1 (New Delhi: External Publicity Division, Ministry of External Affairs, 1959), 98-105; Panikkar, *In Two Chinas*, 102, 170-71, 174-75; B.M. Mullik, *The Chinese Betrayal: My Years with Nehru* (Bombay: Allied Publishers, 1971), 146-53.

11 India, Parliamentary Debates, 5, pt. 1, 155-56 quoted in Lall, *Aksaichin and Sino-Indian Conflict*, 237.

12 Hoffman, *India and the China Crisis*, 25-30.

13 Shri Prakash, "The Sixth Meeting of the India-China Joint Working Group on the Boundary Question," *China Report: A Journal of East Asian Studies* 30, 1 (January-March 1994): 90-91.

14 Government of India, Ministry of External Affairs, *Report of the Officials of the Government of India and the People's Republic of China on the Boundary Question* (New Delhi: External Publicity Division, Ministry of External Affairs, 1961), 8.

15 Han, *Diplomacy of Contemporary China*, 218.

16 J.N. Dixit, *Across Borders: Fifty Years of India's Foreign Policy* (New Delhi: Picus Books, 1998), 354.

17 Gopal, *Jawaharlal Nehru*, 2: 176-81; Hoffman, *India and the China Crisis*, 32-33.

18 Mullik, *The Chinese Betrayal*, 151.

19 Pei Jianzhang, ed., *Yanjiu Zhou Enlai – waijiao sixiang yu shijian* [Research on Zhou Enlai: diplomatic thought and practice] (Beijing: Shijie zhishi chubanshe, 1989), 7.

20 Sarvepalli Gopal, *Jawaharlal Nehru: A Biography, Volume 3: 1956-1964* (Cambridge, MA: Harvard University Press, 1984), 90, 101.

21 Dipankar Gupta, *The Context of Ethnicity: Sikh Ethnicity in a Comparative Perspective* (Delhi: Oxford University Press, 1996), 17.

22 *ITAR-TASS*, 9 September 1959, in *Current Digest of the Soviet Press*, 11, 36 (7 October 1959): 14.

23 Xie, *Zhongguo waijiao shi ... 1949-1979*, 291.

24 Chen Xiaolu, "Chen Yi and China's Diplomacy," paper presented at the Woodrow Wilson Center for International Scholars conference, 7-9 July 1992.

25 G.V. Matveyev, "Peking's Political Machinations on the Hindustan Peninsula," *Problemy Dalnego Vostoka* 4 (December 1972): 39-45, abstract trans. in *Current Digest of the Soviet Press* 25, 11 (11 April 1973): 4.

26 John W. Garver, *Protracted Contest: Sino-Indian Rivalry in the Twentieth Century* (Seattle: University of Washington Press, 2001), 101.

27 Han, *Diplomacy of Contemporary China*, 219; *White Paper* 1: 75-76. This interpretation was also corroborated by interviews with Chinese scholars at both the China Institute of International Studies and the China Institutes of Contemporary International Relations in July 1994.
28 Garver, *Protracted Contest*, 102, citing Xu Yan, *Zhong-Yin bianjie zhi zhan lishi zhenxiang* [The true history of the Sino-Indian border war] (Hong Kong: Tiandi tushu gongsi, 1993), 54.
29 United States Consulate General, Hong Kong, *Current Background*, 559 (1959).
30 Xie, *Zhongguo waijiao shi ... 1949-1979*, 151.
31 *White Paper* 1: 1-4; G.V. Ambekar and V.P. Divekar, eds., *Documents on China's Relations with South and South-East Asia (1949-1962)* (Bombay: Allied Publishers, 1964), 119; *Documents on the Sino-Indian Boundary Question*, 9-10 and 78-79; John Rowland, *A History of Sino-Indian Relations: Hostile Co-Existence* (Princeton, NJ: D. Van Nostrand, 1967), 85.
32 *White Paper* 1: 49; Ambekar and Divekar, *Documents on China's Relations with South and South- East Asia*, 111-12; Government of India, Ministry of External Affairs, *Report of the Officials*, CR-29-30, 163; Rowland, *A History of Sino-Indian Relations*, 95.
33 Hoffman, *India and the China Crisis*, 35.
34 Ibid., 35-36.
35 *China Pictorial* 95 (July 1958): 20-21; Han, *Diplomacy of Contemporary China*, 218; *White Paper* 1: 47-54; Ambekar and Divekar, *Documents on China's Relations with South and South-East Asia*, 118; *Documents on the Sino-Indian Boundary Question*, 7-8; Government of India, Ministry of External Affairs, *Report of the Officials*, CR-29-30; Mullik, *The Chinese Betrayal*, 150-51; Alastair Lamb, *Asian Frontiers: Studies in a Continuing Problem* (New York: Praeger, 1968), 121-22; Harold C. Hinton, *Communist China in World Politics* (Boston: Houghton Mifflin, 1966), 285.
36 After 1975, when India annexed Sikkim, a fourth sector was created, but China tacitly accepted the annexation of Sikkim in 2003 and the border is no longer an issue.
37 Yang Gongsu, *Zhonghua Renmin Gongheguo waijiao lilun yu shijian* [The theory and practice of People's Republic of China diplomacy] (Beijing: Beijing daxue guoji guanxi xueyuan, 1997), 171-74.
38 Garver, *Protracted Contest*, 103.
39 Yang, *Zhonghua Renmin Gongheguo waijiao lilun yu shijian*, 175.
40 *White Paper* 1: 47-51; Ambekar and Divekar, *Documents on China's Relations with South and South-East Asia*, 112-16; Government of India, Ministry of External Affairs, *Report of the Officials*, CR-29-30, 163.
41 Government of India, Ministry of External Affairs, *Report of the Officials*, 240-50 and CR-12-32.
42 Garver, *Protracted Contest*, 94-95.
43 Chen Xiaolu, "Chen Yi and China's Diplomacy," 122.
44 "Quarterly Chronicle and Documentation," *China Quarterly* 1 (January-March 1960): 110.
45 *White Paper* 1: 49-50; Government of India, Ministry of External Affairs, *India China Border Problem* (New Delhi: External Publicity Division, Ministry of External Affairs, 1962), 5; Hoffman, *India and the China Crisis*, 37.
46 *White Paper* 1: 46-57; *White Paper* 2: 27-47.
47 *White Paper* 1: 48; *White Paper* 2: 35; Ambekar and Divekar, *Documents on China's Relations with South and South-East Asia*, 113; *Documents on the Sino-Indian Boundary Question*, 77-78 and 101-2; Government of India, Ministry of External Affairs, *Report of the Officials*, CR-30-31.

48 *White Paper* 2: 27-33; *Documents on the Sino-Indian Boundary Question*, 1-13.

49 *Renmin ribao*, 19 April 1959, 4; Government of India, Ministry of External Affairs, *White Paper* 3 (New Delhi: External Publicity Division, Ministry of External Affairs, 1959), 45-51; *Documents on the Sino-Indian Boundary Question*, 14-17 and 129-38; Neville Maxwell, "China and India: 'The Un-Negotiated Dispute,'" *China Quarterly* 43 (July-September 1970): 62; Olaf Caroe, "The Sino-Indian Frontier Dispute," *Asian Review* 59, 218 (April 1963).

50 Gopal, *Jawaharlal Nehru*, 3: 98.

51 *White Paper* 1: 52; Ambekar and Divekar, *Documents on China's Relations with South and South-East Asia*, 118.

52 *White Paper* 2: 31; *Documents on the Sino-India Boundary Question*, 9.

53 Yang, *Zhonghua Renmin Gongheguo waijiao lilun yu shijian*, 187.

54 "Report at the Second NPC Standing Committee, September 11, 1959," *Peking Review*, 15 September 1959, 13.

55 M. Taylor Fravel, "Regime Insecurity and International Cooperation: Explaining China's Compromises in Territorial Disputes," *International Security* 30, 2 (Fall 2005): 67.

56 Garver, *Protracted Contest*, 101.

57 *White Paper* 3: 45-46; *Documents on the Sino-Indian Boundary Question*, 15.

58 "Premier Chou En-lai in India," *Peking Review*, 26 April 1960, 41.

59 Neville Maxwell, *India's China War* (London: Jonathan Cape, 1970), 156.

60 Yang, *Zhonghua Renmin Gongheguo waijiao lilun yu shijian*, 188; Xie, *Zhongguo waijiao shi ... 1949-1979*, 264; Han, *Diplomacy of Contemporary China*, 225.

61 B.M. Kaul, *The Untold Story* (New Delhi: Allied Publishers, 1967), 367; B.M. Kaul unpublished paper, quoted in Lall, *Aksaichin and Sino-Indian Conflict*, 274; Yaacov Y.I. Vertzberger, *Misperceptions in Foreign Policymaking: The Sino-Indian Conflict, 1959-1962* (Boulder, CO: Westview Press, 1984), 101-2, 121-22, 149-50.

62 Gopal, *Jawaharlal Nehru*, 3: 97.

63 S.V. Chervonenko, "Memorandum of Conversation with the General Secretary of the CCP Deng Xiaoping, 6 November 1959," *Cold War International History Project Bulletin* 10 (March 1998): 171.

64 "Record of Conversation between Chinese Premier Zhou Enlai and Mongolian Leader J. Zedenbal" (26 December 1962), Cold War International History Project, *Digital Archive*, *Mongolia in the Cold War*, http://digitalarchive.wilsoncenter.org/document/112072.

65 Gopal, *Jawaharlal Nehru*, 3: 136.

66 *Peking Review*, 3 May 1960, 18-19.

67 Maxwell, *India's China War*, 161-69; Hoffman, *India and the China Crisis*, 86-87.

68 Interview with a former associate of Krishna Menon. For corroborating evidence, see T.J.S. George, *Krishna Menon: A Biography* (London: Jonathan Cape, 1964), 254-55; Michael Brecher, *India and World Politics: Krishna Menon's View of the World* (New York: Praeger, 1968), 150-51, 169-70.

69 Lall, *Aksaichin and Sino-Indian Conflict*, 251, 266-67.

70 Quoted in ibid., 269.

71 "Premier Chou En-lai's Written Statement," *Peking Review*, 3 May 1960, 18; Government of India, Ministry of External Affairs, *Prime Minister on Sino-Indian Relations*, vol. 1, *In Parliament* (New Delhi: External Publicity Division, Ministry of External Affairs, 1961), 59.

72 Gopal, *Jawaharlal Nehru*, 3: 133-34.

73 Government of India, Ministry of External Affairs, *Report of the Officials*.

74 Cheng Youshu, "Wo he Yindu," in *Nü waijiaoguan* [Female diplomats], ed. Cheng Xiangjun (Beijing: Renmin tiyu chubanshe, 1995), 88, paraphrased in Xiaohong Liu, *Chinese*

Ambassadors: The Rise of Diplomatic Professionalism since 1949 (Seattle: University of Washington Press, 2001), 133.

75 Government of India, Ministry of External Affairs, *White Paper* 6 (New Delhi: External Publicity Division, Ministry of External Affairs, 1962), 188; Allen S. Whiting, *The Chinese Calculus of Deterrence: India and Indochina* (Ann Arbor: University of Michigan Press, 1975), 45.

76 Hoffman, *India and the China Crisis*, 90-91.

77 Gopal, *Jawaharlal Nehru*, 3: 213-14; P.C. Joshi, "Chinese Dogmatism and the Border Dispute," *New Age* 11, 4 (27 January 1963): 10-11.

78 Arthur Lall, *The Emergence of Modern India* (New York: Columbia University Press, 1981), 155-58.

79 Lall, *Aksaichin and Sino-Indian Conflict*, 251.

80 Kaul, *The Untold Story*, 386-87.

81 Vladislav M. Zubok, "The Mao-Khrushchev Conversations, 31 July – 3 August 1958 and 2 October 1959," *Cold War International History Project Bulletin*, Issue 12/13 (Fall/Winter 2001): 248 Xue Mouhong and Pei Jianzhang, eds., *Dangdai Zhongguo waijiao* [Contemporary Chinese diplomacy] (Beijing: Zhongguo shehui kexue yuan, 1988), 617.

82 Quoted in Zubok, "The Mao-Khrushchev Conversations," 248; From the Journal of Ambassador S.F. Antonov, Summary of a Conversation with the Chairman of the CC CPC Mao Zedong" (14 October 1959), http://digitalarchive.wilsoncenter.org/document/114788.

83 Government of India, Ministry of External Affairs, *White Paper* 8 (New Delhi: External Publicity Division, Ministry of External Affairs, 1963), 1-5.

84 Ibid., 17-24; *Peking Review*, 30 November 1962, 47-48.

85 Quoted in Chen, "Chen Yi and China's Diplomacy," 123.

86 Surjit Mansingh, *India's Search for Power: Indira Gandhi's Foreign Policy, 1966-1982* (New Delhi: Sage Publications, 1984), 204.

87 Quoted in Geng Nien, "Sino-Indian Relations: Retrospect and Prospect," *South Asian Studies* [Chengdu] 3-4 (1981): 3.

88 *New York Times*, 12 June 1978, A6.

89 Foreign Broadcast Information Service [hereafter FBIS], *Daily Report: China*, 25 June 1980, F1-2.

90 John W. Garver, "Sino-Indian Rapprochement and the Sino-Pakistan Entente," *Political Science Quarterly* 11, 2 (Summer 1996): 326-29.

91 Xie, *Zhongguo waijiao shi: Zhonghua Renmin Gongheguo shiqi 1979-1994* [A diplomatic history of China: the period of the People's Republic of China, 1979-1994] (Zhengzhou: Henan renmin chubanshe, 1995), 125-26; *Asian Recorder*, 6-12 August 1981, 161-62.

92 Garver, *Protracted Contest*, 103.

93 "Mr. Huang Hua's Visit to New Delhi – Agreement to Discuss Border Question," *Keesing's Contemporary Archives* 27 (October 1981): 31153.

94 Chen Tiqiang, "ZhongYin bianjie wenti de falu fangmian" [Legal aspects of the Sino-Indian boundary issue], *Guoji wenti yanjiu* 1 (1982): 13.

95 Surjit Mansingh and Steven I. Levine, "China and India: Moving beyond Confrontation," *Problems of Communism* 38, 2-3 (March-June 1989): 38; John W. Garver, "The Indian Factor in Recent Sino-Soviet Relations," *China Quarterly* 125 (March 1991): 74-75.

96 Garver, "Sino-Indian Rapprochement and the Sino-Pakistan Entente," 343.

97 FBIS, *Daily Report: China*, 15 December 1986, F1.

98 Xie, *Zhongguo waijiao shi ... 1979-1994*, 126-27; Nayan Chanda, "Heading for a Conflict," *Far Eastern Economic Review*, 4 June 1987, 42-43; *United Press International* New Delhi,

3 November 1992; *Christian Science Monitor,* 15 December 1988, 15, and 19 December 1988, 28; *China Report* 23, 4 (1987): 477-78.

99 FBIS, *Daily Report: China,* 15 December 1986, F1.

100 Robert G. Sutter and Richard P. Cronin, *China-India Border Friction,* CRS Report 87-514F (Washington, DC: Congressional Research Service, 1987).

101 *China Daily,* 17 June 1987.

102 Sumit Ganguly, "The Sino-Indian Border Talks, 1981-1989," *Asian Survey* 29, 12 (December 1989): 1128.

103 Salamat Ali, "A Shot in the Arm," *Far Eastern Economic Review,* 1 December 1988, 38.

104 Paul H. Kreisberg, "The Indian-Chinese Summit," *Christian Science Monitor,* 15 December 1988, 16.

105 Mira Sinha Bhattacharjea, "Indian Prime Minister's Visit to China," *China Report: A Journal of East Asian Studies* 30, 1 (January-March 1994): 85-86; "Sino-Indian Joint Press Communiqué" (23 December 1988), http://www.fmprc.gov.cn/eng/wjdt/2649/t15800.htm.

106 *Zhonghua Renmin Gongheguo bianjie shiwu tiaoyueji: ZhongYin ZhongBu juan;* "Agreement on the Maintenance of Peace along the Line of Actual Control in the India-China Border" (7 September 1993), 59-67.

107 *Reuters* Beijing, 7 September 1993.

108 *Xinhua,* 8 March 1994; *Agence France-Presse,* 19 July 1994.

109 Waheguru Pal Singh Sidhu and Jin-dong Yuan, "Resolving the Sino-Indian Border Dispute: Building Confidence through Cooperative Monitoring," *Asian Survey* 41, 2 (March/April 2001): 359-60; *South China Morning Post,* 28 April 1998.

110 Wang Hongwei, "Gong jian mianxiang 21 shiji jianshexing hezuo huoban guanxi" [Jointly build relations of constructive cooperative partnership facing the twenty-first century], *Waiguo wenti yanjiu [International Studies]* 1 (gen. issue 46) (1997): 37-41, quoted in Garver, *Protracted Contest,* 7.

111 *New York Times,* 5 May 1998, A6, and 13 May 1998, A14; *Times of India,* 4 May 1998; *South China Morning Post,* 5 May 1998.

112 Stratfor, "Analysis: China Tilts toward India," *Asia Times Online,* 18 June 1999, http://www.atimes.com/.

113 Ramtanu Maitra, "Prospects Brighten for Kunming Initiative," *Asia Times Online,* 12 February 2003, http://www.atimes.com/.

114 The Chinese Foreign Ministry website listed Sikkim as an independent country with this notation until October 2003.

115 Garver, *Protracted Contest,* 175.

116 *Reuters,* 17 December 1996.

117 *Zhonghua Renmin Gongheguo bianjie shiwu tiaoyueji: ZhongYin ZhongBu juan,* 115-20.

118 Jyoti Malhotra, "For India's Tibet Turn, China to Amend its Sikkim Map," *Indian Express,* 25 June 2003.

119 *Hindustan Times,* 24 June 2003 and 28 June 2003; *New York Times,* 25 June 2003.

120 *Hindustan Times,* 12 April 2005.

121 *Straits Times,* 23 June 2003; *Xinhua,* 24 June 2003; "India and China Agree over Tibet," *BBC News,* 24 June 2003, http://news.bbc.co.uk/go/pr/fr/-/2/hi/south_asia/3015840.stm; *Beijing Review,* 3 July 2003, 17.

122 *Hindustan Times,* 28 June 2003.

123 "Premier Wen Jiabao Meets Indian Prime Minister Vajpayee" (9 October 2003). http://www.fmprc.gov.cn/mfa_eng/wjb_663304/zzjg_663340/yzs_663350/gjlb_663354/2711_663426/2713_663430/t26842.shtml.

124 *Beijing Review*, 3 July 2003, 17.

125 *The Hindu*, 31 July 2003.

126 "Agreement between the Government of India and the Government of the People's Republic of China on the Political Parameters and Guiding Principles for the Settlement of the India-China Boundary Questions," 11 April 2005.

127 V.V. Paranjpe, "Climb over the Wall," *Hindustan Times*, 17 June 2003.

128 *The Hindu*, 11 April 2005; "China and India Sign Border Deal," *BBC News*, 11 April 2005, http://news.bbc.co.uk/2/hi/south_asia/4431299.stm.

129 "Agreement between the Government of the Republic of India and the Government of the People's Republic of China on the Establishment of a Working Mechanism for Consultation and Coordination on India-China Border Affairs," http://peacemaker.un. org/; "India, China to Set Up Working Mechanism on Border Management," *The Hindu*, 17 January 2012, http://www.thehindu.com/.

130 "China, India End Border Standoff," *Xinhuanet*, 6 May 2013, http://news.xinhuanet.com/.

131 Ministry of Foreign Affairs of the People's Republic of China, "Premier Li Keqiang Meets with National Security Adviser Shivshankar Menon of India" (29 June 2013), http://www. fmprc.gov.cn/.

132 "Full Text of Joint Statement by Chinese, Indian Defence Ministers," *Xinhuanet*, 6 July 2013, http://news.xinhuanet.com/.

133 Ganguly, "The Sino-Indian Border Talks," 1127-28, 1134.

134 Ananth Krishnan, "India, China Conclude Talks; to Strengthen Border Mechanism," *The Hindu*, 29 June 2013, http://www.thehindu.com/.

135 George J. Gilboy and Eric Heginbotham, *Chinese and Indian Strategic Behavior: Growing Power and Alarm* (New York: Cambridge University Press, 2012).

136 Ramtanu Maitra, "Prospects Brighten for Kunming Initiative," *Asia Times Online*, 12 February 2003, http://www.atimes.com/.

137 Ouyang Yujing, Foreign Ministry, Department of Treaty and Law division director, quoted in "90% of Land Boundaries Settled," *China Youth Daily*, 5 May 2005, http://www.china. org.cn/archive/.

138 Gopal, *Jawaharlal Nehru*, 3: 133-34.

Chapter 3: The Sino-Burmese Boundary Settlement

1 Du Hengzhi, *Zhong-wai tiaoyue guanxi zhi bianqian* [Changes in Sino-foreign treaty relations] (Taipei: Zhonghua wenwu gongying she, 1981), 87-89; W. Stark Toller, "The Undefined China-Burma Frontier," *Eastern World* 2, 10/11 (October-November 1948): 12.

2 Yang Gongsu, *Zhonghua Renmin Gongheguo waijiao lilun yu shijian* [The theory and practice of People's Republic of China diplomacy] (Beijing: Beijing daxue guoji guanxi xueyuan, 1997), 146; J.R.V. Prescott, *Map of Mainland Asia by Treaty* (Melbourne: Melbourne University Press, 1975), 347-81.

3 Hugh Tinker, *The Union of Burma: A Study of the First Years of Independence*, 4th ed. (London: Oxford University Press, 1967), 339-40; Brendan Whyte, "The Sino-Myanmar Border," in *Beijing's Power and China's Borders: Twenty Neighbors in Asia*, ed. Bruce A. Elleman, Stephen Kotkin, and Clive Schofield (Armonk, NY: M.E. Sharpe, 2013), 191-95; Hugh Tinker, "Burma's Northeast Borderland Problems," *Pacific Affairs* 29, 4 (December 1956): 334; Toller, "The Undefined China-Burma Frontier," 12.

4 Han Nianlong, ed., *Diplomacy of Contemporary China* (Hong Kong: New Horizon Press, 1990), 179; Tinker, "Burma's Northeast Borderland Problems," 338-42.

5 Han, ibid., 179; Xie Yixian, *Zhongguo waijiao shi: Zhonghua Renmin Gongheguo shiqi 1949-1979* [A diplomatic history of China: the period of the People's Republic of China, 1949-1979] (Zhengzhou: Henan renmin chubanshe, 1988), 241-42; Wang Taiping, ed.,

Zhonghua Renmin Gongheguo waijiao shi (2) 1957-1959 [Diplomatic history of the PRC (vol. 2) 1957-1969] (Beijing: Shijie zhishi chubanshe, 1998), 95; Daphne E. Whittam, "The Sino-Burmese Boundary Treaty," *Pacific Affairs* 34, 2 (Summer 1961): 175-77; Toller, "The Undefined China-Burma Frontier," 12-14.

6　*Burma Weekly Bulletin,* 5 May 1960, 2; Han, ibid., 179-80.

7　*Burma Weekly Bulletin,* 5 May 1960, 1-8; Whittam, "The Sino-Burmese Boundary Treaty," 174-75; Wang, *Zhonghua Renmin Gongheguo waijiao shi (2),* 94-95.

8　Thakin Nu, *From Peace to Stability* (Rangoon: Government of the Union of Burma, Ministry of Information, 1951), 197-98.

9　Quoted in ibid., 51.

10　The majority of the Nationalist remnants were eventually evacuated in 1953-54 with the cooperation of the Republic of China, the United States, and Thailand, with United Nations involvement.

11　*A Victory for the Five Principles of Peaceful Coexistence: Documents on the Sino-Burmese Boundary Question* (Peking: Foreign Language Press, 1960), 17.

12　Quoted in Shen-yu Dai, "Peking and Rangoon," *China Quarterly* 5 (January-March 1961): 131.

13　*People's China* 1, 2 (16 January 1950): 3.

14　*New China News Agency,* 23 November 1949.

15　*Premier Reports to the People* (Rangoon: Government of the Union of Burma, 1958), 35-36.

16　*Zhonghua Renmin Gongheguo fensheng ditu* (Shanghai: Shanghai ditu chubanshe, 1953), map 46 note; *A Victory for the Five Principles of Peaceful Coexistence,* 17.

17　Harold Hinton, *China's Relations with Burma and Vietnam: A Brief Survey.* (New York: Institute of Pacific Relations, 1958), 45; Tinker, "Burma's Northeast Borderland Problems," 345; J. Stephen Hoadley, "The China-Burma Border Settlement: A Retrospective Evaluation," *Asian Forum* 2, 2 (April-June 1970): 106.

18　*Burma Weekly Bulletin,* 9 September 1950, 133.

19　*The Nation,* 6 December 1960.

20　*Shijie zhishi shouce* [World knowledge handbook] (Beijing: Shijie zhishi chubanshe, 1954), 340; U Nu, "Speech at the Burmese Parliament, March 8, 1951," in Thakin Nu, *From Peace to Stability,* 198; Harold Hinton, *Communist China in World Politics* (Boston: Houghton Mifflin, 1966), 310-11; Whittam, "The Sino-Burmese Boundary Treaty," 175.

21　*Asian Recorder,* 21-27 January 1956, 633; 4-10 August 1956, 961.

22　Han, *Diplomacy of Contemporary China,* 179-80; Wang, *Zhonghua Renmin Gongheguo waijiao shi (2),* 95-97.

23　Thakin Nu, *From Peace to Stability,* 198; *New York Times,* 9 March 1951; Hinton, *China's Relations with Burma and Vietnam,* 40.

24　Xie, *Zhongguo waijiao shi ... 1949-1979,* 152; *New China News Agency,* 30 June 1954.

25　*New China News Agency,* 12 December 1954; *Burma Weekly Bulletin,* 15 December 1954; 5 May 1960, 1.

26　Whittam, "The Sino-Burmese Boundary Treaty," 175-78; Dorothy Woodman, *The Making of Burma* (London: Cresset Press, 1962), 524-26; Hinton, *China's Relations with Burma and Vietnam,* 41, 53; William C. Johnstone, *Burma's Foreign Policy: A Study in Neutralism* (Cambridge, MA: Harvard University Press, 1963), 191-92; Frank N. Trager, "Burma and China," *Journal of Southeast Asian History* 5, 1 (March 1964): 44-46; Wang, *Zhonghua Renmin Gongheguo waijiao shi (2),* 95.

27　*New York Times,* 1 June 1959.

28　*Economist,* 8 August 1956, 570-71.

29　Xie, *Zhongguo waijiao shi ... 1949-1979,* 242; Wang, *Zhonghua Renmin Gongheguo waijiao shi (2),* 95.

30 *Burma Weekly Bulletin,* 5 May 1960, 2.
31 Frank N. Trager, "Burma's Foreign Policy, 1948-1956: Neutralism, Third Force and Rice," *Journal of Asian Studies* 16 (November 1956): 92 fn.
32 *New China News Agency,* 4 August 1956; Whittam, "The Sino-Burmese Boundary Treaty," 177.
33 Woodman, *Making of Burma,* 535-36.
34 A detailed first-hand account of the negotiations is given by U Nu, "Sino-Burmese Boundary Agreement and Treaty of Friendship and Mutual Non-Aggression," *Burma Weekly Bulletin,* 5 May 1960, 1-8.
35 Quoted in Han, *Diplomacy of Contemporary China,* 179.
36 *Burma Weekly Bulletin,* 5 May 1960, 2-3; *New China News Agency,* 22 October 1956; 25 October 1956; 9 November 1956; *Survey of China Mainland Press,* no. 1420 (November 1956): 32; Woodman, *Making of Burma,* 529-30.
37 Woodman, ibid., 530-31; U Nu, *U Nu – Saturday's Son,* trans. U Law Yone, ed. U Kyaw Win (New Haven, CT: Yale University Press, 1975), 258-59; Richard J. Kozicki, "The Sino-Burmese Frontier Problem," *Far Eastern Survey* 26, 3 (March 1957): 33-38.
38 Xie, *Zhongguo waijiao shi ... 1949-1979,* 245; *A Victory for the Five Principles of Peaceful Coexistence,* 16-27.
39 *Burma Weekly Bulletin,* 5 May 1960, 4-5.
40 Woodman, *Making of Burma,* 534.
41 *Burma Weekly Bulletin,* 5 May 1960, 6; *The Nation,* 29 April 1960; Woodman, ibid., 536.
42 *Peking Review,* 26 February 1960, 9-16; *Survey of China Mainland Press,* no. 2188 (3 February 1960): 47; *Asian Recorder,* 10-16 September 1960, 3527; Richard Butwell, "The Sino-Burmese Border Truce," *New Leader* 43, 9 (29 February 1960): 15-16; U Maung Maung, *Burma and General Ne Win* (New York: Asia Publishing House, 1969): 265-70.
43 Maung Maung, "The Burma-China Boundary Settlement," *Asian Survey* 1, 1 (March 1961): 38-43; Whittam, "The Sino-Burmese Boundary Treaty," 174-83; Trager, "Burma and China," 29-61.
44 *United Press International* Rangoon, 5 December 1960.
45 *Burma Weekly Bulletin,* 5 May 1960, 5-7.
46 D.G.E. Hall, *Burma* (London: Hutchison University Library, 1960), 160; Frank N. Trager, "Communist China: The New Imperialism," *Current History* 41, 241 (September 1961): 136-40; Whittam, "The Sino-Burmese Boundary Treaty," 182.
47 Wang, *Zhonghua Renmin Gongheguo waijiao shi (2),* 97.
48 *Burma Weekly Bulletin,* 7 July 1960, 75-77; 21 July 1960, 90; 28 July 1960, 98; 11 August 1960, 114; 15 September 1960, 155.
49 *New China News Agency,* 1 October 1960; *Peking Review,* 4 October 1960, 29-34.
50 Trager, "Communist China: The New Imperialism," 136-40; Amry Vandenbosch, "Chinese Communism for Export," *Current History* 39, 232 (December 1960): 333-38.
51 Yang, *Zhonghua Renmin Gongheguo waijiao lilun yu shijian,* 154-55; *New China News Agency,* 22, 27, 30 April 1959.
52 *Peking Review,* 12 April 1960.
53 *Renmin ribao,* 1 October 1960.
54 Tinker, *The Union of Burma,* 373.
55 *Renmin ribao,* 1 February 1960.
56 Frederick Joss, "China Penetrates the Shan Region of Burma," *Eastern World* (London) 20, 1/2 (January-February 1966): 14-16; Woodman, *Making of Burma,* 522-23; Toller, "The Undefined China-Burma Frontier," 14.
57 U Raschid, "Speech at the Burmese Chamber of Commerce, February 18, 1956," *Burma Weekly Bulletin,* 23 February 1956.

58 Johnstone, *Burma's Foreign Policy,* 199-200.
59 Daniel Wolfstone, "Fast Work on the Sino-Burmese Border," *Far Eastern Economic Review,* 18 August 1960, 368-74.
60 Ibid.; Tinker, *The Union of Burma,* 369.
61 Robert A. Holmes, "The Sino-Burmese Rift: A Failure for China," *Orbis* 16, 1 (Spring 1972): 220-21.
62 *New York Times,* 30 December 1963; *New China News Agency,* 12 July 1964.

Chapter 4: Boundary Settlements with Nepal, Sikkim, and Bhutan

1 A.S. Bhasin, ed., *Documents on Nepal's Relations with India and China, 1949-1966* (Bombay: Academic Books, 1970), 18-22; Ram Rahul, "China's Other Boundaries," *Australian Journal of Politics and History* 9, 2 (May-November 1963): 162.
2 Han Nianlong, ed., *Diplomacy of Contemporary China* (Hong Kong: New Horizon Press, 1990), 182-83; Xie Yixian, *Zhongguo waijiao shi: Zhonghua Renmin Gongheguo shiqi 1949-1979* [A diplomatic history of China: the period of the People's Republic of China, 1949-1979] (Zhengzhou: Henan renmin chubanshe, 1988), 250.
3 Chinese Peoples' Institute of Foreign Affairs, ed. *New Developments in Friendly Relations between China and Nepal* (Peking: Foreign Language Press, 1960), 55; Leo E. Rose, *Nepal: Strategy for Survival* (Berkeley: University of California Press, 1971), 209-10; Leo E. Rose, "Sino-Indian Rivalry and the Himalayan Border States," *Orbis* 5, 2 (Summer 1961): 206-8.
4 Chinese Peoples' Institute of Foreign Affairs, ibid., 7-14; Bhasin, *Documents on Nepal's Relations,* 185.
5 *Asian Recorder* 1, 59 (11 February 1956): 678; S.D. Muni, *Foreign Policy of Nepal* (Delhi: National Publishing House, 1973), 104.
6 Arthur Lall, *How Communist China Negotiates* (New York: Columbia University Press, 1968), 199-200; Guy Searls, "Communist China's Border Policy: Dragon Throne Imperialism?" *Current Scene* 2, 12 (15 April 1963): 11-12.
7 Chinese Peoples' Institute of Foreign Affairs, *New Developments,* 15; Muni, *Foreign Policy of Nepal,* 104; Rose, *Nepal: Strategy for Survival,* 223.
8 *Peking Review,* 25 February 1960, 10.
9 Quoted in Rose, *Nepal: Strategy for Survival,* 225.
10 *New York Times,* 22 March 1960, 1.
11 PRC Foreign Ministry and CCP Central Document Research Office, eds., *Mao Zedong waijiao wenxuan* [Selected foreign policy documents of Mao Zedong] (Beijing: Zhongyang wenxian chubanshe/Shijie zhishi chubanshe, 1994), 395-97; Han, *Diplomacy of Contemporary China,* 184; Xie, *Zhongguo waijiao shi ... 1949-1979,* 251.
12 *Zhonghua Renmin Gongheguo bianjie shiwu tiaoyueji: ZhongNi juan* [The People's Republic of China boundary affairs treaty collection: China-Nepal volume] (Beijing: Shijie zhishi chubanshe, 2004).
13 Muni, *Foreign Policy of Nepal,* 105-6, 112.
14 *Peking Review,* 29 March 1960, 6-10; Bhasin, *Documents on Nepal's Relations,* 266-68; *Far Eastern Economic Review,* 16 June 1960, 1246-48.
15 Han, *Diplomacy of Contemporary China,* 183-84.
16 Chinese Peoples' Institute of Foreign Affairs, *New Developments,* 35, 69-71; *Survey of China Mainland Press,* no. 2218 (17 March 1960): 39-42; 347 (1962): 25; *Associated Press,* Kathmandu, 30 April 1960; Muni, *Foreign Policy of Nepal,* 107, fn. 30.
17 *New York Times,* 22 April 1960, 3.
18 *Peking Review,* 3 May 1960, 12-13.
19 Xie, *Zhongguo waijiao shi ... 1949-1979,* 251.

20　*Peking Review,* 31 May 1960, 4; 7 June 1960, 21-22.

21　Kenneth Conboy and James Morrison, *The CIA's Secret War in Tibet* (Lawrence: University Press of Kansas, 2002), and S. Mahmud Ali, *Cold War in the High Himalayas: The USA, China and South Asia in the 1950s* (New York: St. Martin's Press, 1999), 110-14; Muni, *Foreign Policy of Nepal,* 107-8, esp. fn. 34.

22　*New China News Agency,* 2 July 1960; Koirala interview in *Sunday Post-Herald* (Hong Kong), 18 September 1960.

23　*Asian Recorder,* 23-29 July 1960, 3449-51; 10-16 September 1960, 3536; *China Today* 5, 32 (7 July 1960): 4-5.

24　*Zhonghua Renmin Gongheguo bianjie shiwu tiaoyueji: ZhongNi juan.*

25　*Peking Review,* 20 October 1961, 5-8; Arthur Lall, *How Communist China Negotiates,* 199-200.

26　*Hong Kong Standard* and *Sunday Post-Herald,* 27 January 1963.

27　Quoted in Rose, *Nepal: Strategy for Survival,* 220.

28　Muni, *Foreign Policy of Nepal,* 109-11.

29　Rose, *Nepal: Strategy for Survival,* 220-21, 224.

30　*Peking Review,* 3 May 1960, 12-24.

31　Ibid., 6 October 1961, 11-2; 20 October 1961, 5.

32　Bhasin, *Documents on Nepal's Relations,* 276-78; *New China News Agency,* 29 April 1955.

33　*Peking Review,* 12 October 1962, 6.

34　Rose, *Nepal: Strategy for Survival,* 213-14.

35　Bhasin, *Documents on Nepal's Relations,* 263.

36　*Survey of China Mainland Press,* no. 1395 (1956): 45.

37　Quoted in Francis Watson, *The Frontiers of China* (New York: Praeger, 1966), 137-38.

38　*Peking Review,* 20 October 1961, 5.

39　Ibid., 3 May 1960, 8.

40　*Documents on the Sino-Indian Boundary Question* (Peking: Foreign Language Press, 1960), 67; Government of India, Ministry of External Affairs, *White Paper* 3 (New Delhi: External Publicity Division, Ministry of External Affairs, 1959), 79.

41　Xie, *Zhongguo waijiao shi ... 1949-1979,* 408.

42　G.S. Bajpai, *China's Shadow over Sikkim: The Politics of Intimidation* (New Delhi: Lancer Publishers, 1999), 107-9.

43　Yang Gongsu, *Zhonghua Renmin Gongheguo waijiao lilun yu shijian* [The theory and practice of PRC diplomacy] (Beijing: Beijing daxue guoji guanxi xueyuan, 1997), 146; Government of India, Ministry of External Affairs, *White Paper* 1 (New Delhi: External Publicity Division, Ministry of External Affairs, 1959), 55.

44　The Chinese Foreign Ministry website listed Sikkim as an independent country until October 2003.

45　*Documents on the Sino-Indian Boundary Question,* 7, 67; Government of India, Ministry of External Affairs, *White Paper* 2 (New Delhi: External Publicity Division, Ministry of External Affairs, 1959), 30; Government of India, Ministry of External Affairs, *White Paper* 6 (New Delhi: External Publicity Division, Ministry of External Affairs, 1962), 6.

46　"Sikkim Leader Doubts Red China Will Attack," *New York Times,* 6 September 1959, 3.

47　Bajpai, *China's Shadow over Sikkim,* 129.

48　Bajpai, *China's Shadow over Sikkim,* 129-33; Xie, *Zhongguo waijiao shi ... 1949-1979,* 408-9; *Survey of China Mainland Press,* no. 3536 (14 September 1965): 30-31; Yaacov Y.I. Vertzberger, *China's Southwestern Strategy: Encirclement and Counterencirclement* (New York: Praeger, 1985), 50; Leo E. Rose, "Sikkim and the Sino-Indian Dispute," *Political Science Review* 8, 1 (January-March 1969): 46-51.

49 John W. Garver, *Protracted Contest: Sino-Indian Rivalry in the Twentieth Century* (Seattle: University of Washington Press, 2001), 175.

50 *Reuters,* 17 December 1996.

51 Jyoti Malhotra, "For India's Tibet Turn, China to Amend Its Sikkim Map," *Indian Express,* 25 June 2003.

52 *Hindustan Times,* 24 June 2003 and 28 June 2003; *New York Times,* 25 June 2003.

53 *Hindustan Times,* 12 April 2005.

54 Ram Rahul, *The Himalaya Borderland* (New Delhi: Vikas Publications, 1970), 62-64.

55 Until the early 1970s, Indian maps indicated only an "administrative" border, not an "international" boundary between India and Bhutan.

56 T.T. Poulose, "Bhutan's External Relations and India," *International and Comparative Law Quarterly* 20, 2 (April 1971): 195-212; Leo E. Rose, "Bhutan's External Relations," *Pacific Affairs* 47, 2 (Summer 1974): 192-208.

57 Garver, *Protracted Contest,* 176; Girja Kumar and V.K. Arora, eds., *Documents on Indian External Affairs* (Bombay: Asia Publishing House, 1965), 337.

58 Thierry Mathou, "Bhutan-China Relations: Towards a New Step in Himalayan Politics," in *The Spider and the Piglet: Proceedings of the First International Seminar on Bhutanese Studies* (Thimphu: Centre for Bhutan Studies, 2004), 391-92; R.C. Misra, *The Emergence of Bhutan* (Jaipur: Sandarbh Prakashan, 1989), 72-73; Leo E. Rose, *The Politics of Bhutan* (Ithaca, NY: Cornell University Press, 1977), 61-62; Ram Rahul, *Modern Bhutan* (Delhi: Vikas Publications, 1971), 101-2; George N. Patterson, *Peking versus Delhi* (New York: Praeger, 1964), 207.

59 Rose, *The Politics of Bhutan,* 82.

60 Garver, *Protracted Contest,* 177.

61 "Economic and Political Relations between Bhutan and Neighboring Countries," Monograph 12, A Joint Research Project of the Centre for Bhutan Studies and the Institute of Developing Economics, Japan External Trade Organization (April 2004), 76.

62 K.J. Holsti, "From Isolation to Dependence: Bhutan, 1958-62," in *Why Nations Realign: Foreign Policy Restructuring in the Postwar World,* ed. K.J. Holsti (London: George Allen and Unwin, 1982), 35; Pradyumna P. Karan, "Geopolitical Structure of Bhutan," *India Quarterly* 19, 3 (July-September 1963): 212-13; *New York Times,* 24 August 1959.

63 Mahendra P. Lama, "Nepal and Bhutan," in *Security in South Asia: Comprehensive and Cooperative,* ed. Dipankar Banerjee (New Delhi: Manas Publications, 1999), 154; Rose, *The Politics of Bhutan,* 74-80; K. Krishna Moorthy, "Bhutan's Blank Cheque to Nehru," *Far Eastern Economic Review,* 9 March 1961, 429.

64 "Nehru Asserts India Has Duty to Defend Bhutan and Sikkim," *New York Times,* 26 August 1959.

65 Mathou, "Bhutan-China Relations," 394; Holsti, "From Isolation to Dependence: Bhutan, 1958-62," 27; Rose, ibid., 95.

66 Holsti, ibid., 21.

67 *China Pictorial,* 7 (July 1958): 20-21; "Bhutan Sends Protest to Red China on Border," *New York Times,* 17 March 1960, 14.

68 *Documents on the Sino-Indian Boundary Question,* 7, 67; *White Paper* 2: 29-30.

69 George N. Patterson, "Recent Chinese Policies in Tibet and towards the Himalayan Border States," *China Quarterly* 12 (October-December 1962): 199; Watson, *The Frontiers of China,* 143-44; Rose, "Bhutan's External Relations," 204.

70 K. Krishna Moorthy, "Bhutan: Thoughts of Sovereignty," *Far Eastern Economic Review,* 16 February 1961, 297; Patterson, *Peking versus Delhi,* 218.

71 Moorthy, "Bhutan: Thoughts of Sovereignty," 297.

72 Manorama Kohli, *From Dependency to Interdependence: A Study of Indo-Bhutan Relations* (New Delhi: Vikas Publishing House, 1993), 156; Searls, "Communist China's Border Policy," 11.

73 Moorthy, "Bhutan: Thoughts of Sovereignty," 297.

74 *Hong Kong Standard,* 31 August 1962.

75 Misra, *The Emergence of Bhutan,* 74; Patterson, *Peking versus Delhi,* 198-99; Rose, "Bhutan's External Relations," 198-200; Rose, "Sino-Indian Rivalry and the Himalayan Border States," 214-15; *China News Analysis* 534 (25 September 1964): 7.

76 *The Sino-Indian Boundary Question,* enlarged ed. (Peking: Foreign Language Press, 1962); *The Times,* 27 October 1962, 8.

77 A.R. Field, letter to the editor, *Washington Post,* 11 January 1963, A14; Harold C. Hinton, *Communist China in World Politics* (Boston: Houghton Mifflin, 1966), 322-23.

78 Rahul, *The Himalaya Borderlands,* 65; Karma Ura, "Perceptions of Security," *Journal of Bhutan Studies* 5 (Winter 2001): 138, fn. 26; Neville Maxwell, *India's China War* (London: Jonathan Cape, 1970), 115-16.

79 *Renmin ribao,* 22 October 1962, 1.

80 Rose, "Bhutan's External Relations," 197-98; Ura, "Perceptions of Security," 129.

81 Mathou, "Bhutan-China Relations," 397.

82 Pei Jianzhang, ed., *Xin Zhongguo waijiao fengyun: Zhongguo waijiaoguan huiyilu* [New China's diplomatic challenges: recollections of Chinese diplomats], vol. 2 (Beijing: Shijie zhishi chubanshe, 1991), 175, quoted in Garver, *Protracted Contest,* 181.

83 Rose, *The Politics of Bhutan,* 93-94; Mathou, "Bhutan-China Relations," 399; Dorji Penjore, "Security of Bhutan: Walking between the Giants," *Journal of Bhutan Studies* 10 (Summer 2004): 116.

84 Garver, *Protracted Contest,* 183; Kohli, 159.

85 *Kathmandu Post,* 17 January 1997 and 20 January 1999.

86 Kohli, "From Dependency to Interdependence," 169-70.

87 *Zhonghua Renmin Gongheguo bianjie shiwu tiaoyueji: ZhongYin ZhongBu juan* [The People's Republic of China boundary affairs treaty collection: China-India China-Bhutan volume] (Beijing: Shijie zhishi chubanshe, 2004).

88 Xie Yixian, *Zhongguo waijiao shi: Zhonghua Renmin Gongheguo shiqi 1979-1994* [A diplomatic history of China: the period of the People's Republic of China, 1979-1994] (Zhengzhou: Henan renmin chubanshe, 1995), 129-31; *Zhongguo waijiao: 1998 nianban* [Chinese foreign policy: 1998 edition] (Beijing: Shijie zhishi chubanshe, 1998), 113; *Zhongguo waijiao: 1999 nianban* [Chinese foreign policy: 1999 edition] (Beijing: Shijie zhishi chubanshe, 1999); *Beijing Review,* 30 April 1984, 11; Friedrich Kratochwil, Paul Rohrlich, and Harpreet Mahajan, *Peace and Disputed Sovereignty: Reflections on Conflict over Territory* (Lanham, MD: University Press of America, 1985), 140.

89 "Assembly Discusses Boundary Issues," *Kuenselonline,* 5 July 2002; "Assembly Pressures the Government to Step Up Boundary Discussions with China," *Kuenselonline,* 28 November 2005; Mathou, "Bhutan-China Relations," 402-3, 405; Mathou, "Tibet and Its Neighbors: Moving toward a New Chinese Strategy in the Himalayan Region," *Asian Survey* 45, 4 (2005): 515, fnn. 15 and 16.

90 "Assembly Members Alarmed by Road Construction across Northern Boundary," *Kuenselonline,* 8 June 2005.

91 "Bhutan-China Boundary Must Be Finished," *Kuenselonline,* 24 June 2006.

92 "China, Bhutan Want to Establish Diplomatic Ties," *Indian Express,* 22 June 2012.

93 Mathou, "Tibet and Its Neighbors," 515.

Chapter 5: The Sino-Pakistani Boundary Settlement

1 Anwar Hussain Syed, *China and Pakistan: Diplomacy of an Entente Cordiale* (Amherst: University of Massachusetts Press, 1974); Gurnam Singh, *Sino-Pakistan Relations: The Ayub Era* (Amritsar: Guru Nanak Dev University Press, 1987).

2 Xie Yixian, *Zhongguo waijiao shi: Zhonghua Renmin Gongheguo shiqi 1949-1979* [A diplomatic history of China: the period of the People's Republic of China, 1949-1979] (Zhengzhou: Henan renmin chubanshe, 1988), 252-53.

3 Mujtaba Razvi, *The Frontiers of Pakistan: A Study of Frontier Problems in Pakistan's Foreign Policy* (Karachi: National Publishing House, 1971), 179-81.

4 Ibid., 178.

5 Alastair Lamb, *Asian Frontiers: Studies in a Continuing Problem* (New York: Praeger, 1968), 102-3; Alastair Lamb, *The China-India Border: The Origins of the Disputed Boundaries* (London: Oxford University Press, 1964), 181-82; Alastair Lamb, "The Sino-Pakistan Boundary Agreement of 2 March 1963," *Australian Outlook* 18, 3 (December 1964): 301-6.

6 Quoted in United Nations, General Assembly, Delegation from China, *China Fights for Peace and Freedom* (New York: n.p., 1951), 71-72.

7 Harold C. Hinton, *Communist China in World Politics* (London: Macmillan, 1966), 45; B.N. Goswami, *Pakistan and China: A Study of Their Relations* (New Delhi: Allied Publishers, 1971), 18-20; Razvi, *Frontiers of Pakistan*, 169.

8 S.M. Burke, "Sino-Pakistan Relations," *Orbis* 8, 2 (Summer 1964): 392; Razvi, ibid., 166.

9 "Chou En-lai's Report on Visits to Eleven Countries in Asia and Europe Given to the Third Session of the CPPCC, May 3, 1957," in *China-South Asian Relations (1947-1980) Documents* 2, ed. R.K. Jain (New Delhi: Radiant Publishers, 1981), 15.

10 *Survey of China Mainland Press*, no. 818 (1954): 17-18; no. 829 (1954): 21; no. 845 (1954): 28-30; no. 864 (1954): 1-2.

11 Li Ming and Liu Qiang, eds., *Zhou Enlai de waijiao yishu* [Zhou Enlai's art of diplomacy] (Jinan: Shandong daxue chubanshe, 1992), 160; Arvin R. Field, "Strategic Development in Sinkiang," *Foreign Affairs* 39, 2 (January 1961): 312-18.

12 *Survey of China Mainland Press*, no. 1965 (4 March 1959): 39.

13 *Peking Review*, 28 July 1959, 18-23.

14 Mohammed Ayub Khan, "Pakistan Perspective," *Foreign Affairs* 38, 4 (July 1960): 556.

15 *Survey of China Mainland Press*, no. 1971 (12 March 1959): 54; *Peking Review*, 10 March 1959; quote in Neville Maxwell, *India's China War* (London: Jonathan Cape, 1970), 274.

16 Mohammed Ayub Khan, *Friends Not Masters: A Political Autobiography* (London: Oxford University Press, 1967), 164.

17 *Peking Review*, 28 December 1962, 8.

18 *Documents on the Sino-Indian Boundary Question* (Peking: Foreign language Press, 1960), 1-13; Francis Watson, *The Frontiers of China* (New York: Praeger, 1966), 140.

19 *Dawn* (Karachi), 3 October 1959.

20 Ibid., 24 October 1959.

21 *Pakistan Times*, 24 October 1959.

22 *Survey of China Mainland Press*, no. 2063 (1959): 35.

23 Khan, *Friends Not Masters*, 161.

24 Goswami, *Pakistan and China*, 85; Razvi, *Frontiers of Pakistan*, 171-72.

25 Neville Maxwell, "Settlements and Disputes: China's Approach to Territorial Issues," *Economic and Political Weekly*, 9 September 2006, 3875.

26 Han Nianlong, ed., *Diplomacy of Contemporary China* (Hong Kong: New Horizon Press, 1990), 187-88; Wang Taiping, ed., *Zhonghua Renmin Gongheguo waijiao shi (2) 1957-1959*

[Diplomatic history of the PRC (vol. 2) 1957-1969] (Beijing: Shijie zhishi chubanshe, 1998), 103; Xie, *Zhongguo waijiao shi ... 1949-1979*, 252; Khan, *Friends Not Masters*, 162-63; K. Sarwar Hasan, ed., *China, India, Pakistan* (Documents on the Foreign Relations of Pakistan Series) (Karachi: Pakistan Institute of International Affairs, 1966), 365.

27   *Peking Review*, 11 May 1962, 10.

28   Han, *Diplomacy of Contemporary China*, 188; Watson, *Frontiers of China*, 166; Razvi, *Frontiers of Pakistan*, 176-77; Wang, *Zhonghua Renmin Gongheguo waijiao shi*, 103.

29   *Zhonghua Renmin Gongheguo bianjie shiwu tiaoyueji: ZhongA ZhongBa juan* [The People's Republic of China boundary affairs treaty collection: China-Afghanistan China-Pakistan volume] (Beijing: Shijie zhishi chubanshe, 2004); *Peking Review*, 15 March 1963, 67-70; Lamb, "The Sino-Pakistani Boundary Agreement of 2 March 1963," 299-312; Wang, ibid., 104.

30   Razvi, *Frontiers of Pakistan*, 177.

31   Khan, *Friends Not Masters*, 163. For Pakistan, a significant (and for India, disconcerting) result of the treaty was that China recognized that Kashmir was a disputed area and gave credence to Pakistan's claims.

32   Mao Tse-tung, *Selected Works of Mao Tse-tung*, vol. 4 (Peking: Foreign Language Press, 1965), 98-99; Xie, *Zhongguo waijiao shi ... 1949-1979*, 3; Li and Liu, *Zhou Enlai de waijiao yishu*, 155.

33   Goswami, *Pakistan and China*, 66.

34   Khan, *Friends Not Masters*, 116-17.

35   *Dawn* (Karachi), 20 December 1961.

36   Quoted in G.W. Choudhury, "Reflections on Sino-Pakistan Relations," *Pacific Community* 7, 2 (January 1976): 251.

37   Ibid., 249-50.

38   Geoffrey Wheeler, "Sinkiang and the Soviet Union," *China Quarterly* 16 (October-December 1963): 59; Khalid Bin Sayeed, "Pakistan and China: The Scope and Limits of Convergent Policies," in *Policies toward China: Views from Six Continents*, ed. A.M. Halpern (New York: McGraw Hill, 1965), 243.

39   Xie, *Zhongguo waijiao shi ... 1949-1979*, 253; Yaacov Y.I. Vertzberger, *The Enduring Entente: Sino-Pakistan Relations, 1960-1980* (New York: Praeger, 1983), 26-27.

40   Razvi, *Frontiers of Pakistan*, 174-74; Margaret W. Fisher, Leo E. Rose, and Robert A. Huttenbeck, *Himalayan Battleground: Sino-Indian Rivalry in Ladakh* (New York: Praeger, 1963), 140-42; W.M. Dobell, "Ramification of the China-Pakistan Border Treaty," *Pacific Affairs* 37, 3 (Fall 1964): 284.

41   Razvi, ibid., 173-4.

42   Khan, *Friends Not Masters*, 162.

43   *New York Times*, 26 May 1962, 6; 25 November 1962, 1; 26 November 1962, 2.

44   Razvi, *Frontiers of Pakistan*, 171; Goswami, *Pakistan and China*, 76.

45   Syed, *China and Pakistan*, 244, fn. 60; Goswami, ibid., 80.

46   Zulfikar Ali Bhutto, *Foreign Policy of Pakistan: A Compendium of Speeches Made in the National Assembly of Pakistan, 1962-64* (Karachi: Pakistan Institute of International Affairs, 1964), 31.

47   Ibid., 10; Choudhury, "Reflections on Sino-Pakistan Relations," 253-54; Syed, *China and Pakistan*, 244, fn. 60.

48   Bhutto, *Foreign Policy of Pakistan*, 75.

49   Quoted in Choudhury, "Reflections on Sino-Pakistan Relations," 255.

50   *Renmin ribao*, 30 July 1983, 6, quoted in John W. Garver, "Sino-Indian Rapprochement and the Sino-Pakistan Entente," *Political Science Quarterly* 111, 2 (Summer 1996): 330.

51   Khan, *Friends Not Masters*, 162.

52 *Morning News,* 14 January 1962.
53 Khan, *Friends Not Masters,* 163-64; Syed, *China and Pakistan,* 91-2.
54 *Survey of China Mainland Press,* no. 705 (1953): 20-22; no. 3955 (1967): 45; *Peking Review,* 28 January 1966, 21; 18 February 1966, 10; 16 December 1966, 38.
55 *Peking Review,* 5 March 1965, 6.
56 *Peking Review,* 28 February 1964, 5-9.
57 Razvi, *Frontiers of Pakistan,* 187, esp. fn. 1; Lawrence L. Whetten, "Moscow's Anti-China Pact," *World Today* 25, 9 (September 1969): 385-93; *Peking Review,* 25 July 1969, 9.
58 Zulfikar Ali Bhutto, *The Myth of Independence* (London: Oxford University Press, 1969), 69.
59 *Peking Review,* 4 February 1966, 11.

Chapter 6: The Sino-Afghan Boundary Settlement

1 Yang Gongsu, *Zhonghua Renmin Gongheguo waijiao lilun yu shijian* [The theory and practice of People's Republic of China diplomacy] (Beijing: Beijing daxue guoji guanxi xueyuan, 1997), 166-67; Xie Yixian, *Zhongguo waijiao shi: Zhonghua Renmin Gongheguo shiqi 1949-1979* [A diplomatic history of China: the period of the People's Republic of China, 1949-1979] (Zhengzhou: Henan renmin chubanshe, 1988), 373 (China claims that Russia occupied approximately 13,000 square miles).
2 W.K. Fraser-Tytler, *Afghanistan: A Study of Political Developments in Central and South Asia* (London: Oxford University Press, 1950), 169, 343.
3 Yang, *Zhonghua Renmin Gongheguo waijiao lilun yu shijian,* 167.
4 Fraser-Tytler, *Afghanistan,* 345.
5 J.R.V. Prescott, *Map of Mainland Asia by Treaty* (Melbourne: Melbourne University Press, 1975), 238.
6 *China News Analysis* 116 (20 January 1956): 4.
7 Rosemary Foot, "Sino-Soviet Rivalry in Kabul," *Round Table* 280 (October 1980): 434-42.
8 *Survey of China Mainland Press,* no. 1456 (23 January 1957): 44; no. 1459 (28 January 1957): 33.
9 Ibid., no. 1460 (29 January 1957): 22.
10 Foot, "Sino-Soviet Rivalry," 438.
11 *Peking Review,* 30 August 1960, 9.
12 Ibid., 22 September 1959, 21; *Survey of Mainland China Press* 2064 (6 September 1959); *New China News Agency,* 13 September 1959; *New York Times,* 6 September 1959.
13 *Peking Review,* 30 August 1960, 6-11; 20 December 1960, 18-20; *Asian Recorder* 6, 38 (17-23 September 1960): 3539.
14 *Renmin ribao,* 7 March 1959.
15 *New York Times,* 6 September 1959.
16 *Peking Review,* 30 August 1960, 10-11.
17 *New China News Agency,* 2 March 1963; *Peking Review,* 15 March 1963, 5.
18 *China News Analysis* 129 (27 April 1956): 5-6. This issue discusses maps of China and changes made since 1949, and includes reproductions of the maps.
19 *Wenhuibao,* 24 October 1957, cited in Shen-yu Dai, "China and Afghanistan," *China Quarterly* 25 (January-March 1966): 220, fn. 23; Harold C. Hinton, *Communist China in World Politics* (Boston: Houghton Mifflin, 1966): 320-21.
20 Wang Taiping, ed., *Zhonghua Renmin Gongheguo waijiao shi (2) 1957-1969* [Diplomatic history of the PRC (vol. 2) 1957-1969] (Beijing: Shijie zhishi chubanshe, 1998), 105.
21 *Renmin ribai,* 18 October 1963; *China News Analysis* 496 (6 December 1963): 6.
22 *Zhonghua Renmin Gongheguo bianjie shiwu tiaoyueji: ZhongA ZhongBa juan* [The People's Republic of China boundary affairs treaty collection: China-Afghanistan China-Pakistan volume] (Beijing: Shijie zhishi chubanshe, 2004).

23 Xie, *Zhongguo waijiao shi ... 1949-1979*, 253-54.
24 Han Nianlong, ed., *Diplomacy of Contemporary China* (Hong Kong: New Horizon Press, 1990), 189.
25 John W. Garver, "The Sino-Soviet Dispute in the Pamir Mountains Region," *China Quarterly* 85 (March 1981): 107-18.
26 *Peking Review*, 15 March 1963, 5.
27 *Renmin ribai*, 8 March 1963.
28 *New York Times*, 29 September 1961; Louis Dupree, *Afghanistan* (Princeton, NJ: Princeton University Press, 1980), 544-46.
29 *Peking Review*, 20 November 1964, 17; Sreedhar, "Sino-Afghan Economic Relations," *China Report* 12, 5-6 (September 1976): 7-9; Dai, "China and Afghanistan," 219-21.
30 *Peking Review*, 6 November 1964, 6.
31 "Nehru Receives Afghan Welcome," *New York Times*, 15 September 1959, 7; Hasan Ali Shah Jafri, *Indo-Afghan Relations (1947-67)* (New Delhi: Sterling Publishers, 1976), 77-80.

Chapter 7: Sino-Soviet/Russian Relations and the Boundary Settlement
1 Elizabeth Wishnick, *Mending Fences: The Evolution of Moscow's China Policy from Brezhnev to Yeltsin* (Seattle: University of Washington Press, 2001), 18.
2 Xie Yixian, *Zhongguo waijiao shi: Zhonghua Renmin Gongheguo shiqi 1949-1979* [A diplomatic history of China: the period of the People's Republic of China, 1949-1979] (Zhengzhou: Henan renmin chubanshe, 1988), 373.
3 Yang Gongsu, *Zhonghua Renmin Gongheguo waijiao lilun yu shijian* [The theory and practice of People's Republic of China diplomacy] (Beijing: Beijing daxue guoji guanxi xueyuan, 1997), 166-67; Xie, ibid., 373.
4 Quoted in Allen S. Whiting, *Soviet Policies in China: 1917-1925* (New York: Columbia University Press, 1954), 273.
5 John M. Maki, *Selected Documents: Far Eastern International Relations (1689-1951)* (Seattle: University of Washington Press, 1951), 203-10; Fang Ming, "Guanyu SuE liangci duiHau xuanyan he feichu ZhongE bupingdeng taioyue" [The two declarations of the Soviet government toward China and the abolition of Sino-Russian unequal treaties], *Lishi yanjiu* 6 (1980): 74.
6 Xie, *Zhongguo waijiao shi ... 1949-1979*, 372.
7 Tian Zengpei, ed., *Gaige kaifang yilai de Zhongguo waijiao* [Chinese foreign policy since opening up and reform] (Beijing: Shijie zhishi chubanshe, 1993), 329; *RA Report* 14 (January 1993): 34-35.
8 *Zhongguo waijiao: 1998 nianban* [Chinese foreign policy: 1998 edition] (Beijing: Shijie zhishi chubanshe, 1998), 361.
9 Craig Seibert, trans., "Stalin's Dialogue with Mao Zedong" (S.N. Goncharov interview with Ivan V. Kovalev), *Journal of Northeast Asian Studies* 10, 4 (Winter 1991): 69.
10 *Peking Review*, 3 May 1960, 13; Chinese Peoples' Institute of Foreign Affairs, ed., *New Developments in Friendly Relations between China and Nepal* (Peking: Foreign Language Press, 1960), 75.
11 *Renmin ribao* editorial, 8 March 1963.
12 Han Nianlong, ed., *Diplomacy of Contemporary China* (Hong Kong: New Horizon Press, 1990), 299.
13 Xie, *Zhongguo waijiao shi ... 1949-1979*, 373; Han, ibid., 299.
14 "Quarterly Chronicle and Documentation," *China Quarterly* 59 (July-September 1974): 656.
15 Jiang Yan, "Our Sacred Land: Heixiazidao Island," *Dili zhishi* 1 (1975): 5-7; Jeanne L. Wilson, *Strategic Partners: Russian-Chinese Relations in the Post-Soviet Era* (New York: M.E. Sharpe, 2004), 43.

16 Xiaoyuan Liu, *Reins of Liberation: An Entangled History of Mongolian Independence, Chinese Territoriality, and Great Power Hegemony, 1911-1950* (Stanford, CA: Stanford University Press, 2006), 388-89.

17 Douglas Johnson and Hungdah Chiu, eds., *Agreements of the People's Republic of China, 1949-1967: A Calendar* (Cambridge, MA: Harvard University Press, 1968), 5, 57, 76.

18 *Current Digest of the Soviet Press* 16, 34 (6 September 1964): 5-7; Nikita Sergeyevich Khrushchev, *Khrushchev Remembers: The Last Testament* (Boston: Little, Brown, 1974), 284-89; A. Kruchinin and V. Olgin, *Territorial Claims of Mao Tse-tung: History and Modern Times* (Moscow: Novosti Press Agency Publishing House, 1971), 25.

19 *Asahi Shimbun*, 1 August 1964, in Dennis J. Doolin, *Territorial Claims in the Sino-Soviet Conflict: Documents and Analysis,* Hoover Institution Studies 7 (Stanford, CA: Hoover Institution on War, Revolution and Peace, Stanford University Press, 1965), 45-46.

20 "Statement of the Government of the People's Republic of China, May 24, 1969," *Peking Review*, 30 May 1969, 7; Oton Ambroz, *Realignment of World Power: The Russo-Chinese Schism under the Impact of Mao Tse-tung's Last Revolution,* vol. 1 (New York: Robert Speller and Sons, 1972), 127.

21 "Premier Chou En-lai's Press Conference in Kathmandu," *Peking Review,* 3 May 1960, 13; Liu, *Reins of Liberation*, 389.

22 Thomas W. Robinson, *The Sino-Soviet Border Dispute: Background, Development and the March 1969 Clashes* (Santa Monica, CA: Rand Corporation, 1970), 7.

23 *Peking Review,* 13 September 1963.

24 *Pravda*, 13 December 1962, in *Current Digest of the Soviet Press* 14, 52 (23 January 1963): 4.

25 "A Comment on the Statement of the Communist Party of the USA," *Peking Review,* 15 March 1963, 58-62.

26 "Dangerous Seat of Tension in Asia," *Pravda*, 19 September 1963, in *Soviet News* 4895 (1963): 157-58.

27 Khrushchev, *Khrushchev Remembers*, 286.

28 Interviews with Vladimir S. Miasnikov and Yuri M. Galenovitch of the Russian Academy of Sciences, Institute for Far Eastern Studies, November 1993.

29 *Pravda,* 2 September 1964, in *Current Digest of the Soviet Press* 16, 34 (6 September 1964): 6-7.

30 Alexei D. Voskressenski, *Russia and China: A Theory of Inter-State Relations* (London: RoutledgeCurzon, 2003), 173.

31 *Current Digest of the Soviet Press* 16, 34 (16 September 1964): 4; 38 (14 October 1964): 6.

32 Sergey S. Radchenko, "The Soviets' Best Friend in Asia: The Mongolian Dimension of the Sino-Soviet Dispute," Cold War International History Project, Working Paper 42 (Washington, DC: Woodrow Wilson International Center for Scholars, 2003): 8; "Record of Conversation between the Mongolian People's Republic Government Delegation and the Deputy Chairman of the People's Republic of China State Council, Foreign Minister Chen Yi" (20 November 1964), Cold War International History Project, *Digital Archive, Mongolia in the Cold War,* http://digitalarchive.wilsoncenter.org/document/112517.

33 "Note of the Ministry of Foreign Affairs of the People's Republic of China to the Soviet Embassy in China, March 2, 1969," *Peking Review,* 7 March 1969, 5 and 7; "Chenpao Island Has Always Been Chinese Territory," *Peking Review,* 14 March 1969, 14-16; "Chinese Foreign Ministry's March 15 Urgent and Strong Protest Note," *Peking Review,* 21 March 1969, 8; "Soviet Note of Protest, March 15, 1969," *Studies in Comparative Communism* 2, 3-4 (July-October 1969): 165-66.

34 Henry Kissinger, *The White House Years* (Boston: Little, Brown 1979), 183-84.

35 "Statement of the Government of the People's Republic of China, May 24, 1969," *Peking Review*, 30 May 1969, 7; Xie, *Zhongguo waijiao shi ... 1949-1979*, 374.

36 *Pravda*, 14 June 1969, 1-2, in *Current Digest of the Soviet Press* 21, 24 (1969): 10; *Down with the New Tsars! Soviet Revisionists' Anti-China Atrocities on the Heilung and Wusuli Rivers* (Peking: Foreign Language Press, 1969).

37 "On Settling Frontier Disputes: Statement by the Government of the USSR to the Government of the People's Republic of China," *Reprints from the Soviet Press* 9, 2 (25 July 1969): 56-58; "Report to the Tenth National Congress of the Communist Party of China, August 24, 1973," *Peking Review*, 7 September 1973, 23.

38 *Peking Review*, 8 May 1964, 20-21; "Statement of the Government of the People's Republic of China, May 24, 1969," *Peking Review*, 30 May 1969, 8; "USSR Government Statement on Soviet-Chinese Border Incidents, March 30, 1969," *Reprints from the Soviet Press* 8, 9 (2 May 1969): 20; William E. Griffith, *Sino-Soviet Relations: 1964-1965* (Cambridge, MA: MIT Press, 1967), 181-82; Robinson, *Sino-Soviet Border Dispute*, 11-17.

39 Han, *Diplomacy of Contemporary China*, 152.

40 M.A. Suslov, *Marxism-Leninism: The International Teaching of the Working Class* (Moscow: Progress Publishers, 1975), 173.

41 "Statement of the Government of the People's Republic of China, May 24, 1969," *Peking Review*, 30 May 1969, 8.

42 Lyle J. Goldstein, "Return to Zhenbao Island: Who Started the Shooting and Why It Matters," *China Quarterly* 168 (December 2001): 989; Christian F. Ostermann, "New Evidence on the Sino-Soviet Border Dispute, 1969-71," *Cold War International History Project Bulletin*, issues 6-7 (Winter 1995/96): 187.

43 "Statement of the Government of the People's Republic of China, May 24, 1969," *Peking Review*, 30 May 1969, 3-9.

44 "On Settling Frontier Disputes: Statement by the Government of the USSR to the Government of the People's Republic of China," *Reprints from the Soviet Press* 9, 2 (25 July 1969): 51.

45 Roderick MacFarquhar, "The Succession to Mao and the End of Maoism, 1969-82," in *The Politics of China: The Eras of Mao and Deng*, 2nd ed., ed. Roderick MacFarquhar (Oxford: Oxford University Press, 1997), 263.

46 Xie, *Zhongguo waijiao shi ... 1949-1979*, 377; Shi Yuxin,"Bo huangyan zhizaozhe: guanyu ZhongSu bianjie de ruogan wenti" [Refuting lie-fabricators: regarding several issues on the Sino-Soviet boundary], *Lishi yanjiu* 1 (1974): 128; Li Huichuan, "The Crux of the Sino-Soviet Boundary Question" [pt. 2], *Peking Review*, 3 August 1981, 13 (Chinese version in *Guoji wenti yanjiu* 1 [July 1981]); *Renmin ribao*, 20 October 1969.

47 Interviews with Vladimir S. Miasnikov and Yuri M. Galenovitch, Russian Academy of Sciences, Institute of Far Eastern Studies, November 1993.

48 Ibid.

49 "Document of the Ministry of Foreign Affairs of the People's Republic of China, October 8, 1969," *Peking Review*, 10 October 1969, 8-15.

50 Shi, "Bo huangyan zhizaozhe," 128.

51 Interview with Yuri M. Galenovitch, Russian Academy of Sciences, Institute of Far Eastern Studies, November 1993.

52 *Peking Review*, 10 October 1969, 8; *Dagong bao*, 9 January 1970; Li Huichuan, "The Crux of the Sino-Soviet Boundary Question"; Yang, *Zhonghua Renmin Gongheguo waijiao lilun yu shijian*, 168-69.

53 *Peking Review*, 10 October 1969, 15.

54 "On Settling Frontier Disputes: Statement of the Government of the USSR to the Government of the People's Republic of China," *Reprints from the Soviet Press* 9, 2 (25 July 1969): 56.

55 *Pravda,* 1 April 1978; Kenneth Lieberthal, *The Sino-Soviet Conflict in the 1970s: Its Evolution and Implications for the Strategic Triangle* (Santa Monica, CA: Rand, 1978), 11, fn. 23; Central Intelligence Agency, "Sino-Soviet Exchanges, 1969-84" (EA 84-10069), 4; "Territorial Issues in the Sino-Soviet Dispute" (GCR RP 75-31), 4-5.

56 Quoted in Alexander Lukin, *The Bear Watches the Dragon: Russia's Perceptions of China and the Evolution of Russian-Chinese Relations since the Eighteenth Century* (Armonk, NY: M.E. Sharpe, 2003), 145.

57 *Far Eastern Economic Review,* 31 March 1983, 22-24.

58 Interview with Russian Foreign Ministry official, 10 April 1995.

59 Edgar Snow, "The Open Door," *New Republic,* 27 March 1971, 23; Li Huichuan, "The Crux of the Sino-Soviet Boundary Question."

60 Xie Yixian, *Zhongguo waijiao shi: Zhonghua Renmin Gongheguo shiqi 1979-1994* [A diplomatic history of China: the period of the People's Republic of China, 1979-1994] (Zhengzhou: Henan renmin chubanshe, 1995), 12-13; Han, *Diplomacy of Contemporary China,* 411-14; Qian Qichen, *Waijiao shiji* [Ten foreign policy events] (Beijing: Shijie zhishi chubanshe, 2003), 6-8.

61 Alexei D. Voskressenski, "Current Concepts of Sino-Russian Relations and Frontier Problems in Russia and China," *Central Asian Survey* 13, 3 (1994): 378-79.

62 Wishnick, *Mending Fences,* 15-17.

63 Xie, *Zhongguo waijiao shi ... 1979-1994,* 41-42; Qian, *Waijiao shiji,* 25.

64 Interviews with Russian Foreign Ministry officials, November 1993 and 10 April 1995.

65 Xie, *Zhongguo waijiao shi ... 1979-1994,* 49; Tian, *Gaige kaifang yilai de Zhongguo waijiao,* 327-29; "Sino-Soviet Communiqué," *Xinhua,* 18 May 1989; *New York Times,* 8 February 1987, 3; 10 February 1987, 5; 8 August 1987, 3; 25 September 1987, 12; *Boston Globe,* 22 August 1987, 3; *Christian Science Monitor,* 1 November 1988, 2.

66 *China News Digest,* 23 October 1994.

67 Interview with Russian Foreign Ministry official, 10 April 1995.

68 Liu Dexi, Sun Yan, and Liu Songbin, *Sulian jietihou de ZhongE guanxi* [Sino-Russian relations after the breakup of the Soviet Union] (Harbin: Heilongjiang jiaoyu chubanshe, 1996), 197; Yang, *Zhonghua Renmin Gongheguo waijiao lilun yu shijian,* 165-66; Cheng Faren, *ZhongE guojietu kao* [A study of Sino-Soviet border maps] (Taipei: Meng Zang weiyuanhui, 1969), 84.

69 Interview with a Russian Foreign Ministry official, 10 April 1995.

70 Koreans maintain that the Qing Dynasty had no authority to cede "Noktun-do," a Korean-claimed island in the Tumen River, to Russia by the Treaty of Beijing, and has demanded its return. http://www.dbpia.co.kr/Journal/ArticleDetail/400378.

71 Zhai Wenqi and Tang Chengyun, "Tumen jiang kaifa yu dongbeiya guoji guanxi" [Tumen River development and the international relations of northeast Asia], *Qinghai Shifan daxue xuebao* 1 (1999), http://www.cnki.com.cn/Article/CJFDTotal-QHSZ901. 002.htm.

72 *Asahi Shimbun,* 7 December 1991, 7; interviews with Victor L. Larin, Russian Academy of Sciences, Far Eastern Branch, Institute of History, Archaeology and Ethnography of the Peoples of the Far East, November 1993; and with Russian Foreign Ministry official, 10 April 1995; Lukin, *The Bear Watches the Dragon,* 171 and 175; *China News Digest,* 25 April 1995.

73   Tian, *Gaige kaifang yilai de Zhongguo waijiao*, 329; *Washington Post*, 17 March 1991, A11; *Survey of China Mainland Press* (16-21 May 1991).

74   *Zhonghua Renmin Gongheguo bianjie shiwu tiaoyueji: ZhongE juan* 1 [The People's Republic of China boundary affairs treaty collection: China-Russia volume 1] (Beijing: Shijie zhishi chubanshe, 2005); Peng Xiaoming, "Tumen jiang chuhaikou chengle Zhongguo ren yongjiu de quru" [The mouth of the Tumen River has become an eternal humiliation for the Chinese] (30 September 2003), http://www.kanzhongguo.com/.

75   *China News Digest*, 25 April 1995.

76   *RA Report* 17 (July 1994): 48; Wishnick, *Mending Fences*, 182.

77   *RA Report*, ibid., 46.

78   Suzanne Crow, "Russia Debates Its National Interests," *RFE/RL Research Report* 1, 28 (10 July 1992): 43, 45; Jingjie Li, "From Good Neighbors to Strategic Partners," in *Rapprochement or Rivalry? Russia-China Relations in a Changing Asia*, ed. Sherman W. Garnett (Washington, DC: Carnegie Endowment for International Peace, 2000), 74-77. Goncharov specialized in Sino-Soviet Relations at the Institute of the Far East and later served in the Russian Federation embassy in Beijing.

79   Gaye Christoffersen, "Nesting the Sino-Russian Border and the Tumen Project in the Asia-Pacific: Heilongjiang's Regional Relations," *Asian Perspectives* 20, 2 (Fall-Winter 1996): 278; "Resignation over Land," *Moscow Times*, 6 April 1996; International Boundary Research Unit, *Boundary and Security Bulletin* 4, 2 (Summer 1996): 44.

80   *China News Digest*, 2 March 1995; Xiaoquan Ni, "Recent Developments in China's Relations with Russia and the United States," *Institute Reports* (East Asian Institute, Columbia University), April 1995, 7.

81   *ITAR-TASS News Agency (World Service)*, Moscow, 24 April 1996; International Boundary Research Unit, *Boundary and Security Bulletin* 4, 2 (Summer 1996): 44.

82   *Xinhua News Agency*, Beijing, 25 April 1996.

83   Li, "From Good Neighbors to Strategic Partners," 88.

84   Akihiro Iwashita, "The Russo-Chinese 'Strategic Partnership' and the Border Negotiations: Then and Now," *Yamaguchi kenritsu daigaku daigakuyinronshu* [Bulletin of the Graduate School of Yamaguchi Prefecture University] 2 (March 2001), 1-10.

85   Lukin, *The Bear Watches the Dragon*, 172-77; Wishnick, *Mending Fences*, 176-77 and 180.

86   Genrikh Kireev, "Demarcation of the Border with China," *International Affairs* (Moscow) 45, 2 (1999): 98-109; Sergei Blagov, "Russian Border Checks Glitch," *South China Morning Post*, 2 July 1999; Wishnick, ibid., 178.

87   Sergei Blagov, "Russia Hails Border Deal with China Despite Criticism," *Eurasia Daily Monitor* 2, 102 (May 2005); *Los Angeles Times*, 14 October 2008; *Xinhua*, 14 October 2008.

88   "China, Russia Complete Boundary Delimitation," *People's Daily*, 15 October 2004, http://english1.people.com.cn/; Ministry of Foreign Affairs of the People's Republic of China (14 October 2004), http://www.fmprc.gov.cn/eng/wjb/zzjg/dozys/xw1b/t165266.htm; Embassy of the People's Republic of China in India, http://www.chinaembassy.org.in/ong/zghd/t164561.htm.

89   "Russia Hails Border Settlement" (15 November 2004), http://www.china.org.cn/.

90   Interview with Jiang Yi, Chinese Academy of Social Sciences, November 2004.

91   Yan Jiaqi, "Jiang Zemin chumai 'tudi' huan 'linmu': ping Zhong-E mulin youhao hezuo tiaoyue" [Jiang Zemin sold out territory for good neighbourly relations: a critique of the Sino-Russian treaty of friendship and cooperation], http://www.kanzhongguo.com/; Cao Changqing, "Jiang Zemin qianyue songtudi" [Jiang Zemin signed a treaty to hand over territory], http://www.kanzhongguo.com/.

92 Li Xiang, "Return of Heixiasi Island Marks End of Border Dispute," *China Daily*, 15 October 2008, http://chinadaily.com.cn/.

93 Interview with Yuri M. Galenovitch, Russian Academy of Sciences, Institute of Far Eastern Studies, November 1993.

94 Wishnick, *Mending Fences*, 181.

95 Vladimir S. Miasnikov, "Present Issues between Russian and China: Realties and Prospects," *Sino-Soviet Affairs* 18, 2 (Summer 1994): 24; Wishnick, ibid., 154-56.

96 "Information Note of Romanian Embassy from Beijing to Ministry of Foreign Affairs" (23 May 1989), Cold War International History Project, *Digital Archive*, http://digitalarchive.wilsoncenter.org/document/113148; *Deng Xiaoping wenxuan* [Selected works of Deng Xiaoping] (Peking: Foreign Language Press, 1992), 3, 409, fn. 104.

97 Lukin, *The Bear Watches the Dragon*, 234-35.

98 Wishnick, *Mending Fences*, 189.

99 Lukin, *The Bear Watches the Dragon*, 234-35.

100 Zhu Chenghu, *ZhongMei quanxi de fazhan bianhua ji qi qushi* [The development, transformation, and trends in Sino-American relations] (Nanjing: Jiangsu renmin chubanshe, 1998), 341-46.

101 *Survey of China Mainland Press* (16-21 May 1991).

102 Tian, *Gaige kaifang yilai de Zhongguo waijiao*, 327-28.

103 *Zhonghua Renmin Gongheguo bianjie shiwu tiaoyueji: ZhongChao juan* [The People's Republic of China boundary affairs treaty collection: China-Korea volume] (Beijing: Shijie zhishi chubanshe, 2004); Daniel Gomà Pinilla, "Border Disputes between China and North Korea," *China Perspectives* 52 (March-April 2004): 2-8.

104 Seo Dong-shin, "NK Slams China for Koguryo Distortion," *Korea Times*, 15 September 2004.

105 Gari Ledyard, "Cartography in Korea," in *The History of Cartography*, vol. 2, book 2, ed. J.B. Harley and David Woodward (Chicago: University of Chicago Press, 1987), 289.

106 Yonson Ahn, "Competing Nationalisms: The Mobilisation of History and Archaeology in the Korea-China Wars over Koguryo/Gaoguoli," *Asia-Pacific Journal: Japan Focus*, http://www.japanfocus.org/; Austin Ramzy, "Rewriting History: China and the Koreas Feud over the Ancient Kingdom of Koguryo," *Times Asia*, 16 August 2004; James Brooke, "Seeking Peace in a Once and Future Kingdom," *New York Times*, 25 August 2004, A-3.

107 Ledyard, "Cartography in Korea," 301.

108 Quoted in Marion Eggert, "A Borderline Case: Korean Travelers' Views of the Chinese Border (Eighteenth to Nineteenth Century)," in *China and Her Neighbours: Borders, Visions of the Other, Foreign Policy 10th to 19th Century*, ed. Sabine Dabringhaus and Roderich Ptak (Wiesbaden: Harrassowitz Verlag, 1997), 51-52.

109 J.R.V. Prescott, *Map of Mainland Asia by Treaty* (Melbourne: Melbourne University Press, 1975), 499-508; Ledyard, "Cartography in Korea," 302; Zhang Cunwu [Chang Ts'un-wu], "Qingdai Zhong-Han bianwu wenti tanyuan" [An investigation of the Sino-Korean border question during the Qing dynasty], *Zhongyang yanjiuyuan jindaishi yanjiusuo jikan* (Taipei) 2 (1971): 463-503.

110 Interview with a former Chinese Foreign Ministry official who served as an ambassador, Beijing, November 1993.

111 *Facts about Korea* (Pyongyang: Foreign Language Publishing House, 1961), 1-4; *China Pictorial* 11 (November 1961): 30-31.

112 *Zhonghua Renmin Gongheguo bianjie shiwu tiaoyueji: ZhongChao juan*, 65-92.

113 Unless otherwise noted, the details of the negotiations and settlement are based on a confidential interview with a former Chinese Foreign Ministry official who served as an

ambassador, Beijing, November 1993. For corroboration, see Chae-Jin Lee, *China and Korea: Dynamic Relations* (Stanford, CA: Hoover Institution, 1996), 99-100.

114 Zhou Enlai confirmed this settlement to Prime Minister Tsedenbal of Mongolia in December 1962 when concluding the Sino-Mongolian boundary treaty: "Record of Conversation between Chinese Premier Zhou Enlai and Mongolian leader J. Tsedenbal" (26 December 1962), Cold War International History Project, *Digital Archive, Mongolia in the Cold War,* http://digitalarchive.wilsoncenter.org/document/112072. For a Korean view, see "What Is Hwanggumpyong Island?" http://english.chosun.com/site/data/html_dir/2011/06/10/2011061001158.html. In 2011, a PRC-DPRK joint development project for a special economic zone on the islands was inaugurated.

115 Gomà Pinilla, "Border Disputes between China and North Korea," 2.

116 Lee, *China and Korea,* 99.

117 *Nav Bharat Times,* 14 July 1965, cited in Kim Deuk Hwang, *Paektusan-gua Bukbang-ganggye* [Mt. Paektu and the northern border] (Seoul: Sa Sa Yon Publishers, 1988), 28; *Indian Express,* 20 July 1965, cited in Thomas An, "New Winds in Pyongyang?" *Problems of Communism* 15, 4 (July-August 1966): 68; Chin O. Chung, *P'yŏngyang between Peking and Moscow: North Korea's Involvement in the Sino-Soviet Dispute, 1958-1975* (Tuscloosa: University of Alabama Press, 1978), 120.

118 Mitchell Lerner, "'Mostly Propaganda in Nature': Kim Il Sung, the Juche Ideology, and the Second Korean War," North Korea International Documentation Project Working Paper 3 (Washington, DC: Woodrow Wilson International Center for Scholars, December 2010), 35-36.

119 *Sunday Times,* 25 May 1969, 9; Kim, *Paektusan-gua Bukbangganggye,* 28; Lee, *China and Korea,* 101.

120 Nena Vreeland et al., *Area Handbook for North Korea,* 2nd ed. (Washington, DC: US Government Printing Office, 1976), 207-8.

121 *New York Times,* 23 November 1970, 5; Prescott, *Map of Mainland Asia by Treaty,* 502.

122 Kim, *Paektusan-gua Bukbangganggye,* 29-30; Jilin Provincial Map (Zhongguo ditu chubanshe, May 1998).

123 Tai Sung An, *North Korea in Transition: From Dictatorship to Dynasty* (Westport, CT: Greenwood Press, 1983), 112. Some Chinese scholars speculate that the PLA has raised questions regarding the alignment of the boundary and China's border security.

124 *Zhonghua Renmin Gongheguo bianjie shiwu tiaoyueji: ZhongChao juan;* Sébastien Colin, "A Border Opening onto Numerous Geopolitical Issues," *China Perspectives* 48 (July-August 2003).

125 Yang Zhaoquan, *Zhongchao bianjie shi* [History of the China-Korea border] (Jilin: Wenshi chubanshe, 1993), 527-35; Daniel Gomà, "The Chinese-Korean Border Issue," *Asian Survey* 46, 6 (November/December 2006): 877.

126 In the eyes of many Koreans, both China and Russia have imperial pasts and imperial ambitions. South Korean commentators speculate that if the Pyongyang regime falls, China will come as a "thief in the night" seeking more Korean territory. Just as Russia has an older brother/younger brother relationship with Ukraine and is unwilling to lose this buffer zone, China assumes a similar relationship with North Korea. See Cho Guangdong, "Crimea, a Significant for Korean Reunification," http://www.newdaily.co.kr/news/article.html?no=197196.

Chapter 8: The Sino-Mongolian Boundary Settlement

1 Xiaoyuan Liu, *Reins of Liberation: An Entangled History of Mongolian Independence, Chinese Territoriality, and Great Power Hegemony, 1911-1950* (Stanford, CA: Stanford University Press, 2006), 85, 377-78, 389.

2   *Records of the Department of State Relating to Political Relations between Russia (and the Soviet Union) and Other States, 1910-29,* National Archives Microfilm Publications, Microcopy 340, 761.93/88 (1961).
3   Ibid.
4   "Declaration and Exchange of Notes Respecting Mongolia, October 23/November 5, 1913," *American Journal of International Law Supplement* 10, 4 (October 1916): 246-58.
5   Girard M. Friters, *Outer Mongolia and Its International Position* (New York and Baltimore: Johns Hopkins University Press, 1957).
6   Ibid., 186.
7   Eric Hyer, "'The Great Game': Mongolia between Russia and China," *Mongolian Journal of International Affairs* 4 (1997): 89-104.
8   The Republic of China rescinded this recognition following Soviet recognition of the People's Republic of China in 1949. Belatedly, the Republic of China again accepted Mongolian independence in 2002.
9   Edgar Snow, *Red Star over China* (New York: Modern Library, 1944), 96.
10 Andre Ledovsky, "Mikoyan's Secret Mission to China in January and February 1949," *Far Eastern Affairs* 23, 2 (1995): 88-89.
11 Craig Seibert, trans., "Stalin's Dialogue with Mao Zedong" (S.N. Goncharov interview with Ivan V. Kovalev), *Journal of Northeast Asian Studies* 10, 4 (Winter 1991): 69.
12 Andrei Ledovsky, "The Moscow Visit of a Delegation of the Communist Party of China in June to August 1949," *Far Eastern Affairs* 24, 4 (1996): 82-84.
13 See Robert A. Rupen, "The Mongolian People's Republic and Sino-Soviet Competition," in *Communist Strategies in Asia,* ed. A Doak Barnett (New York: Praeger, 1963), 288.
14 "China–Union of Soviet Socialist Republics: Communiqué," *American Journal of International Law* 44, 3 (July 1950): 83-84.
15 *New China Daily* (Nanjing), 5 March 1950, cited in Rupen, "The Mongolian People's Republic and Sino-Soviet Competition," 288-89.
16 Shi Bo, *Waimenggu duli neimu* [Inside story of Outer Mongolia's independence] (Beijing: Renmin Zhongguo chubanshe, 1993), ch. 8; Nikita Sergeyevich Khrushchev, *Khrushchev Remembers: The Last Testament* (Boston: Little, Brown, 1974), 285.
17 *Pravda,* 2 September 1964, in *Current Digest of the Soviet Press* 16, 34 (16 September 1964): 5-7.
18 Li Haiwen, "A Distortion of History: An Interview with Shi Zhe about Kovolev's Memoirs," *Chinese Historians* 5, 2 (Fall 1992): 61-62.
19 Felix Chuev, *Molotov Remembers: Inside Kremlin Politics* (Chicago: Ivan R. Dee, 1993), 71.
20 "Information Memorandum: 'About the Claims of the Chinese Leader with Regard to the Mongolian People's Republic'" (30 January 1964), Cold War International History Project, *Digital Archive, Mongolia in the Cold War,* http://digitalarchive.wilsoncenter. org/document/113098; "Excerpts from Tsedenbal's Diary on His Conversations with Soviet Leader Anastas Mikoyan" (24 February 1956), ibid., http://digitalarchive.wilson center.org/document/110480.
21 C.L. Sulzberger, "India and Russia – A Study in Contrasts," *New York Times,* 14 February 1955, 18; Alexander Kaznacheev, *Inside a Soviet Embassy: Experiences of a Russian Diplomat in Burma* (Philadelphia: Lippincott, 1962), 142.
22 *Christian Science Monitor,* 9 August 1957, 9; Harrison E. Salisbury, "Chinese-Mongol Tension Rising; Ulan Bator Charges Subversion," *New York Times,* 22 May 1964, 12.
23 Harrison E. Salisbury, *To Moscow and Beyond* (New York: Harper and Brothers, 1959), 228; Harrison E. Salisbury, "Soviet Influence in Mongolia Rises," *New York Times,* 17

December 1961, 32; 25 April 1964, 3; 22 May 1964, 12; Foreign Broadcast Information Service, *Daily Report, Far East* 83 (28 April 1964): FFF1.

24 *Renmin ribao*, 30 August 1956, in *Survey of China Mainland Press*, no. 1363 (August 1956): 20, and no. 1439 (28 December 1957): 36; *People's China* 18 (16 September 1956): 40; *Christian Science Monitor*, 9 August 1957, 9.

25 *Renmin ribao*, 4 October 1957; *Survey of China Mainland Press*, no. 1631 (15 October 1957): 42-44; *Joint Publication Research Service* 45,465 (23 May 1968): 33-35; *Peking Review*, 30 December 1958, 22.

26 P.H.M. Jones, "Mongolia between Two Fires," *Far Eastern Economic Review*, 17 August 1961, 307.

27 Harrison E. Salisbury, *War between Russia and China* (New York: W.W. Norton, 1969), 17-18.

28 Robert A. Rupen, "The Mongolian People's Republic and Inner Mongolia," *China News Analysis* 540 (13 November 1964): 2; Rupen, "The Mongolian People's Republic and Sino-Soviet Competition," 265.

29 *The Times*, 30 September 1958, 10; *Survey of China Mainland Press*, no. 1870 (8 October 1958): 56.

30 *Current Digest of the Soviet Press* 9, 20 (26 June 1957): 27-28.

31 Zbigniew Brzezinski, *The Soviet Bloc: Unity and Conflict* (New York: Praeger, 1961), 424.

32 Seymour Topping, "Red Bloc Speeds Economic Unity," *New York Times*, 9 June 1962, 1; Philip E. Uren, "Economic Relations among Communist States," in *The Communist States at the Crossroads*, ed. Adam Bromke (New York: Praeger, 1965): 204.

33 Tsedendambyn Batbayar, *Modern Mongolia: A Concise History* (Ulaanbaatar: Mongolian Center for Scientific and Technological Information, 1996), 55; *New York Times*, 17 December 1961, 33.

34 *Zhonghua Renmin Gongheguo bianjie shiwu tiaoyueji: ZhongMeng juan* [The People's Republic of China boundary affairs treaty collection: China-Mongolia volume] (Beijing: Shijie zhishi chubanshe, 2004); *Renmin ribao*, 24 December 1962, 1; *Survey of China Mainland Press*, no. 2889 (2 January 1963): 32-37; *China News Analysis*, 18 January 1963, 6-7.

35 Han Nianlong, ed., *Diplomacy of Contemporary China* (Hong Kong: New Horizon Press, 1990), 185; Wang Taiping, ed., *Zhonghua Renmin Gongheguo waijiao shi (2) 1957-1959* [Diplomatic history of the PRC (vol. 2) 1957-1969] (Beijing: Shijie zhishi chubanshe, 1998), 100.

36 *Renmin ribao*, 27 December 1962, in *Survey of China Mainland Press*, no. 2889 (2 January 1963): 38; Wang, ibid., 100.

37 *Christian Science Monitor*, 9 August 1957, 9; 6 January 1964, 2; Theodore Shabad, "Soviet and Chinese Disagree on Maps," *New York Times*, 26 February 1961, 20; *China News Analysis*, 2 March 1962, 5; O. Chuluun, "The Two Phases in Mongolian-Chinese Relations (1949-1972)," *Far Eastern Affairs* 1 (1974): 26-27.

38 Wang, *Zhonghua Renmin Gongheguo waijiao shi*, 100-1.

39 *Reuters* (Peking), 24 December 1962, cited by Guy Searls, "Communist China's Border Policy: Dragon Throne Imperialism?" *Current Scene* 2, 13 (15 April 1963): 104; Wang, ibid., 101-2.

40 *Renmin ribao*, 27 December 1962, in *Survey of China Mainland Press*, no. 2889 (2 January 1963): 38-39; *New York Times*, 28 December 1962, 3; Han, *Diplomacy of Contemporary China*, 186; "Record of Conversation between Chinese Premier Zhou Enlai and Mongolian Leader J. Zedenbal" (26 December 1962), Cold War International History Project, *Digital Archive, Mongolia in the Cold War*, http://digitalarchive.wilsoncenter.org/document/112072.

41 *Renmin ribao,* 27 December 1962, in *Survey of China Mainland Press,* no. 2889 (2 January 1963): 38-39; *Renmin ribao,* 9 March and 26 March 1963, in *Joint Publication Research Service* 18730 (15 April 1963): 1-18, and United States Consulate General, Hong Kong, *Current Background* 707 (9 August 1963): 1-13; *Joint Publication Research Service* 19279 (17 May 1963): 1-30.

42 *Renmin ribao,* 3 July 1964, 3.

43 Ibid., 27 December 1962, 3; *China News Analysis* 452 (18 January 1963): 7; *Survey of China Mainland Press,* no. 2889 (2 January 1963): 37; Henry S. Bradsher, "Sino-Soviet Rift Catches Mongolia," *Christian Science Monitor,* 6 January 1964, 2; Alastair Lamb, *Asian Frontiers: Studies in a Continuing Problem* (New York: Praeger, 1968), 202; Batbayar, *Modern Mongolia,* 57.

44 A.J.K. Sanders, *The People's Republic of Mongolia* (London: Oxford University Press, 1968), 42-43; *New York Times,* 24 May 1964, 6; Wang, *Zhonghua Renmin Gongheguo waijiao shi,* 102.

45 *Unen,* 11 August 1967, 30.

46 Chuluun, "The Two Phases in Mongolian-Chinese Relations," 26.

47 Sergey S. Radchenko, "The Soviets' Best Friend in Asia: The Mongolian Dimension of the Sino-Soviet Dispute," Cold War International History Project, Working Paper 42 (Washington, DC: Woodrow Wilson International Center for Scholars, 2003), 6.

48 *Current Digest of the Soviet Press* 9, 2 (26 June 1957): 28.

49 Robert A. Rupen, *Mongols of the Twentieth Century* (Bloomington: Indiana University Press, 1964), 272.

50 *New York Times,* 22 August 1959, 3; 11 September 1959, 3; 22 October 1959, 3; David Floyd, *Mao against Khrushchev: A Short History of the Sino-Soviet Conflict* (New York: Praeger, 1963), 261-62; C.R. Bawden, "Mongolian People's Republic, Number 3," *China News Analysis* 493 (15 November 1963): 1.

51 Constitution of the Mongolian People's Republic (reprinted in Rupen, *Mongols of the Twentieth Century,* 413-26).

52 *China News Analysis* 410 (2 March 1962): 4 and 6; Rupen, "The Mongolian People's Republic and Inner Mongolia," 2-4; Tsedendamba Batbayar, "Mongolia's Foreign Policy in the 1990s: New Identity and New Challenges," *Regional Security Issues and Mongolia* (Institute for Strategic Studies, Ulaanbaatar) 17 (2002): 123; Batbayar, *Modern Mongolia,* 59.

53 *China News Analysis* 534 (25 September 1964): 2.

54 *Renmin ribao,* 25 December 1962, in *Survey of China Mainland Press,* no. 2888 (31 December 1962): 39.

55 *Survey of China Mainland Press,* no. 2889 (2 January 1963): 28-40 passim.

56 After concluding boundary treaties with Russia, on 24 June 1996, China and Mongolia negotiated two protocols demarcating the China-Russia-Mongolia trijunctions *(Zhonghua Renmin Gongheguo bianjie shiwu tiaoyueji: ZhongMeng juan).*

57 *Renmin ribao,* 27 December 1962, 3; *Current Digest of the Soviet Press* 14, 52 (23 January 1963): 35; *Survey of China Mainland Press,* no. 2889 (2 January 1963): 37-40; *New York Times,* 26 December 1962, 1.

58 *Current Digest of the Soviet Press* 15, 2 (6 February 1963): 20.

59 *Joint Publication Research Service* 26544 (24 September 1964): 14.

60 MPRP official statement in *Novosti Mongolii,* 22 October 1963, cited in Robert A. Rupen, "Recent Trends in the Mongolian People's Republic," *Asian Survey* 4, 4 (April 1964): 812; Tsedenbal statement in *Current Digest of the Soviet Press* 16, 37 (7 October 1964): 15.

61 *Renmin ribao,* 22 March 1963; *South China Morning Post,* 23 March 1963, 18; *Current Digest of the Soviet Press* 16, 37 (7 October 1964): 15.

62 *New York Times,* 6 September 1964, IV:3; *Current Digest of the Soviet Press* 16, 34 (16 September 1964): 3-7.
63 *Christian Science Monitor,* 5 March 1963, 8; *China News Analysis* 468 (17 May 1963): 5.
64 *China News Analysis* 534 (25 September 1964): 4.
65 *Renmin ribao,* 8 April 1964, 3; *China News Analysis,* ibid., 4.
66 "Information Note of Romanian Embassy from Beijing to Ministry of Foreign Affairs" (23 May 1989), Cold War International History Project, *Digital Archive,* http://digital archive.wilsoncenter.org/document/113148.
67 "China Stakes a Claim to All the Mongolias," *International Herald Tribune,* 30 April 1992; Batbayar, "Mongolia's Foreign Policy in the 1990s," 128-29.
68 *South China Morning Post,* 1 July 1992, 12.

Chapter 9: The Sino-Japanese Senkaku/Diaoyu Islands Dispute
1 "Senkaku Islands" has become the most common and widely used name for the islands. Other Chinese variations are rendered as "Tiaoyuyu" or "Tiaoyutai."
2 Quoted in Han Nianlong, ed., *Diplomacy of Contemporary China* (Hong Kong: New Horizon Press, 1990), 249.
3 Xie Yixian, *Zhongguo waijiao shi: Zhonghua Renmin Gongheguo shiqi 1949-1979* [A diplomatic history of China: the period of the People's Republic of China, 1949-1979] (Zhengzhou: Henan renmin chubanshe, 1988), 325.
4 Quoted in Han, *Diplomacy of Contemporary China,* 253.
5 "The Struggle of the People of Ryukyu Opposing American Occupation," *Renmin ribao,* 8 January 1953.
6 K.O. Emery et al., "Geological Structure and Some Water Characteristics of the East China Sea and Yellow Sea," *Technical Bulletin* 2 (1969): 39.
7 "Red China, Japan Claim Oil Islands," *Washington Post,* 5 December 1970, A-10.
8 "Agreement with Japan Concerning the Ryukyu Islands and Daito Islands: Hearing before the Senate Committee on Foreign Relations," 92nd Congress, 1st Session (Washington, DC: 1971), 91; *Congressional Record,* 92nd Congress, 1st Session (9 November 1971).
9 *Peking Review,* 1 January 1972, 12-13.
10 *Peking Review,* 10 March 1972, 16; Xie, *Zhongguo waijiao shi ... 1949-1979,* 424-25.
11 *Peking Review,* 12 May 1972, 18-22; 26 May 1972, 14.
12 Foreign Broadcast Information Service (FBIS), *Daily Report: Asia and Pacific,* 7 April 1971, C1; *New York Times,* 23 May 1971, IV:7; 21 June 1971, 14; 23 April 1972, 17; *Washington Post,* 19 June 1971, A19.
13 Ministry of Foreign Affairs of Japan, "The Japan-China Summit Meeting between Prime Minister Kakuei Tanaka and Premier Zhou Enlai on September 27, 1972," http://www.mofa.go.jp/region/asia-paci/senkaku/qa_1010.html#qa14.
14 *Peking Review,* 3 November 1978, 16; Besshi Yukio, "Nitchu kokko seijoka no seiji katei: seisaku ketteisha to sono kodo no haikei" [Political process of the normalization of Sino-Japanese diplomatic relations: decision makers and the background of their behaviour], *Kokusai seiji* 66, 3 (1980): 3; Xie, *Zhongguo waijiao shi ... 1949-1979,* 526, 536.
15 Ministry of Foreign Affairs of Japan, "Fact Sheet on the Senkaku Islands (November 2012), http://www.mofa.go.jp/; Mamoru Ishida, "Finding Common Ground on the Senkakus Dispute," *Japan Times,* 19 March 2013, http://www.japantimes.co.jp/.
16 Takemura Kenichi, "Sonoda gaiso ni chokugeki intabyu" [A hard-hitting interview of Foreign Minister Sonoda], *Jiyu minshu* 273 (10 October 1978), 49-50.
17 FBIS, *Daily Report: Communist China,* 4 December 1970, A15-17; 7 December 1970, A8.
18 Ibid., 29 December 1970, A7.
19 *New York Times,* 20 March 1972, 13.

20 Besshi, "Nitchu kokko seijoka no seiji katie," 3-7.
21 FBIS, *Daily Report: Asia and Pacific*, 2 October 1972, C1-2.
22 *Peking Review*, 17 March 1972, 11.
23 FBIS, *Daily Report: PRC*, 8 October 1974, A8; Ueji Tatsunori, *Senkaku retto to Takeshima* (Tokyo: Kyoikusha, 1978), 81.
24 Ibid., 17-21.
25 FBIS, *Daily Report: Asia and Pacific*, 12 April 1978, C3.
26 Ibid., 17 April 1978, C4.
27 Ibid., 14 April 1978, C1.
28 FBIS, *Daily Report: China*, 17 April 1978, A6-8; *New York Times*, 16 April 1978, 8.
29 FBIS, *Daily Report: Asia and Pacific*, 17 April 1978, C2; 18 April 1978, C1.
30 FBIS, *Daily Report: PRC*, 25 April 1978, A7.
31 Ibid., 24 April 1978, C1.
32 Ibid., 2 May 1978, A9.
33 Ibid., 11 May 1978, A17-18.
34 Kenichi, "Sonoda gaiso ni chokugeki intabyu," 49-50.
35 FBIS, *Daily Report: PRC*, 14 August 1978, A7.
36 Ministry of Foreign Affairs of Japan, "Fact Sheet on the Senkaku Islands"; Ishida, "Finding Common Ground on the Senkakus Dispute."
37 FBIS, *Daily Report: Asia and Pacific*, 16 August 1978, C2-3;Takemura Kenichi, "Sonoda gaiso ni chokugeki intabyu," 49.
38 Yang Gongsu, *Zhonghua Renmin Gongheguo waijiao lilun yu shijian* [Theory and practice of People's Republic of China diplomacy] (Beijing: Beijing daxue guoji guanxi xueyuan, 1997), 275-79; "Chairman of Chinese Delegation T'eng Hsiao-ping's [Three Worlds] Speech," *Peking Review*, 19 April 1974, 6-11; "Chairman Mao's Theory of the Differentiation of the Three Worlds Is a Major Contribution to Marxism-Leninism," *Peking Review*, 4 November 1977, 10-41.
39 Joseph Y.S. Cheng, "Normalization of Sino-Japanese Relations: China's Bargaining Position Regarding the Taiwan Question," *Asia Quarterly* 4 (1980): 258-59.
40 FBIS, *Daily Report: Asia and Pacific*, 13 April 1978, C9.
41 Ibid., C6-9; *Mainichi shimbun*, 8 April 1978, 2.
42 FBIS, ibid., 17 April 1978, C4.
43 Ibid., C3-4.
44 Ibid., C2-3.
45 FBIS, *Daily Report: China*, 25 April 1978, A7.
46 Ibid., 31 May 1979, D5.
47 Daniel Tretiak, "Peking's Policy toward Sinkiang: Trouble on the 'New Frontier,'" *Current Scene* 11, 24 (15 November 1963).
48 FBIS, *Daily Report: Asia and Pacific*, 13 April 1978, C6.
49 FBIS, *Daily Report: China*, 19 May 1978, N2.
50 Ibid., 17 August 1978, N1.
51 *Renmin ribao*, 16 April 1978, 3; FBIS, *Daily Report: PRC*, 11 May 1978, A17-18.
52 *Peking Review*, 3 November 1978, 16; Ministry of Foreign Affairs of Japan, "Fact Sheet on the Senkaku Islands."
53 The CCP issued an internal document in September 1996 ordering university officials to stop student protests over the Diaoyu Islands dispute. See *China News Digest*, 18 September 1996; Liu Binyan, "Big Drama about Small Islands," *China Focus* 4, 10 (1 October 1996): 1; "Activists Warned to Halt Diaoyu Protests," *South China Morning Post*, 29 May 1997. More recent efforts are detailed in M. Taylor Fravel, "Explaining Stability in the Senkaku (Diaoyu) Islands Dispute," in *Getting the Triangle Straight: Managing*

China-Japan-US Relations, ed. Gerald Curtis, Ryosei Kokubun, and Wang Jisi (Baltimore: Brookings Institution Press, 2010), 153-55.

54 Ministry of Foreign Affairs of Japan, "The Basic View on the Sovereignty over the Senkaku Islands" (May 2013), http://www.mofa.go.jp/region/.

55 State Council Information Office of the People's Republic of China, "Full Text: Diaoyu Dao, an Inherent Territory of China" (September 2012), http://english.gov.cn/.

56 After 17 years of negotiations, in April 2013 Japan and Taiwan (ROC) concluded a fisheries agreement after setting aside the Diaoyu/Senkaku issue which was excluded from the scope of the agreement. See "Taiwan, Japan Reach Milestone Fisheries Agreement," *Taiwan Panorama* (38, 6 (June 2013): 53-55.

57 Ministry of Foreign Affairs of Japan, "Q&A on the Senkaku Islands," http://www.mofa.go.jp/region/asia-paci/senkaku/qa_1010.html#qa16.

58 Liu Jiangyong, "New Situation and Prospect of Disputes over Diaoyu Dao," *Foreign Affairs Journal,* issue 106 (Winter 2012): 39.

59 James Manicom, "The State of Cooperation in the East China Sea," *NBR Analysis Brief,* 30 April 2013.

60 Ministry of Foreign Affairs of the People's Republic of China, "China and Japan Reach Principled Consensus on the East China Sea Issue" (18 June 2008), http://www.fmprc.gov.cn/; Xinjun Zhang, "China's 'Peaceful Rise,' 'Harmonious' Foreign Relations, and Legal Confrontation and Lesson from the Sino-Japanese Dispute over the East China Sea," Foreign Policy Research Institute, Philadelphia, *E-Notes,* 16 April 2010, 6. China unilaterally started development in 2013. See "Japan Complains over China Drill Rig Near Disputed Gas Field," *BBC News,* 3 July 2013, http://www.bbc.co.uk/.

61 Ministry of Foreign Affairs of the People's Republic of China, "China and Japan Reach Principled Consensus on the East China Sea Issue"; Martin Fackler, "China and Japan in Deal over Contested Gas Fields," *New York Times,* 19 June 2008; "Tokyo Nixed Joint Senkaku Exploitation," *Japan Times,* 22 October 2010, http://info.japantimes.co.jp/.

62 "Backing Off Not an Option for China," *Global Times,* 15 September 2012, http://www.globaltimes.cn/.

63 Jane Perlez, "Chinese President to Seek New 'Power Relationship' in Talks with Obama," *New York Times,* 29 May 2013, A6; Lin Hongyu, "Zhongguo haiyang zhanlue kunjing: chengyin yu duice" [The predicament of Chinese maritime strategy: causes and counter-measures], *Xiandai Guoji Guanxi* 8 (2012): 7.

64 FBIS, *Daily Report: China,* 31 May 1979, D6 (emphasis added).

65 FBIS, *Daily Report: East Asia,* 2 October 1990, 11-12; 23 October 1990, 3; 24 October 1990, 2; "Chinese Foreign Ministry Spokesman on Diaoyu Islands," *Xinhua Overseas News Service,* 25 October 1990.

66 FBIS, *Daily Report: China,* 27 February 1992, 15-16.

67 "Qian Qichen News Conference," *BBC Summary of World Broadcasts,* 29 March 1991; "Jiang Zemin Tells Japanese Journalists Whole Party behind Economic Reforms," *BBC Summary of World Broadcasts,* 6 April 1992; Xie, *Zhongguo waijiao shi: Zhonghua Renmin Gongheguo shiqi 1979-1994* [A diplomatic history of China: the period of the People's Republic of China, 1979-1994] (Zhengzhou: Henan renmin chubanshe, 1995), 141-42.

68 *Associated Press–Dow Jones,* 10 September 1993, via *China News Digest,* 14 September 1993; 9 December 1993.

69 Erica Strecker Downs and Phillip C. Saunders, "Legitimacy and the Limits of Nationalism: China and the Diaoyu Islands," *International Security* 23, 3 (Winter 1998-99): 117; Phil Deans, "Contending Nationalisms and the Diaoyutai/Senkaku Dispute," *Security Dialogue* 31, 1 (2000): 119-31.

70 http://www.fmprc.gov.cn/mfa_eng/zxxx_662805/t1208360.shtml.
71 M. Taylor Fravel, "Explaining Stability in the Senkaku (Diaoyu) Islands Dispute," 157-59; Suisheng Zhao, "Foreign Policy Implication of Chinese Nationalism Revisited: The Strident Turn," *Journal of Contemporary China* 22, 82 (2013): 553.

Chapter 10: The Sino-Vietnamese Territorial and Boundary Settlements
1 Xiaohong Liu, *Chinese Ambassadors: The Rise of Diplomatic Professionalism since 1949* (Seattle: University of Washington Press, 2001), 136.
2 Zbigniew Brzezinski, *Power and Principle: Memoirs of the National Security Advisor, 1977-81* (New York: Farrar, Straus and Giroux, 1983), 409.
3 Nguyen Manh Hung, "The Sino-Vietnamese Conflict: Power Play among Communist Neighbors," *Asian Survey* 19, 11 (November 1979): 1038.
4 Han Nianlong, ed., *Diplomacy of Contemporary China* (Hong Kong: New Horizon Press, 1990), 344-46; Bruce Burton, "Contending Explanations of the 1979 Sino-Vietnamese War," *International Journal* 34, 4 (Autumn 1979): 704.
5 Allen S. Whiting, *The Chinese Calculus of Deterrence: India and Indochina* (Ann Arbor: University of Michigan Press, 1975), 186-98.
6 Han, *Diplomacy of Contemporary China*, 346-7.
7 Ibid., 330-31.
8 "Note Sent by the Chinese Foreign Ministry to the Vietnamese Embassy in China, June 23, 1980," United Nations Document S/14047; Ramses Amer, "Assessing Sino-Vietnamese Relations through the Management of Contentious Issues," *Contemporary Southeast Asia* 26, 2 (August 2004): 321.
9 Xie Yixian, *Zhongguo waijiao shi: Zhonghua Renmin Gongheguo shiqi 1949-1979* [A diplomatic history of China: the period of the People's Republic of China, 1949-1979] (Zhengzhou: Henan renmin chubanshe, 1988), 516-21.
10 "Memorandum Dated 15 March 1979 of the Ministry of Foreign Affairs of the Socialist Republic of Viet Nam Concerning the Chinese Authorities' Provocations and Territorial Encroachments in the Border Region of Viet Nam," United Nations Document S/13234; "Speech Made by Han Nianlong, Head of the Chinese Government Delegation and Vice-Minister for Foreign Affairs, at the Fourth Plenary Meeting of the Sino-Vietnamese Negotiations on 12 May 1979," United Nations Document S/13318; *Beijing Review,* 25 May 1979, 20; Pao-min Chang, "The Sino-Vietnamese Territorial Dispute," *Asia Pacific Community* 8 (Spring 1980); John B. Allcock et al., eds., *Border and Territorial Disputes,* 3rd ed. (Essex, UK: Longman Current Affairs, 1992), 465; Yang Gongsu, *Zhonghua Renmin Gongheguo waijiao lilun yu shijian* [Theory and practice of People's Republic of China diplomacy] (Beijing: Beijing daxue guoji guanxi xueyuan, 1997), 349.
11 *Beijing Review,* 25 May 1979, 19-20.
12 J.R.V. Prescott, *Map of Mainland Asia by Treaty* (Melbourne: Melbourne University Press, 1975), 453. See also Han, *Diplomacy of Contemporary China,* 335; Xie, *Zhongguo waijiao shi ... 1949-1979,* 519.
13 Han, ibid., 337; Xie, ibid., 132-33; "Memorandum Dated 15 March 1979 of the Ministry of Foreign Affairs of the Socialist Republic of Viet Nam Concerning the Chinese Authorities' Provocations and Territorial Encroachments in the Border Region of Viet Nam," United Nations Document S/13234; "Speech Made by Han Nianlong, Head of the Chinese Government Delegation and Vice-Minister for Foreign Affairs, at the Fourth Plenary Meeting of the Sino-Vietnamese Negotiations on 12 May 1979," United National Document S/13318.
14 "Memorandum on Vice-Premier Li Xiannian's Talks with Premier Pham Van Dong, 10 June 1977," *Beijing Review,* 30 March 1979, 17-22.

15 *Beijing Review,* 25 May 1979, 16-18.
16 Xie, *Zhongguo dangdai waijiao shi,* 338.
17 *Beijing Review,* 25 May 1979, 21; *On Vietnam's Expulsion of Chinese Residents* (Beijing: Foreign Language Press, 1978), 71-72, 103-6; "Memorandum Outlining Vice-Premier Li Xiannian's Talk with Premier Pham Van Dong on 10 June 1977," United Nations Document S/13255; "Memorandum Dated 14 February 1979 of the Ministry of Foreign Affairs of the Socialist Republic of Viet Nam on the Chinese Authorities' Intensified Armed Activities on the Viet Nam Border and Their Frantic War Preparations against Viet Nam," United Nations Document S/13093; "Statement Issued by the Xinhua News Agency on 17 February 1979 on Authorization of the Chinese Government," United Nations Document S/13094; Xie, *Zhongguo dangdai waijiao shi,* 340.
18 Xie, ibid., 503-5, 523-25; Yang, *Zhonghua Renmin Gongheguo waijiao lilun yu shijian,* 345-46.
19 Foreign Broadcast Information Service (FBIS), *Daily Report: PRC,* 12 February 1979, A7.
20 Ibid., 6 February 1979, A2.
21 Ibid., 21 February 1979, A4; 23 February 1979, A11.
22 "Statement Issued by the Xinhua News Agency on 17 February 1979 upon Authorization of the Chinese Government," United Nations Document S/13094; "Note Dated 1 March 1979 from the Ministry of Foreign Affairs of China to the Vietnamese Embassy in China," United Nations Document S/13129.
23 Burton, "Contending Explanations of the 1979 Sino-Vietnamese War," 699.
24 Xiaoming Zhang, "China's 1979 War with Vietnam: A Reassessment," *China Quarterly* 184 (December 2005): 856; Amer, "Assessing Sino-Vietnamese Relations through the Management of Contentious Issues," 324; Nayan Chanda, *Brother Enemy: The War after the War* (New York: Harcourt Brace Jovanovich, 1986), 261.
25 FBIS, *Daily Report: PRC,* 18 September 1978, A13.
26 FBIS, ibid., 26 December 1978, A13-16; Zhang, "China's 1979 War with Vietnam," 855-57, 868-69.
27 Brzezinski, *Power and Principle,* 409.
28 "Note Dated 2 March 1979 from the Ministry of Foreign Affairs of the Socialist Republic of Viet Nam to the Ministry of Foreign Affairs of the People's Republic of China," United Nations Document S/13134.
29 "Note Sent by the Ministry of Foreign Affairs of the People's Republic of China to the Minister of Foreign Affairs of the Socialist Republic of Vietnam, 31 March 1979," United Nations Document S/13212.
30 Xie, *Zhongguo waijiao shi ... 1949-1979,* 522.
31 FBIS, *Daily Report: PRC,* 14 September 1978, A12-14; 13 November 1978, A8-9; 9 January 1979, A21-22.
32 "Speech by the Head of the Delegation of the Government of the Socialist Republic of Viet Nam, Dinh Nho Liem, at the First Meeting of the Second Round of Viet Nam–China talks (28 June 1979)," United Nations Document S/13434.
33 *Beijing Review,* 4 May 1979, 28.
34 "Speech by Vice-Foreign Minister Han Nianlong, Head of the Chinese Government Delegation, at the 13th Plenary Meeting of the Sino-Vietnamese Negotiations on 19 October 1979," United Nations Document S/13583; Xie, *Zhongguo waijiao shi ... 1949-1979,* 523-24.
35 "Note Sent by the Chinese Foreign Ministry to the Vietnamese Embassy in China, 23 June 1980," United Nations Document S/14047; "Note Addressed by the Ministry of

Foreign Affairs of the Socialist Republic of Viet Nam to the Ministry of Foreign Affairs of the People's Republic of China, 3 July 1980," United Nations Document S/14054.

36 "Memorandum Outlining Vice-Premier Li Xiannian's Talk with Premier Pham Van Dong on 10 June 1977," United Nations Document S/13255; *Beijing Review,* 25 May 1979, 16-17.

37 Nayan Chanda, "China and Cambodia: In the Mirror of History," *Asia-Pacific Review* 9, 2 (2002): 5.

38 Tian Zengpei, ed., *Gaige kaifang yilai de Zhongguo waijiao* [Chinese foreign policy since opening up and reform] (Beijing: Shijie zhishi chubanshe, 1993), 81-82; *New York Times,* 4 November 1991, A4.

39 *China News Digest,* 27 January 1998. Overall trade grew from US$32 million in 1991 to US$2.5 billion in 2000.

40 Nguyen Quy Binh, Ministry of Foreign Affairs interview, 26 May 1995, Hanoi; *United Press International,* 28 August 1993; *Kyodo News Service,* 19 November 1993; *China News Digest,* 23 December 1993 and 22 November 1994.

41 "Talks to Tackle Border Tensions," *South China Morning Post,* 16 July 1997; *China News Digest,* 22 October 1998.

42 "Border Deal Struck with Vietnam," *South China Morning Post,* 3 December 1999; "Vietnamese Border Agreement Signed," *South China Morning Post,* 31 December 1999.

43 Amer, "Assessing Sino-Vietnamese Relations through the Management of Contentious Issues," 331.

44 *Associated Press,* 16 September 2002; "China, Vietnam Settle Land Border Issue," *China Daily,* 24 February 2009, http://www.chinadaily.com.cn/.

45 FBIS, *Daily Report, East Asia,* 6 July 1994, 66; 20 October 1994, 84.

46 Ramses Amer, "The Sino-Vietnamese Approach to Managing Boundary Disputes," *Maritime Briefing* 3, 5 (2002): 41-42.

47 "Joint China-Vietnam Statement for Comprehensive Cooperation," http://www.fmprc. gov.cn/eng/6939.html; Xiao Jianguo, "Drawing the Line," http://www.bjreview.com.cn/ 200432/World-200432(A).htm.

48 Nguyen Quy Binh, Ministry of Foreign Affairs interview, 26 May 1995, Hanoi; Amer, "The Sino-Vietnamese Approach to Managing Boundary Disputes," 8.

49 Martin Stuart-Fox and Mary Kookyman, *Historical Dictionary of Laos* (London: Scarecrow Press, 1992), 22.

50 Han, *Diplomacy of Contemporary China,* 205-8; *Peking Review,* 28 April 1961, 7-8; 7 December 1962, 20.

51 Alastair Lamb, *Asian Frontiers: Studies in a Continuing Problem* (New York: Praeger, 1968), 175-80.

52 Prescott, *Map of Mainland Asia by Treaty,* 447-51.

53 Tian, *Gaige kaifang yilai de Zhongguo waijiao,* 87.

54 Lamb, *Asian Frontiers,* 175, fn.

55 Interviews with Chinese scholars at both the China Institute of International Studies and the China Institutes of Contemporary International Relations, July 1994.

56 Tian, *Gaige kaifang yilai de Zhongguo waijiao,* 87, 361; FBIS, *Daily Report, East Asia,* 12 February 1991, 37; 18 March 1991, 48.

57 *Zhonghua Renmin Gongheguo bianjie shiwu tiaoyueji: ZhongLao juan* [The People's Republic of China boundary affairs treaty collection: China-Laos volume] (Beijing: Shijie zhishi chubanshe, 2004), 155-74.

58 Ian Townsend-Gault, "The China-Laos Boundary: Lan Xang Meets the Middle Kingdom," in *Beijing's Power and China's Border: Twenty Neighbors in Asia,* ed. Bruce A. Elleman, Stephen Kotkin, and Clive Schofield (Armonk, NY: M.E. Sharpe, 2013), 150.

Chapter 11: Boundary Settlements with Eurasian States

1 Hasan H. Karrar, *The New Silk Road Diplomacy: China's Central Asian Foreign Policy since the Cold War* (Vancouver: UBC Press, 2009), 3.

2 Ibid., 54.

3 Marlène Laruelle and Sébastien Peyrouse, *China as a Neighbor: Central Asian Perspectives and Strategies* (Washington, DC: John Hopkins University–SAIS, Central Asia–Caucasus Institute and Silk Road Studies Program, 2009), 24.

4 Bonnie Glaser, "China's Security Perceptions: Interests and Ambitions," *Asian Survey* 33, 3 (March 1993): 252-71; James Hsiung, "China's Omni-directional Diplomacy: Realignment to Cope with Monopolar US Power," *Asian Survey* 35, 6 (June 1995): 573-86; Tariq Mahmud Ashraf, "Afghanistan in Chinese Strategy toward South and Central Asia," *China Brief* 8, 10 (13 May 2008): 2.

5 *Beijing Review,* 2-8 May 1994, 19.

6 *Renmin ribao,* 5 July 1998.

7 Tarique Niazi, "The Ecology of Strategic Interests: China's Quest for Energy Security from the Indian Ocean and the South China Sea to the Caspian Sea Basin," *China and Eurasia Forum Quarterly* 6, 4 (November 2006): 111; Niklas Swanström, "China and Central Asia: A New Great Game or Traditional Vassal Relations?" *Journal of Contemporary China* 14, 45 (November 2005): 569-84.

8 Quoted in Keith Martin, "China and Central Asia: Between Seduction and Suspicion," *RFE/RL Research Report* 3, 24 (24 June 1994): 33.

9 *Beijing Review,* 23-29 March 1992, 12; *The Independent* (London), 13 January 1992.

10 Xu Tao and He Xichuan, "Gongtong gozhu mianxiang ershiyi shiji de chuanmian hezuo huoban guanxi: Zhong-Ha shuangbian guanxi fazhan qingkuang" [Mutually building a comprehensive cooperative partnership for the twenty-first century: the development of Sino-Kazakh relations], *Xiandai guoji guanxi* 10 (1997): 3-5.

11 *Xinhua General Overseas News Service,* 8 September 1992.

12 *Xinhua,* 11 April 1996 and 27 April 1996.

13 *Wenhui bao* (Hong Kong), 26 April 1992.

14 Zhang Wenmu, "America's Oil Geostrategy and the Security of Tibet and Xinjiang: Considering New Trends in US Foreign Policy toward South and Central Asia," *Zhanlue yu guanli [Strategy and Management]* 2 (1998): 100-1.

15 Ibid., 103-4.

16 *Beijing Review,* 1-7 June 1992, 30; Foreign Broadcast Information Service [hereafter FBIS], *Daily Report: China,* 3 September 1992; 22 December 1992), 51; Gaye Christoffersen, "Xinjiang and the Great Islamic Circle: The Impact of Transnational Forces on Chinese Regional Economic Planning," *China Quarterly* 133 (March 1993): 130-51.

17 Evan A. Feigenbaum, "Central Asia Contingencies," in *Managing Instability on China's Periphery,* ed. Paul B. Stares, Scott A. Snyder, Joshua Kurlantzick, Daniel Markey, and Evan A. Feigenbaum. (New York: Council on Foreign Relations, Center for Preventive Action, 2011), 65.

18 Niazi, "The Ecology of Strategic Interests," 109-14; Pan Guang, "China and Central Asia: Charting a New Course for Regional Cooperation," *Jamestown Foundation China Brief* 7, 3 (5 February 2007):1-4.

19 "Chinese Challenge," *Economist,* 12 May 1994, 30; *Beijing Review,* 1-7 June 1992, 30; 23-29 January 1995, 23; FBIS, *Daily Report: China,* 29 October 1992, 8; 18 June 1993, 8; 21 June 1993, 12; Nicolas Becquelin, "A New Xinjiang for a New Central Asia," *China Perspectives* 15 (January-February 1998): 13, 16; *Xinhua,* 26 August 1999; *Xinhua Economic News Service,* 31 March 2005; Jonson, Lena, *Tajikistan in the New Central Asia: Geopolitics, Great Power Rivalry and Radical Islam* (London: I.B. Tauris, 2006), 86-87.

20 Many speculate that China's real objective is to link Uzbekistan, viewed by many Chinese as Central Eurasia's regional leader, to China.

21 *Beijing Review,* 9-15 May 1994, 5.

22 "China's Strike," *Economist,* 16 August 1997, 32-33; *Beijing Review,* 27 October – 2 November 1997, 27.

23 "Kazakhstan's Pipeline to Prosperity," *The Economist,* 11 October 1997, 47; Becquelin, "A New Xinjiang," 15; Marat Yermukanov, "A Thorny Road to Sino-Kazakh Partnership," *China Brief* 4, 14 (8 July 2004): 6; Niazi, "The Ecology of Strategic Interests," 112.

24 *Beijing Review,* 3-9 August 1992, 12-13.

25 Han Nianlong, ed., *Diplomacy of Contemporary China* (Hong Kong: New Horizon Press, 1990), 176-77.

26 Xie Yixian, *Zhongguo waijiao shi: Zhonghua Renmin Gongheguo shiqi 1949-1979* [A diplomatic history of China: the period of the People's Republic of China, 1949-1979] (Zhengzhou: Henan renmin chubanshe, 1988), 373.

27 Han, *Diplomacy of Contemporary China,* 299.

28 Xie, *Zhongguo waijiao shi: Zhonghua Renmin Gongheguo shiqi 1979-1994* [A diplomatic history of China: the period of the People's Republic of China, 1979-1994] (Zhengzhou: Henan renmin chubanshe, 1995), 32, fn. 1.

29 Li Huichuan, "The Crux of the Sino-Soviet Boundary Question" [pt. 2], *Peking Review,* 3 August 1981, 16. See also Li Huichuan, "The Crux of the Sino-Soviet Boundary Question" [pt. 1], *Peking Review,* 2 July 1981, 12-17.

30 Qian Qichen, *Waijiao shiji* [Ten foreign policy events] (Beijing: Shijie zhishi chubanshe, 2003), 231.

31 *Xinhua,* 15 April 1993; *BBC Worldwide Monitoring Central Asia Unit,* 7 July 2001; Necati Polat, *Boundary Issues in Central Asia* (Ardsley, NY: Transnational Publishers, 2002), 19-20.

32 "China is Quietly Occupying Kazakhstan," Chinese translation of article published in *Pacific Star News,* 15 January 1998; Research Institute for Peace and Security, *Asian Security: 1996-97* (Washington, DC: Brassey's, 1997), 202; Becquelin, "A New Xinjiang for a New Central Asia," 13.

33 *BBC Summary of World Broadcasts,* 11 August 1992; *BBC Monitoring/BBC Global News Wire – Asia Africa Intelligence Wire,* 22 July 2005.

34 Xu and He, "Gongtong gozhu mianxiang ershiyi shiji de chuanmian hezuo huoban guanxi," 3.

35 Ibid., 4.

36 *Zhonghua Renmin Gongheguo bianjie shiwu tiaoyueji: ZhongHa juan* [The People's Republic of China boundary affairs treaty collection: China-Kazakhstan volume] (Beijing: Shijie zhishi chubanshe, 2005); *BBC Monitoring/BBC Global News Wire – Asia Africa Intelligence Wire,* 3 August 2002, 27 November 2002, 13 February 2004, 22 July 2005.

37 *WPS Russian Media Monitoring Agency,* 18 June 1999; *BBC Monitoring/BBC Global News Wire – Asia Africa Intelligence Wire,* 8 January 2002.

38 *Beijing Review,* 9-15 May 1994, 5; *BBC Worldwide Monitoring Central Asia Unit/BBC Worldwide Monitoring,* 15 April 2000; *BBC Monitoring/BBC Global News Wire – Asia Africa Intelligence Wire,* 9 July 2003.

39 Allen Carlson, "Constructing the Dragon's Scales: China's Approach to Territorial Sovereignty and Border Relations in the 1980s and 1990s," *Journal of Contemporary China* 12, 37 (November 2003): 690; *WPS Russian Media Monitoring Agency,* 18 June 1999; *BBC Monitoring/BBC Global News Wire – Asia Africa Intelligence Wire,* 18 January 2002.

40 *Renmin ribao,* 5 July 1998.

41 *BBC Summary of World Broadcasts,* 2 May 1994.
42 Ibid., 13 January 1996.
43 *Xinhua,* 4 July 1996.
44 *Renmin ribao,* 29 April 1998.
45 *BBC Monitoring/BBC Global News Wire – Asia Africa Intelligence Wire,* 3 August 2002; *Associated Press,* 20 February 2003.
46 *BBC Worldwide Monitoring Central Asia Unit,* 9 May 2001, 22 June 2001, 28 June 2001.
47 Ibid., 7 May 2002.
48 "Kyrgyz Legislature Continues to Discuss Chinese Border Controversy," *RFE/RL Newsline* 5, 119 (22 June 2001).
49 *Xinhua Domestic Service,* 26 August 1999; *ITAR-TASS News Agency,* 26 August 1999; Zhao Zongwei, "Border Accord Signed," *China Daily,* 27 August 1999.
50 Dmitri Plenseev, "Kyrgyz Border Pact with China Stirs Tension in Bishkek" (17 May 2002), http://www.eurasianet.org; *Deutsche Presse-Agentur,* 16 May 2002; *ITAR-TASS News Agency,* 17 May 2002; *Associated Press,* 20 February 2003.
51 *BBC Monitoring/BBC Monitoring International Reports – Asia Africa Intelligence Wire,* 27 November 2002; Sergei Luzianin, "Materials and Documents on the Kyrgyzstan-China Border," *Far Eastern Affairs* 33, 1 (January-March 2005): 153-54.
52 *Zhonghua Renmin Gongheguo bianjie shiwu tiaoyueji: ZhongJi juan* [The People's Republic of China boundary affairs treaty collection: China-Kyrgyzstan volume] (Beijing: Shijie zhishi chubanshe, 2005).
53 Tian Zengpei, ed., *Gaige kaifang yilai de Zhongguo waijiao* [Chinese foreign policy since opening up and reform] (Beijing: Shijie zhishi chubanshe, 1993), 329.
54 Xie, *Zhongguo waijiao shi ... 1979-1994,* 32, fn. 1.
55 *Zhonghua Renmin Gongheguo bianjie shiwu tiaoyueji: ZhongTa juan* [The People's Republic of China boundary affairs treaty collection: China-Tajikistan volume] (Beijing: Shijie zhishi chubanshe, 2005); Gu Guanfu, "1996-1997 nian ZhongYa xingshi baogao" [1996-1997 report on the situation in Sino–Central Asia relations], in *Zhongguo zhanlue yu guanli yanjiu hui, guoji xingshi fenxi baogao, 1996-1997,* 74; *BBC Monitoring Central Asia Unit/BBC Worldwide Monitoring,* 7 April 2000; *BBC Monitoring/BBC Global News Wire – Asia Africa Intelligence Wire,* 3 August 2002.
56 *China Central Television,* 26 April 1996; *BBC Monitoring/BBC Global News Wire – Asia Africa Intelligence Wire,* 31 July 2002.
57 Gregory Gleason, "Why Russia Is in Tajikistan," *Comparative Strategy* 20 (2001): 84.
58 *BBC Monitoring Central Asia Unit/BBC Worldwide Monitoring,* 21 December 2001.
59 *Xinhua,* 12 January 1996.
60 *Agence France-Presse,* 31 October 1997; *BBC Monitoring Central Asia Unit,* 3 August 2002.
61 *Xinhua,* 13 August 1999; *China Daily,* 14 August 1999; *BBC Monitoring/BBC Global News Wire – Asia Africa Intelligence Wire,* 27 November 2002; Gleason, "Why Russia Is in Tajikistan," 84; Jonson, *Tajikistan in the New Central Asia,* 85-86.
62 John C.K. Daly, "Sino-Kyrgyz Relations after the Tulip Revolution," *China Brief* 5, 9 (26 April 2005): 6-7; Kambiz Arman, "US Geopolitical Position Takes a Hit in Tajikistan" (13 July 2004), http://www.eurasianet.org.
63 Polat, *Boundary Issues in Central Asia,* 45; "People's Republic of China–Tajikistan Joint Communiqué," http://www.people.com.cn/GB/paper464/938/130357.html.
64 *Dagong bao* (Hong Kong), 24 September 2001, in FBIS, *Daily Report: China,* 26 September 2001.
65 *BBC Monitoring – Asia Pacific – Political,* 26 December 2001.

66 Ministry of Foreign Affairs of the People's Republic of China, "China's Territorial and Boundary Affairs" (30 June 2003), http://fmprc.gov.cn/.

67 Buzurgmehr Ansori, "Tajikistan Defines Border with China: Country Ceded 1,100 Sq. Km. to China," *Central Asia Online*, 29 January 2011, http://centralasiaonline.com/.

68 "Jiang Zemin – chumai Zhongguo lingtu zhuchuan maiguozei daibiao" [Jiang Zemin – a national traitor who sold out China's territorial sovereignty], http://kanzhongguo.com/news/gb/articles/3/9/29/51772p.html.

69 *Renmin ribao*, 5 July 1998.

70 Ibid.

71 *BBC Worldwide Monitoring Central Asia Unit*, 9 May 2001, 22 June 2001, 28 June 2001.

72 *Xinhua*, 4 July 1996.

73 Gu, "1996-1997 nian ZhongYa xingshi baogao," 74; *BBC Monitoring Central Asia Unit/BBC Worldwide Monitoring*, 7 April 2000; *BBC Monitoring/BBC Global News Wire – Asia Africa Intelligence Wire*, 3 August 2002.

74 Yu Lei, "Five-Way Border Pledge Signed," *China Daily*, 27 April 1996.

75 *BBC Monitoring/BBC Global News Wire – Asia Africa Intelligence Wire*, 3 August 2002.

76 Becquelin, "A New Xinjiang for a New Central Asia," 13.

77 Antoine Blua, "Central Asia: Some in Region Worried about Growing Chinese Power," *Radio Free Europe/Radio Liberty*, 16 June 2003.

78 Ronald N. Montaperto, "Whither China? Beijing's Policies for the 1990s," *Strategic Review* 20, 3 (Summer 1992): 30.

79 Lillian Craig Harris, "Xinjiang, Central Asia, and the Implications for China's Policy in the Islamic World," *China Quarterly* 133 (1993): 127-28.

80 Laruelle and Peyrouse, *China as a Neighbour*, 114-18, 146-48; Allen Carlson, *Unifying China, Integrating with the World: Securing Chinese Sovereignty in the Reform Era* (Stanford, CA: Stanford University Press, 2005), 237.

Chapter 12: The South China Sea Territorial Disputes

1 Over forty thousand ships transit the South China Sea annually, twice as many as pass through the Suez Canal and triple the number passing through the Panama Canal.

2 Li Xiaokun, "Special Agency Set Up to Handle Sea, Land Disputes," *China Daily*, 5 May 2009, http://www.chinadaily.com.cn/.

3 The Republic of China (Taiwan) claim is spelled out in Second Workshop on Managing Potential Conflicts in the South China Sea (Bandung, Indonesia, 8 July 1991), *Second Workshop Report* (1991), 289-90.

4 John B. Allcock et al., eds., *Border and Territorial Disputes*, 3rd ed. (Essex, UK: Longman Current Affairs, 1992), 542-45.

5 *Zhou Enlai waijiao wenxuan* [Selected works of Zhou Enlai on diplomacy] (Beijing: Zhongyang wenxian chubanshe, 1990), 40.

6 Han Nianlong, ed., *Diplomacy of Contemporary China* (Hong Kong: New Horizon Press, 1990), 332-33; Allcock et al., *Border and Territorial Disputes*, 469-71.

7 M. Taylor Fravel, *Strong Borders, Secure Nation: Cooperation and Conflict in China's Territorial Disputes* (Princeton, NJ: Princeton University Press, 2008), 62.

8 *Peking Review*, 18 June 1976, 4.

9 Pao-min Chang, "The Sino-Vietnamese Territorial Dispute," *Asia Pacific Community* 8 (Spring 1980): 144.

10 *Beijing Review*, 30 March 1979, 21.

11 Ibid., 21; "Memorandum Outlining Vice-Premier Li Xiannian's Talk with Premier Pham Van Dong on 10 June 1977," United Nations Document S/13255, 8, fn. d; Yang Gongsu,

Zhonghua Renmin Gongheguo waijiao lilun yu shijian [The theory and practice of People's Republic of China diplomacy]. Beijing: Beijing daxue guoji guanxi xueyuan, 1997), 349.

12 *Beijing Review,* 30 March 1979, 17-22; "Memorandum Outlining Vice-Premier Li Xiannian's Talk with Premier Pham Van Dong on 10 June 1977," ibid.

13 Foreign Broadcast Information Service [FBIS], *Daily Report: PRC,* 29 December 1978, A5.

14 Xie Yixian, ed., *Zhongguo dangdai waijiao shi* [History of contemporary Chinese diplomacy] (Beijing: Zhongguo qingnian chubanshe, 1997), 436.

15 The Permanent Mission of the People's Republic of China to the United Nations, 14 April 2011 note to the Secretary General with reference to the Republic of the Philippines' note verbale dated 5 April 2011, http://www.un.org/depts/los/clcs_new/submissions_files/mysvnm33_09/chn_2011_re_phl_e.pdf.

16 Pan Shiying, "The Nansha Islands: A Chinese Point of View," *Window,* 3 September 1993, 25.

17 Interview with scholars at China Institutes of Contemporary International Relations, 5 July 1994.

18 Chen Jie, "China's Spratly Policy: With Special Reference to Its Approach to the Philippines and Malaysia," *Asian Survey* 3, 10 (October 1994): 893-94; *Business Times* (Singapore), 29 October 1992.

19 Joint Statement RP-PRC Consultations on the South China Sea and on Other Areas of Cooperation, 9-10 August 1995; *New York Times,* 5 April 1995, 8; *Far Eastern Economic Review,* 6 April 1995, 14-15; *South China Morning Post,* 5 August 1998.

20 *South China Morning Post,* 6 November 1998, 7 November 1998; *Yangzi wanbao,* 11 June 1999, 8; Wilfrido V. Villacorta, "The Philippines Territorial Claim in the South China Sea," in *Fishing in Troubled Waters,* ed. R.D. Hill, Norman G. Owen, and E.V. Roberts (Hong Kong: Centre for Asian Studies, University of Hong Kong, 1991), 207-15.

21 In May 2013, the Philippines coast guard fired on an unarmed Chinese fishing trawler operating in disputed waters, killing the captain of the boat.

22 Khadijah Muhamed and Tunku Shamsul Bahrin, "Scramble for the South China Sea: The Malaysian Perspective," in Hill, Owen, and Roberts, *Fishing in Troubled Waters,* 237.

23 *China News Digest,* 26 March 1995.

24 "Chinese Ships Patrol Area Contested by Malaysia," *Reuters,* 26 January 2014.

25 *Deng Xiaoping wenxuan* [Selected works of Deng Xiaoping], 3, 49.

26 Xie Yixian, *Zhongguo waijiao shi: Zhonghua Renmin Gongheguo shiqi 1979-1994* [A diplomatic history of China: the period of the People's Republic of China, 1979-1994] (Zhengzhou: Henan renmin chubanshe, 1995), 136, 139.

27 FBIS, *Daily Report: East Asia,* 24 March 1988, 44-45; 25 March 1988, 51-54; FBIS, *Daily Report: China,* 31 March 1988, 7-8; *Knight-Ridder,* 19 May 1994; *New York Times,* 20 May 1994, 5; *South China Morning Post,* 26 July 1994; *China Daily,* 16 November 1995, 1; Xie, *Zhongguo waijiao shi ... 1979-1994,* 4, 137.

28 "Offering to Aid Talks, U.S. Challenges China on Disputed Islands," *New York Times,* 23 July 2010; "Clinton Statement on South China Sea," http://translations.state.gov/st/english/texttrans/2011/07/20110723125330su0.9067433.html#axzz2Ja44foKJ.

29 *Japan Economic Newswire,* 25 July 1993; *Free China Journal,* 27 August 1993, 3.

30 Quoted in Eric Hyer, "The South China Sea Disputes: Implications of China's Earlier Territorial Settlements," *Pacific Affairs* 68, 1 (Spring 1995): 34; *Japan Economic Newswire,* 19 May 1993; *United Press International,* 14 July 1993.

31 FBIS, *Daily Reports: East Asia,* 13 August 1990, 36; Nayan Chanda and Tai Ming Cheung, "Reef Knots," *Far Eastern Economic Review,* 30 August 1990, 11; 4 July 1991, 19; *New Straits Times,* 13 August 1990; Xie, *Zhongguo waijiao shi ... 1979-1994,* 258-60. Chinese

statements are inconsistent, alternating between "shelving the territorial dispute" *(gezhi lingtu zhengduan)*, "shelving the dispute over sovereignty" *(gezhi zhuquan zhengyi)*, and "shelving the dispute" *(gezhi zhengyi)*.

32 *United Press International,* 13 May 1994; *China News Digest,* 22 November 1994; *China Daily,* 16 November 1995, 1.

33 *Japan Economic Newswire,* 19 May 1993.

34 Cai Penghong, "Reflections on Joint Development of Disputed Maritime Territory," *Strategy and Management* 2 (1995): 73-82.

35 *Free China Journal,* 19 July 1991, 1; 2 July 1992, 2.

36 "Offering to Aid Talks, US Challenges China on Disputed Islands," *New York Times,* 23 July 2010; Peter Lee, "US Goes Fishing for Trouble," *Asian Times Online,* 29 July 2010, http://www.atimes.com/.

37 "China's Warning on Spratlys Raises Spectre of Armed Clashes," *Straits Times,* 11 March 1992.

38 Law of the People's Republic of China on the Territorial Sea and the Contiguous Zone (Beijing: Legislative Affairs Commission of the Standing Committee of the National People's Congress of the People's Republic of China, 1992); Xie, *Zhongguo waijiao shi ... 1979-1994,* 259-60.

39 B.A. Hamzah, "China's Strategy," *Far Eastern Economic Review,* 13 August 1992, 22.

40 "ASEAN Declaration on the South China Sea," 22 July 1992.

41 *New York Times,* 18 June 1992; *Free China Journal,* 2 July 1992, 2; 7 July 1992, 1; *United Press International,* 13 July 1993; *Agence France-Presse,* 19 April 1994.

42 Interview with scholars at China Institutes of Contemporary International Relations, 5 July 1994.

43 *Free China Journal,* 19 July 1991, 1; 13 September 1991, 1; 29 May 1992, 2; *Far Eastern Economic Review,* 4 July 1991, 19.

44 *China News Digest,* 20 April 1995.

45 *United Press International,* 16 May 1993; *Associated Press,* 15 January 1993.

46 *Japan Economic Newswire,* 18 January 1993. The Chinese name for the South China Sea is *Nanhai* (South Sea) and only on English maps is the term "South China Sea" used.

47 *New China News Agency,* 16 July 1971.

48 *Beijing Review,* 26 September 1983, 8.

49 Chi-kin Lo, *China's Policy towards Territorial Disputes: The Case of the South China Sea Islands* (New York: Routledge, 1989), 38-39, 94.

50 Nayan Chanda, "Fear of the Dragon," *Far Eastern Economic Review,* 13 April 1995, 24.

51 *New York Times,* 21 July 1994; *South China Morning Post,* 26 July 1994; *China News Digest,* 22 July 1994.

52 Nayan Chanda, "Territorial Imperative," *Far Eastern Economic Review,* 23 February 1995, 14.

53 "Philippine Chief of Staff General Angelo Reyes Speaks Out on China" (3 December 1999), http://asia.biz.yahoo.com.

54 Chen Jie, "China's Spratly Policy: With Special Reference to Its Approach to the Philippines and Malaysia," *Asian Survey* 3, 10 (October 1994): 893.

55 *Xisha chundao he Nansha chundao zigu yilai jiushi Zhongguo di lingtu* [The Xisha and Nansha Islands have been Chinese territory since ancient times (Beijing: Renmin chubanshe, 1981)]; Pan Shiying, "The Nansha Islands: A Chinese Point of View," *Window* (3 September 1993), 23-27; *China News Digest,* 22 March 1995.

56 Xie, *Zhongguo waijiao shi ... 1979-1994,* 259; Michael Leifer, "Chinese Economic Reform and Security Policy: The South China Sea Connection," *Survival* 37, 2 (Summer 1995): 51.

57 Chen Jie, "China's Spratly Policy," 893.
58 *The Truong Sa and Hoang Sa Archipelagoes and International Law* (Hanoi: Socialist Republic of Vietnam, Ministry of Foreign Affairs, 1988), 21; Leifer, "Chinese Economic Reform and Security Policy," 53.
59 B.A. Hamzah, *The Spratlies: What Can Be Done to Enhance Confidence* (Kuala Lumpur: Institute of Strategic and International Studies (ISIS) Malaysia, 1990), 13.
60 *China News Digest,* 19 April 1995.
61 Quoted in Joseph Chin Yong Liow, "Malaysia-China Relations in the 1990s: The Maturing of a Partnership," *Asian Survey* 40, 4 (July-August 2000): 681.
62 *China News Daily,* 17 December 1997; Nayan Chanda and Tai Ming Cheung, "Reef Knots," *Far Eastern Economic Review,* 30 August 1990, 11.
63 *China News Digest,* 28 April1994, 6 April 1995.
64 Guoxing Ji, "China versus South China Sea Security," *Security Dialogue* 29, 1 (1998): 101-12.
65 Scott Snyder, "The South China Sea Dispute: Prospects for Preventive Diplomacy," a special report of the United States Institute of Peace (Washington, DC: United States Institute of Peace, August 1996), 14.
66 "Declaration on the Conduct of Parties in the South China Sea" (4 November 2002), http://www.asean.org/asean/external-relations/china/item/declaration-on-the-conduct-of-parties-in-the-south-china-sea.
67 Andrew Jacobs, "China Warns US to Stay Out of Islands Dispute," *New York Times,* 26 July 2010.
68 This conclusion is based on interviews with PLA officers and Foreign Ministry officials. For details on the miscommunication with the United States and the media-driven public controversy, see Michael D. Swaine, "China's Assertive Behavior Part One: On 'Core Interests,'" *China Leadership Monitor* 34 (Winter 2011): 8-10.
69 Ming Yang, "Taking Advantage of China's Peaceful Stance," *China Daily,* 30 June 2012, http://www.chinadaily.com.cn/.
70 "Don't Take Peaceful Approach for Granted," *Global Times,* 25 October 2011, http://www.globaltimes.cn/.
71 Ministry of Foreign Affairs of the People's Republic of China, "Foreign Ministry Spokesperson Jiang Yu's Regular Press Conference on October 25, 2011," http://www.fmprc.gov.cn/.
72 Shao Feng, "Security Strategies for China's Maritime Domain" (13 July 2012), http://english.caixin.com/2012-07-13/100410946_all.html.
73 Quoted in Willy Lam, "China's Hawks in Command," *Wall Street Journal,* 1 July 2012, http://online.wsj.com/.
74 "China-Philippines Cooperation Depends on Proper Settlement of Maritime Disputes," *Xinhuanet,* 31 August 2011, http://news.xinhuanet.com/.
75 Edward Wong, "China Hedges Over Whether South China Sea Is a 'Core Interest' Worth War," *New York Times,* 30 March 2011.
76 "Guidelines for the Implementation of the Declaration on the Conduct of Parties in the South China Sea," http://www.asean.org/4979.htm; Li Mingjiang, *Chinese Debates of the South China Sea Policy: Implication for Future Developments,* RSIS Working Paper 239 (Singapore: S. Rajaratnam School of International Studies, Nanyang Technological University, 17 May 2012), 9-11, 17; Barry Wain, "A South China Sea Charade: China Continues Stalling Multilateral Efforts to Resolve Territorial Disputes," *Wall Street Journal,* 22 August 2011.

77 Ministry of Foreign Affairs of the People's Republic of China, "Foreign Ministry Spokesperson Liu Weimin's Regular Press Conference on October 12, 2011," http://www.fmprc.gov.cn/.

78 "South China Sea Conflict," *Global Times*, http://www.globaltimes.cn/SPECIAL COVERAGE/SouthChinaSeaConflict.aspx.

79 "Declaration of the Republic of China on the Outer Limits of Its Continental Shelf" (12 May 2009), http://www.mofa.gov.tw/EnOfficial/ArticleDetail/DetailDefault/ad125edc -048e-45de-93bc-11427232687b?arfid=7b3b4d7a-8ee7-43a9-97f8-7f3d313ad781&opno =84ba3639-be42-4966-b873-78a267de8cf1.

80 *Free China Journal*, 10 September 1993, 2; 6 May 1994, 6; *China News Digest*, 18 April 1995.

81 *China News Digest*, 30 March 1995.

82 Shim Jae Hoon, "Blood Thicker than Politics: Taiwan Indicates a Military Preparedness to Back China," *Far Eastern Economic Review*, 5 May 1988, 26; "Five-Handed Poker in the Spratlys," *The Economist*, 21 May 1988, 36.

83 In February 2008, President Chen Shui-bian (Democratic Progressive Party) became the first ROC (Taiwan) head of state to visit Taiping (Itu Aba) Island, where he announced a Spratly Islands initiative. He visited the Pratas Islands twice while president from 2000 to 2008.

84 *Straits Times*, 22 July 1993, 23 July 1992; Xie, *Zhongguo waijiao shi ... 1979-1994*, 260.

85 Francesco Sisci, "The Spratlys Pact: Beijing's Olive Branch," *Asia Times Online*, 6 November 2002, http://www.atimes.com.

86 Treaty of Amity and Cooperation in Southeast Asia (24 February 1976), http://www.asean.org/news/item/treaty-of-amity-and-cooperation-in-southeast-asia-indonesia -24-february-1976-3.

87 "China, ASEAN Set 'Guidelines' on Sea Row but No Deal Expected," *Reuters*, 20 July 2011, http://www.reuters.com/.

88 Allen Carlson, "Constructing the Dragon's Scales: China's Approach to Territorial Sovereignty and Border Relations in the 1980s and 1990s," *Journal of Contemporary China* 12, 37 (November 2003): 697.

89 Michael G. Gallagher, "China's Illusory Threat to the South China Sea," *International Security* 19, 1 (Summer 1994): 169-94.

90 "Five-Handed Poker in the Spratlys," *The Economist*, 21 May 1988, 36; *Straits Times*, 22 January 1992.

91 Xinjun Zhang, "China's 'Peaceful Rise,' 'Harmonious' Foreign Relations, and Legal Confrontation and Lesson from the Sino-Japanese Dispute over the East China Sea," Foreign Policy Research Institute, Philadelphia, *E-Notes*, 16 April 2010, 4.

92 Michael D. Swaine and Ashley J. Tellis, *Interpreting China's Grand Strategy: Past, Present, and Future* (Santa Monica: RAND, 2000), 131-33.

93 Li Mingjiang, "Chinese Debates of South China Sea Policy: Implications for Future Developments," RSIS Working Paper 239 (17 May 2012), 25.

94 James Reilly, *Strong Society, Smart State: The Rise of Public Opinion in China's Japan Policy* (New York: Columbia University Press, 2012), 8-9.

95 Michael D. Swaine, "China's Assertive Behavior Part Three: The Role of the Military in Foreign Policy," *China Leadership Monitor* 36 (Winter 2012): 5.

96 *New York Times*, 11 May 2012, A12.

97 "Phl and China Seek Diplomatic Solution on Scarborough Issue," http://news.pia.gov.ph/index.php?article=2271335414573. In January 2013, the Philippines took the case to the

International Tribunal for the Law of the Sea, seeking to invalidate China's nine-dash line. Beijing rejected this third-party arbitration. "The Republic of the Philippines v. The People's Republic of China," http://www.pca-cpa.org/showpage.asp?pag_id=1529. See Ian Story, "Manila Ups the Ante in the South China Sea," *China Brief* 13, 3 (1 February 2013); Ministry of Foreign Affairs of the People's Republic of China, "Foreign Ministry Spokesperson Hua Chunying's Remarks on the Philippines' Statement on the South China Sea" (16 July 2013), http://www.fmprc.gov.cn/; "China Refutes Philippines' South China Sea Accusation," *Xinhuanet*, 17 July 2013, http://news.xinhuanet.com/.

98 Minghao Zhao, "The Predicaments of Chinese Power," *New York Times*, 12 July 2012.
99 "Road Map toward China's Maritime Peace," *Global Times*, 27 July 2010, http://www.globaltimes.cn/.
100 "Exploring the Path of Major-Country Diplomacy with Chinese Characteristics," remarks by Foreign Minister Wang Yi at the Luncheon of the Second World Peace Forum (27 June 2013), http://www.fmprc.gov.cn/mfa_eng/wjdt_665385/zyjh_665391/t1053908.shtml.
101 "Statement by H.E. Mr. Wang Yi, Minister of Foreign Affairs of the People's Republic of China at the General Debate of the 68th Session of the United Nations General Assembly (New York, 27 September 2013)," http://www.fmprc.gov.cn/mfa_eng/wjdt_665385/zyjh_665391/t1082330.shtml.
102 "China Vows to Defend 'Every Inch of Territory,'" http://www.npc.gov.cn/englishnpc/Special_12_2/2014-03/09/content_1846605.htm; http://news.xinhuanet.com/english/special/2014-03/08/c_133170657.htm.

Conclusion

1 M. Taylor Fravel, "The Dangerous Math of Chinese Island Disputes," *Wall Street Journal*, 29 October 2012, 15.
2 Michael D. Swaine and Ashley J. Tellis, *Interpreting China's Grand Strategy: Past, Present, and Future* (Santa Monica, CA: RAND, 2000), 131-33.
3 Suisheng Zhao, "Foreign Policy Implication of Chinese Nationalism Revisited: The Strident Turn," *Journal of Contemporary China* 22, 82 (2013): 535-53.
4 "Press Conference of the PRC State Council Information Office for Contacts between Central Gov't, Dalai Lama," *Xinhua*, 11 February 2010, http://news.xinhuanet.com/.
5 "Chinese Surveillance Ships Enter Diaoyu Waters," *Global Times*, http://www.globaltimes.cn/.
6 M. Taylor Fravel, "International Relations Theory and China's Rise: Assessing China's Potential for Territorial Expansion," *International Studies Review* 12, 4 (2010):507, 526.
7 Ernest R. May, "The Nature of Foreign Policy: The Calculated versus the Axiomatic," *Daedalus* 91, 4 (Fall 1962): 653-67.

Bibliography

Government Publications and Documents

"Agreement between the Government of India and the Government of the People's Republic of China on the Political Parameters and Guiding Principles for the Settlement of the India-China Boundary Questions." 11 April 2005.

"Agreement between the Government of the Republic of India and the Government of the People's Republic of China on the Establishment of a Working Mechanism for Consultation and Coordination on India-China Border Affairs." http://peacemaker.un.org/.

"Agreement on the Maintenance of Peace along the Line of Actual Control in the India-China Border." 7 September 1993.

"Agreement with Japan Concerning the Ryukyu Islands and Daito Islands: Hearing before the Senate Committee on Foreign Relations." 92nd Congress, 1st Session. Washington, DC: 1971.

Ambekar, G.V., and V.D. Divekar, eds. *Documents on China's Relations with South and South-East Asia (1949-1962)*. Bombay: Allied Publishers, 1964.

"ASEAN Declaration on the South China Sea." 22 July 1992.

Bhutto, Zulfikar Ali. *Foreign Policy of Pakistan: A Compendium of Speeches Made in the National Assembly of Pakistan, 1962-64*. Karachi: Pakistan Institute of International Affairs, 1964.

–. *The Myth of Independence*. London: Oxford University Press, 1969.

Central Intelligence Agency. "Sino-Soviet Exchanges, 1969-84" (EA 84-10069). See http://www.foia.cia.gov/sites/default/files/document_conversions/89801/DOC_0000497181.pdf; CIA Historical Review Program, declassified in 1999 but produced in 1984, evidently by the Directorate of Intelligence.

–. "Territorial Issues in the Sino-Soviet Dispute" (GCR RP 75-31). See http://www.foia.cia.gov/sites/default/files/document_conversions/89801/DOC_0000498588.pdf; CIA Historical Review Program, declassified in 1999. ("This paper was produced by the Office of Geographic and Cartographic Research and coordinated within the Directorate for Intelligence and with the Geographer." No date was given but the document was produced in November 1975.)

Chinese Peoples' Institute of Foreign Affairs, ed. *New Developments in Friendly Relations between China and Nepal*. Peking: Foreign Language Press, 1960.

Congressional Record. 92nd Congress, 1st session. 9 November 1971.

Constitution of the People's Republic of China, *Documents of the First Session of the First National People's Congress of the CPR*. Peking: Foreign Language Press, 1955.

"Declaration and Exchange of Notes Respecting Mongolia, October 23/November 5, 1913," *American Journal of International Law Supplement* 10, 4 (October 1916): 246-58.

"Declaration of the Republic of China on the Outer Limits of Its Continental Shelf" (12 May 2009). http://www.mofa.gov.tw/EnOfficial/ArticleDetail/DetailDefault/ad125 edc-048e-45de-93bc-11427232687b?arfid=7b3b4d7a-8ee7-43a9-97f8-7f3d313 ad781&opno=84ba3639-be42-4966-b873-78a267de8cf1.

Documents of the First Session of the First National People's Congress of the CPR. Peking: Foreign Language Press, 1955.

Documents on the Sino-Indian Boundary Question. Peking: Foreign Language Press, 1960.

Down with the New Tsars! Soviet Revisionists' Anti-China Atrocities on the Heilung and Wusuli Rivers. Peking: Foreign Language Press, 1969.

"Economic and Political Relations between Bhutan and Neighboring Countries," Monograph 12. A Joint Research Project of the Centre for Bhutan Studies and the Institute of Developing Economics, Japan External Trade Organization (April 2004).

"Excerpts from Tsedenbal's Diary on His Conversations with Soviet Leader Anastas Mikoyan" (24 February 1956). Cold War International History Project, *Digital Archive, Mongolia in the Cold War.* http://digitalarchive.wilsoncenter.org/document/110480.

"Exploring the Path of Major-Country Diplomacy with Chinese Characteristics." Remarks by Foreign Minister Wang Yi at the Luncheon of the Second World Peace Forum (27 June 2013). http://www.fmprc.gov.cn/mfa_eng/wjdt_665385/zyjh_665391/t1053908.shtml.

Foreign Broadcast Information Service. *Daily Report: Asia and Pacific*

–. *Daily Report: China*

–. *Daily Report: Communist China*

–. *Daily Report: East Asia*

–. *Daily Report: PRC*

Government of India, Ministry of External Affairs. *India China Border Problem.* New Delhi: External Publicity Division, Ministry of External Affairs, 1962.

–. *Prime Minister on Sino-Indian Relations.* Vol. 1: *In Parliament.* New Delhi: External Publicity Division, Ministry of External Affairs, 1961.

–. *Report of the Officials of the Government of India and the People's Republic of China on the Boundary Question.* New Delhi: External Publicity Division, Ministry of External Affairs, 1961.

–. *White Papers,* 14 vols. New Delhi: External Publicity Division, Ministry of External Affairs, 1959-68.

"Information Memorandum: 'About the Claims of the Chinese Leader with Regard to the Mongolian People's Republic'" (30 January 1964). Cold War International History Project, *Digital Archive, Mongolia in the Cold War.* http://digitalarchive.wilsoncenter. org/document/113098.

"Information Note of Romanian Embassy from Beijing to Ministry of Foreign Affairs" (23 May 1989). Cold War International History Project, *Digital Archive,* http://digital archive.wilsoncenter.org/document/113148.

Joint Statement RP-PRC Consultations on the South China Sea and on Other Areas of Cooperation, 9-10 August 1995.

Law of the People's Republic of China on the Territorial Sea and the Contiguous Zone. Beijing: Legislative Affairs Commission of the Standing Committee of the Nation People's Congress of the People's Republic of China, 1992.

Ministry of Foreign Affairs of Japan. "The Japan-China Summit Meeting between Prime Minister Kakuei Tanaka and Premier Zhou Enlai on September 27, 1972." http://www. mofa.go.jp/region/asia-paci/senkaku/qa_1010.html#qa14.

Ministry of Foreign Affairs of the People's Republic of China. "Premier Li Keqiang Meets with National Security Adviser Shivshankar Menon of India" (29 June 2013), http://www.fmprc.gov.cn/.

Ministry of Foreign Affairs of the People's Republic of China and Communist Party of China Central Document Research Office, eds. *Mao Zedong waijiao wenxuan* [Selected foreign policy documents of Mao Zedong]. Beijing: Zhongyang wenxian chubanshe/ Shijie zhishi chubanshe, 1994.

The Permanent Mission of the People's Republic of China to the United Nations, 14 April 2011 note to the Secretary General with reference to the Republic of the Philippines' note verbale dated 5 April 2011. http://www.un.org/depts/los/clcs_new/submissions_files/mysvnm33_09/chn_2011_re_phl_e.pdf.

"Record of Conversation between Chinese Premier Zhou Enlai and Mongolian leader J. Zedenbal" (26 December 1962). Cold War International History Project, *Digital Archive, Mongolia in the Cold War.* http://digitalarchive.wilsoncenter.org/document/112072.

"Record of Conversation between the Mongolian People's Republic Government Delegation and the Deputy Chairman of the People's Republic of China State Council, Foreign Minister Chen Yi" (20 November 1964). Cold War International History Project, *Digital Archive, Mongolia in the Cold War.* http://digitalarchive.wilsoncenter.org/document/112517.

Records of the Department of State Relating to Political Relations between Russia (and the Soviet Union) and Other States, 1910-29. National Archives Microfilm Publications, Microcopy 340, 761.93/88 (1961).

"Sino-India Joint Press Communiqué" (23 December 1988). http://www.fmprc.gov.cn/eng/wjdt/2649/t15800.htm; http://in.china-embassy.org/eng/zygxc/wx/t762866.htm.

The Sino-Indian Boundary Question, enlarged ed. Peking: Foreign Language Press, 1962.

"Statement of the Government of the People's Republic of China, May 24, 1969." *Peking Review,* 30 May 1969, 7.

"Statement by H.E. Mr. Wang Yi, Minister of Foreign Affairs of the People's Republic of China at the General Debate of the 68th Session of the United Nations General Assembly (New York, 27 September 2013)." http://www.fmprc.gov.cn/mfa_eng/wjdt_665385/zyjh_665391/t1082330.shtml.

Sutter, Robert G., and Richard P. Cronin. *China-India Border Friction.* CRS Report 87-514F. Washington, DC: Congressional Research Service, 1987.

Thakin Nu. *From Peace to Stability.* Rangoon: Government of the Union of Burma, Ministry of Information, 1951.

Treaty of Amity and Cooperation in Southeast Asia (24 February 1976). http://www.asean.org/news/item/treaty-of-amity-and-cooperation-in-southeast-asia-indonesia-24-february-1976-3.

The Truong Sa and Hoang Sa Archipelagoes and International Law. Hanoi: Socialist Republic of Vietnam, Ministry of Foreign Affairs, 1988.

United Nations, General Assembly, Delegation from China. *China Fights for Peace and Freedom.* New York: n.p., 1951.

United States Consulate General, Hong Kong. *Current Background.*

United States Senate, Committee on the Judiciary, Subcommittee to Investigate the Administration of the Internal Security Act and Other Internal Security Laws (91st Cong., 1st sess.). *The Amerasia Papers: A Clue to the Catastrophe of China* 2. Washington, DC: Government Printing Office, 1970.

A Victory for the Five Principles of Peaceful Coexistence: Documents on the Sino-Burmese Boundary Question. Beijing: Foreign Language Press, 1960.

Vreeland, Nena, Rinn-Sup Shinn, Peter Just, and Philip W. Moeller, eds. *Area Handbook for North Korea,* 2nd ed. Washington, DC: US Government Printing Office, 1976.

Zhong-Su youhao guanxi xuexi shouce [Sino-Soviet friendly relations study handbook]. Shanghai: Zhanwang zhoukan, 1950.

Zhonghua Renmin Gongheguo bianjie shiwu tiaoyueji: ZhongA ZhongBa juan [The People's Republic of China boundary affairs treaty collection: China-Afghanistan China-Pakistan volume]. Beijing: Shijie zhishi chubanshe, 2004.

Zhonghua Renmin Gongheguo bianjie shiwu tiaoyueji: ZhongChao juan [The People's Republic of China boundary affairs treaty collection: China-Korea volume]. Beijing: Shijie zhishi chubanshe, 2004.

Zhonghua Renmin Gongheguo bianjie shiwu tiaoyueji: ZhongE juan 1 & 2 [The People's Republic of China boundary affairs treaty collection: China-Russia volumes 1 and 2]. Beijing: Shijie zhishi chubanshe, 2005.

Zhonghua Renmin Gongheguo bianjie shiwu tiaoyueji: ZhongHa juan [The People's Republic of China boundary affairs treaty collection: China-Kazakhstan volume]. Beijing: Shijie zhishi chubanshe, 2005.

Zhonghua Renmin Gongheguo bianjie shiwu tiaoyueji: ZhongJi juan [The People's Republic of China boundary affairs treaty collection: China-Kyrgyzstan volume]. Beijing: Shijie zhishi chubanshe, 2005.

Zhonghua Renmin Gongheguo bianjie shiwu tiaoyueji: ZhongLao juan [The People's Republic of China boundary affairs treaty collection: China-Laos volume]. Beijing: Shijie zhishi chubanshe, 2004.

Zhonghua Renmin Gongheguo bianjie shiwu tiaoyueji: ZhongMeng juan [The People's Republic of China boundary affairs treaty collection: China-Mongolia volume]. Beijing: Shijie zhishi chubanshe, 2004.

Zhonghua Renmin Gongheguo bianjie shiwu tiaoyueji: ZhongNi juan [The People's Republic of China boundary affairs treaty collection: China-Nepal volume]. Beijing: Shijie zhishi chubanshe, 2004.

Zhonghua Renmin Gongheguo bianjie shiwu tiaoyueji: ZhongTa juan [The People's Republic of China boundary affairs treaty collection: China-Tajikistan volume]. Beijing: Shijie zhishi chubanshe, 2005.

Zhonghua Renmin Gongheguo bianjie shiwu tiaoyueji: ZhongYin ZhongBu juan [The People's Republic of China boundary affairs treaty collection: China-India China-Bhutan volume]. Beijing: Shijie zhishi chubanshe, 2004.

Zhonghua Renmin Gongheguo bianjie shiwu tiaoyueji: ZhongYue juan [The People's Republic of China boundary affairs treaty collection: China-Vietnam volume]. Beijing: Shijie zhishi chubanshe, 2004.

Books, Articles, and Digital Sources

"90% of Land Boundaries Settled." *China Youth Daily,* 5 May 2005. http://www.china.org.cn/archive/.

Ahn, Yonson. "Competing Nationalisms: The Mobilisation of History and Archaeology in the Korea-China Wars over Koguryo/Gaoguoli." *Asia-Pacific Journal: Japan Focus.* http://www.japanfocus.org/.

Ali, S. Mahmud. *Cold War in the High Himalayas: The USA, China and South Asia in the 1950s.* New York: St. Martin's Press, 1999.

Ali, Salamat. "A Shot In the Arm." *Far Eastern Economic Review,* 1 December 1988, 38-42.

Allcock, John B., Guy Arnold, Alan J. Day, D.S. Lewis, Lorimer Poultnoy, Roland Rance, and D.J. Sagar, eds. *Border and Territorial Disputes,* 3rd ed. Essex, UK: Longman Current Affairs, 1992.

Ambroz, Oton. *Realignment of World Power: The Russo-Chinese Schism under the Impact of Mao Tse-tung's Last Revolution,* 2 vols. New York: Robert Speller and Sons, 1972.

Amer, Ramses. "Assessing Sino-Vietnamese Relations through the Management of Contentious Issues." *Contemporary Southeast Asia* 26, 2 (August 2004): 320-45.

—. "The Sino-Vietnamese Approach to Managing Boundary Disputes." *Maritime Briefing* 3, 5 (2002): 41-42.

An, Tai Sung. *North Korea in Transition: From Dictatorship to Dynasty.* Westport, CT: Greenwood Press, 1983.

An, Thomas. "New Winds in Pyongyang?" *Problems of Communism* 15, 4 (July-August 1966): 68-71.

Anderson, Malcolm. *Frontiers: Territory and State Formation in the Modern World.* Cambridge: Polity Press, 1996.

Ashraf, Tariq Mahmud. "Afghanistan and Chinese Strategy toward South and Central Asia." Jamestown Foundation *China Brief* 7, 10 (13 May 2008).

—. "Afghanistan in Chinese Strategy toward South and Central Asia." *China Brief* 8, 10 (13 May 2008). http://www.jamestown.org/programs/chinabrief/single/?tx_ttnews% 5Btt_news%5D=4915&tx_ttnews%5BbackPid%5D=168&no_cache=1#.U2LiIfldXRw.

Bajpai, G.S. *China's Shadow over Sikkim: The Politics of Intimidation.* New Delhi: Lancer Publishers, 1999.

Banerjee, Banerjee, ed. *Security in South Asia: Comprehensive and Cooperative.* New Delhi: Manas Publications, 1999.

Barnett, A. Doak. *The Making of Foreign Policy in China: Structure and Process.* Boulder, CO: Westview Press, 1985.

Barnett, A. Doak, ed. *Communist Strategies in Asia.* New York: Praeger, 1963.

Batbayar, Tsedendamba. *Mongolia's Foreign Policy in the 1990s: New Identity and New Challenges.* Ulaanbaatar: Institute for Strategic Studies, 2002.

Batbayar, Tsedendambyn. *Modern Mongolia: A Concise History.* Ulaanbaatar: Mongolian Center for Scientific and Technological Information, 1996.

Bawden, C.R. "Mongolian People's Republic, Number 3." *China News Analysis* 493 (15 November 1963): 1-7.

Becquelin, Nicolas. "A New Xinjiang for a New Central Asia." *China Perspectives* 15 (January-February 1998): 10-21.

Besshi, Yukio. "Nitchu kokko seijoka no seiji katie: seisaku ketteisha to sono kodo no haikei" [Political process of the normalization of Sino-Japanese diplomatic relations: decision makers and the background of their behaviour]. *Kokusai seiji* 66, 3 (1980): 1-18.

Bhasin, A.S., ed. *Documents on Nepal's Relations with India and China, 1949-1966.* Bombay: Academic Books, 1970.

Bhattacharjea, Mira Sinha. "China's Strategy for the Determination and Consolidation of Its Territorial Boundaries: A Preliminary Investigation." *China Report* 23, 4 (1987): 397-419.

—. "Indian Prime Minister's Visit to China." *China Report: A Journal of East Asian Studies* 30, 1 (January-March 1994): 85-86.

Blagov, Sergei. "Russia Hails Border Deal with China Despite Criticism." *Eurasia Daily Monitor* 2, 102 (May 2005). http://www.jamestown.org/programs/edm/single/?tx_ ttnews%5Btt_news%5D=30445&tx_ttnews%5BbackPid%5D=176&no_cache=1#. U2Las_ldXRw.

Brandt, Conrad, Benjamin Schwartz, and John K. Fairbank, eds. *A Documentary History of Chinese Communism.* New York: Athenaeum, 1966.

Brecher, Michael. *India and World Politics: Krishna Menon's View of the World.* New York: Praeger, 1968.

Bromke, Adam, ed. *The Communist States at the Crossroads.* New York: Praeger, 1965.

Brzezinski, Zbigniew. *Power and Principle: Memoirs of the National Security Advisor, 1977-81.* New York: Farrar, Straus and Giroux, 1983.

—. *The Soviet Bloc: Unity and Conflict.* New York: Praeger, 1961.

Burke, S.M. "Sino-Pakistani Relations." *Orbis* 8, 2 (Summer 1964): 391-404.

Burles, Mark. *Chinese Policy toward Russia and the Central Asian Republics.* Santa Monica, CA: RAND, 1999.

Burton, Bruce. "Contending Explanations of the 1979 Sino-Vietnamese War." *International Journal* 34, 4 (Autumn 1979): 699-722.

Butwell, Richard. "The Sino-Burmese Border Truce." *New Leader* 43, 9 (29 February 1960): 15-16.

–. *U Nu of Burma.* Stanford, CA: Stanford University Press, 1963.

Cai, Penghong. "Reflections on Joint Development of Disputed Maritime Territory." *Strategy and Management* 2 (1995): 73-82.

Cao Changqing. "Jiang Zemin qianyue songtudi" [Jiang Zemin signed a treaty to hand over territory]. http://www.kanzhongguo.com/.

Carlson, Allen. "Constructing the Dragon's Scales: China's Approach to Territorial Sovereignty and Border Relations in the 1980s and 1990s." *Journal of Contemporary China* 12, 37 (November 2003): 677-98.

–. *Unifying China, Integrating with the World: Securing Chinese Sovereignty in the Reform Era.* Stanford, CA: Stanford University Press, 2005.

Caroe, Olaf. "The Sino-Indian Frontier Dispute." *Asian Review* 59, 218 (April 1963): 67-81.

Chanda, Nayan. *Brother Enemy: The War after the War.* New York: Harcourt Brace Jovanovich, 1986.

–. "China and Cambodia: In the Mirror of History." *Asia-Pacific Review* 9, 2 (2002): 1-11.

–. "Fear of the Dragon." *Far Eastern Economic Review,* 13 April 1995, 24-25.

–. "Heading for a Conflict." *Far Eastern Economic Review,* 4 June 1987, 42-43.

–. "Territorial Imperative." *Far Eastern Economic Review,* 23 February 1995, 14-15.

Chanda, Nayan, and Tai Ming Cheung. "Reef Knots." *Far Eastern Economic Review,* 30 August 1990, 11.

Chang, Chih-i. *A Discussion of the National Question in the Chinese Revolution and of Actual Nationalities Policy (Draft).* Translated in George Moseley, *The Party and the National Question in China* (Cambridge, MA: MIT Press, 1966).

Chang, Pao-min. *The Sino-Vietnamese Territorial Dispute.* New York: Praeger, 1985.

–. "The Sino-Vietnamese Territorial Dispute." *Asia Pacific Community* 8 (Spring 1980): 130-65.

Chen, Agnes Fang-chin. "Chinese Frontier Diplomacy: The Eclipse of Manchuria." *Yenching Journal of Social Studies* 5, 1 (July 1950): 69-141.

Chen, Jie. "China's Spratly Policy: With Special Reference to its Approach to the Philippines and Malaysia." *Asian Survey* 3, 10 (October 1994): 893-903.

Chen, Xiaolu. "Chen Yi and China's Diplomacy." Paper presented at the Woodrow Wilson Center for International Scholars conference, 7-9 July 1992.

Chen Tiqiang. "ZhongYin bianjie wenti de falu fangmian" [Legal aspects of the Sino-Indian boundary issue]. *Guoji wenti yanjiu* 1 (1982): 11-82.

Cheng, Joseph. Y.S. "Normalization of Sino-Japanese Relations: China's Bargaining Position Regarding the Taiwan Question." *Asia Quarterly* 4 (1980): 258-59.

Cheng Faren. *ZhongE guojietu kao* [A study of Sino-Soviet border maps]. Taipei: Meng Zang weiyuanhui, 1969.

Cheng Xiangjun, ed. *Nü waijiaoguan* [Female diplomats]. Beijing: Renmin tiyu chubanshe, 1995.

Chervonenko, S.V. "Memorandum of Conversation with the General Secretary of the CCP Deng Xiaoping, 6 November 1959." *Cold War International History Project Bulletin* 10 (March 1998): 169-71.

"China, India End Border Standoff." *Xinhuanet,* 6 May 2013. http://news.xinhuanet.com/.

"China, Russia Complete Boundary Delimitation." *People's Daily,* 15 October 2004. http://english1.people.com.cn/.

"China–Union of Soviet Socialist Republics: Communiqué." *American Journal of International Law* 44, 3 (July 1950): 83-84.

"China and India Sign Border Deal." *BBC News,* http://news.bbc.co.uk/2/hi/south_asia/4431299.stm.

"China Vows to Defend 'Every Inch of Territory.'" http://www.npc.gov.cn/englishnpc/Special_12_2/2014-03/09/content_1846605.htm; http://news.xinhuanet.com/english/special/2014-03/08/c_133170657.htm.

Chiu, Hungdah. *Comparison of the Nationalist and Communist Chinese Views of Unequal Treaties.* Harvard Law School Studies in Chinese Law No. 19. Cambridge, MA: Harvard Law School, 1972.

"Chou En-lai's Report on Visits to Eleven Countries in Asia and Europe Given to the Third Session of the CPPCC, May 3, 1957." In *China-South Asian Relations (1947-1980) Documents* 2, ed. R.K. Jain. New Delhi: Radiant Publishers, 1981.

Choudhury, G.W. "Reflections on Sino-Pakistan Relations." *Pacific Community* 7, 2 (January 1976): 248–70 .

Christoffersen, Gaye. "Nesting the Sino-Russian Border and the Tumen Project in the Asia-Pacific: Heilongjiang's Regional Relations." *Asian Perspectives* 20, 2 (Fall-Winter 1996): 265-99.

–. "Xinjiang and the Great Islamic Circle: The Impact of Transnational Forces on Chinese Regional Economic Planning." *China Quarterly* 133 (March 1993): 130-51.

Chuev, Felix. *Molotov Remembers: Inside Kremlin Politics.* Chicago: Ivan R. Dee, 1993.

Chuluun, O. "The Two Phases in Mongolian-Chinese Relations (1949-1972)." *Far Eastern Affairs* 1 (1974): 24-32.

Chung, Chien-peng. "The Defense of Xinjiang." *Harvard International Review* 25, 2 (Summer 2003): 58-62.

–. *Domestic Politics, International Bargaining and China's Territorial Disputes.* New York: RoutledgeCurzon, 2004.

Chung, Chin O. *Pyongyang between Peking and Moscow: North Korea's Involvement in the Sino-Soviet Dispute, 1958-1975.* Tuscaloosa: University of Alabama Press, 1978.

Cohen, Jerome Alan, ed. *China's Practice of International Law: Some Case Studies.* Cambridge, MA: Harvard University Press, 1972.

Colin, Sébastien. "A Border Opening onto Numerous Geopolitical Issues." *China Perspectives* 48 (July-August 2003): 4-20.

Conboy, Kenneth, and James Morrison. *The CIA's Secret War in Tibet.* Lawrence: University Press of Kansas, 2002.

Cranmer-Byng, John. "The Chinese View of Their Place in the World: An Historical Perspective." *China Quarterly* 53 (January-March 1973).

Crow, Suzanne. "Russia Debates Its National Interests." *RFE/RL Research Report* 1, 28 (10 July 1992): 43, 45.

Curtis, Gerald, Ryosei Kokubun, and Wang Jisi, eds., *Getting the Triangle Straight: Managing China-Japan-US Relations.* Baltimore: Brookings Institution Press, 2010.

Dabringhaus, Sabine, and Roderich Ptak, eds. *China and Her Neighbours: Borders, Visions of the Other, Foreign Policy 10th to 19th Century.* Wiesbaden: Harrassowitz Verlag, 1997.

Dai, Shen-yu. "China and Afghanistan." *China Quarterly* 25 (January-March 1966): 213-21.

–. "Peking and Rangoon." *China Quarterly* 5 (January-March 1961): 131-44.

Daly, John C.K. "Sino-Kyrgyz Relations after the Tulip Revolution." *China Brief* 5, 9 (26 April 2005): 6-7.

Deans, Phil. "Contending Nationalisms and the Diaoyutai/Senkaku Dispute." *Security Dialogue* 31, 1 (2000): 119-31.

Deng Xiaoping wenxuan [Selected works of Deng Xiaoping]. Peking: Foreign Language Press, 1992.

Diehl, Paul F., ed. *A Road Map to War: Territorial Dimensions of International Conflict.* Nashville: Vanderbilt University Press, 1999.

Dittmer, Lowell. "The Strategic Triangle: An Elementary Game-Theoretical Analysis." *World Politics* 33, 4 (July 1981): 485-515.

Dixit, J.N. *Across Borders: Fifty Years of India's Foreign Policy.* New Delhi: Picus Books, 1998.

Dobell, W. M. "Ramifications of the Chinese-Pakistan Border Treaty." *Pacific Affairs* 37, 3 (Fall 1964): 283-95.

Donaldson, Robert H. *The Soviet-Indian Alignment: Quest for Influence.* Denver: Graduate School of International Studies, University of Denver, 1979.

Doolin, Dennis J. *Territorial Claims in the Sino-Soviet Conflict: Documents and Analysis.* Hoover Institution Studies 7. Stanford, CA: Hoover Institution on War, Revolution and Peace, Stanford University Press, 1965.

Downs, Erica Strecker, and Phillip C. Saunders. "Legitimacy and the Limits of Nationalism: China and the Diaoyu Islands." *International Security* 23, 3 (Winter 1998-99): 114-46.

Du Hengzhi. *Zhongwai tiaoyue guanxi zhi bianqian* [Changes in Sino-foreign treaty relations]. Taipei: Zhonghua wenwu gongying she, 1981.

Dupree, Louis. *Afghanistan.* Princeton, NJ: Princeton University Press, 1980.

Dutt, Vidya Prakash. *China and the World: An Analysis of Communist China's Foreign Policy.* New York: Praeger, 1966.

Elleman, Bruce A., Stephen Kotkin, and Clive Schofield, eds. *Beijing's Power and China's Border: Twenty Neighbors in Asia.* Armonk, NY: M.E. Sharpe, 2013.

Emery, K.O., et al. "Geological Structure and Some Water Characteristics of the East China Sea and Yellow Sea." *Technical Bulletin* 2 (1969).

Facts about Korea. Pyongyang: Foreign Language Publishing House, 1961.

Fairbank, John K. "China's Foreign Policy in Historical Perspective." *Foreign Affairs* 47, 3 (April 1969): 449-63.

–, ed. *The Chinese World Order: Traditional China's Foreign Relations.* Cambridge, MA: Harvard University Press, 1968.

Fang Ming. "Guanyu SuE liangci duiHau xuanyan he feichu ZhongE bupingdeng taioyue" [The two declarations of the Soviet government toward China and the abolition of Sino-Russian unequal treaties]. *Lishi yanjiu* 6 (1980): 63-75.

Feigenbaum, Evan A. "Central Asia Contingencies." In *Managing Instability on China's Periphery*, ed. Paul B. Stares, Scott A. Snyder, Joshua Kurlantzick, Daniel Markey, and Evan A. Feigenbaum. New York: Council on Foreign Relations, Center for Preventive Action, 2011, 60-70.

Feng, Huiyun. *Chinese Strategic Culture and Foreign Policy Decision Making: Confucianism, Leadership and War.* New York: Routledge, 2007.

Field, Arvin R. "Strategic Development in Sinkiang." *Foreign Affairs* 39, 2 (January 1961): 312-18.

Fisher, Margaret W., Leo E. Rose, and Robert A. Huttenbeck. *Himalayan Battleground: Sino-Indian Rivalry in Ladakh.* New York: Praeger, 1963.

Floyd, David. *Mao against Khrushchev: A Short History of the Sino-Soviet Conflict.* New York: Praeger, 1963.

Foot, Rosemary. "Sino-Soviet Rivalry in Kabul." *Round Table* 280 (October 1980): 434-42.

Franke, Herbert, and Denis Twitchett, eds. *The Cambridge History of China.* Vol. 6, *Alien Regimes and Border States, 907-1368.* Cambridge: Cambridge University Press, 1994.

Fraser-Tytler, W.K. *Afghanistan: A Study of Political Developments in Central and South Asia.* London: Oxford University Press, 1950.

Fravel, M. Taylor. "The Dangerous Math of Chinese Island Disputes." *Wall Street Journal,* 29 October 2012.

–. "Explaining Stability in the Senkaku (Diaoyu) Islands Dispute." In *Getting the Triangle Straight: Managing China-Japan-US Relations,* ed. Gerald Curtis, Ryosei Kokubun, and Wang Jise, 144-64. Washington, DC: Brookings Institution Press, 2010.

–. "International Relations Theory and China's Rise: Assessing China's Potential for Territorial Expansion." *International Studies Review* 12, 4 (2010): 505-32.

–. "Regime Insecurity and International Cooperation: Explaining China's Compromises in Territorial Disputes." *International Security* 30, 2 (Fall 2005): 46-83.

–. *Strong Borders, Secure Nation: Cooperation and Conflict in China's Territorial Disputes.* Princeton, NJ: Princeton University Press, 2008.

Friters, Girard M. *Outer Mongolia and Its International Position.* New York and Baltimore: Johns Hopkins University Press, 1957.

"Full Text of Joint Statement by Chinese, Indian Defence Ministers." *Xinhuanet,* 6 July 2013, http://news.xinhuanet.com/.

Gallagher, Michael G. "China's Illusory Threat to the South China Sea." *International Security* 19, 1 (Summer 1994): 169-94.

Ganguly, Sumit. "The Sino-Indian Border Talks, 1981-1989." *Asian Survey* 29, 12 (December 1989): 1123-35.

Garnett, Sherman W., ed. *Rapprochement or Rivalry? Russia-China Relations in a Changing Asia.* Washington, DC: Carnegie Endowment for International Peace, 2000.

Garver, John W. "The Indian Factor in Recent Sino-Soviet Relations." *China Quarterly* 125 (March 1991): 74-75.

–. *Protracted Contest: Sino-Indian Rivalry in the Twentieth Century.* Seattle: University of Washington Press, 2001.

–. "Sino-Indian Rapprochement and the Sino-Pakistan Entente." *Political Science Quarterly* 111, 2 (Summer 1996): 326-29.

–. "The Sino-Soviet Dispute in the Pamir Mountains Region." *China Quarterly* 85 (March 1981): 107-18.

Geng, Nien. "Sino-Indian Relations: Retrospect and Prospect." *South Asian Studies* [Chengdu] 3-4 (1981): 1-5.

George, T.J.S. *Krishna Menon: A Biography.* London: Jonathan Cape, 1964.

Gibler, Douglas M. "Alliances that Never Balance: The Territorial-Settlement Treaty." In *A Road Map to War: Territorial Dimensions of International Conflict,* ed. Paul F. Diehl, 181-204. Nashville: Vanderbilt University Press, 1999.

Gilboy, George J., and Eric Heginbotham. *Chinese and Indian Strategic Behavior: Growing Power and Alarm.* New York: Cambridge University Press, 2012.

Gittings, John. *The World and China, 1922-1972.* New York: Harper and Row, 1974.

Glaser, Bonnie. "China's Security Perceptions: Interests and Ambitions." *Asian Survey* 33, 3 (March 1993): 252-71.

Gleason, Gregory. "Why Russia Is in Tajikistan." *Comparative Strategy* 20 (2001): 77-89.

Goldstein, Lyle J. "Return to Zhenbao Island: Who Started the Shooting and Why It Matters." *China Quarterly* 168 (December 2001): 985-97.

Gomà, Daniel. "The Chinese-Korean Border Issue." *Asian Survey* 46, 6 (November/December 2006): 867-80.

Gomà Pinilla, Daniel. "Border Disputes between China and North Korea." *China Perspectives* 52 (March-April 2004): 2-8.

Gopal, Sarvepalli. *Jawaharlal Nehru: A Biography.* Vol. 2, *1947-1956.* Cambridge, MA: Harvard University Press, 1979.

–. *Jawaharlal Nehru: A Biography.* Vol. 3, *1956-1964.* Cambridge, MA: Harvard University Press, 1984.

Goswami, B.N. *Pakistan and China: A Study of their Relations.* New York: Allied Publishers, 1971.

Griffith, W.E. *Sino-Soviet Relations: 1964-1965.* Cambridge, MA: MIT Press, 1967.

Gu Guanfu. "1996-1997 nian ZhongYa xingshi baogao" [1996-1997 report on the situation in Sino–Central Asia relations]. *Zhongguo zhanlue yu guanli yanjiu hui, guoji xingshi fenxi baogao, 1996-1997.* Beijing: Zhongguo zhanlue yu guanli yanjiu hui [China Institute of Strategy and Manaagement], 1997.

Gupta, Dipankar. *The Context of Ethnicity: Sikh Ethnicity in a Comparative Perspective.* Delhi: Oxford University Press, 1996.

Hall, D.G.E. *Burma.* London: Hutchison University Library, 1960.

Halpern, A.M., ed. *Policies toward China: Views from Six Continents.* New York: McGraw Hill, 1965.

Hamrin, Carol Lee. "Elite Politics and the Development of China's Foreign Relations." In *Chinese Foreign Policy: Theory and Practice,* ed. Thomas W. Robinson and David Shambaugh, 70-114. New York: Oxford University Press, 1994.

Hamrin, Carol Lee, and Suisheng Zhao, eds. *Decision-Making in Deng's China: Perspectives from Insiders.* Armonk, NY: M.E. Sharpe, 1995.

Hamzah, B.A. "China's Strategy." *Far Eastern Economic Review,* 13 August 1992.

–. *The Spratlies: What Can Be Done to Enhance Confidence.* Kuala Lumpur: Institute of Strategic and International Studies (ISIS) Malaysia, 1990.

Han, Nianlong, ed. *Diplomacy of Contemporary China.* Hong Kong: New Horizon Press, 1990.

Harding, Harry, ed. *China's Foreign Relations in the 1980s.* New Haven, CT: Yale University Press, 1984.

Harris, Lillian Craig. "Xinjiang, Central Asia, and the Implications for China's Policy in the Islamic World." *China Quarterly* 133 (1993): 111-29.

Hasan, K. Sarwar, ed. *China, India, Pakistan.* Documents on the Foreign Relations of Pakistan Series. Karachi: Pakistan Institute of International Affairs, 1966.

Hill, R.D., Norman G. Owen, and E.V. Roberts, eds. *Fishing in Troubled Waters.* Hong Kong: Centre for Asian Studies, University of Hong Kong, 1991.

Hinton, Harold. *China's Relations with Burma and Vietnam: A Brief Survey.* New York: Institute of Pacific Relations, 1958.

–. *Communist China in World Politics.* Boston: Houghton Mifflin, 1966.

–, ed. *The People's Republic of China, 1949-1979: A Documentary Survey.* 5 vols. Wilmington, DE: Scholarly Resources, 1980.

Ho, Ping-ti. "The Significance of the Ch'ing Period in Chinese History." *Journal of Asian Studies* 26, 2 (February 1967): 189-95.

Hoadley, J. Stephen. "China-Burma Border Settlement: A Retrospective Evaluation." *Asian Forum* 2, 2 (April-June 1970): 104-16.

Hoffman, Steven A. *India and the China Crisis.* Berkeley: University of California Press, 1990.

Holmes, Robert A. "The Sino-Burmese Rift: A Failure for China." *Orbis* 16, 1 (Spring 1972): 211-36.

Holsti, K.J., ed. *Why Nations Realign: Foreign Policy Restructuring in the Postwar World.* London: George Allen and Unwin, 1982.

Hoon, Shim Jae. "Blood Thicker than Politics: Taiwan Indicates a Military Preparedness to Back China." *Far Eastern Economic Review,* 5 May 1988, 26-27.

Hsiung, James. "China's Omni-directional Diplomacy: Realignment to Cope with Monopolar US Power." *Asian Survey* 35, 6 (June 1995): 573-86.

Hua, Di. "China's Comprehensive Strategic Doctrine." In *The Role of Technology in Meeting the Defense Challenges of the 1980s: Report of a Conference,* ed. William Perry and Hua Di, 67-104. Stanford, CA: Arms Control and Disarmament Program, Stanford University, 1981.

Hudson, G.F. "The Nationalities of China." *St. Antony's Papers* 7 (1960): 51-61.

Hunt, Michael H. "Chinese Foreign Relations in Historical Perspective." In *China's Foreign Relations in the 1980s,* ed. Harry Harding, 1-42. New Haven, CT: Yale University Press, 1984.

Huth, Paul K. "Enduring Rivalries and Territorial Disputes, 1950-1990." *Conflict Management and Peace Science* 15, 1 (1996): 14-15.

–. *Standing Your Ground: Territorial Disputes and International Conflict.* Ann Arbor: University of Michigan Press, 1996.

Hyer, Eric. "'Dangerous Shoals': An Introduction to the South China Sea Disputes." *American Asian Review* 12, 4 (Winter 1994): 7-22.

–. "'The Great Game': Mongolia between Russia and China." *Mongolian Journal of International Affairs* 4 (1997): 89-104.

–. "The Sino-Russian Boundary Settlement." *Boundary and Security Bulletin* 4, 2 (Summer 1996): 90-94.

–. "The South China Sea Disputes: Implications of China's Earlier Territorial Settlements." *Pacific Affairs* 68, 1 (Spring 1995): 34-54.

"India, China to Set Up Working Mechanism on Border Management." *The Hindu,* 17 January 2012. http://www.thehindu.com/.

"India and China Agree over Tibet." *BBC News,* 24 June 2003. http://news.bbc.co.uk/go/pr/fr/2/hi/south_asia/3015840.stm.

Iwashita, Akihiro. "The Russo-Chinese 'Strategic Partnership' and the Border Negotiations: Then and Now." *Yamaguchi kenritsu daigaku daigakuyinronshu* [Bulletin of the Graduate School of Yamaguchi Prefecture University] 2 (March 2001): 1-10.

Jafri, Hasan Ali Shah. *Indo-Afghan Relations (1947-1967).* New Delhi: Sterling Publishers, 1976.

Jain, R.K., ed. *China-South Asian Relations (1947-1980) Documents,* Vol. 2. New Delhi: Radiant Publishers, 1981.

Ji, Guoxing. "China versus South China Sea Security." *Security Dialogue* 29, 1 (1998): 101-12.

Jiang Junzhang. *Zhongguo bianjiang yu guofang* [China's frontiers and national defence]. Taipei: Liming wenhua, 1979.

Jiang Yan. "Our Sacred Land: Heixiazidao Island." *Dili zhishi* 1 (1975): 5-7.

Johnson, Douglas, and Hungdah Chiu, eds. *Agreements of the People's Republic of China, 1949-1967: A Calendar.* Cambridge, MA: Harvard University Press, 1968.

Johnstone, William C. *Burma's Foreign Policy: A Study in Neutralism.* Cambridge, MA: Harvard University Press, 1963.

Jones, P.H.M. "Mongolia between Two Fires." *Far Eastern Economic Review,* 17 August 1961, 15-17.

Jonson, Lena. *Tajikistan in the New Central Asia: Geopolitics, Great Power Rivalry and Radical Islam*. London: I.B. Tauris, 2006.

Joshi, P.C. "Chinese Dogmatism and the Border Dispute." *New Age* 11, 4 (27 January 1963): 10-11.

Joss, Frederick. "China Penetrates the Shan Region of Burma." *Eastern World* (London) 20, 1/2 (January-February 1966): 14-16.

Kao, Ting-tsz. *The Chinese Frontiers*. Aurora, IL: Chinese Scholarly Publishing, 1980.

Karan, Pradyumna P. "Geopolitical Structure of Bhutan." *India Quarterly* 19, 3 (July-September 1963): 203-13.

Karrar, Hasan H. *The New Silk Road Diplomacy: China's Central Asian Foreign Policy since the Cold War*. Vancouver: UBC Press, 2009.

Kaul, B.M. *The Untold Story*. New Delhi: Allied Publishers, 1967.

Kaznacheev, Alexander. *Inside a Soviet Embassy: Experiences of a Russian Diplomat in Burma*. Philadelphia: Lippincott, 1962.

Khan, Mohammed Ayub. *Friends Not Masters: A Political Autobiography*. London: Oxford University Press, 1967.

–. "Pakistan Perspective." *Foreign Affairs* 38, 4 (July 1960): 547-56.

Khrushchev, Nikita Sergeyevich. *Khrushchev Remembers: The Last Testament*. Boston: Little, Brown, 1974.

Kim Deuk Hwang. *Paektusan-gua Bukbangganggye* [Mt. Paektu and the northern border]. Seoul: Sa Sa Yŏn Publishers, 1988.

Kireev, Genrikh. "Demarcation of the Border with China." *International Affairs* (Moscow) 45, 2 (1999): 98-109.

Kissinger, Henry. *The White House Years*. Boston: Little, Brown, 1979.

–. *A World Restored: Metternich, Castlereagh and the Problems of Peace, 1812-22*. New York: Houghton Mifflin, 1957.

Kohli, Manorama. *From Dependency to Interdependence: A Study of Indo-Bhutan Relations*. New Delhi: Vikas Publishing House, 1993.

Kozicki, Richard J. "The Sino-Burmese Frontier Problem." *Far Eastern Survey* 26 (March 1957): 33-38.

Kratochwil, Friedrich, Paul Rohrlich, and Harpreet Mahajan. *Peace and Disputed Sovereignty: Reflections on Conflict over Territory*. Lanham, MD: University Press of America, 1985.

Kreisberg, Paul H. "The Indian-Chinese Summit." *Christian Science Monitor*, 15 December 1988, 16.

Krishnan, Ananth. "India, China Conclude Talks; to Strengthen Border Mechanism." *The Hindu*, 29 June 2013. http://www.thehindu.com/.

Kruchinin, A., and V. Olgin. *Territorial Claims of Mao Tse-tung: History and Modern Times*. Moscow: Novosti Press Agency Publishing House, 1971.

Kumar, Girja, and V.K. Arora, eds. *Documents on Indian External Affairs*. Bombay: Asia Publishing House, 1965.

Kun, Bela. *Fundamental Laws of the Chinese Soviet Republic*. New York: International Publishers, 1934.

"Kyrgyz Legislature Continues to Discuss Chinese Border Controversy." *RFE/RL Newsline* 5, 119 (22 June 2001).

Lall, Arthur. *The Emergence of Modern India*. New York: Columbia University Press, 1981.

–. *How Communist China Negotiates*. New York: Columbia University Press, 1968.

Lall, John. *Aksaichin and Sino-Indian Conflict*. New Delhi: Allied Publishers, 1989.

Lama, Mahendra P. "Nepal and Bhutan." In *Security in South Asia: Comprehensive and Cooperative*, ed. Dipankar Banerjee, 150-201. New Delhi: Manas Publications, 1999.

Lamb, Alastair. *Asian Frontiers: Studies in a Continuing Problem*. New York: Praeger, 1968.
–. *The China-India Border: The Origins of the Disputed Boundaries*. London: Oxford University Press, 1964.
–. "The Sino-Pakistan Boundary Agreement of 2 March 1963." *Australian Outlook* 18, 3 (December 1964): 299-312.
Lampton, David M. "China: Outward Bound but Inner-Directed." *SAISPHERE 2006*, http://www.sais-jhu.edu/pressroom/publications/saisphere/2006/lampton.htm.
Laruelle, Marlène, and Sébastien Peyrouse. *China as a Neighbor: Central Asian Perspectives and Strategies*. Washington, DC: John Hopkins University–SAIS, Central Asia–Caucasus Institute and Silk Road Studies Program, 2009.
Ledovsky, Andrei. "Mikoyan's Secret Mission to China in January and February 1949." *Far Eastern Affairs* 23, 2 (1995): 88-89.
–. "The Moscow Visit of a Delegation of the Communist Party of China in June to August 1949." *Far Eastern Affairs* 24, 4 (1996): 64-86.
Ledyard, Gari. "Cartography in Korea." In *The History of Cartography*, vol. 2, book 2, ed. J.B. Harley and David Woodward, 235-345. Chicago: University of Chicago Press, 1994.
Lee, Chae-Jin. *China and Korea: Dynamic Relations*. Stanford, CA: Hoover Institution, 1996.
Lee, Kuan Yew. Speech given at "The 1996 Architect of the New Century Dinner." Nixon Center, Washington, DC, 24 November 1996. http://www.nixoncenter.org/publications/YEW96.html.
Leifer, Michael. "Chinese Economic Reform and Security Policy: The South China Sea Connection." *Survival* 37, 2 (Summer 1995): 44-60.
Lerner, Mitchell. "'Mostly Propaganda in Nature': Kim Il Sung, the Juche Ideology, and the Second Korean War." North Korea International Documentation Project Working Paper 3. Washington, DC: Woodrow Wilson International Center for Scholars, December 2010.
Li, Haiwen. "A Distortion of History: An Interview with Shi Zhe about Kovolev's Memoirs." *Chinese Historians* 5, 2 (Fall 1992): 58-65.
Li Huichuan. "The Crux of the Sino-Soviet Boundary Question" [pt. 1]. *Peking Review*, 2 July 1981, 12-17.
–. "The Crux of the Sino-Soviet Boundary Question" [pt. 2]. *Peking Review*, 3 August 1981, 13-16.
Li, Jijun. "Traditional Military Thinking and the Defensive Strategy of China." *Letort Paper* 1. Carlisle, PA: Strategic Studies Institute, United States Army War College, 1997.
Li, Jingjie. "From Good Neighbors to Strategic Partners." In *Rapprochement or Rivalry? Russia-China Relations in a Changing Asia*, ed. Sherman W. Garnett, 71-98. Washington, DC: Carnegie Endowment for International Peace, 2000.
Li, Mingjiang. "Chinese Debates of South China Sea Policy: Implications for Future Developments." RSIS Working Paper 239. Singapore: S. Rajaratnam School of International Studies, Nanyang Technological University, 17 May 2012.
Li Ming and Liu Qiang, eds. *Zhou Enlai de waijiao yishu* [Zhou Enlai's art of diplomacy]. Jinan: Shandong daxue chubanshe, 1992.
Li Xiang. "Return of Heixiasi Island Marks End of Border Dispute." *China Daily*, 15 October 2008. http://chinadaily.com.cn/.
Lieberthal, Kenneth. *The Sino-Soviet Conflict in the 1970s: Its Evolution and Implications for the Strategic Triangle*. Santa Monica, CA: Rand, 1978.
Lin Hongyu. "Zhongguo haiyang zhanlue kunjing: chengyin yu duice" [The predicament of Chinese maritime strategy: causes and countermeasures]. *Xiandai Guoji Guanxi* 8 (2012): 7-43.

Liow, Joseph Chin Yong. "Malaysia-China Relations in the 1990s: The Maturing of a Partnership." *Asian Survey* 40, 4 (July-August 2000): 672-91.

Liu, Binyan. "Big Drama about Small Islands." *China Focus* 4, 10 (1 October 1996): 1-5.

Liu, Xiaohong. *Chinese Ambassadors: The Rise of Diplomatic Professionalism since 1949.* Seattle: University of Washington Press, 2001.

Liu, Xiaoyuan. *Reins of Liberation: An Entangled History of Mongolian Independence, Chinese Territoriality, and Great Power Hegemony, 1911-1950.* Stanford, CA: Stanford University Press, 2006.

Liu, Xuecheng. *The Sino-Indian Border Dispute and Sino-Indian Relations.* Lanham, MD: University Press of America, 1994.

Liu Dexi, Sun Yan, and Liu Songbin. *Sulian jietihou de ZhongE guanxi* [Sino-Russian relations after the breakup of the Soviet Union]. Harbin: Heilongjiang jiaoyu chubanshe, 1996.

Liu Jiangyong. "New Situation and Prospect of Disputes over Diaoyu Dao." *Foreign Affairs Journal* [China], issue 106 (Winter 2012): 32-50.

Liu Peihua. *Zhongguo jindai shi* [Modern Chinese history]. Beijing: Yichang shuju, 1954.

Liu Shaoqi. *Collected Works of Liu Shao-ch'i, 1958-1967.* Hong Kong: Union Research Institute, 1968.

Lo, Chi-kin. *China's Policy towards Territorial Disputes: The Case of the South China Sea Islands.* New York: Routledge, 1989.

Lukin, Alexander. *The Bear Watches the Dragon: Russia's Perceptions of China and the Evolution of Russian-Chinese Relations since the Eighteenth Century.* Armonk, NY: M.E. Sharpe, 2003.

Luzianin, Sergei. "Materials and Documents on the Kyrgyzstan-China Border." *Far Eastern Affairs* 33, 1 (January-March 2005): 153-54.

MacFarquhar, Roderick, ed. *The Politics of China: The Eras of Mao and Deng,* 2nd ed. Oxford: Oxford University Press, 1997.

–, ed. *The Politics of China: Sixty Years of the People's Republic of China,* 3rd ed. Oxford: Cambridge University Press, 2011.

Maitra, Ramtanu. "Prospects Brighten for Kunming Initiative." *Asia Times Online,* 12 February 2003. http://www.atimes.com/.

Maki, John M. *Selected Documents: Far Eastern International Relations (1689-1951).* Seattle: University of Washington Press, 1951.

Malhotra, Jyoti. "For India's Tibet Turn, China to Amend its Sikkim Map." *Indian Express,* 25 June 2003. http://archive.indianexpress.com/oldStory/26444/.

Mancall, Mark. *China at the Center: 300 Years of Foreign Policy.* New York: Free Press, 1984.

–. "The Persistence of Tradition in Chinese Foreign Policy." *Annals of the American Academy of Political and Social Science* 349 (September 1963): 17-20.

Manicom, James. "The State of Cooperation in the East China Sea." *NBR Analysis Brief,* 30 April 2013.

Mansingh, Surjit. *India's Search for Power: Indira Gandhi's Foreign Policy, 1966-1982.* New Delhi: Sage Publications, 1984.

Mansingh, Surjit, and Steven I. Levine. "China and India: Moving beyond Confrontation." *Problems of Communism* 38, 2-3 (March-June 1989): 31-49.

Mao, Tse-tung. *China: The March toward Unity.* New York: Workers Library Publishers, 1937.

–. *Selected Works of Mao Tse-tung.* Vol. 4. Peking: Foreign Language Press, 1965.

Mao Zedong. *Zhongguo geming yu Zhongguo gongchandang* [The Chinese revolution and the Chinese Communist Party]. Zhangjiakou: Xinhua shudian, 1945. Revised ed.: Renmin chubanshe, 1952.

Martin, Keith. "China and Central Asia: Between Seduction and Suspicion." *RFE/RL Research Report* 3, 24 (24 June 1994): 26-36.

Mathou, Thierry. "Bhutan-China Relations: Towards a New Step in Himalayan Politics." In *The Spider and the Piglet: Proceedings of the First International Seminar on Bhutanese Studies,* ed. Karma Ura and Sonam Kinga, 388-411. Thimphu: Centre for Bhutan Studies, 2004.

—. "Tibet and Its Neighbors: Moving toward a New Chinese Strategy in the Himalayan Region." *Asian Survey* 45, 4 (2005): 503-21.

Matveyev, G.V. "Peking's Political Machinations on the Hindustan Peninsula." *Problemy Dalnego Vostoka* 4 (December 1972): 39-45. Abstract trans. in *Current Digest of the Soviet Press* 25, 11 (11 April 1973): 4.

Maung, Maung. "The Burma-China Boundary Settlement." *Asian Survey* 1, 1 (March 1961): 38-43.

Maung Maung U. *Burma and General Ne Win.* New York: Asia Publishing House, 1969.

Maxwell, Neville. "China and India: 'The Un-Negotiated Dispute.'" *China Quarterly* 43 (July-September 1970): 47-80.

—. *India's China War.* London: Jonathan Cape, 1970.

—. "Settlements and Disputes: China's Approach to Territorial Issues." *Economic and Political Weekly,* 9 September 2006, 3873-81.

May, Ernest R. "The Nature of Foreign Policy: The Calculated versus the Axiomatic." *Daedalus* 91, 4 (Fall 1962): 653-67.

Mearsheimer, John J. *The Tragedy of Great Power Politics.* New York: W.W. Norton, 2001.

Menon, Krishna P.S. *Delhi-Chungking: A Travel Diary.* Bombay: Oxford University Press, 1947.

Miasnikov, Vladimir S. "Present Issues between Russian and China: Realties and Prospects." *Sino-Soviet Affairs* 18, 2 (Summer 1994).

Miller, Alice. "Dilemmas of Globalization and Governance." In *The Politics of China: Sixty Years of the People's Republic of China,* 3rd ed., ed. Roderick MacFarquhar, 538-99. New York: Cambridge University Press, 2011.

Misra, R.C. *The Emergence of Bhutan.* Jaipur: Sandarbh Prakashan, 1989.

Montaperto, Ronald N. "Whither China? Beijing's Policies for the 1990s." *Strategic Review* 20, 3 (Summer 1992): 23-33.

Moorthy, K. Krishna. "Bhutan: Thoughts of Sovereignty." *Far Eastern Economic Review,* 16 February 1961, 13-15.

—. "Bhutan's Blank Cheque to Nehru." *Far Eastern Economic Review,* 9 March 1961, 38.

Moraes, Frank. *Witness to an Era: India, 1920 to the Present Day.* London: Weidenfeld and Nicolson, 1973.

Mozingo, David P. "Communist China: Its Southern Border Lands." *SAIS Review* 12, 2 (Winter 1968): 43-54.

"Mr. Huang Hua's Visit to New Delhi – Agreement to Discuss Border Question." *Keesing's Contemporary Archives* 27 (October 1981): 31153.

Mullik, B.M. *The Chinese Betrayal: My Years with Nehru.* Bombay: Allied Publishers, 1971.

Muni, S.D. *Foreign Policy of Nepal.* Delhi: National Publishing House, 1973.

Nguyen Manh Hung. "The Sino-Vietnamese Conflict: Power Play among Communist Neighbors." *Asian Survey* 19, 11 (November 1979): 1037-52.

Ni, Xiaoquan. "Recent Developments in China's Relations with Russia and the United States." *Institute Reports* (East Asian Institute, Columbia University), April 1995.

Niazi, Tarique. "The Ecology of Strategic Interests: China's Quest for Energy Security from the Indian Ocean and the South China Sea to the Caspian Sea Basin." *China and Eurasia Forum Quarterly* 6, 4 (November 2006): 97-116.

Nu, U. *U Nu – Saturday's Son*, trans. U Law Yone, ed. U Kyaw Win. New Haven, CT: Yale University Press, 1975.

On Vietnam's Expulsion of Chinese Residents. Beijing: Foreign Language Press, 1978.

Ó Tuathail, Gearóid. *Critical Geopolitics: The Politics of Writing Global Space*. Minneapolis : University of Minnesota Press, 1996.

Ostermann, Christian F. "New Evidence on the Sino-Soviet Border Dispute, 1969-71." *Cold War International History Project Bulletin*, issues 6-7 (Winter 1995): 186-206.

Pan, Guang. "China and Central Asia: Charting a New Course for Regional Cooperation." *Jamestown Foundation China Brief* 7, 3 (5 February 2007). http://www.jamestown.org/programs/chinabrief/single/?tx_ttnews%5Btt_news%5D=32468&tx_ttnews%5Bback Pid%5D=197&no_cache=1#.UzeIIfldXRw.

Pan, Shiying. "The Nansha Islands: A Chinese Point of View." *Window*, 3 September 1993.

Panikkar, K.M. *In Two Chinas: Memoirs of a Diplomat*. London: George Allen and Unwin, 1955.

Patterson, George N. *Peking versus Delhi*. New York: Praeger, 1964.

–. "Recent Chinese Policies in Tibet and towards the Himalayan Border States." *China Quarterly* 12 (October-December 1962): 191-202.

Pei Jianzhang. *Xin Zhongguo waijiao fengyun: Zhongguo waijiaoguan huiyilu* [New China's diplomatic challenges: recollections of Chinese diplomats]. Vols. 1-3. Beijing: Shijie zhishi chubanshe, 1990-94.

–, ed. *Yanjiu Zhou Enlai – waijiao sixiang yu shijian* [Research on Zhou Enlai: diplomatic thought and practice]. Beijing: Shijie zhishi chubanshe, 1989.

Peng Xiaoming. "Tumen jiang chuhaikou chengle Zhongguo ren yongjiu de quru" [The mouth of the Tumen River has become an eternal humiliation for the Chinese] (30 September 2003). http://www.kanzhongguo.com/.

Penjore, Dorji. "Security of Bhutan: Walking between the Giants." *Journal of Bhutan Studies* 10 (Summer 2004): 108-31.

Perdue, Peter C. "Boundaries, Maps, and Movement: Chinese, Russian, and Mongolian Empires in Early Modern Central Eurasia." *International History Review* 20, 2 (June 1998): 263-86.

–. "Comparing Empires: Manchu Colonialism." *International History Review* 20, 2 (June 1998): 255-62.

Perry, William, and Hua Di, eds. *The Role of Technology in Meeting the Defense Challenges of the 1980s: Report of a Conference*. Stanford, CA: Arms Control and Disarmament Program, Stanford University, 1981.

Polat, Necati. *Boundary Issues in Central Asia*. Ardsley, NY: Transnational Publishers, 2002.

Poulose, T.T. "Bhutan's External Relations and India." *International and Comparative Law Quarterly* 20, 2 (April 1971): 195-212.

Prakash, Shri. "The Sixth Meeting of the India-China Joint Working Group on the Boundary Question." *China Report: A Journal of East Asian Studies* 30, 1 (January-March 1994): 90-91.

"Premier Wen Jiabao Meets Indian Prime Minister Vajpayee" (9 October 2003). http://www.fmprc.gov.cn/mfa_eng/wjb_663304/zzjg_663340/yzs_663350/gjlb_663354/2711_663426/2713_663430/t26842.shtml.

Prescott, J.R.V. *Map of Mainland Asia by Treaty*. Melbourne: Melbourne University Press, 1975.

Qian Qichen. *Waijiao shiji* [Ten foreign policy events]. Beijing: Shijie zhishi chubanshe, 2003.

"Quarterly Chronicle and Documentation." *China Quarterly* 59 (July-September 1974): 625-61.

Radchenko, Sergey S. "The Soviets' Best Friend in Asia: The Mongolian Dimension of the Sino-Soviet Dispute." Cold War International History Project, Working Paper 42. Washington, DC: Woodrow Wilson International Center for Scholars, 2003.

Rahul, Ram. "China's Other Boundaries." *Australian Journal of Politics and History* 9, 2 (May-November 1963): 150-66.

—. *The Himalaya Borderland.* New Delhi: Vikas Publications, 1970.

—. *Modern Bhutan.* Delhi: Vikas Publications, 1971.

Raschid, U. "Speech at the Burmese Chamber of Commerce, February 18, 1956." *Burmese Weekly Bulletin,* 23 February 1956.

Razvi, Mujtaba. *The Frontiers of Pakistan: A Study of Frontier Problems in Pakistan's Foreign Policy.* Karachi: National Publishing House, 1971.

Reilly, James. *Strong Society, Smart State: The Rise of Public Opinion in China's Japan Policy.* New York: Columbia University Press, 2012.

Research Institute for Peace and Security. *Asian Security: 1996-97.* Washington, DC: Brassey's, 1997.

Robinson, Thomas W. *The Sino-Soviet Border Dispute: Background, Development and the March, 1969 Clashes.* Santa Monica, CA: Rand Corporation, 1970.

Robinson, Thomas W., and David Shambaugh, eds. *Chinese Foreign Policy: Theory and Practice.* Oxford: Clarendon Press, 1994.

Rose, Leo E. "Bhutan's External Relations." *Pacific Affairs* 47, 2 (Summer 1974): 192-208.

—. *Nepal: Strategy for Survival.* Berkeley: University of California Press, 1971.

—. *The Politics of Bhutan.* Ithaca, NY: Cornell University Press, 1977.

—. "Sikkim and the Sino-Indian Dispute." *Political Science Review* 8, 1 (January-March 1969): 41-58.

—. "Sino-Indian Rivalry and the Himalayan Border States." *Orbis* 5, 2 (Summer 1961): 198-215.

Rowland, John. *A History of Sino-Indian Relations: Hostile Co-Existence.* Princeton, NJ: D. Van Nostrand, 1967.

Rupen, Robert A. "The Mongolian People's Republic and Inner Mongolia." *China News Analysis* 540 (13 November 1964): 1-7.

—. "The Mongolian People's Republic and Sino-Soviet Competition." In *Communist Strategies in Asia,* ed. A. Doak Barnett, 262-92. New York: Praeger, 1963.

—. *Mongols of the Twentieth Century.* Bloomington: Indiana University Press, 1964.

—. "Recent Trends in the Mongolian People's Republic." *Asian Survey* 4, 4 (April 1964): 812-20.

Salisbury, Harrison E. *To Moscow and Beyond.* New York: Harper and Brothers, 1960.

—. *War between Russia and China.* New York: W.W. Norton, 1969.

Sanders, A.J.K. *The People's Republic of Mongolia.* London: Oxford University Press, 1968.

Sayeed, Khalid Bin. "Pakistan and China: The Scope and Limits of Convergent Policies." In *Policies toward China: Views from Six Continents,* ed. A.M. Halpern, 229-61. New York: McGraw Hill, 1965.

Schram, Stuart. *Mao Tse-tung.* New York: Penguin Books, 1977.

Searls, Guy. "Communist China's Border Policy: Dragon Throne Imperialism?" *Current Scene* 2, 12 (15 April 1963): 1-22.

Second Workshop on Managing Potential Conflicts in the South China Sea (Bandung, Indonesia, July 8, 1991). *Second Workshop Report* (1991).

Seibert, Craig, trans. "Stalin's Dialogue with Mao Zedong" (S.N. Goncharov interview with Ivan V. Kovalev), *Journal of Northeast Asian Studies* 10, 4 (Winter 1991): 45-77.

Shi Bo. *Waimenggu duli neimu* [Inside story of Outer Mongolia's independence]. Beijing: Renmin Zhongguo chubanshe, 1993.

Shi Yuxin. "Bo huangyan zhizaozhe: guanyu ZhongSu bianjie de ruogan wenti" [Refuting lie-fabricators: regarding several issues on the Sino-Soviet boundary]. *Lishi yanjiu* 1 (1974): 113-28.

Shijie zhishi shouce [World Knowledge Handbook]. Beijing: Shijie zhishi chubanshe, 1954.

Sidhu, Waheguru Pal Singh, and Jin-dong Yuan. "Resolving the Sino-Indian Border Dispute: Building Confidence through Cooperative Monitoring." *Asian Survey* 41, 2 (March/April 2001): 359-60.

Singh, Gurnam. *Sino-Pakistan Relations: The Ayub Era.* Amritsar: Guru Nanak Dev University Press, 1987.

Smith, Richard J. *Chinese Maps: Images of "All under Heaven."* London: Oxford University Press, 1996.

Snow, Edgar. "The Open Door." *New Republic,* 27 March 1971, 20-23.

–. *Red Star over China.* New York: Modern Library, 1944.

Snyder, Scott. "The South China Sea Dispute: Prospects for Preventive Diplomacy." A special report of the United States Institute of Peace. Washington, DC: United States Institute of Peace, August 1996.

"Soviet Note of Protest, March 15, 1969." *Studies in Comparative Communism* 2, 3-4 (July-October 1969): 165-66.

Sreedhar. "Sino-Afghan Economic Relations." *China Report* 12, 5-6 (September 1976): 7-9.

Stares, Paul B., Scott A. Snyder, Joshua Kurlantzick, Daniel Markey, and Evan A. Feigenbaum, eds. *Managing Instability on China's Periphery.* New York: Council on Foreign Relations, Center for Preventive Action, 2011.

Stratfor. "Analysis: China Tilts toward India." *Asia Times Online,* 18 June 1999. http://www.atimes.com/.

Stuart-Fox, Martin, and Mary Kookyman. *Historical Dictionary of Laos.* London: Scarecrow Press, 1992.

Suslov, M.A. *Marxism-Leninism: The International Teaching of the Working Class.* Moscow: Progress Publishers, 1975.

Swaine, Michael D. "China's Assertive Behavior Part One: On 'Core Interests.'" *China Leadership Monitor* 34 (Winter 2011): 1-25.

–. "China's Assertive Behavior Part Three: The Role of the Military in Foreign Policy." *China Leadership Monitor* 36 (Winter 2012): 1-17.

Swaine, Michael D., and Ashley J. Tellis. *Interpreting China's Grand Strategy: Past, Present, and Future.* Santa Monica, CA: RAND, 2000.

Swanström, Niklas. "China and Central Asia: A New Great Game or Traditional Vassal Relations?" *Journal of Contemporary China* 14, 45 (November 2005): 569-84 .

Syed, Anwar Hussain. *China and Pakistan: Diplomacy of an Entente Cordiale.* Amherst: University of Massachusetts Press, 1974.

"Taiwan, Japan Reach Milestone Fisheries Agreement." *Taiwan Panorama* 38, 6 (June 2013): 53-55.

Takemura, Kenichi. "Sonoda gaiso ni chokugeki intabyu" [A hard-hitting interview of Foreign Minister Sonoda]. *Jiyu minshu* 273 (10 October 1978): 44-51.

Tang, Shiping. "From Offensive to Defensive Realism: A Social Evolutionary Interpretation of China's Security Strategy." In *China's Ascent: Power, Security, and the Future of International Politics,* ed. Robert Ross and Zhu Feng, 141-63. Ithaca, NY: Cornell University Press, 2008.

Tatsunori, Ueji. *Senkaku retto to Takeshima.* Tokyo: Kyoikusha, 1978.

Terrill, Ross. *The New Chinese Empire.* New York: Basic Books, 2003.

Tian Zengpei, ed. *Gaige kaifang yilai de Zhongguo waijiao* [Chinese foreign policy since opening up and reform]. Beijing: Shijie zhishi chubanshe, 1993.

Tinker, Hugh. "Burma's Northeast Borderland Problems." *Pacific Affairs* 29, 4 (December 1956): 324-47.

–. *The Union of Burma: A Study of the First Years of Independence,* 4th ed. London: Oxford University Press, 1967.

Toller, W. Stark. "The Undefined China-Burma Frontier." *Eastern World* 2, 10/11 (October-November 1948): 12-14.

Trager, Frank N. "Burma and China." *Journal of Southeast Asian History* 5, 1 (March 1964): 29-61.

–. "Burma's Foreign Policy, 1948-1956: Neutralism, Third Force, and Rice." *Journal of Asian Studies* 16 (November 1956): 89-102.

–. "Communist China: The New Imperialism." *Current History* 41, 241 (September 1961): 136-40.

Tretiak, Daniel. "Peking's Policy toward Sinkiang: Trouble on the 'New Frontier.'" *Current Scene* 2, 24 (15 November 1963): 1-13.

Tu, Wei-ming. "Cultural China: The Periphery as the Center." *Daedalus* 120, 2 (Spring 1991): 145-67.

Ura, Karma. "Perceptions of Security." *Journal of Bhutan Studies* 5 (Winter 2001): 113-39.

Ura, Karma, and Sonam Kinga, eds. *The Spider and the Piglet: Proceedings of the First International Seminar on Bhutanese Studies.* Thimphu: Centre for Bhutan Studies, 2004.

Uren, Philip E. "Economic Relations among the Communist States." In *The Communist States at the Crossroads,* ed. Adam Bromke, 199-218. New York: Praeger, 1965.

Vandenbosch, Amry. "Chinese Communism for Export." *Current History* 39, 232 (December 1960): 333-50.

Vasquez, John A. *The War Puzzle.* Cambridge: Cambridge University Press, 1993.

Vertzberger, Yaacov Y.I. *China's Southwestern Strategy: Encirclement and Counter-encirclement.* New York: Praeger, 1985.

–. *The Enduring Entente: Sino-Pakistan Relations, 1960-1980.* New York: Praeger, 1983.

–. *Misperceptions in Foreign Policymaking: The Sino-Indian Conflict, 1959-1962.* Boulder, CO: Westview Press, 1984.

Voskressenski, Alexei D. "Current Concepts of Sino-Russian Relations and Frontier Problems in Russia and China." *Central Asian Survey* 13, 3 (1994): 361-81.

–. *Russia and China: A Theory of Inter-State Relations.* London: RoutledgeCurzon, 2003.

Waltz, Kenneth N. *Theory of International Politics.* Reading, MA: Addison-Wesley, 1979.

Wang, Dong. *China's Unequal Treaties: Narrating National History.* Lanham, MD: Lexington Books, 2005.

Wang Jisi. "International Relations Theory and the Study of Chinese Foreign Policy: A Chinese Perspective." In *Chinese Foreign Policy: Theory and Practice,* ed. Thomas W. Robinson and David Shambaugh, 481-505. New York: Oxford University Press, 1994.

Wang, Yuan-Kang. *Harmony and War: Confucian Culture and Chinese Power Politics.* New York: Columbia University Press, 2011.

Wang Hongwei. "Gong jian mianxiang 21 shiji jianshexing hezuo huoban guanxi" [Jointly build relations of constructive cooperative partnership facing the twenty-first century]. *Waiguo wenti yanjiu* 1 (gen. issue 46) (1997): 37-41.

Wang Taiping, ed. *Zhonghua Renmin Gongheguo waijiao shi (2) 1957-1969* [Diplomatic history of the PRC (vol. 2) 1957-1969]. Beijing: Shijie zhishi chubanshe, 1998.

Watson, Francis. *The Frontiers of China.* New York: Praeger, 1966.

Weng Tu-chien. "China's Policy on National Minorities." *People's China* 1, 7 (1 April 1950): 6-7.

"What Is Hwanggumpyong Island?" http://english.chosun.com/site/data/html_dir/2011/06/10/2011061001158.html.

Wheeler, Geoffrey. "Sinkiang and the Soviet Union." *China Quarterly* 16 (October-December 1963): 56-61.

Whetten, Lawrence L. "Moscow's Anti-China Pact." *World Today* 25, 9 (September 1969): 385-93.

Whiting, Allen S. *The Chinese Calculus of Deterrence: India and Indochina.* Ann Arbor: University of Michigan Press, 1975.

—. "Forecasting Chinese Foreign Policy: IR Theory vs. the Fortune Cookie." In *Chinese Foreign Policy: Theory and Practice,* ed. Thomas W. Robinson and David Shambaugh, 506-23. Oxford: Clarendon Press, 1994.

—. "Leaping the Great Wall between Security Studies and China Studies." *Security Studies* 6, 4 (Summer 1997): 183-96.

—. *Soviet Policies in China, 1917-1925.* New York: Columbia University Press, 1954.

Whittam, Daphne E. "The Sino-Burmese Boundary Treaty." *Pacific Affairs* 34, 2 (Summer 1961): 174-83.

Whyte, Brendan. "The Sino-Myanmar Border." In *Beijing's Power and China's Borders: Twenty Neighbors in Asia,* ed. Bruce A. Elleman, Stephen Kotkin, and Clive Schofield, 191-203. Armonk, NY: M.E. Sharpe, 2013.

Wilson, Jeanne L. *Strategic Partners: Russian-Chinese Relations in the Post-Soviet Era.* New York: M.E. Sharpe, 2004.

Wishnick, Elizabeth. *Mending Fences: The Evolution of Moscow's China Policy from Brezhnev to Yeltsin.* Seattle: University of Washington Press, 2001.

Wolfstone, Daniel. "Fast Work on the Sino-Burmese Border." *Far Eastern Economic Review,* 18 August 1960, 368-74.

Woodman, Dorothy. *The Making of Burma.* London: Cresset Press, 1962.

Wright, David Curtis. *From War to Diplomatic Parity in Eleventh-Century China: Sung's Foreign Relations with Kitan Liao.* Leiden, Netherlands: Brill, 2005.

Wright, Quincy. *A Study of War.* Chicago: University of Chicago Press, 1965.

Xie Bin. *Zhongguo sangdi shi* [History of China's lost territory]. Shanghai: Zhonghua shuju, 1925.

Xie Yixian, ed., *Zhongguo dangdai waijiao shi* [History of contemporary Chinese diplomacy]. Beijing: Zhongguo qingnian chubanshe, 1997.

—. *Zhongguo waijiao shi: Zhonghua Renmin Gongheguo shiqi 1949-1979* [A diplomatic history of China: the period of the People's Republic of China, 1949-1979]. Zhengzhou: Henan renmin chubanshe, 1988.

—. *Zhongguo waijiao shi: Zhonghua Renmin Gongheguo shiqi 1979-1994* [A diplomatic history of China: the period of the People's Republic of China, 1979-1994]. Zhengzhou: Henan renmin chubanshe, 1995.

Xisha chundao he Nansha chundao zigu yilai jiushi Zhongguo di lingtu [The Xisha and Nansha Islands have been Chinese territory since ancient times]. Beijing: Renmin chubanshe, 1981.

Xu Tao and He Xichuan. "Gongtong gozhu mianxiang ershiyi shiji de chuanmian hezuo huoban guanxi: Zhong-Ha shuangbian guanxi fazhan qingkuang" [Mutually building a comprehensive cooperative partnership for the twenty-first century: the development of Sino-Kazakh relations]. *Xiandai guoji guanxi* 10 (1997): 3-5.

Xu Yan. *Zhong-Yin bianjie zhi zhan lishi zhenxiang* [The true history of the Sino-Indian border war]. Hong Kong: Tiandi tushu gongsi, 1993.

Xue Mouhong and Pei Jianzhang, eds. *Dangdai Zhongguo waijiao* [Contemporary Chinese diplomacy]. Beijing: Zhongguo shehui kexue yuan, 1988.

Yan Jiaqi. "Jiang Zemin chumai 'tudi' huan 'linmu': ping Zhong-E mulin youhao hezuo tiaoyue" [Jiang Zemin sold out territory for good neighbourly relations: a critique of the Sino-Russian treaty of friendship and cooperation]. http://www.kanzhongguo.com/.

Yang, Lian-sheng. "Historical Notes on the Chinese World Order." In *The Chinese World Order: Traditional China's Foreign Relations*, ed. John King Fairbank, 20-23. Cambridge, MA: Harvard University Press, 1968.

Yang Gongsu. *Zhonghua Renmin Gongheguo waijiao lilun yu shijian* [The theory and practice of People's Republic of China diplomacy]. Beijing: Beijing daxue guoji guanxi xueyuan, 1997.

Yang Zhaoquan. *Zhongchao bianjie shi* [History of the China-Korea border]. Jilin: Wenshi chubanshe, 1993.

Yermukanov, Marat. "A Thorny Road to Sino-Kazakh Partnership." *China Brief* 4, 14 (8 July 2004).

Zhai Wenqi and Tang Chengyun. "Tumen jiang kaifa yu dongbeiya guoji guanxi" [Tumen River development and the international relations of northeast Asia]. *Qinghai Shifan daxue xuebao* 1 (1999). http://www.cnki.com.cn/Article/CJFDTotal-QHSZ901.002. htm.

Zhang, Qingmin. "Towards an Integrated Theory of Chinese Foreign Policy: Bringing Leadership Personality Back In." *Journal of Contemporary China* 23, 89 (2014): 902.

Zhang, Xiaoming. "China's 1979 War with Vietnam: A Reassessment." *China Quarterly* 184 (December 2005): 851-74.

Zhang, Xinjun. "China's 'Peaceful Rise,' 'Harmonious' Foreign Relations, and Legal Confrontation and Lesson from the Sino-Japanese Dispute over the East China Sea." Foreign Policy Research Institute, Philadelphia, *E-Notes*, 16 April 2010.

Zhang Cunwu. "Qingdai Zhong-Han bianwu wenti tanyuan" [An investigation of the Sino-Korean border question during the Qing dynasty]. *Zhongyang yanjiuyuan jindaishi yanjiusuo jikan* (Taipei) 2 (1971): 463-53.

Zhang Wenmu. "America's Oil Geostrategy and the Security of Tibet and Xinjiang: Considering New Trends in US Foreign Policy toward South and Central Asia." *Zhanlue yu guanli [Strategy and Management]* 2 (1998): 100-1.

Zhao, Suisheng. "Foreign Policy Implication of Chinese Nationalism Revisited: The Strident Turn." *Journal of Contemporary China* 22, 82 (2013): 535-53.

Zhongguo waijiao: 1998 nianban [Chinese foreign policy: 1998 edition]. Beijing: Shijie zhishi chubanshe, 1998.

Zhongguo waijiao: 1999 nianban [Chinese foreign policy: 1999 edition]. Beijing: Shijie zhishi chubanshe, 1999.

Zhonghua Renmin Gongheguo fensheng ditu. Shanghai: Shanghai ditu chubanshe, 1953.

Zhou Enlai waijiao wenxuan [Selected works of Zhou Enlai on diplomacy]. Beijing: Zhongyang wenxian chubanshe, 1990.

Zhu Chenghu. *ZhongMei quanxi de fazhan bianhua ji qi qushi* [The development, transformation, and trends in Sino-American relations]. Nanjing: Jiangsu renmin chubanshe, 1998.

Zubok, Vladislav M. "The Mao-Khrushchev Conversations, 31 July – 3 August 1958 and 2 October 1959." *Cold War International History Project Bulletin*, issue 12/13 (Fall/Winter 2001): 243-72.

Index

Note: "(m)" after a page number indicates a map. Page numbers enclosed in square brackets indicate textual references for endnotes

Glen Peterson, *The Power of Words: Literacy and Revolution in South China, 1949-95*

Wing Chung Ng, *The Chinese in Vancouver, 1945-80: The Pursuit of Identity and Power*

Yijiang Ding, *Chinese Democracy after Tiananmen*

Diana Lary and Stephen MacKinnon, eds., *Scars of War: The Impact of Warfare on Modern China*

Eliza W.Y. Lee, ed., *Gender and Change in Hong Kong: Globalization, Postcolonialism, and Chinese Patriarchy*

Christopher A. Reed, *Gutenberg in Shanghai: Chinese Print Capitalism, 1876-1937*

James A. Flath, *The Cult of Happiness: Nianhua, Art, and History in Rural North China*

Erika E.S. Evasdottir, *Obedient Autonomy: Chinese Intellectuals and the Achievement of Orderly Life*

Hsiao-ting Lin, *Tibet and Nationalist China's Frontier: Intrigues and Ethnopolitics, 1928-49*

Xiaoping Cong, *Teachers' Schools and the Making of the Modern Chinese Nation-State, 1897-1937*

Diana Lary, ed., *The Chinese State at the Borders*

Norman Smith, *Resisting Manchukuo: Chinese Women Writers and the Japanese Occupation*

Hasan H. Karrar, *The New Silk Road Diplomacy: China's Central Asian Foreign Policy since the Cold War*

Richard King, ed., *Art in Turmoil: The Chinese Cultural Revolution, 1966-76*

Blaine R. Chiasson, *Administering the Colonizer: Manchuria's Russians under Chinese Rule, 1918-29*

Emily M. Hill, *Smokeless Sugar: The Death of a Provincial Bureaucrat and the Construction of China's National Economy*

Kimberley Ens Manning and Felix Wemheuer, eds., *Eating Bitterness: New Perspectives on China's Great Leap Forward and Famine*

Helen M. Schneider, *Keeping the Nation's House: Domestic Management and the Making of Modern China*

James A. Flath and Norman Smith, eds., *Beyond Suffering: Recounting War in Modern China*

Elizabeth R. VanderVen, *A School in Every Village: Educational Reform in a Northeast China County, 1904-31*

Norman Smith, *Intoxicating Manchuria: Alcohol, Opium, and Culture in China's Northeast*

Juan Wang, *Merry Laughter and Angry Curses: The Shanghai Tabloid Press, 1897-1911*

Richard King, *Milestones on a Golden Road: Writing for Chinese Socialism, 1945-80*

David Faure and Ho Ts'ui-P'ing, eds., *Chieftains into Ancestors: Imperial Expansion and Indigenous Society in Southwest China*

Yunxiang Gao, *Sporting Gender: Women Athletes and Celebrity-Making during China's National Crisis, 1931-45*

Peipei Qiu, with Su Zhiliang and Chen Lifei, *Chinese Comfort Women: Testimonies from Imperial Japan's Sex Slaves*

Julia Kuehn, Kam Louie, and David M. Pomfret, eds., *Diasporic Chineseness after the Rise of China: Communities and Cultural Production*

Bridie Andrews, *The Making of Modern Chinese Medicine, 1850-1960*

Kelvin E.Y. Low, *Remembering the Samsui Women: Migration and Social Memory in Singapore and China*

Jiayan Zhang, *Coping with Calamity: Environmental Change and Peasant Response in Central China, 1736-1949*

Alison R. Marshall, *Cultivating Connections: The Making of Chinese Prairie Canada*

Ruoyun Bai, *Staging Corruption: Chinese Television and Politics*

Christopher G. Rea and Nicolai Volland, *The Business of Culture: Cultural Entrepreneurs in China and Southeast Asia, 1900-65*